Unreal Engine Projects for Non-coders

A guide to Unreal Engine's visual environment asset pipelines and basic VR concepts

Myron Mortakis

bpb

www.bpbonline.com

First Edition 2025

Copyright © BPB Publications, India

ISBN: 978-93-65896-350

To View Complete
BPB Publications Catalogue
Scan the QR Code:

www.bpbonline.com

Dedicated to

*My beloved wife **Nicole***

*My parents, **Ioannis** and **Jennie***

and

The spirit of persistence and dedication

About the Author

A Greek-Brazilian-American developer and entrepreneur, **Myron** is HELM Systems' (a South Florida-based independent game development studio) founder, CEO, and lead developer, with more than 20 years of experience in interactive software development and an expert in Unreal Engine, which he has been working with since its first generation. He is knowledgeable in a vast multitude of development roles, making him the perfect individual for efficient project planning and management, from conceptualization to launching a finished qualitative product for a plethora of applications and industries, including but not limited to gaming, entertainment, aerospace, industrial, architectural, VR/AR/XR and more.

He has an excellently balanced approach between creative passion and realization of business necessities, with a strong emphasis on efficient and cost-effective development, with product quality and timely delivery being top priorities.

He has been a recipient of the US residency as an alien of extraordinary ability in the field of video game and interactive software development while has also received an IGF award nomination and an Epic Games Unreal DevGrant for work conducted in video game development, as well as press mentions both for his video game development work and an interactive VR end-product visualization application for the aerospace industry. He also served as a panelist and presenter at conferences. In his free time, he is an avid electric guitar player and musician who composes, plays, and produces original music, having an extensive knowledge and a lifelong passion for music production equipment and techniques.

About the Reviewer

Ilya's journey in game development began at a small startup, where the team focused on developing MVPs for presentations while continuously expanding their knowledge through books and online resources to master Unreal Engine 4. After 1.5 years, he accepted an offer from Xtrematic, a company specializing in Unreal Engine 4-based VR projects for arcade VR machines. There, he deepened his expertise in VR development, learning the intricacies of VR systems within Unreal Engine and optimizing both logic and graphics for immersive experiences.

During the COVID-19 period, the company nearly shut down, prompting Ilya to transition to AltwolfSoftware, where he joined an outsourcing team working for Flying Wild Hog on Space Punks. His contributions included gamepad support, UI improvements, and AI enhancements. After the game's release, he took on the role of a lead developer for a small outsourcing team on the decimated project, managing a team of four developers responsible for implementing player character features.

After nearly two years at AltwolfSoftware, Ilya moved to the UK to join Cloud Imperium Games and work on Star Citizen. For the past 2.5 years, he has been part of the mission features team, implementing mission-related functionalities and broader game improvements. In recent updates, he contributed to the UI implementation of mobiGlas and took part in gameplay improvements related to server meshing for the 4.0 update, enabling hundreds of players to interact within a single session.

In addition to his professional work, Ilya teaches Unreal Engine and C++ programming at an online school and runs his own YouTube channel, SikorskiPishet, where he shares his expertise with aspiring game developers.

Acknowledgement

I would like to thank my wife Nicole for standing by me and showing me continuous support while authoring this book as she has with every other aspect of life, and the choices I have made and continue to be making.

Much gratitude to all the people I have learned from or got inspired by in my 20+ year journey so far. I am immensely grateful to the teams I have worked with, as well as the projects I have undertaken and the challenges I have faced, as they have always driven me forward to keep improving, growing, and learning further. Furthermore, I want to give special thanks to certain people I have met along the game development road so far, specifically Christian Allen, Amanda Schade, Marc Brehme, David Jagneuax, James Lay, Nick Calandra, Ricardo Robles Ortiz, Lawrence Nembhard, Mike Herauf, Richard Cowgill, Doug Kennedy, Marc Diana, Mike Poropat, Andru Fratarcangeli and Alain Galvan.

I owe an immense gratitude to the team at BPB Publications for providing guidance and support, but most importantly for being patient with someone that engages in a book authoring endeavor for the very first time. I thank the entire team for their professionalism, communication and guidance, and for the opportunity to complete this endeavor.

Preface

This book is meant to start with very basic introductions to Unreal Engine 5, its core technologies, tools, and workflows. It targets mainly beginners and quickly accelerates their learning to an intermediate level, with a good general understanding of the overall Unreal Engine workflows.

It starts with small, simple, and easy-to-complete projects and then proceeds to a complex project that utilizes everything taught in the earlier chapters of the book.

The book is divided into 16 chapters. It starts with the most basic steps, such as downloading and installing the Unreal Engine and setting up a working environment, explaining the basics of the engine's UI, toolsets, and workflows. It continues with a very basic introductory project that serves as an introduction to the tools and workflows later projects will utilize in more depth, while offering brief and optional examinations of the workflow of external applications and their relation to the Unreal Engine, mainly for asset creation.

Since chapters on external application workflows are optional, the author ensured that all created and exported assets are readily available for the readers should they wish to retain their focus strictly on the Unreal Engine workflows and processes.

Ultimately, the readers are guided through completing a complex project that allows even a beginner user to advance to an intermediate level, while allowing an intermediate user to possibly freshen up or further their knowledge in specific workflows.

Lastly, the book closes with a brief introduction to virtual reality.

Chapter 1: Unleashing the Unreal Engine– This chapter provides the reader with a very brief introduction to the Unreal Engine's various applications and history, as well as the author's and proceeds to show in detail to first-time users how to download, install, and set up Unreal Engine 5 on their machines.

Chapter 2: Unreal Engine UI- Breaks down the basic UI elements of the Unreal Engine's default layout, facilitating first-time users' overcoming of the seemingly overwhelming interface and showing them how to navigate through 3D space.

Chapter 3: Unreal Engine's Building Blocks- Guides the reader through their first project by completing a simple scene. Thus, the book teaches the reader about level design, Static Meshes, Materials, lighting, and Blueprints in a very simple, introductory manner.

Chapter 4: Project Overview and Main Asset Creation for Statue Scene– Analyzes the book's first complex project and breaks it down into parts, proceeding then to an optional in-depth overview of the 3D modeling and overall asset creation workflow, utilizing external applications, namely Reallusion Character Creator 4, ZBrush and Substance 3D Painter, ending the chapter with the preparation and exporting process of the asset, for the Unreal Engine.

Chapter 5: Importing Assets and Setting Up the Statue Scene- Shows the reader how to properly import and organize the previously created assets in Unreal Engine 5. Then, it proceeds to utilize these assets for the creation of Materials and finalization of the Statue Scene within the engine.

Chapter 6: Lighting and Cinematic for the Statue Scene– Explains lighting in further detail, and guides the reader through the steps of lighting up the Statue Scene. Then, it proceeds with utilizing some of the Unreal Engine's tools for the rendering of a short cinematic sequence.

Chapter 7: Fantasy Castle Project Breakdown and Planning– Analyzes and breaks down the book's most complex project. Overall, an introduction to careful project planning of a complex project, which can result in smaller, manageable segments.

Chapter 8: Fantasy Castle Base Mesh Modeling- Is diving into the workflow of creating the base meshes that will later on make up a complete asset pack. This is achieved by looking into the workflow of an external application, namely 3ds Max.

Chapter 9: Fantasy Castle High Poly Mesh Sculpting– Will continue the workflow that Chapter 8 initiated by working on the previously produced base meshes in ZBrush and sculpting them to transform them into high-poly, detailed meshes.

Chapter 10: Fantasy Castle Texturing and Materials– Proceeds with Chapter 9's results, and finalizes their Materials and textures in Substance 3D Painter, ending with finalization and preparation for exporting to the Unreal Engine.

Chapter 11: Fantasy Castle Bringing It All in Unreal– Goes through a step by step process of importing and organizing the previously created assets into the Unreal Engine, then proceeds with finalizing the assets within Unreal, ending the chapter with level design, by placing the created assets in the scene and utilizing Unreal Engine's terrain and Foliage tools.

Chapter 12: Fantasy Castle Character and Interaction Blueprints– Goes deeper into Blueprint utilization, teaching the reader how to create an original playable character within the Unreal Engine, looking briefly into concepts such as retargeting and in-engine animation, ending with assigning the playable character some interesting functions and abilities.

Chapter 13: Fantasy Castle Interactive Blueprint Actors– Continues with further utilization of the Unreal Engine Blueprints, by showing the reader how to create some interactive actors, such a firepit that can be toggled on and off, a teleportation portal.

Chapter 14: Fantasy Castle Mini Game Blueprints– Carrying on with the spirit of the previous two chapters, in this chapter, the reader goes through the steps of creating a mini game and its necessary components, all to be used in the Fantasy Castle Project.

Chapter 15: Fantasy Castle Level Finalization and Packaging– Goes through the steps of finalizing and completing the project, packaging it, and creating an executable format.

Chapter 16: Statue Scene Introduction to VR– Serves as a very brief introduction to virtual reality, by modifying the existing Statue Scene project into a VR project.

Code Bundle and Coloured Images

Please follow the link to download the
Code Bundle and the *Coloured Images* of the book:

https://rebrand.ly/c1m9l39

The code bundle for the book is also hosted on GitHub at
https://github.com/bpbpublications/Unreal-Engine-Projects-for-Non-coders.
In case there's an update to the code, it will be updated on the existing GitHub repository.

We have code bundles from our rich catalogue of books and videos available at
https://github.com/bpbpublications. Check them out!

Errata

We take immense pride in our work at BPB Publications and follow best practices to ensure the accuracy of our content to provide with an indulging reading experience to our subscribers. Our readers are our mirrors, and we use their inputs to reflect and improve upon human errors, if any, that may have occurred during the publishing processes involved. To let us maintain the quality and help us reach out to any readers who might be having difficulties due to any unforeseen errors, please write to us at :

errata@bpbonline.com

Your support, suggestions and feedbacks are highly appreciated by the BPB Publications' Family.

Piracy

If you come across any illegal copies of our works in any form on the internet, we would be grateful if you would provide us with the location address or website name. Please contact us at **business@bpbonline.com** with a link to the material.

If you are interested in becoming an author

If there is a topic that you have expertise in, and you are interested in either writing or contributing to a book, please visit **www.bpbonline.com**. We have worked with thousands of developers and tech professionals, just like you, to help them share their insights with the global tech community. You can make a general application, apply for a specific hot topic that we are recruiting an author for, or submit your own idea.

Reviews

Please leave a review. Once you have read and used this book, why not leave a review on the site that you purchased it from? Potential readers can then see and use your unbiased opinion to make purchase decisions. We at BPB can understand what you think about our products, and our authors can see your feedback on their book. Thank you!

For more information about BPB, please visit **www.bpbonline.com**.

Join our book's Discord space

Join the book's Discord Workspace for Latest updates, Offers, Tech happenings around the world, New Release and Sessions with the Authors:

https://discord.bpbonline.com

Table of Contents

CHAPTER 1
Unleashing the Unreal Engine

Introduction

This chapter will give you a very brief introduction to the Unreal Engine history and the author's journey with it and then will guide you through downloading, installing, and running the Unreal Engine for the very first time. Most importantly, you will familiarize yourself with the Epic Games Launcher, the proper steps to installing the Unreal Engine, and the ability to access and select different engine versions, while you will receive an overview of the different types of project templates the engine offers from the beginning. In addition, you will learn how to properly set up your work environment and the very first project.

Structure

The topics covered in this chapter:

- History of the Unreal Engine and the author's experience with it
- Getting started with Unreal Engine

Objectives

By the end of this chapter, you will have a better understanding of the Unreal Engine's origins, evolution, its different applications to today's industries. You will also be comfortable with downloading and installing the Unreal Engine, while being able to understand and select the different installation options, engine versions and Starter Content.

History of the Unreal Engine and the author's experience with it

The author's first interaction with the Unreal Engine came in 1999, playing *Epic Games Unreal Tournament*. It was a well-balanced, good-looking multiplayer **First Person Shooter (FPS)**, released at a time when titles like *Doom* and *Quake* were dominating the FPS market. As a gamer would say, experiencing the game was thrilling, especially when playing it with friends and family at **local area network (LAN)** parties. There was an immediate interest on the author's behalf to find ways to expand his gaming experience and game time, which eventually led to downloading free, community-made levels for the game. This was quite exciting, as it meant that one could freely expand the game they were already enjoying and experience designs that further contributed to the game's enjoyment.

Having the ability to download custom levels was quite exciting, yet there was even more content to improve and expand one's experience with the default game. There were mods, modifications that would range from something relatively simple, such as introducing a new weapon with different weapon stats, to something complicated and radically transformative, such as a total conversion, which, in essence, would be an entirely new game, running within the original game.

A gamer would certainly be excited about all these possibilities to expand further and enjoy any experience with the game however, upon discovering more about all the available custom-made content, the author's creative curiosity started growing, pushing him towards obtaining more information on how one could go about creating such custom content. While information and learning resources were extremely limited, often vague, and quite difficult to find, determination to learn using the Unreal Engine and the Unreal Editor was at least enough to allow the author to express his creative visions for the original game, initially through custom-built maps, later through modding and total conversions.

At that time, the Unreal Engine was considered an FPS engine since it was widely used for the development of first-person shooter games and content. However, in 2000, *Human Head Studios* released *Rune*, a third-person hack-and-slash action game, which was using the Unreal Engine and offered the opportunity to witness the Unreal Engine's application on a product other than an FPS.

As someone who has always had a soft spot for ancient and medieval world history and an inclination towards fantasy themed IPs, *Rune* elevated the author's curiosity and interest in the Unreal Engine to the highest levels possible, resulting in him spending entire days, weeks, and months in learning as much as possible, building and releasing custom levels and content, and actively participating in the *Rune*'s modding and Unreal Engine communities.

At the same time, the author was actively engaged in the Rune modding scene, eagerly learning and working hard to improve his skills, Epic Games made shockwaves in the gaming world with news of *Unreal Tournament 2003* (in essence, Unreal Tournament 2), which would be the first title to use the — then new — Unreal Engine 2. Early screenshots and sneak preview trailers made both gamers and enthusiast developers drool over the visuals and the overall possibilities of the second generation of the Unreal Engine. At this point, the author was strongly motivated and determined to start bringing his creative visions and aspirations of a dark fantasy world to life. While still a college student working to obtain *Bachelor of Science* degrees in *Liberal Studies* and *Computer Science*, the author proceeded with forming a small game development team of enthusiast and amateur game developers with the purpose of creating our own fantasy total conversion, which would utilize the Unreal Engine 2 and feature controllable dragons, horses, first-person ranged and spell casting combat, third person melee combat. An impossible feat, as described by many we consulted with at the time, and an ambitious project, to say the least, yet also a testament to the Unreal Engine's capabilities as well as our team's determination.

At this period, any custom content, such as a level, a player skin, a weapon pack, or an entire total conversion, could be released only as freely downloadable content and could not be monetized. Only Unreal Engine licensees were able to release and monetize products built with the Unreal Engine, but that did not deter the author and countless others from developing and releasing such projects, especially since they were all in the earlier learning stages of their careers and game development journeys.

In 2005, the author and his team successfully released the first iteration of their total conversion, *The SoulKeeper*, featuring all the mechanics they aimed to include: controllable dragons, horses, three different types of combat, all in a multi-player format, an add-on to Unreal Tournament 2003 and Unreal Tournament 2004. They received mainstream online and print media coverage, were featured on CD compilations, topped several *Most Downloaded* charts on popular gaming websites, and most notably received an *Independent Game Festival Nomination* in 2006 while also being invited by Epic Games and the **Independent Game Developer Association (IGDA)** to showcase their game at **Game Developers' Conference (GDC)** 2006.

All these achievements were great and satisfying motivators, but looking back at those days now, the most valuable takeaway was that they set out to do something challenging and unheard of at the time, and thanks to the Unreal Engine and, of course, thanks to the hard work and dedication, they were able to successfully overcome all the challenges and complete the technical goals they set out to.

While all this was happening, in 2006, Epic Games were heavily promoting and sharing news and information about their — then upcoming — Unreal Engine 3. At GDC 2006, Unreal Engine 3 was the talk of the show, and it was impossible to overlook how good the visuals were, how impressive the lighting, the visual effects, the overall quality, and the overall technology looked. With Unreal Engine 3, Epic Games also introduced an effective node-based method for visual scripting (known as *Kismet*) as well as material shader composition, vastly facilitating, expediting, and, therefore, improving development workflows. Nonetheless, it was very expensive to license, therefore being a commercially feasible option only to AAA studios, backed by AAA publishers, who could afford the expensive licensing fees. Still, the Unreal Engine 3 was, as one would expect, a powerful technological marvel and a highly successful and widely used gaming engine, powering an overwhelming majority of commercially successful, blockbuster AAA games in the years that followed and undisputedly establishing it as an integral and leading technology within the gaming industry. In Unreal Engine 3's lifecycle, **Unreal Development Kit (UDK)** was also released as a freely available educational tool, essentially a lighter version of the fully licensed Unreal Engine 3.

By this point in time, any Unreal Engine announcement about a new generation had become an industry standard, an expected and most certainly anticipated event, so it was only natural that once Epic Games decided to share more information and news about Unreal Engine 4, once again shockwaves were sent out through the entire gaming industry. At GDC 2014, Epic Games launched Unreal Engine 4; however, this time, the innovation was not just at the technical level. Still, Epic Games had also announced a new licensing model, under which anyone who would be willing to become a subscriber for USD $19 per month would be able to license and commercially release products built with Unreal Engine 4. Among the many innovations Unreal Engine 4 introduced, it also shipped an updated and largely improved version of Unreal Engine 3's tools, introducing Unreal Blueprints (an updated and improved version of Unreal Engine 3's Kismet, the node-based, visual scripting tool). Eventually, Epic Games decided to drop the subscription-based licensing model. They made the Unreal Engine freely available and accessible, allowing virtually anyone to create and launch commercial products utilizing the Unreal Engine.

In addition to the innovations mentioned above brought by Unreal Engine's fourth generation, Unreal Engine 4 started finding its way into completely different industries and applications beyond the video gaming industry.

Briefly looking into the author's adventures in a long and still ongoing development journey, in 2015, *HELM Systems*, the author's development company, collaborated with a company in the aerospace industry, building a real-time **virtual reality (VR)** application for the customization and end-product visualization of the fuselage of private jets. They developed this application using Unreal Engine 4, and it was compatible with both the *Occulus Rift* and *HTC Vive* headsets. In 2017, they released an early access VR game, *The SoulKeeper VR*, which was an innovative and daring product in the uncertain and challenging VR gaming landscape at the time, being featured once again in popular mainstream VR gaming publications, as well as receiving an Epic Games Unreal Dev Grant. In the following years, the company utilized Unreal Engine 4 in several ways that went beyond the scope of game development, including architectural visualization applications, training applications, virtual production utilizations, and online convention applications, just to name a few.

The Unreal Engine 4 has made its way into several well-known and mainstream products and brands as well, such as popular car manufacturer user interfaces and vehicle visual customization applications, TV series and films, business and academic applications, architectural visualization, engineering applications, and many more. To this book's authoring date, the Unreal Engine 4 is widely used and can be found in many popular products, even with Unreal Engine's fifth generation already available.

This brings us to this book's authoring present, the latest generation of the Unreal Engine, the main subject of this book's focus, the Unreal Engine 5. Unreal Engine 5 was released in early access in the Spring of 2021 and officially launched a year later, in the Spring of 2022. Once again, Unreal Engine 5 introduces several new and innovative technologies that truly help improve production workflow and creativity and achieve unparalleled levels of realistic, qualitative visuals. We will cover several of those in the following chapters, but some of the most notable innovations are *Nanite* and *Lumen*. Nanite allows, for the first time ever, the importation of high poly geometries in a real-time environment, while Lumen is a powerful dynamic global illumination solution.

Getting started with Unreal Engine

As long and varied as Unreal Engine's history has been thus far, it continues to grow, finding itself in more and more applications and industries, connected with emerging and innovative technologies, so rest assured there are many more chapters and developments yet to be written in this history. And this is the perfect opportunity to begin your journey and become part of this unwritten yet part of the Engine's history. But let us begin with small, conservative, and simple — for now — steps. What better starting point than to first download and install the Engine on your computer. Let us get started with the following steps:

1. First visit Unreal Engine's official documentation website to get detailed hardware and software system requirements to ensure you have the proper system setup that can run Unreal Engine 5: **https://docs.unrealengine.com/5.0/en-US/hardware-and-software-specifications-for-unreal-engine/**

   For your convenience, you can refer to the following three figures (*Figure 1.1, Figure 1,2,* and *Figure 1.3)* as well, all three taken straight from the official documentation website, displaying the minimum hardware requirements for Windows, macOS, and Linux, respectively:

Operating System	Windows 10 64-bit version 1909 revision .1350 or higher, or versions 2004 and 20H2 revision .789 or higher.
Processor	Quad-core Intel or AMD, 2.5 GHz or faster
Memory	8 GB RAM
Graphics Card	DirectX 11 or 12 compatible graphics card
RHI Version	• DirectX 11: Latest drivers • DirectX 12: Latest drivers • Vulkan: AMD (21.11.3+) and NVIDIA (496.76+)

Figure 1.1: Minimum hardware requirements for Windows

The following figure shows the minimum hardware requirements for macOS:

Operating System	Latest MacOS Monterey
Processor	Quad-core Intel, 2.5 GHz or faster
Memory	8 GB RAM
Video Card	Metal 1.2 Compatible Graphics Card

Figure 1.2: Minimum hardware requirements for macOS

The following figure shows the hardware requirements for Linux:

Operating System	Ubuntu 22.04
Processor	Quad-core Intel or AMD, 2.5 GHz or faster
Memory	32 GB RAM
Video Card	NVIDIA GeForce 960 GTX or Higher with latest NVIDIA binary drivers
Video RAM	8 GB or more
RHI Version	• **Vulkan:** AMD (21.11.3+) and NVIDIA (515.48+)

Figure 1.3: Minimum hardware requirements for Linux

2. Once you have confirmed your hardware meets the minimum system requirements, visit Unreal Engine's official website: **https://www.unrealengine.com/** and click **DOWNLOAD** as shown in *Figure 1.4*:

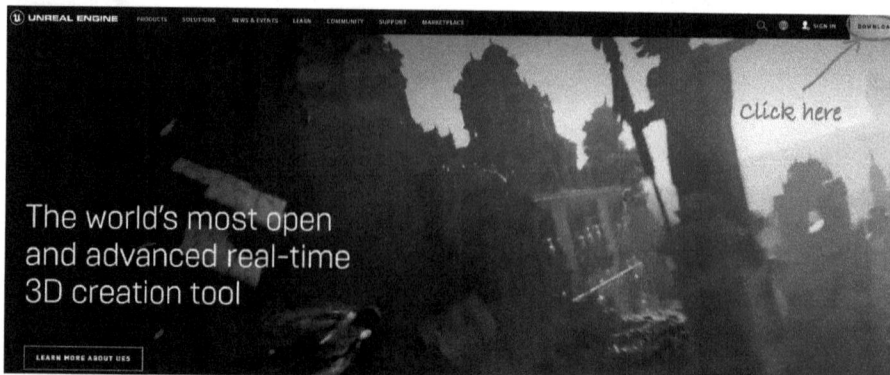

Figure 1.4: Unreal Engine's official website

3. Clicking **DOWNLOAD** will initiate the download for the Epic Installer. Once the download is complete, run the downloaded file and install it either at the default path or a drive/folder of your preference, as depicted in *Figure 1.5*:

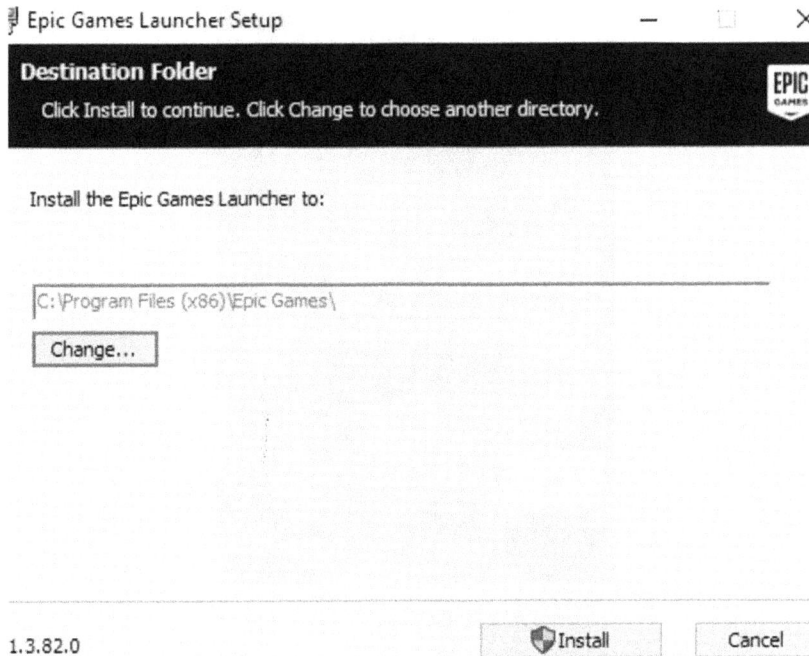

Figure 1.5: Epic Games Launcher installation

Once the Epic Launcher is installed and running, you will be asked to sign in with your **Epic Games** account or Alternatively with other accounts such as *Facebook, Google,* and more. While not a requirement, it is recommended you proceed with creating an Epic Games account. With your account, not only will you be able to actively participate in the Unreal Engine's development community, but you will also be able to purchase or sell on the Unreal Engine Marketplace, currently known as **Fab** (**https://www.fab.com/**), as well as keep track of your purchased or obtained assets in your Vault (essentially your Marketplace Asset Library). At this point, it is worth noting that every month, Epic Games gives the community some amazing assets that can be found on the Marketplace free of charge for the duration of the month. Additionally, you can access Epic Games content, sample projects, learning projects, and much more. Refer to *Figure 1.6* for the Epic Games Launcher's **Sign In** prompt:

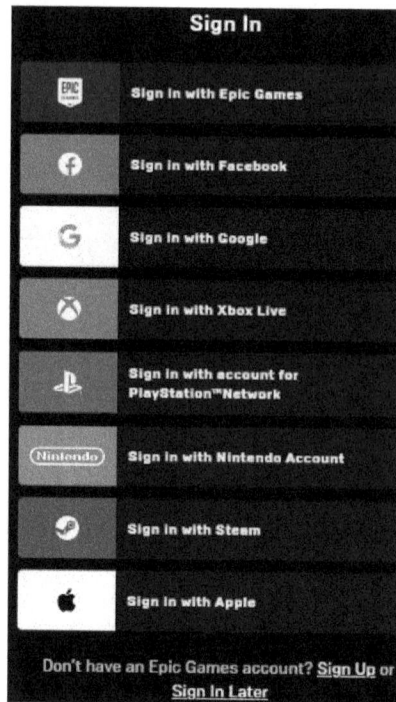

Figure 1.6: Epic Games Launcher Sign In

4. Once you have successfully created your **Epic Games** account, login, and you will be welcomed by the Epic Launcher's initial screen, similar to the one shown in *Figure 1.7*:

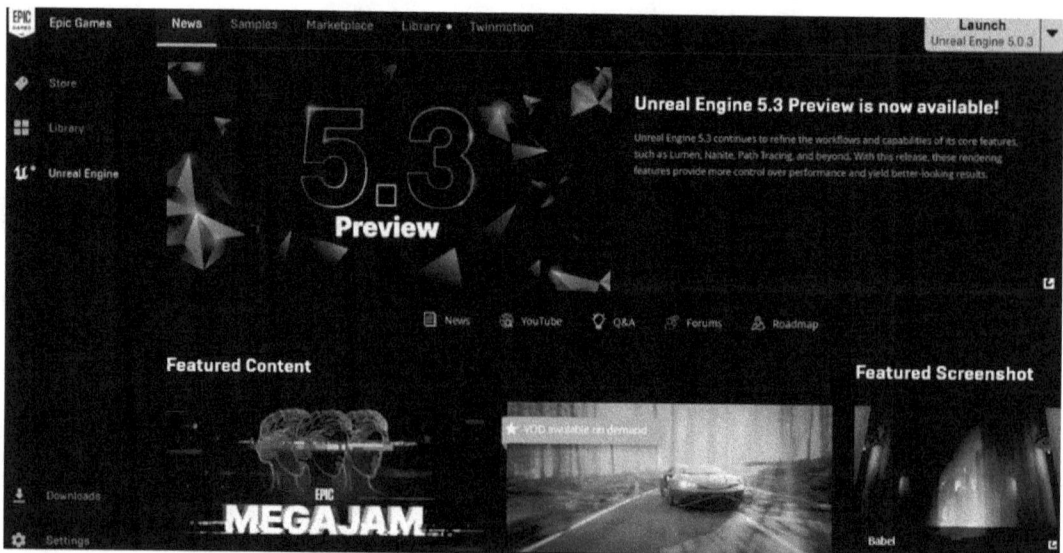

Figure 1.7: Epic Games Launcher home screen

5. On the upper central part of the Epic Launcher's window, click on **Library**. This is where you can add different engine versions, see, and access all the projects you will be creating, as well as access your Vault, where all the Marketplace assets you own can be found and added to different projects. To begin installing the Engine, you can either click the **Install Engine** button on the upper right-hand corner, which will then proceed with installing the latest stable version of the Engine, or you can click on the small + button next to **ENGINE VERSIONS**, and from there select a specific Engine version you want to install, including preview versions, which are not stable, instead they are a preview of an upcoming Engine version, allowing you to already familiarize yourself with upcoming features, as well as report any issues you come across. Please refer to *Figure 1.8* for a visual representation of the different options discussed in this section:

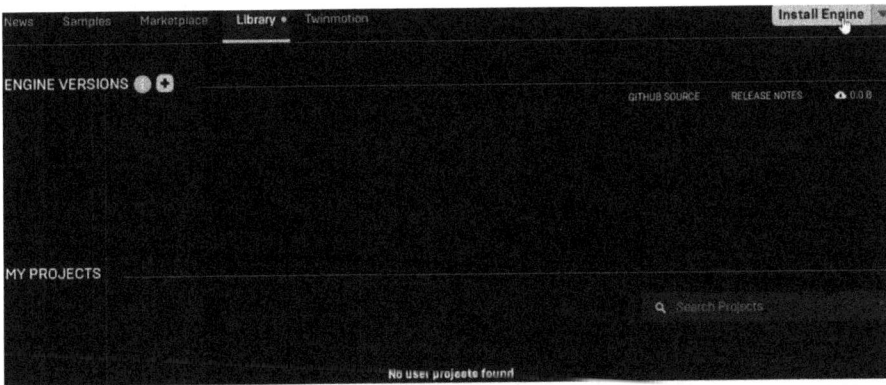

Figure 1.8: Installing the Unreal Engine

6. Once you begin installing the Engine, you will be asked for the path you wish to install it in, as well as the features and settings you want to include. For this book's purposes, it is recommended that the settings shown in *Figure 1.9* are used:

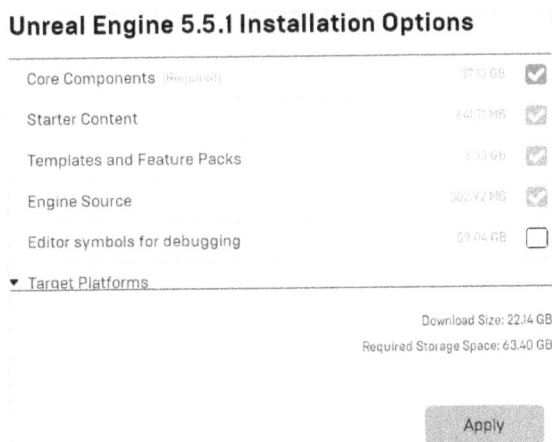

Figure 1.9: Unreal Engine Installation Options

7. While the Epic Launcher is busy installing the Unreal Engine, download Microsoft's Visual Studio — Community Edition. You can download the free Community edition of Visual Studio from this link: **https://visualstudio.microsoft.com/vs/ community/**

Once downloaded, run the executable file and choose the desired installation path. Next, you will be asked to select the **Workloads** and Components you wish to install. Scroll down and make sure the **Game development with C++** box is checked while ensuring on the prompt's right-hand side that you have at least **C++ profiling tools**, **C++ Build Insights**, **C++ AddressSanitizer**, **Windows 11 SDK** (the newest version you can find), **Windows 10 SDK** (once again, the newest version available), **IDE support for Unreal Engine**, **Unreal Engine installer** all checked. For your convenience, refer to *Figure 1.10* for the settings used in the latest Visual Studio installation:

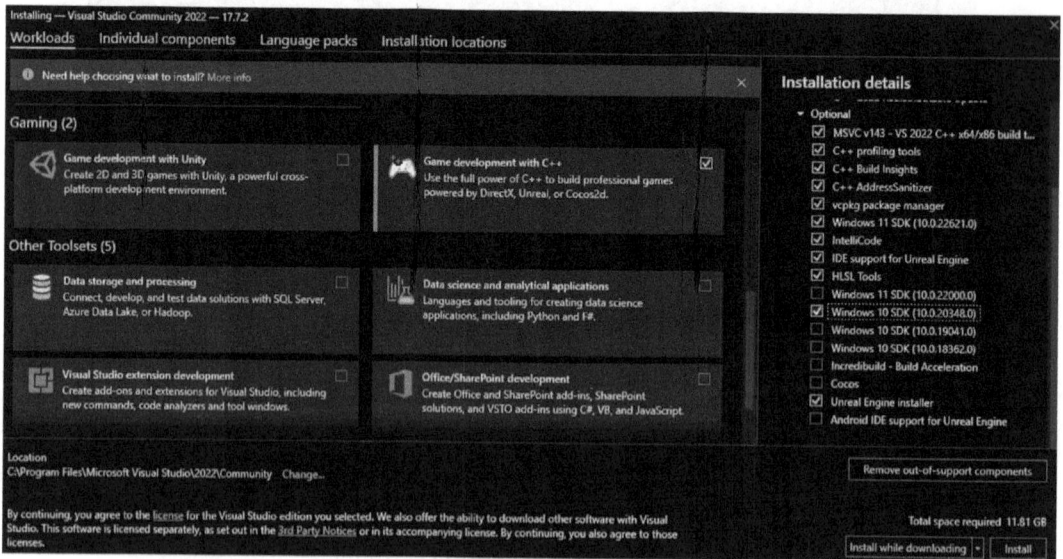

Figure 1.10: Microsoft Visual Studio installation options

8. In addition, you can also check Unreal Engine's official documentation for more detailed information on installing Visual Studio for development with the Unreal Engine: **https://docs.unrealengine.com/4.26/enUS/ProductionPipelines/ DevelopmentSetup/VisualStudioSetup/**

9. With both the Unreal Engine and Visual Studio installed, we are now ready to create our very first project. Since this is the same project we will be working on in *Chapters 4 to 6,* we will want to make sure we name it and set it up appropriately. Click on **Launch** as depicted in *Figure 1.11*:

Figure 1.11: Launching the Unreal Engine

Conclusion

The Unreal Engine has a long history, deeply rooted in game development, yet through the years it has evolved into a technological platform that allows developers to build a variety of applications in a plethora of industries. While some of us have been fortunate enough to have been working with the Engine and witnessed its evolution and growth from the start, there is still a long and bright future ahead of it, with endless possibilities for both technical (even scientific) and artistic applications, and now it is an excellent time to start your own personal journey in the world of the Unreal Engine development.

Having concluded the first chapter, you should be feeling comfortable with installing the Engine on any computer, accessing the different Engine versions and installing the one you prefer, setting up the foundations of your production environment.

In the next chapter, we will go into detail about setting up your very first project while examining some of the available default templates.

Points to remember

Key points learned in this chapter are as follows:

- The Unreal Engine can be utilized to develop a variety of applications for an ever-growing variety of industries.
- Create your free Epic Games account and download and install the Epic Games Launcher.
- Access the different Engine versions and install the one of your preferences (usually the latest).
- Installation options and setup of any required 3rd party libraries or SDKs (specifically Microsoft Visual Studio).

Exercise

1. You can practice everything learned in this chapter by simply repeating the chapter's steps. You can either perform a clean installation on a secondary machine — if available — or simply uninstall and reinstall the Engine on your primary computer.

Join our book's Discord space

Join the book's Discord Workspace for Latest updates, Offers, Tech happenings around the world, New Release and Sessions with the Authors:

https://discord.bpbonline.com

CHAPTER 2

Unreal Engine UI

Introduction

This chapter will help you prepare and launch our very first project. We will briefly cover the different available project templates, choose the one we will need to work with for our first project later, launch it, and then navigate through the Unreal Engine's initial **user interface** (**UI**) and cover the basics, including the different icons, the layouts, and the usability. We will also play around with some basic actor placement, actor scaling and positioning, actor properties just to get a basic grasp of the overall UI utilization. Nothing we do in this chapter will be saved, as we will be repeating all these steps and processes in much more detail in the later chapters.

Structure

The topics covered in this chapter:

- Welcome to an Unreal world
- Project templates
- Project defaults
- The settings for our first project
- UI breakdown

Objectives

By the end of this chapter, you will have a good understanding of the Unreal Engine's most basic and fundamental UI layout and its functions, preparing the ground for the next chapters. You will learn how to prepare your first project and the different templates and options you can use, while you will also be able to understand and instantly recognize the different sections of the initial and default user interface the engine features. At the end of this chapter, you will be ready to start working on a very simple project, which will follow in the next chapter.

Welcome to an Unreal world

The last step we took in the previous chapter was to click on the **Launch** button. Be patient when loading; the Engine will conduct and initialize some processes. If you run this on Windows, you might be asked to Allow Access to some of the Engine's processes. Once it loads, you will be presented with various templates to choose from as your starting point. Depending on the nature and the requirements of each individual project, Epic Games provides you with some solid starting points. There are templates for Games, Film and Live Events, Architecture, Automotive product design and manufacturing, and Simulation, covering different gaming types, **augmented reality** (**AR**) and VR applications, virtual productions, product customization tools, and so much more.

Project templates

For this book's projects, we will be using templates from the Games category. Looking into the Games category, you will find that there are seven templates to choose from:

- **Blank**: This is the cleanest template you can get; only the fundamentals are included

- **First Person**: If you intend to create an FPS or an **First Person** (**FP**) experience, this is the template to use.

- **Third Person**: If **Third Person Shooter** (**TPS**)/3rd person avatar control is needed, this is the template to start with.

- **Top Down**: Commonly used in well-known point and click **Role Playing Games** (**RPGs**), a good starting point for such projects.

- **Vehicle**: For projects requiring vehicle control, such as racing games, this template gives you enough basics, such as vehicle and suspension physics, acceleration, and more.

- **Handheld AR**: Intended for projects that need augmented reality applications on mobile devices.

- **Virtual reality**: Intended for projects meant to be interactive VR applications.

If you are curious about finding more information on each template, all you need to do is click on any of them and read the official description in the upper right-hand corner.

For this chapter, as well as for our first project, we will be using the Blank template. The reason for this selection is that our first project will feature the golden statue of a Goddess placed in a lit scene. Therefore, we do not need any first or third-person avatar control; all we need is to be able to fly through the scene and, later on, render a short movie of the scene.

Project defaults

On the middle right-hand side, you will see there are some project defaults we can select. The first decision you need to make for this section is whether you need your project to be a Blueprint-based project or a C++-based project.

A Blueprint project indicates that the entire project's programming, or code if you prefer, is done through Unreal Engine's node-based, visual scripting feature, the Blueprints. This means any classes you create (for example, a playable character or the character's weapon) will all be created with Blueprints.

A C++ project indicates that you will still have access to the Engine's Blueprints. However, there will be classes and actors you create by coding them in C++.

Whether you decide to go with a Blueprint based or a C++ based project, depends on your development team lineup and their comfort (or your comfort if you are a solo developer) levels with programming in C++.

Given that this book is targeting a wide range of audience that most certainly includes absolute beginners, we will stick to a Blueprint-based project.

The second option you are presented with is your project's target platform. You can select either Desktop or Mobile, the first indicating your intentions to develop an application for desktops. In contrast, the second indicates your intentions to develop an application for mobile devices (possibly lower hardware specifications).

The third option you need to select is the level of quality you want your project to feature. More specifically, it refers to the visual quality. If you opt for a Maximum quality level, your project will demand more powerful hardware to meet the demands for better quality. If you opt for Scalable, then some of the higher-end and more performance-demanding features will be disabled, making your project easier to run regarding performance and hardware requirements.

The next option you can check or uncheck is Starter Content. If you check the box next to this option, then your project will include the default Starter Content, which essentially is a collection of assets such as Static Meshes, material shaders, sound waves, and cues, just enough to get you started. It is usually recommended to be included if the developer(s) are new to the world of development with the Unreal Engine and are trying to educate themselves further. If you are a seasoned developer working on a commercial project, chances are you do not need this included unless you feel there might be some good starting points for some of your original assets, such as Material Instances derived from the Starter Content's Materials and more.

Lastly, you are asked whether you want to include Ray Tracing support or not. This choice should depend on the hardware you intend to use with this project. If your GPU supports raytracing and you want to feature it in your project, then you should include it. If your target hardware does not support raytracing, or you feel that the visual benefits of raytracing are secondary or even less important to your project's performance, then you should exclude it.

The settings for our first project

As mentioned earlier, our first project, at least in terms of functionality, is a rather simple project. In terms of mechanics and features, we do not have any; however, in terms of visual fidelity and quality, we want it to look as best as it can and fit the next gen look that Unreal Engine 5 can offer. So, provided your hardware meets the official minimum system requirements, please refer to *Figure 2.1* for the settings we will be using for our first project:

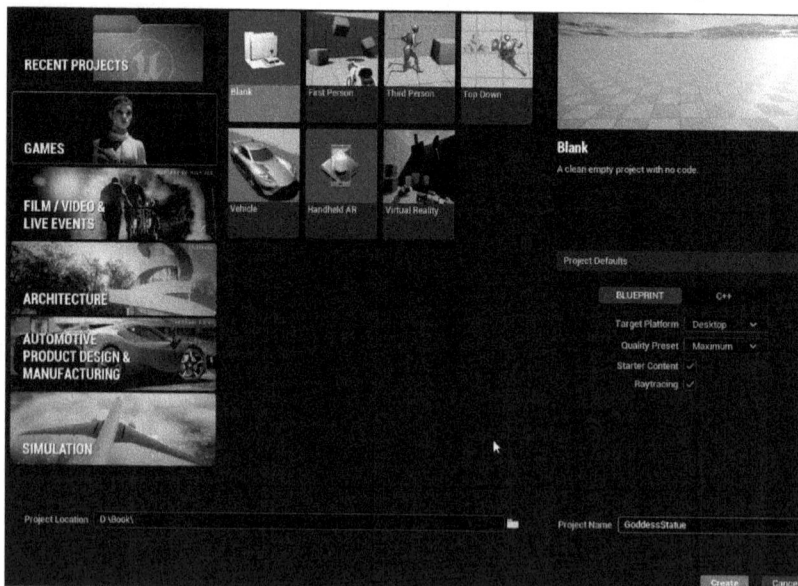

Figure 2.1: *Preparing the first project*

Select the project location of your preference and then use **GoddessStatue** as the project's name. Finally, click on the **Create** button. After you have hit the **Create** button, once again you need to be patient, as the first time a project is created and loaded, it can take a while due to several initializations and shader compilations. Once these have taken place, your project will be loading considerably faster from the second time onward.

UI breakdown

Once the project has finally loaded, you will be greeted with a screen that looks very much like the following *Figure 2.2*:

Figure 2.2: Initial screen

At a first glance, it might be a bit daunting where to begin, but do not despair, it is a lot easier than it looks.

The **Unreal Engine** (**UE**) official documentation has a nice UI layout breakdown you can refer to, like the one posted below, but for this book, we will use a breakdown, slightly different than the one found in the official documentation. The link to the official documentation is included here as well, this way, you have options to follow whichever one you feel is easier for you. The link to the official documentation's UI explanation: **https://docs.unrealengine.com/5.0/en-US/unreal-editor-interface/**.

Back to this book's version, the author has used the following breakdown before, in *Unreal Florida*, the author's local Unreal Engine chapter — the author founded Unreal Florida with other local developers back in 2015. Unreal Florida often introduces and teaches the Unreal Engine to new users with different backgrounds, and so far, using the breakdown displayed further below, has worked well.

Now, it is also a good time to disclaim that the user interface in the Unreal Editor is highly customizable, and every developer will eventually end up using a layout that they feel is most functional to them and their workflow. In this book, we will go through some of the layout customization steps and will eventually modify the layout to fit the one the author is most comfortable with and uses in everyday development. However, you do not have to stick to that layout, as there is no right or wrong layout. The only layout that ultimately matters is the one you are the most comfortable with.

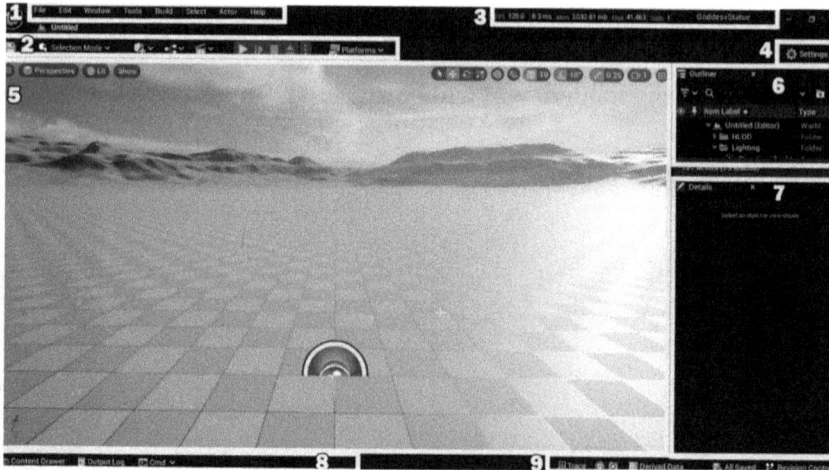

Figure 2.3: UI breakdown

So here is the numbered section breakdown of the initial UI. Let us take a closer look into what each numbered section features:

Section 1: Menu Bar

Much like in any other application, this is where you have the main controls for the entire application, including saving and loading, undo/redo, copy/pasting and deleting, access to project and editor settings, plugin settings, access to different tools and windows with useful features, build options, packaging settings, help resources and more.

Section 2: Main Toolbar

Here, you can quickly save your work and enter different editing modes, such as selecting objects and editing them, working on terrain or Foliage, and a lot more.

Through this section, you can also quickly add actors to your scene, such as a primitive shape or a light.

Additionally, the Main Toolbar provides the user with quick access to different Blueprint-based functions, such as creating a new Blueprint class, editing a Level Blueprint, which is a Blueprint specifically controlling events and functions within the presently opened level, modifying Game Modes, which in essence are classes dictating the basic settings of a game mode, such as what is the default pawn and much more.

This section also provides you with quick access to adding a Level Sequence, which essentially is an actor you will need to render a movie from your scene or control actors through a timeline-based format, in which you can add keys in different frames and determine what sort of events occur at these keys.

You also have quick access to playing through the currently opened level, as well as modifying the settings of such playthroughs, such as conducting it in the main Viewport or opening the playthrough on a new window, as well as setting the resolution and other features that new window will feature, conducting your playthrough in VR mode and much more.

Lastly, but equally importantly, you have quick access to target-specific platform settings and packaging tools, which come in handy once you are ready to package your project and prepare it for distribution.

Section 3: Performance information

And here is our first opportunity to customize the UI a bit. In this section, we have a display of information useful to monitor our performance, such as the framerate or, for example, the memory used. There are other ways to obtain and monitor that information. However, some developers feel it is a lot easier and less intrusive to have some of that information displayed on the title bar. To add this section to your UI, follow the next steps:

1. Click on **Edit** in the Menu Bar (*Section 1* of the UI breakdown), and then select **Editor Preferences**, as indicated in *Figure 2.4*:

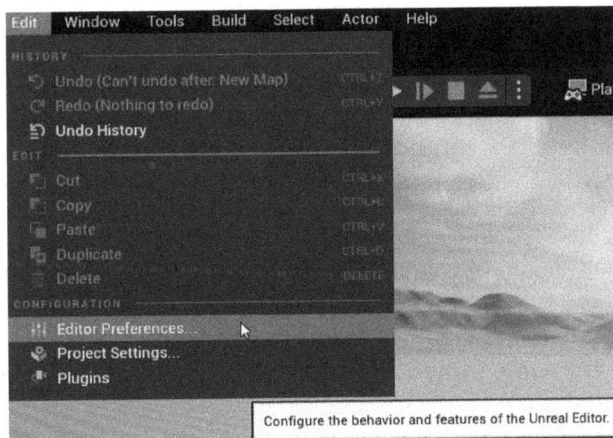

Figure 2.4: Editor Preferences

2. Then, on the left-hand side, find and click **Performance**, as seen in *Figure 2.5*:

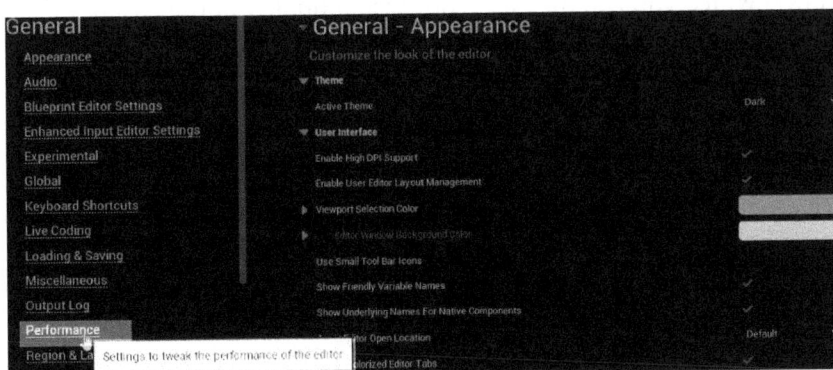

Figure 2.5: Performance settings

3. Next, enable the desired feature by checking the box next to **Show Frame Rate and Memory,** which is found all the way on top, as shown in *Figure 2.6*:

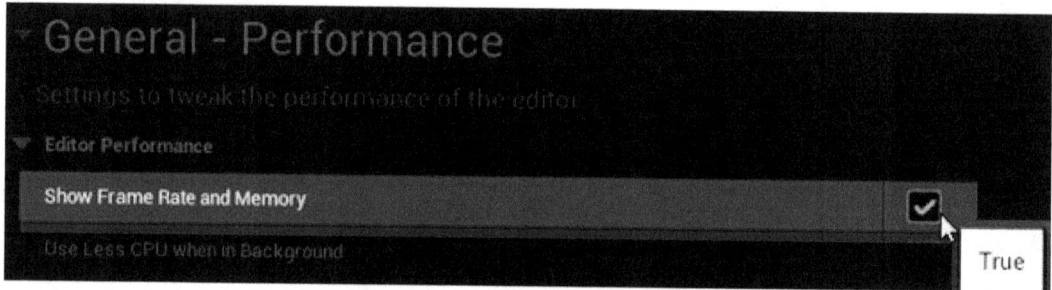

Figure 2.6: Enabling framerate counter

Congratulations, this was your very first UI layout customization! Now, you can keep track of how performance is affected by the activities and events happening in your Viewport. If you are not familiar with framerates, all you need to remember for now is that the higher the number next to the FPS is, the better the performance. The lower the number next to the **milliseconds (ms)**, the better the performance. In other words, **FPS** stands for **frames per second,** Therefore, you know you achieved good performance when you successfully render many frames within a second. The ms is the time measurement unit; therefore, the lower that number is, the less time it takes for your scene to render and the better the performance is.

Lastly, in *Section 3* of our UI breakdown, you can also see the project's name being displayed all the way on top of the right-hand corner. While this might at first seem a bit redundant, it can be quite useful when a developer is working on multiple projects or sometimes even different versions of the same project, therefore, it is useful to easily know exactly which project you are working on.

Section 4: Settings

This is a quick and easy way to access several different settings, such as — once again much like in *Section 1* — project settings and plugins, but also world settings and scalability settings through which you can increase your visual quality at the cost of performance or improve your performance but at the cost of your visual quality. If, at this stage, you find that your framerate (FPS) is low, for instance, below 30FPS, then it is strongly recommended that you change your scalability settings.

Here is how you can do that:

1. Click on **Settings** on the upper right-hand side of the screen, and then hover over **Engine Scalability Settings**, as depicted in *Figure 2.7*:

Figure 2.7: Engine Scalability Settings

2. Select different quality modes, such as **Low**, **Medium** and more or do the same for individual components, such as **Post Processing**, **Shadows,** and so on. You can also move around the **Resolution Scale** slider and decrease it from 100% to a lesser value. If your performance was not as good to begin with, by playing around with these settings, you can increase the performance you have while working on your project, making it easier to work with. If your performance was optimal from the start, you can still use the **Engine Scalability Settings** to preview what your end users will be seeing if you grant them access to these settings.

Section 5: Level Viewport

This is your 3D window to the world you are building. Through the Level Viewport, not only do you add, select and edit different objects and actors, but you also navigate your camera through the 3D space.

Here is how you navigate through the Viewport with your mouse:

- Left-click and drag anywhere in the Viewport while moving your mouse forward, and you will move your Viewport camera forward.

- Left-click and drag anywhere in the Viewport while moving your mouse backward, and you will move your Viewport camera backward.

- Left-click or right-click and drag anywhere in the Viewport while moving your mouse to the right, and you will rotate your Viewport camera to the right.

- Left-click or right-click and drag anywhere in the Viewport while moving your mouse to the left, and you will rotate your Viewport camera to the left.

- Right-click and drag anywhere in the Viewport while moving your mouse forward, and you will rotate your Viewport camera upwards.

- Right-click and drag anywhere in the Viewport while moving your mouse backward, and you will rotate your Viewport camera downwards.

- Left-click and right-click, and drag anywhere in the Viewport while moving your mouse forward, and you will increase your Viewport camera's Altitude.

- Left-click and right-click and drag anywhere in the Viewport while moving your mouse backward, and you will decrease your Viewport camera's Altitude.

- Left-click and right-click, then drag anywhere in the Viewport while moving your mouse to the right, and you will strafe your Viewport camera to the right.

- Left-click and right-click, then drag anywhere in the Viewport while moving your mouse to the left, and you will strafe your Viewport camera to the left.

- Scroll the mouse wheel up anywhere in your Viewport, and you will zoom your Viewport camera in.

- Scroll the mouse wheel down anywhere in your Viewport, and you will zoom your Viewport camera out.

- Click and drag the middle mouse button while moving your mouse forward anywhere in your Viewport, and you will increase your Viewport's camera Altitude.

- Click and drag the middle mouse button while moving your mouse backward anywhere in your Viewport, and you will decrease your Viewport's camera Altitude.

- Click and drag the middle mouse button while moving your mouse to the right anywhere in your Viewport, and you will strafe your Viewport camera to the right.

- Click and drag the middle mouse button while moving your mouse to the left anywhere in your Viewport, and you will strafe your Viewport camera to the left.

The following *Figures 2.8* and *Figure 2.9* below summarize mouse-based Viewport camera navigation:

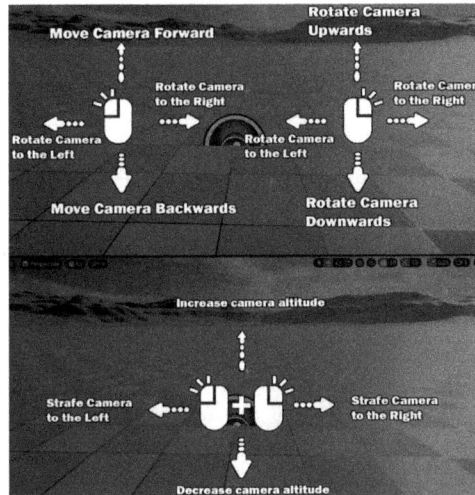

Figure 2.8: *Navigating through the Viewport with the mouse*

The following figure shows the middle mouse button and scroll functions:

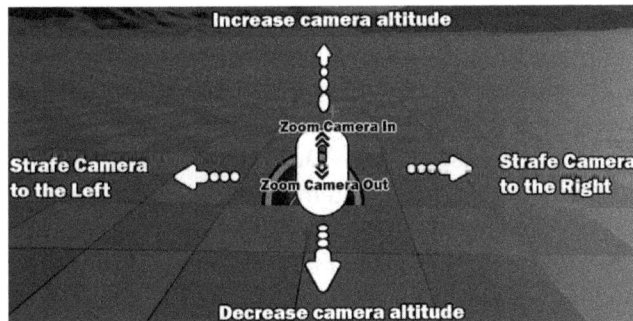

Figure 2.9: *Middle mouse button and scroll functions*

Alternatively, you can use your keyboard arrow keys to move forward, backward, left, and right, as well as *NumPad's* (ensure *NumLock* is turned on) keys *7* and *9* to decrease and increase Altitude, respectively, while *NumPad* keys *1* and *3* will zoom out and in, as long as they are held pressed respectively. However, usually using the mouse rather than the keyboard is preferred to navigate my way through the Viewport, because the keyboard-based navigation feels very rigid and slows the movement down, whereas the mouse-based navigation feels as if it flows smoother and is faster to move around. Try both methods and ultimately decide which one works best for you.

Besides the Viewport camera navigation, this section also houses several useful tools, including different viewing modes, such as perspective or orthographic, lit or unlit, wireframe, and lighting only, among many others, as well as toggling the visibility of different actors and features within. You can modify all these features through the buttons displayed in the *Figure 2.10*:

Figure 2.10: Different display options for the 3D Viewport

Through the Viewport, you can also switch between selection, movement, rotation, or scaling of objects, as well as toggle snap-to-grid functions along with the unit amount you wish to snap to. You can also choose if your 3-dimensional arrow gizmo is aligned with the world or a specific object. In addition to all that, you can also modify your Viewport camera's speed, a function that is quite handy when working with extremely large or extremely tight/small scenes. You can modify all these features through the buttons displayed in *Figure 2.11* below:

Figure 2.11: Different navigation settings for the 3D Viewport

Section 6: Outliner

The entirety of the content placed in your currently loaded level can be seen in the **Outliner**, in the form of a hierarchical tree. Not only can you see an itemized list of your content, but you can also rename it, organize it in folders or groups, toggle its visibility, and delete it. If you click once on any item listed in the **Outliner**, you will be able to quickly see its properties in the **Details** tab (which is *Section 7* of our UI breakdown, thus explained shortly) without having to manually locate the item within the 3D space in the Viewport. If you double-click on any item listed in the **Outliner**, then your Viewport camera will be quickly transferred to the double-clicked item in the 3D world, thus easily and quickly enabling you to find and visualize its presence within the 3D space. The **Outliner** can also show you the total number of actors placed at your level and the total number of actors selected at any given moment, as indicated in *Figure 2.12*:

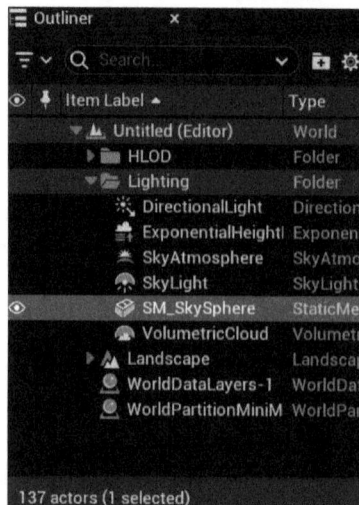

Figure 2.12: The Outliner tab

Section 7: Details

When you select an actor, either through the level Viewport, or the **Outliner**, then this actor's properties show up on the **Details** tab. Depending on the actor, these properties vary, but they will all have a **Transform** section where you can edit their coordinates within the 3D space, their rotation in relation to the 3D space, and their scale in the world. In addition, you will be able to access actor-specific properties, such as Materials used by a Static Mesh, or brightness and radius values assigned to a light, audio volume assigned to a sound cue, and so on. Think of the **Details** tab as your quickest and easiest way to modify specific attributes and properties for every actor or object you place in your 3D world. Please refer to *Figure 2.13* for the **Details** tab:

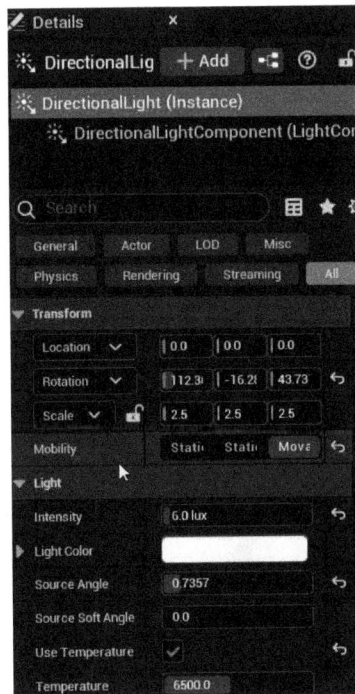

Figure 2.13: The Details tab

Section 8: Content Drawer and Bottom Toolbar

The **Content Drawer** is a great and easy way to quickly access different assets in your project's asset library. If you click it, a window very similar to Windows Explorer pops up, and from there, you can navigate to different folders within your project's content hierarchical structure and access assets such as Static Meshes (think of inanimate objects such as doors and columns or tables and chairs), Skeletal Meshes (think of assets that can be animated, such as human characters or goblins), material shaders and much, much more. Click anywhere back in the Viewport, and the **Content Drawer** withdraws from your view. Alternatively, you can pop it back in the picture and away by pressing *Ctrl+Spacebar*. *Figure 2.14* depicts the **Content Drawer**:

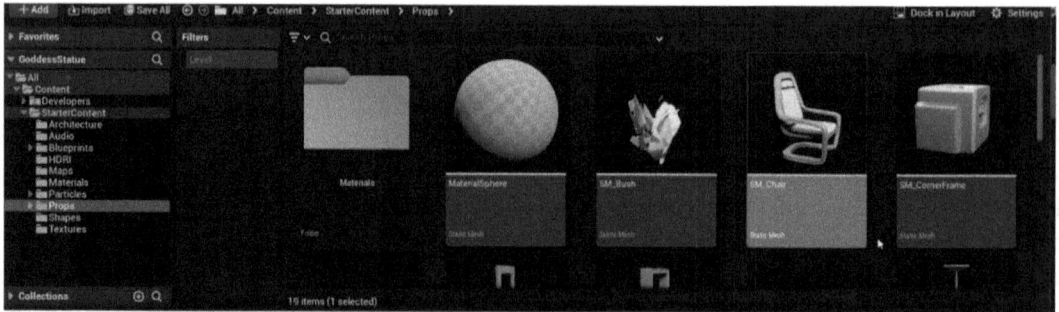

Figure 2.14: The Content Drawer

Next to the **Content Drawer** you will find the **Output Log**, which is a great way to read up on the editor's log, especially useful when something goes wrong and does not work the way it is supposed to. Imagine some actor does not function as it should in runtime, or your project's packaging fails. The **Output Log** will most certainly be a good place to use in your troubleshooting and overall investigation process. A depicted sample of the **Output Log** can be seen in *Figure 2.15*:

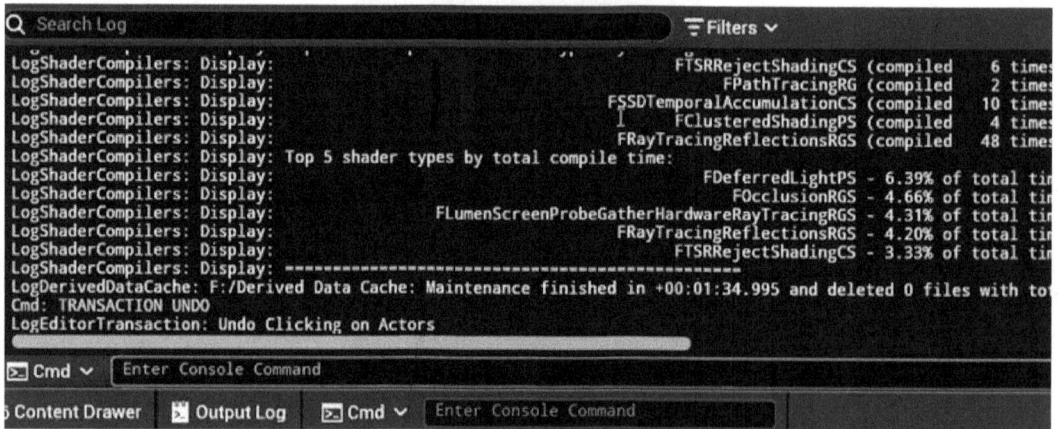

Figure 2.15: The Output Log

Following the **Output Log**, you have the console command (**Cmd**) prompt. This is useful when you need to type in some sort of command that can help you execute a specific function. For example, let us assume you want to have the framerate counter in your level Viewport. All you need to do is type the appropriate **Cmd**, in this case, this would be **stat FPS**, as indicated in *Figure 2.16*:

Figure 2.16: Using the command prompt

Upon executing the **stat FPS** command, you will be able to see the framerate counter in your 3D Viewport, as indicated in *Figure 2.17*:

Figure 2.17: *Displaying a framerate counter through the console command prompt*

Section 9: Right Bottom Toolbar

On the lower right-hand corner, as depicted in *Figure 2.18*, there is the right side of the Bottom Toolbar. In essence, we will not be using any of these features in this book's projects, but overall, this is where the developer can set and check their connection to a source control server, modify properties related to the editor's data cache, check if there are any currently open files that need to be saved before closing the editor. There are also **Trace** server related functionalities, which go far beyond this book's scope and, therefore, will not be discussed in this book.

Figure 2.18: *Right Bottom Toolbar*

Conclusion

You might be rejoicing by thinking we covered all the UI there is to cover in the Unreal Engine's editor, but the truth is we only scratched the surface. There are a lot more tools and functions, each with its unique UI encapsulating different tabs, sections, windows, Viewports, and properties. Worry not, these will be broken down as well and easily understood and memorized by utilizing them when a step in each of our projects requires us to bring them up and use them. As a matter of fact, we will already be exploring some of them in the next chapter!

Nevertheless, now you know how to setup a project and use different templates, as well as have a better understanding of the initial User Interface's layout.

Everything you learned in this chapter, will most certainly be useful in the next chapter, as we will start adding, editing and manipulating content, for the purpose of completing our very first scene.

Points to remember

- Setting up an Unreal Engine project
- Using Unreal Engine templates for your project
- Unreal Engine's Default and initial UI layout
- Engine Scalability Settings
- Framerate monitoring
- 3D Viewport navigation

Exercises

1. You can practice everything you learned in this chapter by setting up a new project using any of the Engine's default templates and then navigating through the 3D Viewport while enabling the framerate counter in your project.

Join our book's Discord space

Join the book's Discord Workspace for Latest updates, Offers, Tech happenings around the world, New Release and Sessions with the Authors:

https://discord.bpbonline.com

CHAPTER 3
Unreal Engine's Building Blocks

Introduction

In this chapter, we perform an introductory mini project in which we build a small building with a room in an empty terrain by using different Static Meshes we bring in from our asset library, only to move them, rotate them, and scale them until we get the results we want. Then we apply different Materials on our Static Meshes, once again taken from our existing asset library. Next, we add and modify some lighting in our scene, only to end it all with Blueprinting that allows the end user to toggle the light on and off when playing our map.

Structure

The topics covered in this chapter:

- Building your very first level
- First interaction with Materials
- Your first Blueprint

Objectives

Once you have completed this chapter, you will have a better understanding of some of the Engine's fundamental tools and workflows, which will be useful for the projects after this chapter.

Building your very first level

Now that we are familiar with the basic layout and location of our fundamentals, let us start creating a very simple scene just to get a basic understanding of the more advanced steps we will be taking in the next chapter.

Typically, there are a few standard actors that we place almost every time we create an environment. One of the most common types of actors, if not the most common, is the **Static Mesh**. The Static Mesh, in essence, is an inanimate, rigid object that we place in a scene. Perhaps the most frequent use of a Static Mesh is for architectural purposes. Imagine you want to build a simple room for example, we need to break down the basic components we would need: four walls, a ceiling, a floor, and at least one entry point, therefore a door frame. If we are to be efficient and smart, we will build a set of modular pieces that can be used and reused for more structures. We have four walls, for instance, we do not necessarily need to build four different models of a wall, we can use the same one four times unless, of course, each wall must have some unique characteristic that the other three do not have, however in our example, we are keeping things simple.

This is where the **StarterContent** we added to our project back in *Chapter 1, Unleashing the Unreal Engine* will come in handy. Let us start building a simple room with some of the **StarterContent** Static Meshes.

Before we decide which Static Meshes we want to use to build our simple room, we first need to locate these assets. In the previous chapter, we talked about the **Content Drawer**. This is where the **Content Drawer** will be our best friend. Let us now begin:

1. Press *Ctrl + Spacebar* to bring up the **Content Drawer**, as depicted in *Figure 3.1*:

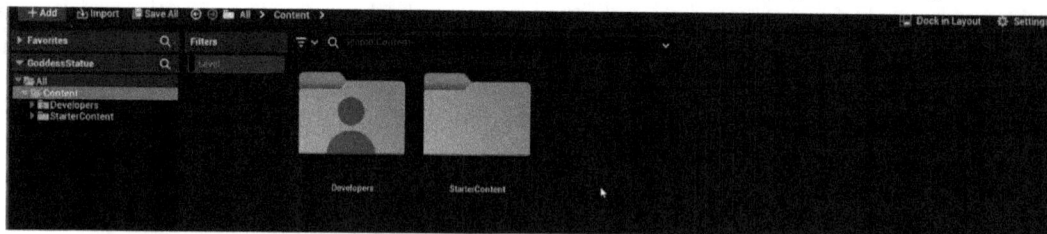

Figure 3.1: Content Drawer

2. Expand the **StarterContent** folder under the **Content** folder in the hierarchical folder tree on the left, and then select the **Props** folder, shown in *Figure 3.2*:

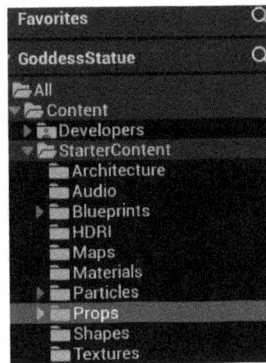

Figure 3.2: StarterContent folder

3. Now click on the add filter icon, which looks like three bars, as indicated in *Figure 3.3*:

Figure 3.3: Using filters in the Content Drawer

4. From all the available filter options you see, check the box next to **Static Mesh**, as depicted in *Figure 3.4*:

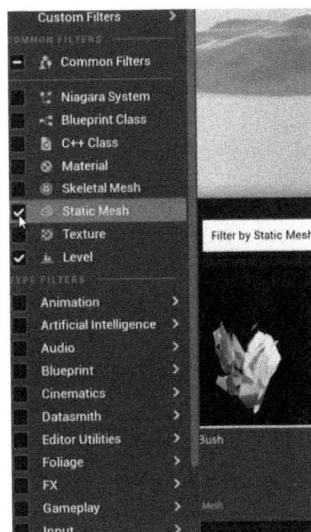

Figure 3.4: Different filter options

5. Now your **Content Drawer** shows you only the Static Meshes within the selected folder, as seen in *Figure 3.5*:

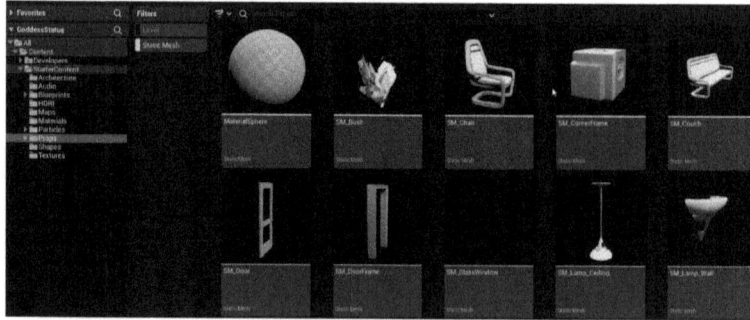

Figure 3.5: *Static Meshes within the selected folder*

6. Let us click and drag the **SM_DoorFrame** Static Mesh into our scene's Level Viewport, as indicated in *Figure 3.6*:

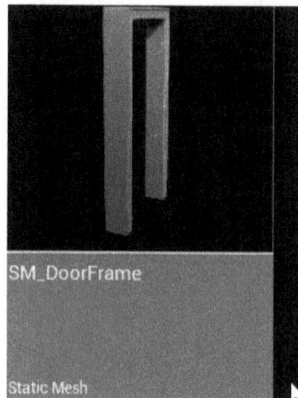

Figure 3.6: *Static Mesh*

The result should resemble *Figure 3.7*:

Figure 3.7: *SM_DoorFrame placed within the 3D Viewport*

7. Repeat the process by clicking and dragging the Static Mesh **SM_Door** from the **Content Drawer** anywhere into the Level Viewport. Most likely you placed it somewhere that is not properly aligned with the door frame. So, it is probably looking somewhat like in *Figure 3.8*:

Figure 3.8: *Door and door frame being misaligned in the 3D space*

8. Let us align the door to the door frame. Select the door frame by simply clicking on it. Alternatively, you can also select it via the Outliner, as described in the previous chapter.

    You will know you have successfully selected it by the yellow outline surrounding the Static Mesh.

9. With the door frame selected, go to the **Details** panel right-click on the **Location** row under the **Transform** section, and select **Copy**, as depicted in *Figure 3.9*:

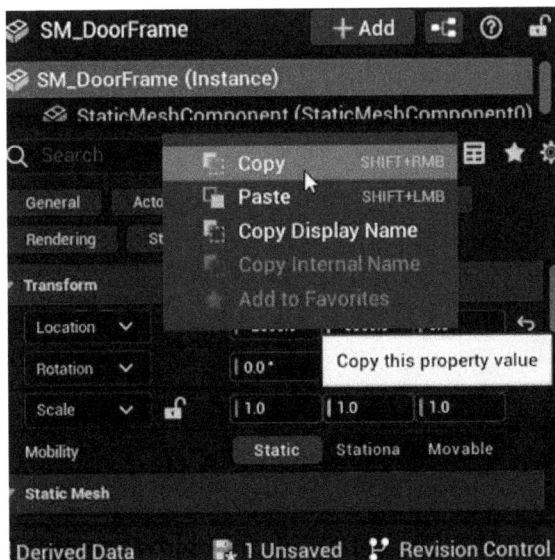

Figure 3.9: *Copying Location coordinates*

10. Now select the door Static Mesh (**SM_Door** if you are selecting it from the Outliner), and once again, in the **Details** panel, under **Transform** right click on the **Location** row and select **Paste**, as displayed in *Figure 3.10:*

Figure 3.10: *Pasting Location coordinates*

Alternatively, if you want to expedite the copy/pasting process, instead of right-clicking you can press *Shift + right* mouse to copy, *Shift + left* mouse to paste.

After copy/pasting, interestingly enough, the result is not what you expected. If you correctly followed the above steps, what you have right now in your Viewport, looks like *Figure 3.11*:

Figure 3.11: *Door mesh still misaligned*

The reason they are still misaligned is because each of these Static Meshes has a different pivot point, and the coordinates are applied to a mesh's pivot point. The door frame's pivot point is centered, and the door's pivot point is on the lower left corner (looking at the *Figure 3.11*). This is not done randomly; the door mesh has the pivot point at its corner because, ideally, at some point, we would want to make it open and close, which consequently would mean it rotates around the Z-axis of its pivot point (the blue arrow pointing upwards, away from the ground).

By copy/pasting the **Location** coordinates from one mesh to the other, however, we achieved perfectly aligning them on the X-axis (red arrow) and the Z-axis (blue arrow), leaving only the Y-axis for us to fix (green arrow). The solution to our problem is quite simple. With the **SM_Door** mesh selected, click and drag the pivot point's green arrow and keep dragging it until it perfectly touches the edge of the door frame mesh, as shown in *Figure 3.12*:

Figure 3.12: Aligning the door mesh to the door frame mesh, yet there is a small gap

11. It looks almost perfect, except for the fact that upon closer inspection there is a small gap between the door and the door frame, on the right side of the door as we are looking at the *Figure 3.12*. Note also that the door mesh's left side overlaps with the door frame mesh's geometry.

To fix that, we need to adjust the number of units we use for snapping any movement on the 3D space's grid. We can do that by clicking **10** next to the grid snapping icon on the upper right corner of the Level Viewport. Click it and then select **5**, as seen in *Figure 3.13*:

Figure 3.13: Modifying the snap grid size

Now that we have modified the snapping grid size to 5 units, we make sure we have the door (**SM_Door**) selected, and once again, we click and drag its pivot point's green arrow (Y-axis) and slightly move it to the right or the left, depending on which side of the door you are looking at, until it is properly aligned with the door frame mesh, as shown in *Figure 3.14*:

Figure 3.14: Perfectly aligning the door with the door frame

Excellent, now we have a door and a door frame, but there are no walls around them. Let us add some walls then. If you got the chance to look around the **Props** folder, where we got our door and door frame meshes from, you probably noticed there are no wall meshes there. That is because in the **StarterContent** folder structure, we can find walls and ceilings within the **Architecture** folder.

12. Once again, open the **Content Drawer** by pressing *Ctrl + Spacebar*, and click on the **Architecture** folder. From there, find, click, and drag the **Wall_Door_400x400** Static Mesh into our Level Viewport, as seen in *Figure 3.15*:

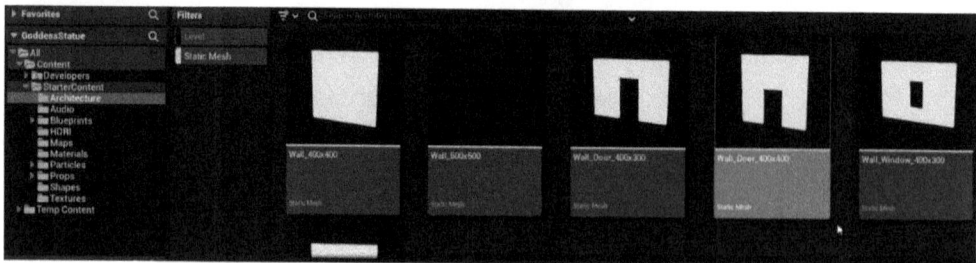

Figure 3.15: Finding Wall_Door_400x400 in the Content Drawer

You probably already noticed that the wall has an opening that should match the door frame perfectly. However, the wall mesh seems to be rotated the wrong way in relation to the door frame and the door. That is easily fixed. With the **Wall_Door_400x400** wall mesh selected, we will switch our mouse cursor into rotation mode while in the Viewport.

There are four modes:

- Select mode, which allows us to select actors in Level Viewport.
- Translate mode, which, in essence, allows us to move selected actors in the Viewport.
- Rotation mode, which allows us to rotate selected actors.
- Scale mode, which allows us to modify the size of a selected actor.

There are three ways to switch between these modes:

- Press *Q* to enter Select mode, *W* for Translate, *E* for Rotate and *R* for Scale.
- Click on each of the different icons shown in *Figure 3.16,* to enter the respective mode.

Figure 3.16: Different actor manipulation modes

- With either Translate, Rotate or Scale modes selected, press *Spacebar* to cycle through these three, will not work with Select mode.

13. Now that you know how to switch into these different modes, once more, with the wall Static Mesh selected in the Level Viewport, enter Rotate mode —the fastest way to do this is by pressing *E* — and you will notice that the transformation gizmo at the mesh's pivot point has changed from having three arrows, into three colorful arched shapes, each one representing rotation along the X, Y, and Z-axis (red, green and blue). Click and drag the blue axis until you have rotated the wall mesh by 90 degrees, as shown in *Figure 3.17*:

Figure 3.17: Rotating a Static Mesh

14. By switching back to the Translate (or move) mode —the fastest way to do that is by pressing *W* — align properly the wall mesh with the door frame mesh. You can achieve that either by manually moving the wall mesh until perfectly positioned around the door frame mesh, or by copying the door frame's location coordinates from its **Details** panel and then pasting them into the wall mesh's location coordinates in the wall's **Details** panel, under the **Transform** section. If you choose to do the latter, do not forget to move the wall mesh manually slightly on the Y (green) axis till properly positioned around the door frame mesh. Your result should look similar to the one in *Figure 3.18*:

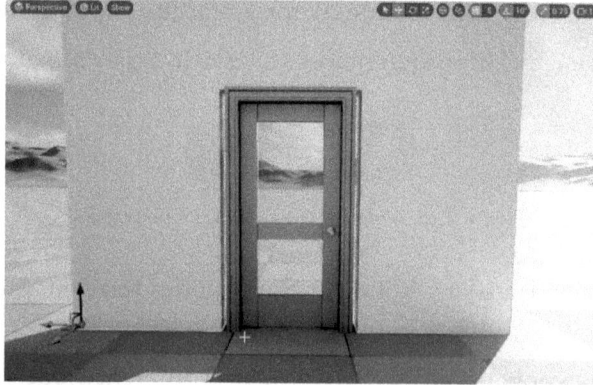

Figure 3.18: *Wall mesh surrounding the door and door frame meshes*

Yet again, it is far from perfect. Note how there is a gap between the wall and the door frame on both sides of the door frame's mesh. To fix this, we will need to move the wall slightly to the right (looking at the picture above) and then switch to Scale mode, just so we can make the wall mesh slightly narrower. To achieve this, you can either keep switching between Translate and Scale modes, provided you modify the scaling's grid size to the smallest possible value, as shown in *Figure 3.19*, which is **0.03125** units, or we can be more efficient and manually enter the correct scaling values in the mesh's Details.

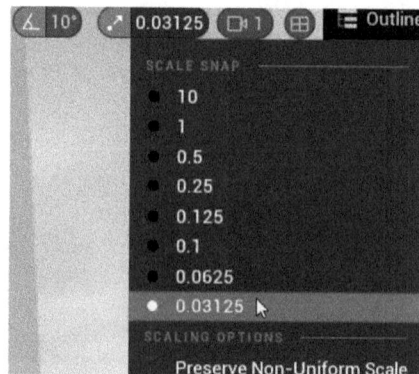

Figure 3.19: *Modifying the scaling units to the smallest value*

Since the scaling work has already been done while preparing this example, the smart approach will be to manually enter the scale values for the mesh. So, select the wall mesh, and then in its **Details**, place the following values for its **Scale**: **0.875** for X (red), **1.0** for Y (green), **1.0** for Z (blue). In other words, we just decreased the mesh's X scale value, to make it essentially narrower. Please refer to *Figure 3.20*:

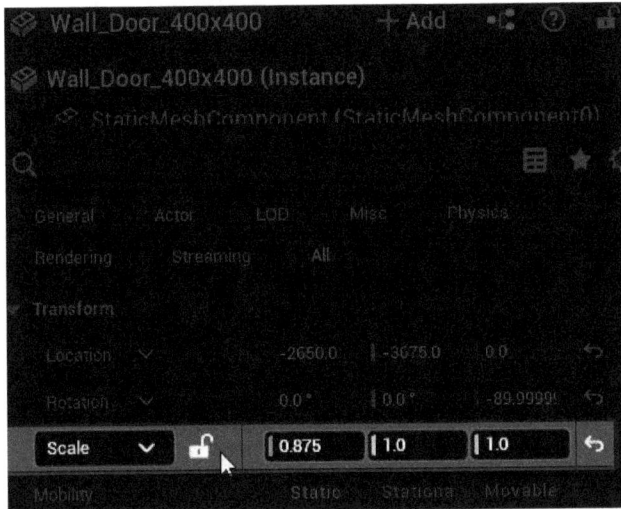

Figure 3.20: Scaling dimensions

Once you have modified the scale values, move the wall around the door frame, until they perfectly match, such as in *Figure 3.21*:

Figure 3.21: Meshes perfectly matching with each other

By now you have learned how to find and access a Static Mesh through the **Content Drawer**, how to place it in the scene through the Level Viewport, how to move it around, rotate it and scale it, until it looks the way you want it to. By using what you just learned, let us find more walls to bring in our scene and finish building this simple room.

Once more, in the **Content Drawer** (*Ctrl + Spacebar*), under the **Architecture** folder, you will find a Static Mesh named **Wall_400x400**, click and drag it into our scene.

By using the Translate mode, position the newly added wall in such a way that it forms a perfect 90 degree angle with the wall mesh surrounding the door frame. It should look like *Figure 3.22*:

Figure 3.22: Having added another wall mesh into the Viewport

Since we need more walls to complete the room, you can keep dragging the same mesh from the **Content Drawer** into the scene, or you can be efficient and instead press *Alt+ Click* and drag the selected wall mesh in the Viewport to the direction of any of the three dimensions (X, Y, Z/ red, green, blue). By performing this action, you are essentially using a shortcut to duplicate the selected Static Mesh. You can also achieve the same result by pressing *Ctrl + D* while having the mesh selected in the Viewport, or keep *Ctrl* pressed and move/drag the mesh to create a new instance, or you can right click on the selected mesh, select **Edit** and then **Duplicate**, much like in the *Figure 3.23*:

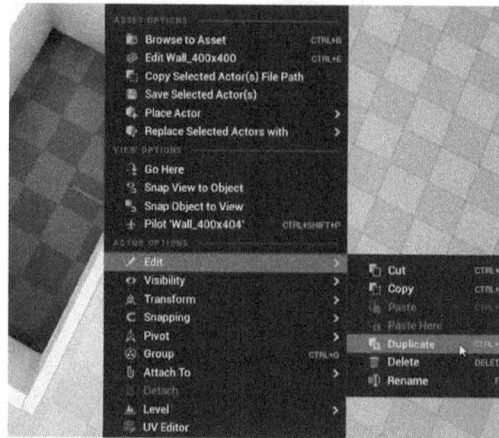

Figure 3.23: Duplicating a mesh through the Viewport

Keep duplicating and moving around the wall mesh, until you have achieved all the steps depicted in the next four *Figures 3.24 to 3.27*:

Figure 3.24: Duplicating and positioning a wall mesh

Keep duplicating and moving around the wall mesh:

Figure 3.25: Yet another wall mesh duplicated and positioned

Figure 3.26: The wall mesh duplication and positioning continue until we have a closed room

In the following figure, a complete closed room is shown:

Figure 3.27: A complete, closed room

Now, it is time to add a floor and a ceiling. For that, we will use the **Floor_400x400** Static Mesh, once again taken from the **Architecture** folder, as seen in *Figure 3.28*. Just like before, *Ctrl + Spacebar* to bring up the **Content Drawer**, so we can click and drag the Static Mesh into our Level Viewport.

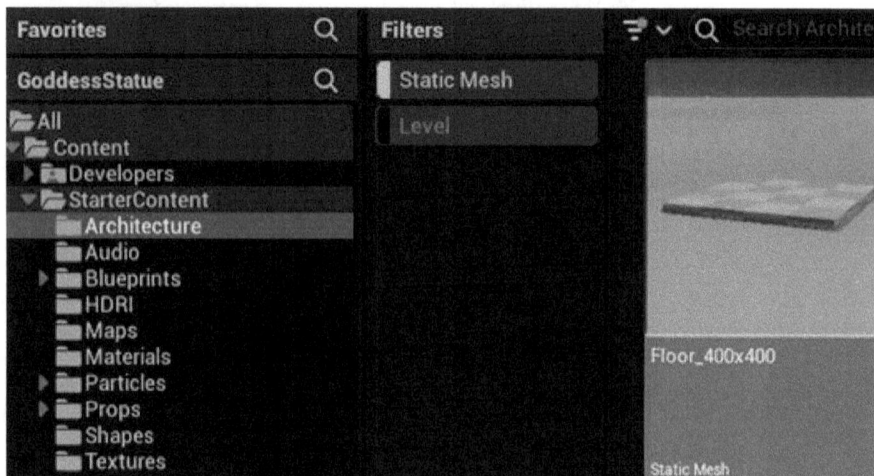

Figure 3.28: The floor mesh

Much like we built the rest of the room so far, again, we use the transform gizmo while having the floor mesh selected in the Viewport, and then we move it, rotate it, and scale it until it is perfectly aligned with our room, pretty much as depicted in *Figure 3.29*:

Figure 3.29: Placing the floor mesh

One thing you probably noticed when you dragged the floor into the Viewport, was how it was overlapping with the existing floor geometry, resulting in a flickering appearance, almost as if the two floors fight each other on which one is visible. The easiest way to fix this is to simply elevate the floor mesh just enough to not overlap with the ground. You can either do this by dragging the mesh up on the Z-axis (blue) or by having the floor mesh selected and then going to its **Transform** section in the **Details** panel and setting the Z value (blue) for its **Location** to anything more than 0, as little as 0.1 will suffice, as indicated in *Figure 3.30*:

Figure 3.30: Fixing surface overlap issues

First interaction with Materials

As you can see in *Figure 3.29*, only half of the room is covered with a floor. To fill up the room's floor, we can either duplicate the floor mesh and move it right next to the existing one, or we can scale the existing one by stretching it along the Y-axis (green). Both methods have their pros and cons.

Stretching the geometry means we also stretch the appearance of its Material shader and the textures used in it. So, if we had a square tiled floor Material applied to this mesh, and we stretched it, we would not have perfectly squared tiles any longer.

To better demonstrate this point, let us find a Material to use on the floor mesh we just placed and moved in our scene.

1. Once again, our best friend, the **Content Drawer** needs to be brought up with *Ctrl + Spacebar*, but this time, we will click on the **Materials** folder under the **StarterContent** folder, as seen in *Figure 3.31*:

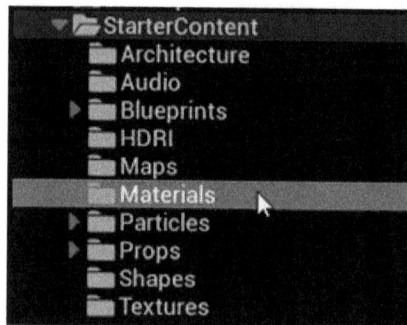

Figure 3.31: The Materials folder within the StarterContent folder

2. Since earlier we had applied the Static Mesh filter, the **Materials** folder will appear empty, as shown in *Figure 3.32*:

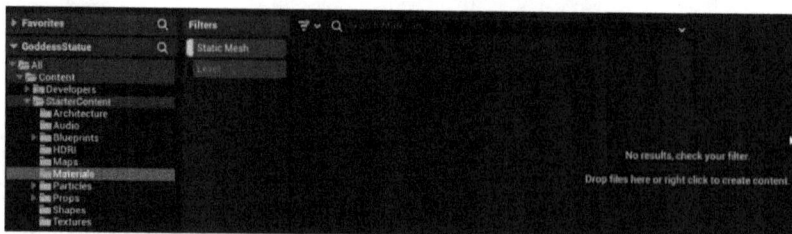

Figure 3.32: Our Content Drawer appears empty

3. All we need to do is click on the **Static Mesh** filter under **Filters**. We will know it is not active because it will be grayed out, much like the **Level** filter in the picture above. Deactivating it will make all the **Material** folder content appear, much like in *Figure 3.33*:

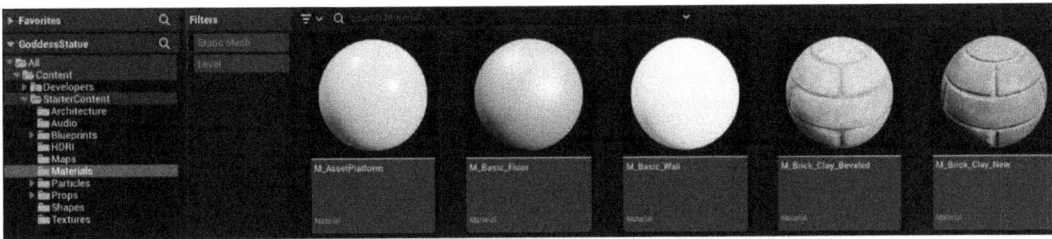

Figure 3.33: Content Drawer does not appear empty any longer

4. Let us find a Material that features square tiles. We are specifically looking for **M_Ceramic_Tile_Checker**. There are two ways to find this Material. The first way is to scroll down in the **Content Drawer**, until we come across this Material, however this can be a daunting task when there are a lot of Materials. In this case the **Content Drawer** informs us that there are 43 items in this folder, so that is a lot of items to sort through to find just one.

Let us use the search bar on the top of the **Content Drawer** to make life a little bit easier. Since you already know the name of the Material we need, just type it in the search bar, as indicated in *Figure 3.34*:

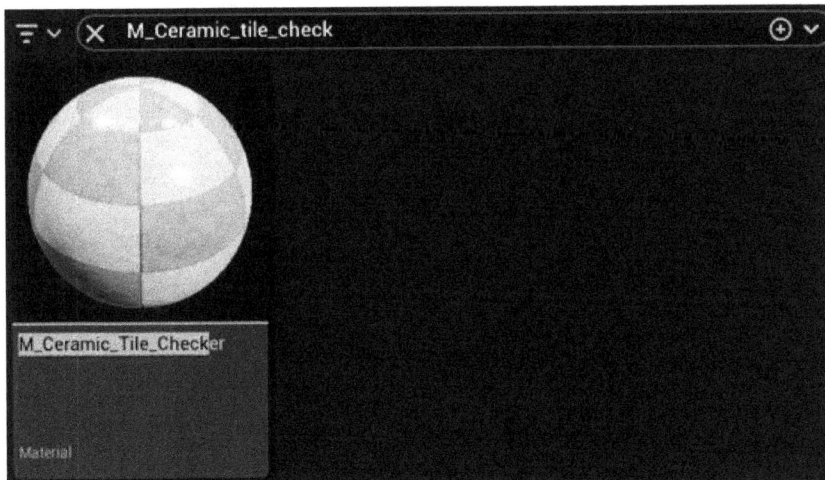

Figure 3.34: Typing the name of the asset we want to find

At this point, it is worth noting that if you know the type of an asset you are trying to find, for example a Material or a Static Mesh, you can just type it in the search bar, and it will show any objects that befit the searched category.

5. There are two ways to apply this Material to our floor mesh in our scene. The first and probably easiest way, is to click and drag the **M_Ceramic_Tile_Checker** directly onto our floor mesh in the Level Viewport, as displayed in the *Figure 3.35*. If you want to use the second way, skip this step and move on to step *6*.

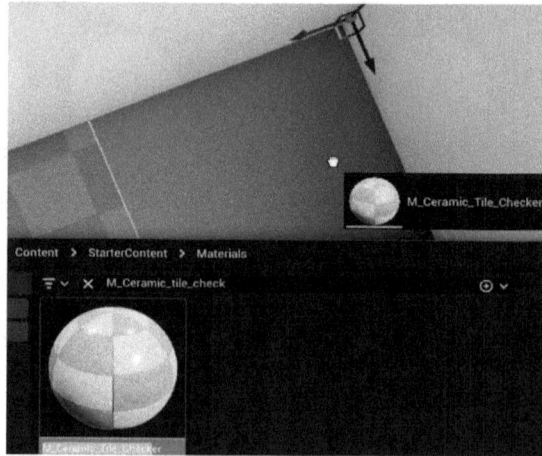

Figure 3.35: Applying a Material on a mesh by clicking and dragging the Material from the Content Drawer directly on to the mesh in the 3D Viewport

6. The second way to apply the selected Material onto our floor mesh, is while having the Material selected with our **Content Drawer** still popped up, click on the floor mesh in our scene, and then scroll further down on its **Details** tab, until you find the **Materials** section. There, you will notice a row titled **Element 0** which is already occupied by the mesh's default Material. Click the small icon depicting a leftwards arrow in a circle, which indicates we want to replace the default Material and instead use whatever Material we have selected in our **Content Drawer**. Doing so will result in (*Figure 3.36*):

Figure 3.36: The Material has been applied to our mesh

7. Now that our floor has a square tiled Material, let us go back to examining the difference between duplicating our mesh and stretching it to cover the room's floor surface. Let us switch to scaling mode, once again the shortcut for that is by pressing *R* while having our floor mesh selected in the Viewport. Now, stretch the

mesh along the Y-axis (green) by simply clicking and dragging the transformation gizmo. Your result should look like *Figure 3.37*:

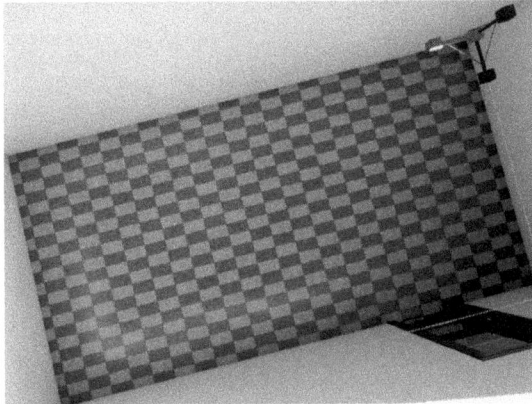

Figure 3.37: Stretched floor mesh

8. While we have successfully covered the room's floor, the tiling does not look that good. Let us hit *Ctrl+Z* to undo the stretch, or simply go to the floor mesh's **Details** tab, scroll all the way up to the **Transform** section, and reset its **Scale** values by pressing the reverse arrow icon next to the values, like shown in *Figure 3.38*:

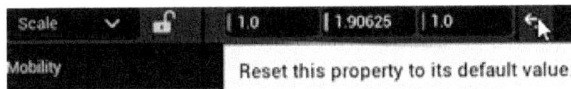

Figure 3.38: Resetting the floor mesh's scale

9. Now switch back to translate or move mode by pressing *W*, and like earlier in this chapter, *Alt+click+drag* the floor mesh along the Y-axis (green arrow), until you have placed the newly generated mesh next to the existing one, in such a way that the entire room is covered with a floor, much like in *Figure 3.39*:

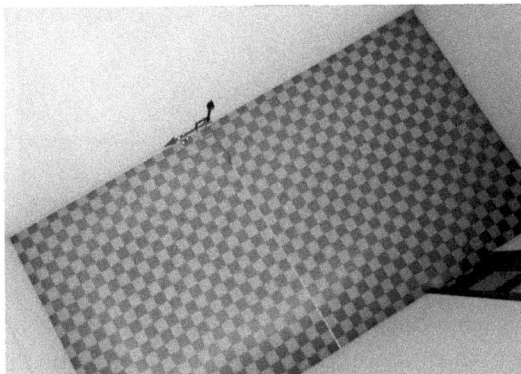

Figure 3.39: Duplicating the floor mesh

While the floor looks great within the room, if we move our Viewport camera outside the room, we will notice that a small part of the floor mesh is bleeding through the walls (*Figure 3.40*):

Figure 3.40: *The floor mesh extends beyond the room's boundaries*

10. While having the second-floor mesh selected in the Viewport, press *Ctrl + Click* on the first-floor mesh. Now you have both selected and highlighted, with the transformation gizmo appearing at the first floor's pivot point, as indicated in *Figure 3.41*:

Figure 3.41: *Having selected both floor meshes*

11. Now press *R* to switch back to scaling mode, and click and drag along the Y-axis (green) of the transformation gizmo, to decrease both floor meshes' width just enough that they fit within the room, as seen in *Figure 3.42*:

Figure 3.42: Scaling the floor meshes down, enough to fit within the room's boundaries

12. Truth be told, you could leave it like this, and the end user would not realize that the tiles are not perfectly square. However, we try to be perfectionists, so let us modify the rest of the scaling values for both meshes. Presently, they are both selected; you know that because the Outliner tells you that there are 2 actors selected. You also know that because you can see each floor mesh highlighted in the level Viewport. Since they both share identical scale values, while having both selected, we can go to the **Details** tab and modify the scale values for both at the same time. Presently, you should have a value of **1.0** for both the X and Z-axis (red and blue), while your Y value (green) should be something less than 1, depending on how much you clicked and drag in the previous step. In my case, it reads **0.9375**. Pretty much, what you see in *Figure 3.43*:

Figure 3.43: The floor mesh's Y (green) scaling should be less than 1

13. Next, look at the little padlock icon next to **Scale**. If it appears locked and we increase the Y (green) value to 1, then both X and Z will increase as well, surpassing the value of 1.0 to maintain the same proportional ratio the floor meshes currently have. However, this is not what we want because we need to modify only the X value. So, if the padlock icon appears locked, click on it, and it will change to unlocked, much like in the previous figure (*Figure 3.43*). With the padlock icon unlocked, now let us copy the Y (green) value, and paste it into the X (red) value, as depicted in *Figure 3.44*:

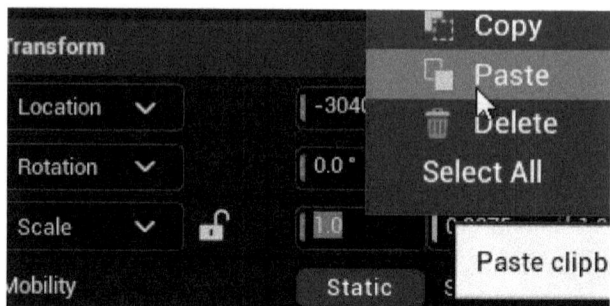

Figure 3.44: Pasting Scale values

14. Your X and Y values now should be the same, less than **1.0,** while the Z value should be exactly **1.0,** similar, to *Figure 3.45*:

Figure 3.45: X (red) and Y (green) values are the same, Z (blue) is 1.0

You may or may not need to move both floors along the X-axis, depending on where they were in relation to the room's walls, but should you notice a small gap between the floor meshes and the wall meshes, simply press W to go into Translate/move mode, and then move the floor meshes accordingly.

Your end result should look similar to *Figure 3.46*:

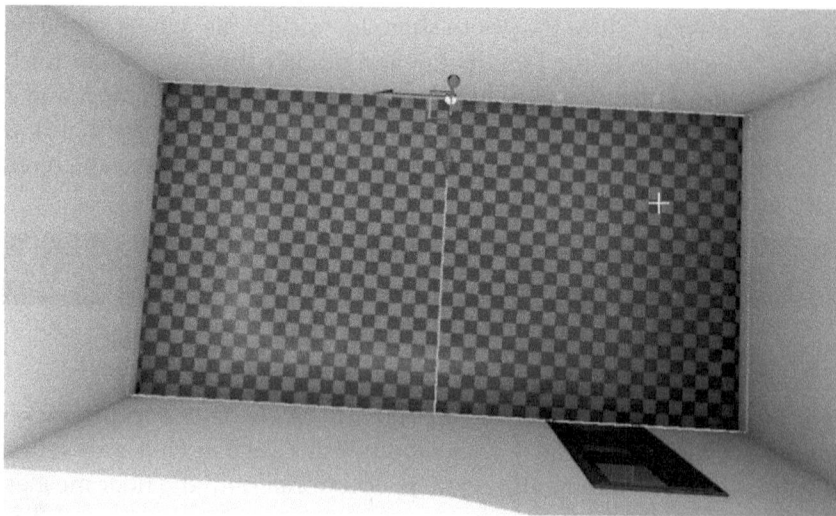

Figure 3.46: A room with a floor

And if we move our Viewport camera outside the room, it should look similar to *Figure 3.47*:

Figure 3.47: A perfectly good room

15. Our room is looking good, but we are missing the ceiling. By utilizing all the previous techniques, we can simply duplicate the two floor meshes and elevate them high enough to function as our ceiling. While having both meshes selected, press *W* to ensure we are in the movement mode and then press *Alt+Click+drag* along the Z-axis (blue arrow) until your result looks much like in *Figure 3.48*:

Figure 3.48: Duplicating the floor meshes to create a ceiling

16. Now let us assign a new Material to the newly generated ceiling meshes, since the squared tile Material is more suitable for the floor meshes. *Ctrl+Spacebar* to bring back the **Content Drawer**. Make sure you delete whatever is typed in the search bar, so that all the Materials can reappear. Let us get a bit more adventurous and go use M_Concrete_Panels on our ceiling. Once again type in **M_Concrete_Panels**

in the search bar, and while having both ceiling meshes selected in the Viewport, click and drag the Material from the **Content Drawer** onto the selected ceiling meshes. The result should resemble *Figure 3.49*:

Figure 3.49: A ceiling mesh with a suitable Material

17. Let us select all the wall meshes now. You can do this either by clicking once on a wall mesh in the Viewport and then while holding *Ctrl* pressed, click all the remaining wall meshes, or you can go in the **Outliner**, type in **wall** in the search bar, click the first row's wall in the **Outliner** and then while holding *Shift* pressed, click on the last row's wall in the **Outliner**, as such (*Figure 3.50*):

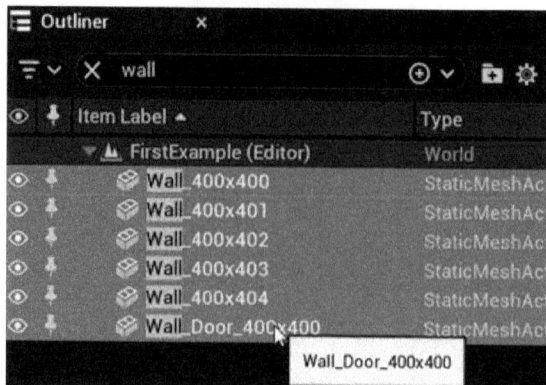

Figure 3.50: Using the Outliner tab's search to filter out specific actors

18. With all of our wall meshes selected, and given that the last thing we had selected in the **Content Drawer** was the Material we used for the ceiling in step *17*, let us go to the **Details** tab, scroll down until we find **Materials, Element 0** and once more click the small icon depicting a leftward arrow in a circle — just like we did earlier in step *6* — this way we use the concrete Material on all of our selected wall meshes, to get this result (*Figure 3.51*):

Figure 3.51: Assigning a realistic Material to our wall meshes

19. Now we have a realistic looking building in front of us. However, if we move the Viewport camera into the interior, we will notice it is quite dark, much like in *Figure 3.52*:

Figure 3.52: The room's interior lighting conditions are currently rather dark

It still looks good thanks to the Unreal Engine's Lumen. You can see the light that comes through the glass sections of the door hits the different surfaces and nicely bounces off them, giving us enough light to be able to see the interior. In addition, you probably noticed that when you first moved your Viewport camera in the interior, it was quite dark, but as time passed it got brighter, in other words the brightness got adjusted, much like it would in real life, when moving from a bright outdoor environment into a dark indoor one, our eyes would need a few seconds to adjust. The amount and the speed of this brightness adjustment can be modified, through post processing, by modifying Auto Exposure values, something we will be looking into more detail in later chapters.

20. For now, let us add some light into this room. Click on the little square with the plus sign icon, next to our Selection Mode, all of which can be found in the Main Toolbar. Should you have forgotten which one that is, just jump back to *Chapter 2, Unreal Engine UI , Page 19,* and look for *Section 2* of the UI breakdown. Back to the little square with the plus sign icon, this is the Quickly Add icon, click it, then hover over to **Lights**, then click on **Point Light**. Refer to the *Figure 3.53.*

Light it up!

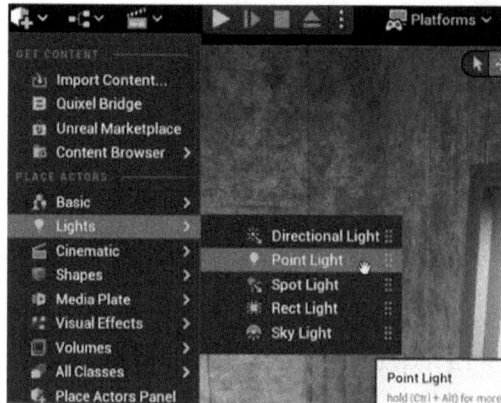

Figure 3.53: Adding a Point Light to our scene

21. This adds a Point Light actor in our scene. Now we will have to use the Point Light's transform gizmo and drag it into our room. The result should look like this (*Figure 3.54*):

Figure 3.54: A Point Light in the scene

22. It looks a little bit too bright. With the Point Light actor selected, let us go over to the **Details** tab and scroll down till we find the **Intensity** row under the **Light** section. The default value is 8.0 and should you wonder these units are Candelas. If you are curious about Candelas, feel free to visit Wikipedia and read up on the Candela unit **https://en.wikipedia.org/wiki/Candela.**

Let us change this value from 8.0 to 0.05. While in the interior, you would not notices much difference in the brightness, and this happens because of the Auto Exposure settings we currently have. Even the lowest intensity values appear to be too bright, as seen in *Figure 3.55*:

Figure 3.55: *Modifying the Light's Intensity value*

23. Let us fix this up, but before we do that, let us make our life a little bit easier and modify our UI layout a bit. Go all the way up on the Menu Bar and click on **Window** and click on **Place Actors**, as displayed in *Figure 3.56*:

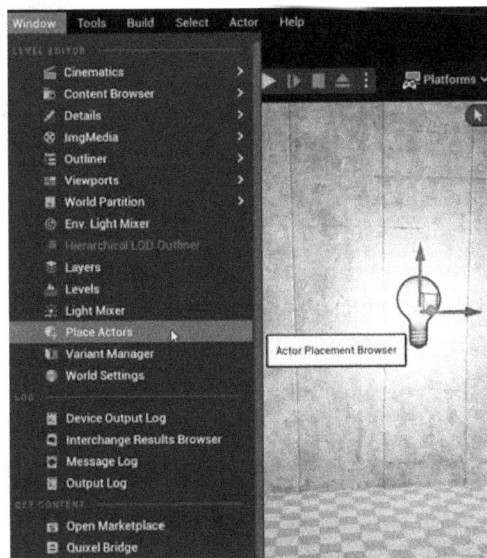

Figure 3.56: *Finding the Place Actors tab*

24. A new tab appears, now click and drag that tab right next to the **Outliner**, as shown in *Figure 3.57*:

Figure 3.57: *Clicking and dragging tabs across the UI*

25. Once you have successfully completed the move, your UI should look like *Figure 3.58*:

Figure 3.58: *The Place Actors tab, is now easily accessible*

The reason we did this is because further down the line, we will be needing to use a lot of actors and items we can quickly obtain through this tab, including lights, primitive geometry, volumes and much more.

26. Next up, click on the **Volumes** icon in the **Place Actors** tab. It looks as shown in *Figure 3.59*:

Figure 3.59: *The Volumes icon*

27. Scroll down until you find **Post Process Volume**, as seen in *Figure 3.60*, which you will then click and drag into the Viewport:

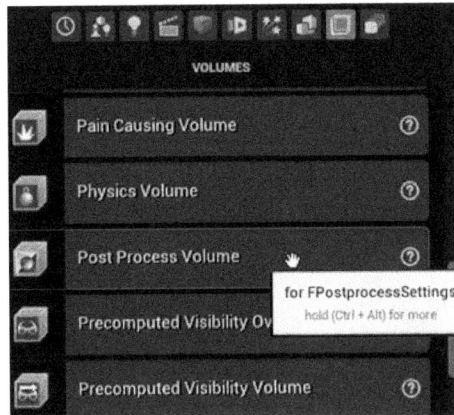

Figure 3.60: *Post Process Volume under the Place Actors tab*

You should now be able to see a yellow wireframed cube in the room we just created something similar to what you see in *Figure 3.61*:

Figure 3.61: *A Post Process Volume in our scene*

What we just did is add a **Post Processing Volume**. This means that we can modify the visuals when within this volume. We can modify for example the brightness, the saturation, the contrast, and so much more. The reason we added this into our room is just so we can modify the Auto Exposure values and be able to achieve darker values for our lights.

We can either have the **Post Process Volume** affect the entire world, or just a specific area. In our case, we want to affect only the interior we just built, so by using movement and scaling modes for our transformation gizmo — while having the post process volume selected — we will roughly size it up to match the shape and dimensions of our interior space. Much like in *Figure 3.62*:

Figure 3.62: *The Post Process Volume's boundaries almost match those of our room*

28. With our post process volume in place and selected, we go to the **Details** tab, and we expand the **Exposure** section. Then we check the boxes for both **Min EV100** and **Max EV100** and modified these parameters to 0 and 10 respectively. With your **Post Process Volume** selected, your details tab should look similar to *Figure 3.63*:

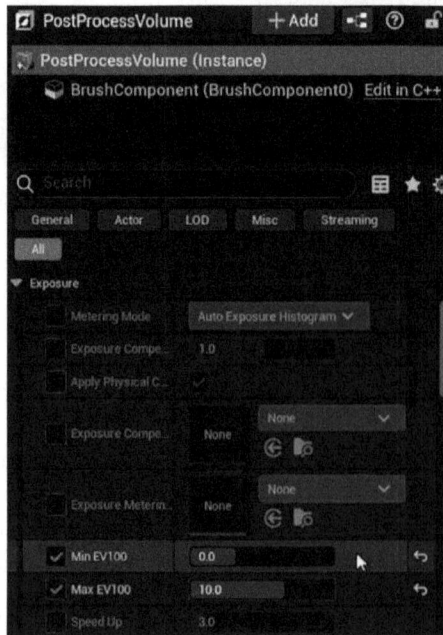

Figure 3.63: *The details of the selected Post Process Volume*

29. Note how dark the room looks now that we modified our exposure values (*Figure 3.64*):

Figure 3.64: The room is extremely dark, even though there is a Point Light in it

30. Select the Point Light and set the **Intensity** value to 1.5 cd (Candelas). Now the room looks a lot brighter, as seen in *Figure 3.65*:

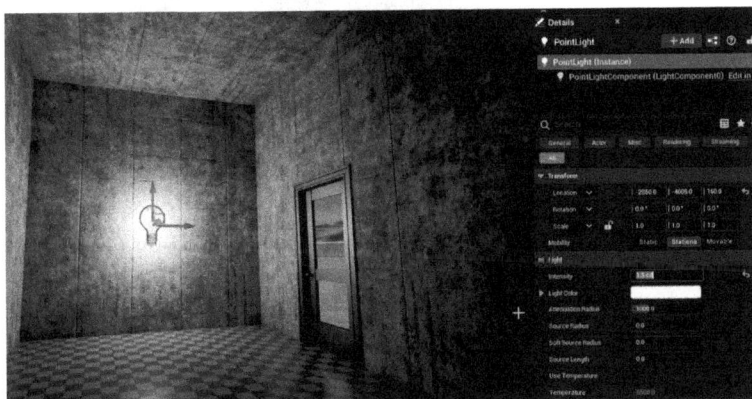

Figure 3.65: The Point Light now appears adequately bright

31. Go back to the **Content Drawer**, and under the **StarterContent** folder, go back into the **Props** folder. In the **Props** folder, look for SM_Lamp_Wall and click and drag it into our scene, close to the wall behind the Point Light, as depicted in *Figure 3.66*:

Figure 3.66: Placing a lamp mesh that indicates a light source

32. By now you should be comfortable selecting, moving, rotating, and scaling up objects in the scene. Rotate and place the lamp mesh properly on the wall, and then move the Point Light right above it, as displayed in *Figure 3.67*:

Figure 3.67: Positioning and aligning our lamp mesh to the wall

33. Select the Point Light — if it is not already selected — and over at the **Details** tab, in the **Transform** section, change its **Mobility** to **Movable**, as seen in *Figure 3.68*. We just converted this light into a dynamic light. That demands more performance, as it allows real time shadow casting, and overall is slower to render. However, in this example we have a very simple scene, and it would not affect our performance.

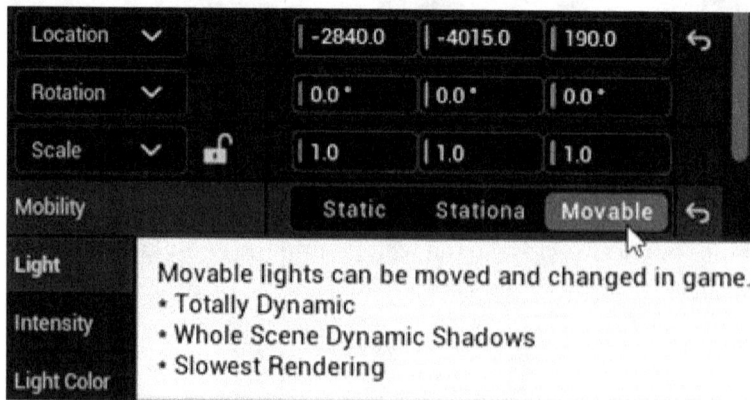

Figure 3.68: Setting the Point Light to Movable (also known as Dynamic)

34. It is probably a good time to save our work thus far. *Ctrl+Spacebar* to bring up the **Content Drawer**, click on the **Content** folder, then click on the +**Add** button on the upper left corner, and click on **New Folder**, as seen in *Figure 3.69*, then name this folder **Level**, as seen in *Figure 3.70*:

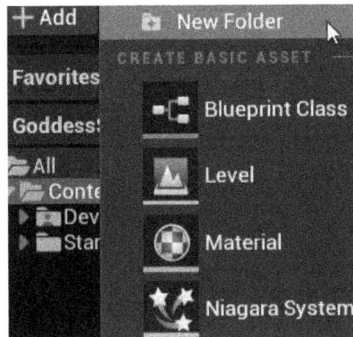

Figure 3.69: Creating a new folder

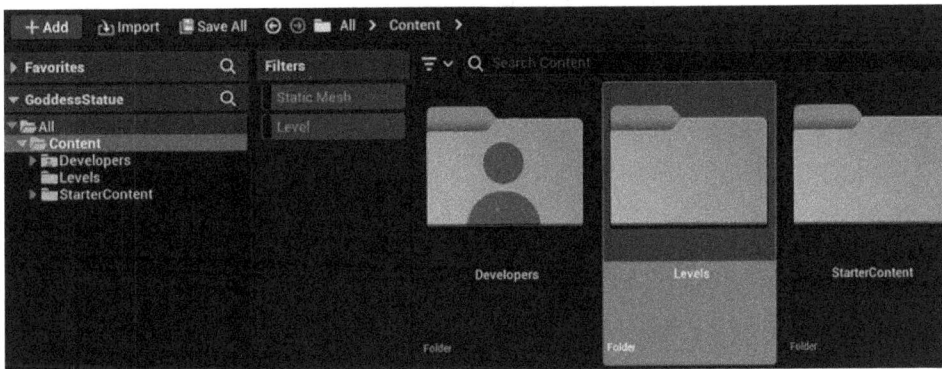

Figure 3.70: Naming the new folder as Levels

35. Now go to the Main Toolbar, click on File, click on **Save Current Level As**, select the **Content/Levels/** folder, and save the level with the **FirstExample** filename. When you are done, your **Content Drawer** folder structure and **Levels** folder should look much like in *Figure 3.71*:

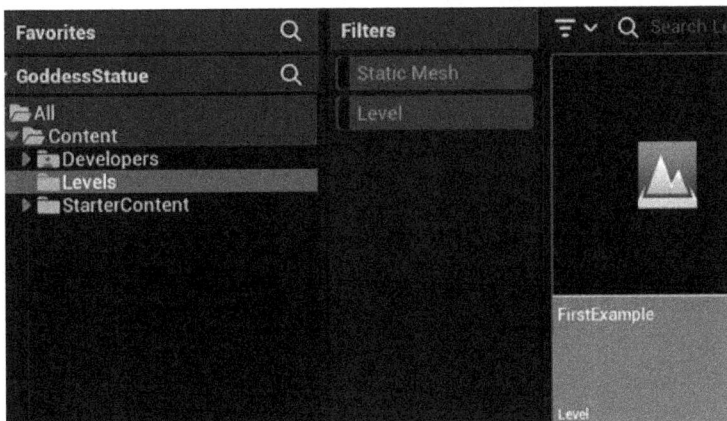

Figure 3.71: FirstExample our saved level within the Content Drawer, under the Levels folder

Congratulations! You have just completed your very first level. You used Static Meshes, you adjusted them to ultimately build some architecture, you applied different Materials to them, you added and edited lights, and added and edited the post processing for the building's interior.

Next, we will have our very first encounter with Blueprints!

Your first Blueprint

Now that we have our first basic level put together, it is a good opportunity to get a simple but fun idea of the power of the Blueprints. To keep it simple, we will work on the Level Blueprint of the FirstExample level we just completed. This way whatever Blueprints we create are affecting only this level and nothing else. They cannot be reused anywhere else, they will not affect anything else, and for now, that is the way we want it.

First, make sure you have loaded and are currently in the FirstExample map. In the previous part, we had just saved it under **Content/Levels/**, which you can find either through the Content Drawer, or by pressing *Ctrl + O* to open a level.

1. Once you have ensured you are in the correct level, open the Level Blueprint by navigating to the Main Toolbar, where you click the little icon that looks like a cluster of nodes connected to each other and then you click on **Open Level Blueprint**, as depicted in *Figure 3.72*:

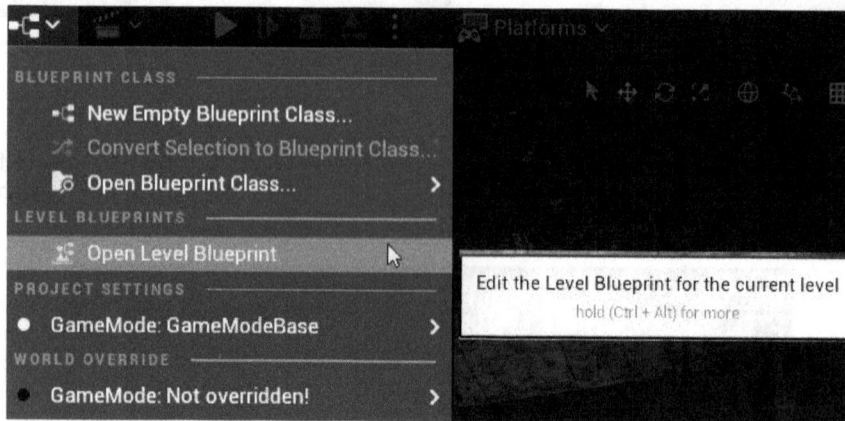

Figure 3.72: Opening up a Level Blueprint

2. Back in the Viewport, select the Point Light in the room we just built. With the Point Light being selected, go back to the Level Blueprint screen, and right click anywhere in the event graph and click **Create a Reference to PointLight**. Your process should be like *Figures 3.73 and 3.74*:

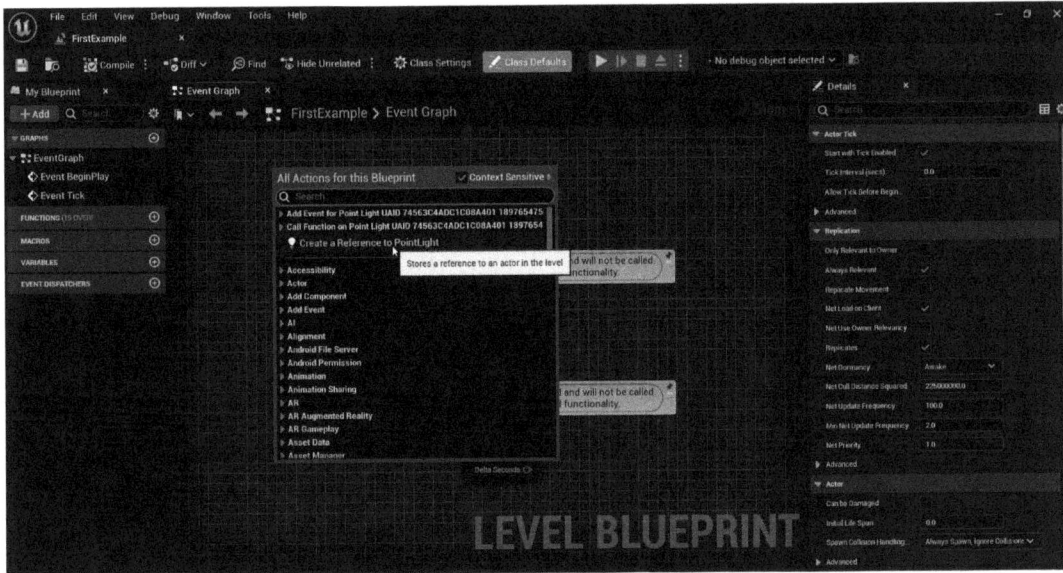

Figure 3.73: Creating a reference of our Point Light in the Level Blueprint

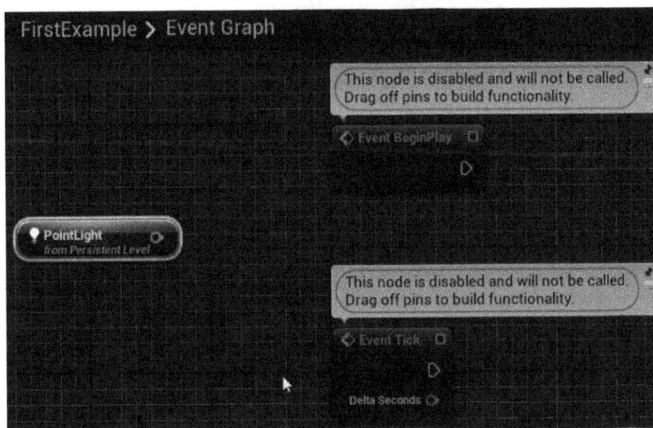

Figure 3.74: The node of the referenced Point Light

Before proceeding any further, here are some tips on navigating through the canvas of the **Event Graph**:

- Right-click and drag will move the canvas towards the same direction you move your mouse while doing so. For example, right-click and drag while moving the mouse right, will move your canvas to the right as well.

- Left-click and drag will begin drawing a selection, any nodes that are touched by this selection, will be included, and once a node is selected it is highlighted. To deselect either press *Ctrl+click* on a selected node or click anywhere on the canvas where there is nothing to be selected.

- Left-click and drag on a selected node: This will move the node wherever you drag it on the canvas.

- Mouse wheel up will zoom in on the spot you have your mouse cursor at.

- Mouse wheel down will zoom out.

- Extra hint! *Mouse wheel up + Ctrl* pressed, will zoom in even further, up to 7 times more.

3. Now that you understand the basic navigation around the Event Graph's canvas, let us move the Point Light reference node we created a bit further from the two red nodes that were already there (the nodes are labeled as Event Begin Play and Event Tick). Click and drag the Point Light node, and place it somewhere relatively far from the other two nodes. If you prefer, you can Alternatively select these two nodes and delete them, as we will not be using them in this example. Your **Event Graph** now should look like this (*Figure 3.75*):

Figure 3.75: A clean Event Graph

4. Click and drag from the Point Light's pin (the small blue circle with the tiny arrow at the edge of the node) anywhere in the **Event Graph** and once you let the click go, type **set intensity** in the search box of the newly popped up window, then select **Set Intensity (PointLightComponent)**, as in *Figure 3.76*:

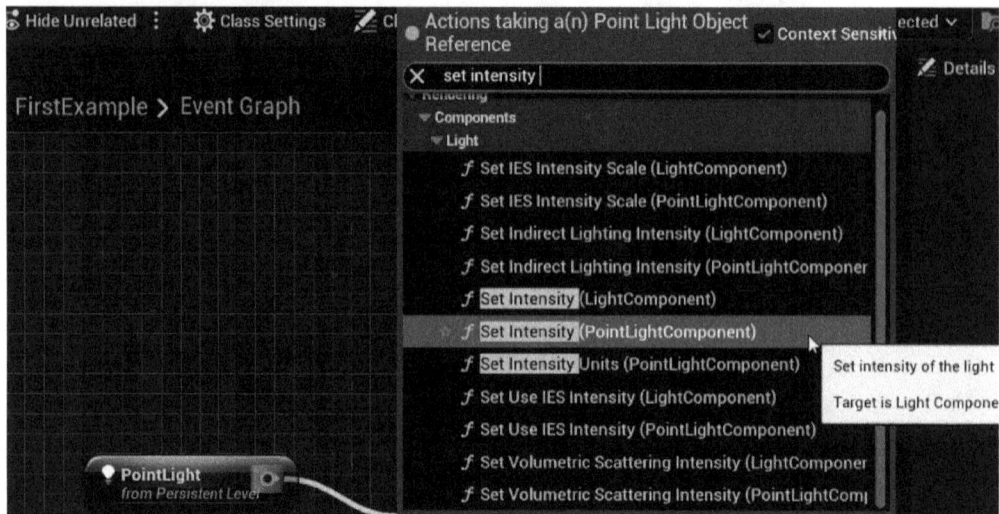

Figure 3.76: Creating the Set Intensity node

5. What you just created is a node that is basically a function that modifies our Point Light's intensity, much like when we did it manually through the **Details** tab earlier in this chapter. Now that you have created that node, it is a good opportunity to tidy up a bit our nodes and their connections, as it can get quite messy if we just leave them as they are. When you are done moving nodes around, your Level Blueprint's Event Graph should look like follows in *Figure 3.77*:

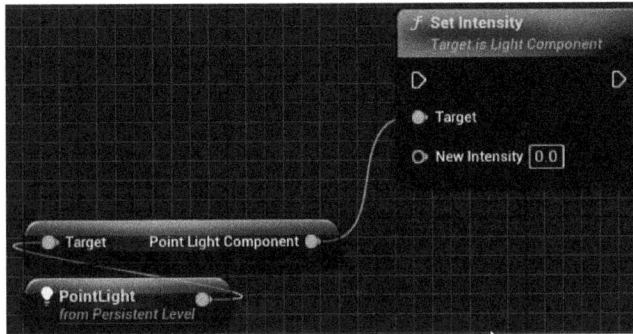

Figure 3.77: The Set Intensity node within the Event Graph

What we have right now is a reference to our Point Light, and a function that can change its intensity, or its brightness if you prefer. What we are currently missing is something that can trigger this intensity change in run-time, in other words something that will modify our Point Light's brightness when we play our level.

To keep things relatively simple, we want the end user to be the one that can trigger this change, by pressing a key on their keyboard, while they are in the game. For this example, let us assign the keyboard key *F* as the one that can trigger the Point Light's change in intensity.

6. Right click anywhere in the Event Graph, and type **Keyboard F** in the search box, then select the **F** key. This process looks similar to *Figure 3.78*:

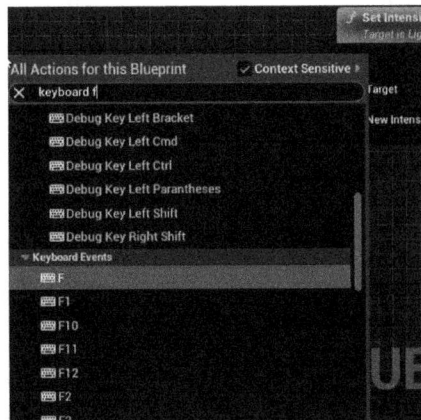

Figure 3.78: Adding a node that refers to the keyboard's F key

Before we can use the *F* key node we just created, there are a couple of adjustments we need to make to it, such as ensure when we use it, it does not get consumed and it can be re-used, as well as ensure it does not override any other bindings we might have — hypothetically speaking — assigned to the *F* key. For example, maybe we had defined the *F* key as the default input for interaction in a game, in which case we would not want to override that, or our player would end up not being able to use it later when needed.

7. Make sure your *F* key node in the **Event Graph** is selected, and then on the right side of the screen go to the **Details** tab (much like the **Details** tab we used in our Level Viewport, but this one is specifically for the Level Blueprint), and under the **Input** section uncheck both **Consume Input** and **Override Parent Binding**. This result should look as below (*Figure 3.79*):

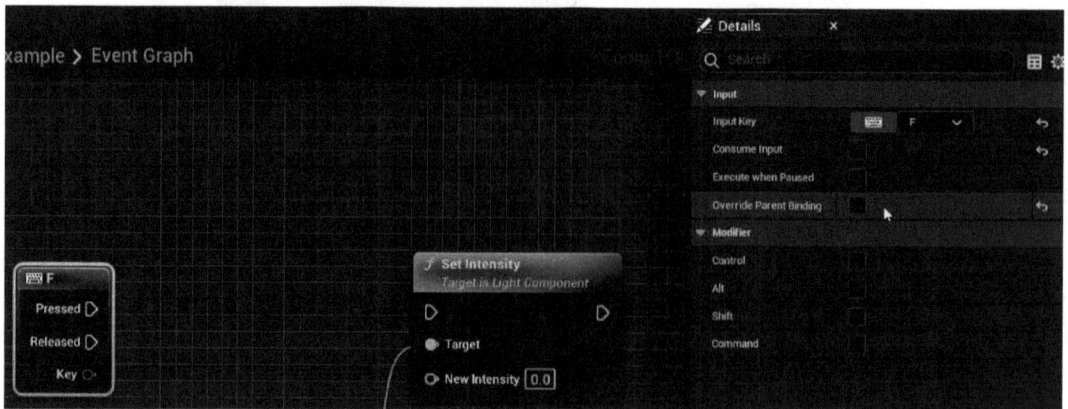

Figure 3.79: Unchecking Consume Input and Override Parent Binding

8. Now we can connect the *F* node's **Pressed** output pin (the large white arrow next to **Pressed**) to the **Set Intensity** function node's input pin (the large white arrow on the node's left side). The result looks much like in *Figure 3.80*:

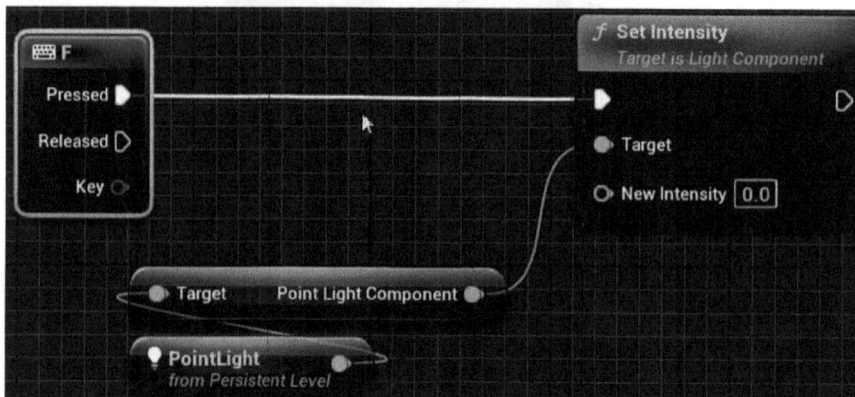

Figure 3.80: The F key node controlling the Point Light's intensity value

9. It finally is time to have a bit of fun playing our map! Minimize the Blueprint window (unless you have a multi-monitor setup, in which case it would be advised having the Blueprint window on any monitor other than the primary) and go back to the Level Viewport. Make sure your Viewport camera is somewhere within the room, looking towards our Point Light. Much like in the *Figure 3.81*:

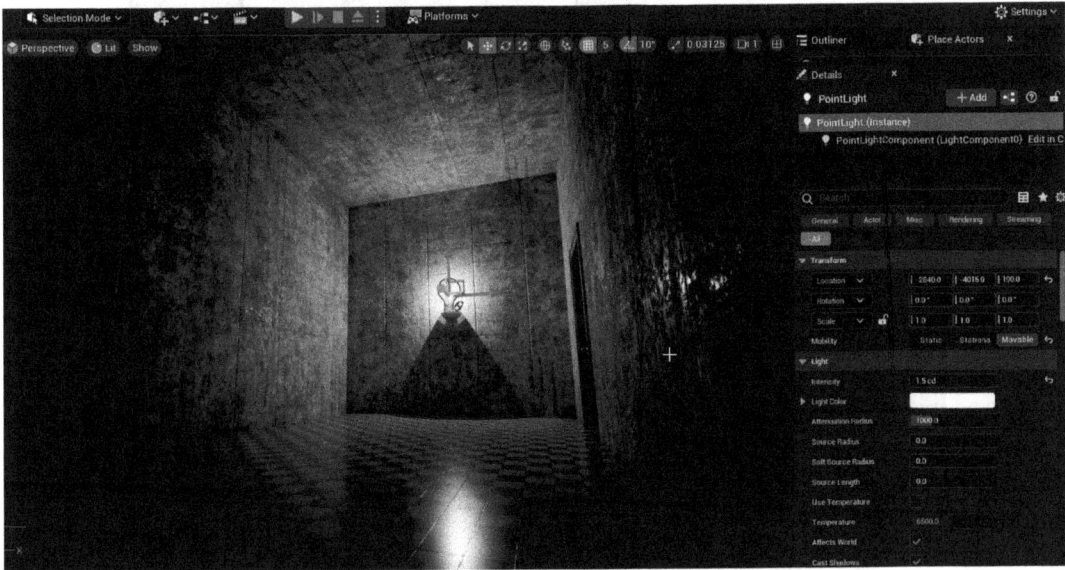

Figure 3.81: Having a general view of the room and the light's effect on it

10. Now, hit the green play button on the Main Toolbar. You will be playing with the map you just created. You can move around using the *W, A, S, D* keys and increase your Altitude with *Spacebar*, while decreasing with *Ctrl*. Use the mouse to rotate the camera.

11. After you have had some fun moving around, make sure you are looking at the Point Light, and whenever you are ready, press *F* and watch the lights go out! That means our Level Blueprint works correctly!

It is certainly cool we can switch off the light, but it is not very practical if we want to switch it back on. What would switching back on mean? It would mean that we are setting the intensity back to a large enough number to make the light bright enough. On second thought, we should probably begin the level with the light switched off, and then allow the user to toggle it on and off with the *F* key. After all, we always conserve energy and switch off the lights when we walk out of a room, so we expect them to be switched off next time we walk back in the room.

12. Then, click on the Point Light in the Viewport, and on the **Details** tab, find its intensity and set it to 0.

13. Go back to the Level Blueprint's Event Graph, and select the Point Light node, the Point Light component node and the set intensity node, much like in *Figure 3.82*.

Once you have selected all three of these nodes — they will be highlighted — right click on any of these nodes and select Copy or simply hit *Ctrl+C* while having them selected.

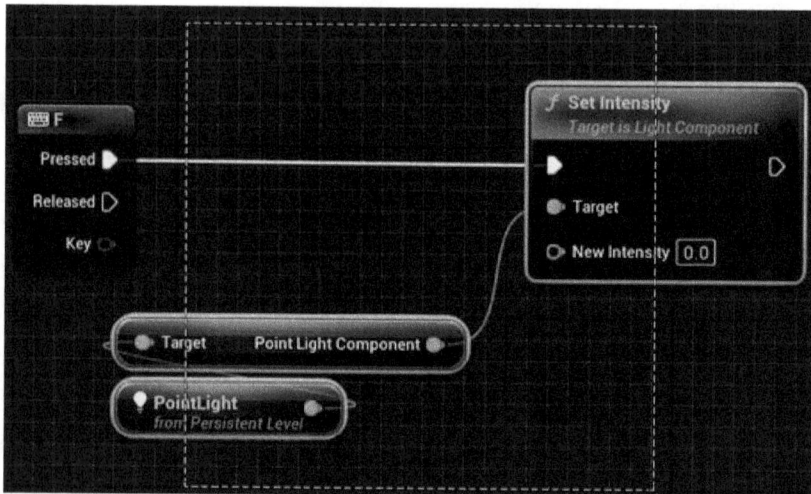

Figure 3.82: Selecting the three nodes

14. Having copied these three nodes, move your mouse cursor a bit further from all these nodes, over an empty spot in the **Event Graph** and hit *Ctrl+V* to paste the nodes we just copied. Your actions so far should result in something that looks approximately like *Figure 3.83*:

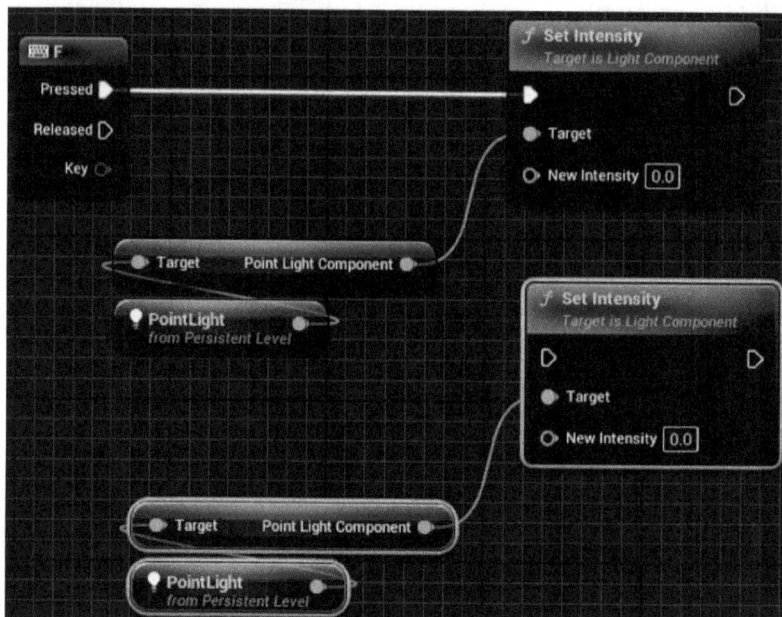

Figure 3.83: Pasted/duplicated nodes in the Event Graph

15. Since this is the same Point Light, with the same Point Light component, let us be a bit more efficient and get rid of the second Point Light and Point Light component nodes. Do keep the second **Set Intensity** node though. Now, your graph should look much like *Figure 3.84:*

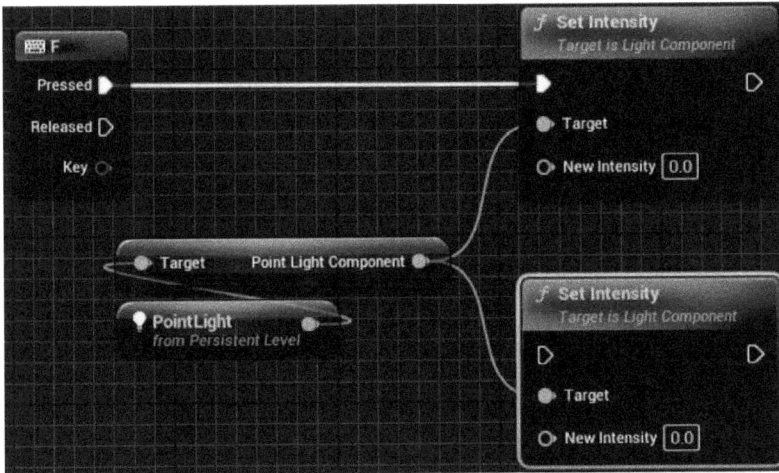

Figure 3.84: Cleaned up light intensity nodes in the Event Graph

16. Since the initial state of the Point Light is dark, in other words we have the intensity's value at 0 by default, the first time we press *F* we want the light to go bright, in other words increase the intensity to a value higher than 0. So set the **New Intensity** value of the first/top **Set Intensity** node to 4. Leave the second one as is, set to 0. Now the node structure must look like in *Figure 3.85:*

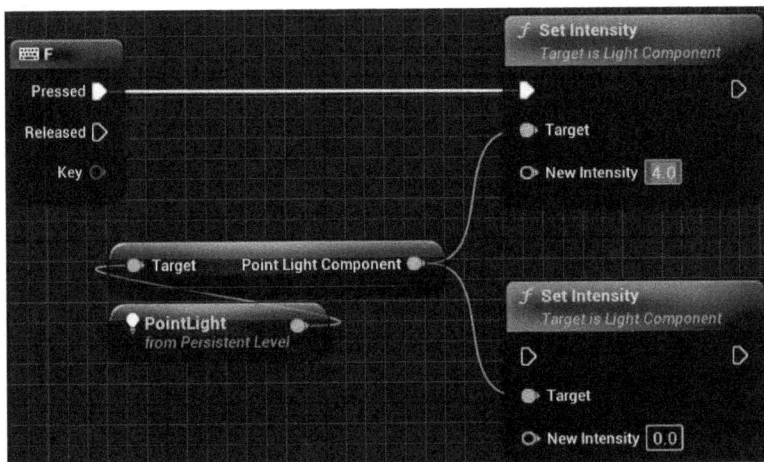

Figure 3.85: First Intensity node changes the light's intensity value to 4, whereas the second to 0

The way it is set up right now, the only thing that will happen if the user presses *F* is change our Point Light's intensity from 0 to 4. We want to allow the user to press

F again and switch the light off, in other words reset the light's intensity value to 0. But we also want them to repeat any of the above steps as often as they would like. To achieve this, we will use a simplistic solution; for this example, we will use a **Flip Flop** switch.

17. Right click anywhere in the **Event Graph** and type **Flip Flop** in the search bar. Select the **Flip Flop** node. Connect the **Pressed** output pin from the *F* node to the **Flip Flop** node's input pin and connect the **Flip Flop** node's output pin **A** to the first **Set Intensity** node with intensity value 4.0, and the **Flip Flop** node's output pin **B** to the first **Set Intensity** node with intensity value 0.0. Your graph now should look approximately like *Figure 3.86*:

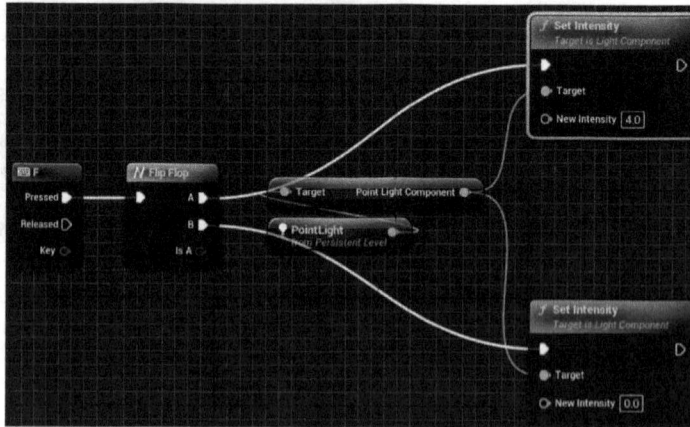

Figure 3.86: *Using the Flip Flop node to interchange between the two intensity values*

18. Let us tide it up a tiny bit. Double click on the first connecting cable/line between **A** and the first **Set Intensity** node. This will result in a small connection pin that you can move around to give a cleaner visual representation to the graph. Repeat that step for the second cable as well (between **B** and the second **Set Intensity** node) and you should be getting something that looks much like in *Figure 3.87*:

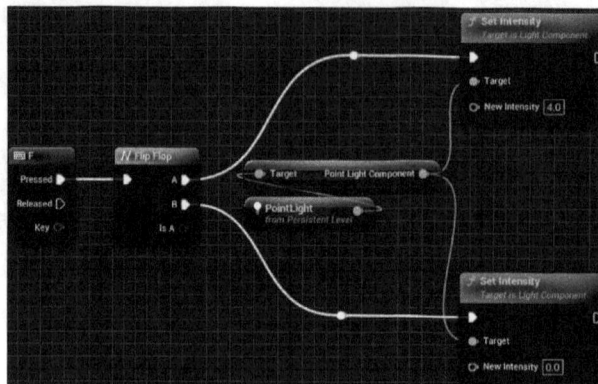

Figure 3.87: *Cleaning up the Event Graph a bit*

19. Now press compile on the top left of the Level Blueprint's window, as shown in *Figure 3.88*. We did not do that before, because when you play a level, the Blueprint compilation takes place automatically, but still, this was a good opportunity to show you this button as well, since you will often want to compile and check for any possible errors or conflicts, prior to going in the game.

Figure 3.88: Compiling the Level Blueprint

If all went smooth you will receive the same icon as in *Figure 3.89*:

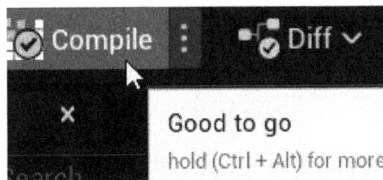

Figure 3.89: The Compile button features a checkmark icon; this indicates it compiled properly

If there was a problem, it would look much like *Figure 3.90*:

Figure 3.90: The Compile button features a bar icon, indicating something went wrong and your Blueprint did not compile

Given the simple nature of our Blueprints, you should not be getting the Compilation Error message. If, however, you do, then try repeating the previous steps from the start.

20. Now, we should be ready to play our level again, and this time, we should be able to toggle the light on and off. Once again, make sure you move your Viewport camera somewhere in the room, looking at the Point Light, since that is where you will spawn, given the way we set up our level. Once you spawn it, press *F* once and check if the light goes on. Then press *F* again to check if it goes back off again. Feel free to keep pressing *F* as many times as you want.

21. If you successfully managed to repeatedly toggle the light on and off, congratulations, not only did you finish your first level, but you also finished your very first Blueprint. Make sure you press *Ctrl+S* to save the map with all these changes.

We certainly covered a lot of ground in this chapter, but we have only scratched the surface. There are still so many things to talk about and look into, such as creating and importing our own Static Meshes, taking advantage of Nanite and making our assets look highly realistic and qualitative, creating our own Materials with texture maps we create, setting up a complete scene that features more advanced lighting that takes advantage of Lumen's power and gives us realistic believable lighting, using ambient sounds and particle effects to give our scene some atmosphere, as well as using Skeletal Meshes that are animated and give our scene some movement and life.

That and much more, will be covered from the next chapter on, where we will begin our first real Unreal project!!

Conclusion

In this chapter, you learned how to place Static Meshes in your scene, how to manipulate and edit different properties of these meshes, while you also learned how to apply Materials to them. You also learned how to add and edit lights in your scene, while you had your very first interaction with Blueprints.

In addition to all of the above, you are now familiar with the Content Drawer and its functions, the Details tab, editing different values under the Details tab for any selected actor.

Most importantly, you have just completed a simple yet important first project!

Thanks to this chapter, now we are ready to tackle our next project, which begins in the next chapter, in which we will cover setting up the project, using proper folder structures, creating and importing the assets we will need, while covering some more advanced topics such as Unreal Engine 5's Nanite.

Points to remember

- Placing objects/actors into a scene
- Positioning, rotating and scaling up those actors
- Duplicating actors
- Using the Content Drawer to find desired assets
- Searching for specific assets in the Content Drawer
- Filtering asset types within the Content Drawer
- Creating your own content folders
- Placing and manipulating Static Meshes
- Placing Materials on Static Meshes
- Placing lights

- Editing lights
- Using the Level Blueprint to allow real time modifications of scene actors

Exercise

1. You are strongly encouraged to try repeating all of this chapter's steps, however this time try complicating your structure a bit. Instead of having a building with one room, using the techniques learned in this chapter, try creating a building with two, or even more, rooms. Connect these rooms with doorways and place a light in each room. Do not be afraid to experiment with different values and scales.

Join our book's Discord space

Join the book's Discord Workspace for Latest updates, Offers, Tech happenings around the world, New Release and Sessions with the Authors:

https://discord.bpbonline.com

CHAPTER 4

Project Overview and Main Asset Creation for Statue Scene

Introduction

In this chapter as well as *Chapters 5, Importing Assets and Setting up the Statue Scene,* and *Chapter 6, Lighting and Cinematic Sequence for the Statue Scene,* we will dedicate our focus on setting up a detailed scene, with assets we create both within the Engine as well import from external applications, as well as assets we will be downloading from Epic Quixel Bridge, which is done within the Unreal Engine.

We will utilize Unreal Engine 5's Nanite, Lumen, while we will also create and render a very short cinematic sequence, by using the Engine's Sequencer tools. Lastly, we will explore some basic foundations for utilizing this scene in virtual reality.

More specifically, we will use an AI generated concept of a golden statue of a Greek God placed in a modern-day garden environment. We will learn how to identify the key elements of the concept, create the assets we need, or download some of them through Quixel Bridge, all to ultimately replicate or even improve the presented concept.

In this first chapter of this project, we will briefly cover the creative process, from concept to realization, however the first couple of parts will be referring to external applications, namely *Reallusion's Character Creator, Maxon's ZBrush* and *Adobe's Substance 3D Painter.* Due to this book's scope, we cannot and will not go into too much detail with utilizing these applications, as each one of them would require and deserve an entire book, so if you do not own or have never used either of these applications, it is recommended you skip this chapter and continue to *Chapter 5, Importing Assets and Setting Up the Statue Scene.*

Structure

The following are the topics discussed in this chapter:

- An overview of our project's concept
- Planning our project's asset creation
- Using Reallusion's Character Creator 4
- Using ZBrush to sculpt our statue
- Using Substance Painter to generate our textures

Objectives

The objectives of this chapter are to create the statue asset from scratch to finish, by utilizing 3 different applications in the process. First, we will analyze and break down the concept we have to work with, then we will identify the different elements we need to create.

We will then begin the process in Character Creator 4 to give ourselves a qualitative base model to begin with, carry our project over to ZBrush where we will sculpt all the details, to finalize the asset creation with Substance Painter, where we will generate the textures, we will need to create the asset's material in Unreal.

An overview of our project's concept

As seen in *Figure 4.1* we have an AI generated concept depicting the golden statue of a Greek God, found in what appears to be a present-day garden-like environment:

Figure 4.1: *The AI generated concept*

Our first task is to analyze and break down the concept into manageable parts. We need to look for and ask ourselves what elements are there, whether any of them are being repeated, and overall plan our strategy in approaching this concept's realization as efficiently as possible. If we look closely at *Figure 4.1* it is easy to break it down into the different elements that compose it, much like in *Figure 4.2*:

Figure 4.2: The concept's breakdown

Let us look at what are the puzzle pieces that put together the bigger picture:

1. The most obvious element is the center of the image and the center of our attention. It is none other than the main theme, which is the golden Greek God Statue.

2. We can easily notice a board leafed plant at the forefront. It appears to be quite dense.

3. In this part, we can notice a fern-like plant, while we also notice light coming through from what appears to be the sky. From this part, we can also understand that it is either early in the day, noon, or early afternoon, but certainly not dusk, dawn, or night. The way the light comes through, in combination with the plants and the structure around, gives away the idea that this is an outdoor space, much like a garden, surrounded by what appears to be a modern-day, concrete — most likely — building.

4. This element, found behind the statue, indicates a modern-day structure. It could be interpreted as some sort of ventilation system, but it could also be interpreted as some kind of concrete-based decorative wall. For our project, we will go with the latter interpretation.

5. Much like in 4, we can see that this is some sort of modern-day building, spanning across the image, and apparently higher than the ground floor.

6. We notice, once again, the same fern-like plant as seen in 3.

7. Same plant as in 2.

8. Same plant as in both 2 and 7.

9. Same plant as in 3 and 6.

At this point, unless you own and have used any of the following software, or are simply curious to get an idea, you might want to consider reading on from *Chapter 5, Importing Assets and Setting Up the Statue Scene*.

If you do read the sections that precede the asset importation steps, then be advised that the workflow conducted in Reallusion Character Creator 4, Maxon's ZBrush, and Adobe's Substance Painter will be very brief and not as explanatory, so unless you have some minimal prior experience with using any of these applications — or similar ones — you might find it very difficult to follow. Do not worry; the assets created within these sections are available for download, so you can perfectly continue with this project in an uninterrupted and seamless way and not deviate from this book's main scope and focus, which is working with the Unreal Engine 5.

The reason for being so brief with the utilization of the other applications is because each one of these applications is an advanced and professional grade tool that can get quite complex and would therefore require a book, or even a series of books, to properly introduce and cover the fundamentals, as well as the more advanced functions they feature.

However, the author decided to dedicate a few pages to each of them within this book, for the purpose of both sparking curiosity to the reader that has never used any of these applications before, as well as to briefly communicate the overall production workflow with the reader that might have utilized these applications prior to reading this book.

With that disclaimer out of the way, let us move on to planning the project's main asset creation, the golden Greek God Statue.

Planning our project's asset creation

Based on our concept's breakdown, it is clear that the statue is quite intricate and detailed, and it is the main theme. Therefore, we will need to create it and then import it into the Unreal Engine. However, the plants and the modern-day building elements are generic, but most importantly, easily and freely found — at high-quality, one might add — on Quixel Bridge within the Unreal Engine, therefore saving us some time while helping us achieve the desired results. Since we are creating the statue, next we need to break down the statue itself into the different elements that compose it, as seen in *Figure 4.3*:

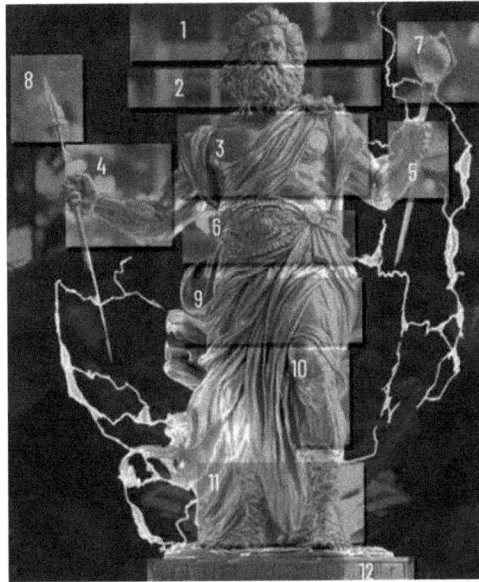

Figure 4.3: The statue's breakdown

Let us analyze the statue's breakdown:

1. The head features some rather lush and detailed hair.
2. The beard is equally detailed and lush.
3. His torso appears to be covered by some cloth.
4. His right arm is tense, and the hand is tightly holding an object.
5. Same as 4, his left arm is also tense, and the hand is holding an object.
6. A heavily ornated belt-like piece connecting the upper garments with the lower garments.
7. The object in the left hand is some sort of scepter with a sphere on its top.
8. The object in the right hand is also some sort of scepter with a pyramid shape on its top.
9. The legs are covered by a cloth that appears to be part of a larger toga.
10. The left knee is exposed and not covered by the toga.
11. He appears to be wearing leather sandals, held together by laces.
12. A subtle and easy to miss, yet important detail, the base of the statue. It is rather ornated.

Knowing the different elements that compose the overall statue, makes it easier for us to break down what appears to be a daunting and complex task, into smaller, manageable, and efficiently feasible subtasks.

Using Reallusion Character Creator 4

The first thing we need to do is give us a female model base, one we can easily edit and pose to resemble our concept. For this, we will be using Reallusion Character Creator 4, which is an excellent and very powerful tool, mainly for creating characters that are fully rigged and ready to use in a plethora of applications, however, it can also work as an efficient way to quickly create a base model, as well as pose that base model, as is the case with statues and this project. In addition, Character Creator features a seamless integration with ZBrush, allowing the user, with the click of a button, to quickly send the posed character to ZBrush for further sculpting and, if needed, back to Character Creator. It is a tool that has been around for quite some time, with the author being an early adopter and vocal supporter of Reallusion's toolsets, using it in the author's professional production environment for game development.

1. Upon loading Character Creator 4, we will double click and load one of their sample projects titled, **CC4 Kevin**, as seen in *Figure 4.4*. This is a sample project that utilizes many of the applications' features, but most importantly for our case, can quickly give us a high-quality base female model.

Figure 4.4: Character Creator 4 – CC4 Kevin project thumbnail

2. We click on the **Scene** tab, select all the elements other than the base model, namely, brows, clothing, etc., as seen in *Figure 4.5*, and delete them:

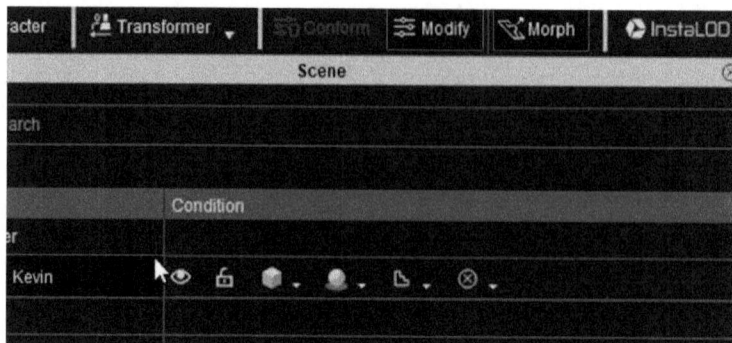

Figure 4.5: Character Creator 4 Scene tab

3. We browse to the **Animation** section of the content library, we expand it and under the **Pose** section, we find the **Calibration** section, within which we find the **A-Pose**, as seen in *Figure 4.6* and we click and drag it onto our model:

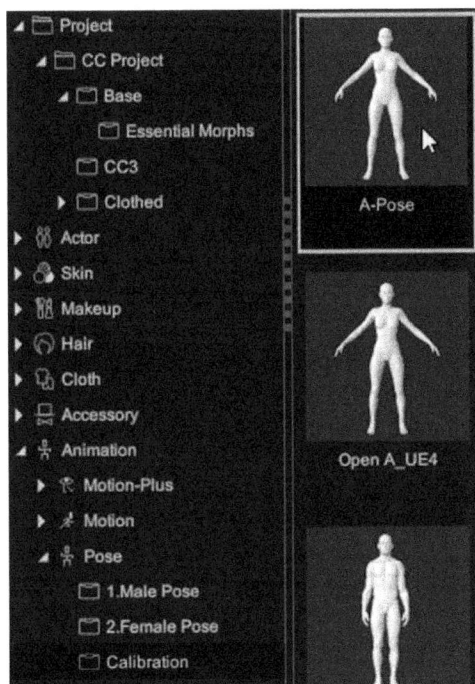

Figure 4.6: *A-Pose*

4. With the character selected in Character Creator 4's main Viewport, we go to the **Motion** tab of our **Modify** panel and click on **Edit Pose**, as seen in *Figure 4.7*:

Figure 4.7: *Editing our base model's pose*

5. We use Character Creator 4's intuitive interface to select different bones and position them, either by rotating them or moving them. *Figure 4.8* shows the UI as well as the Viewport:

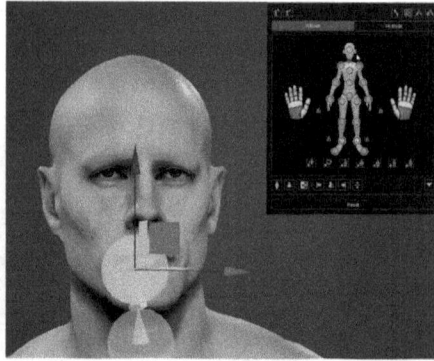

Figure 4.8: *Editing the pose UI — Character Creator 4*

6. *Figures 4.9* and *Figure 4.10* show how we pose the right hand and the legs to resemble the pose of our concept:

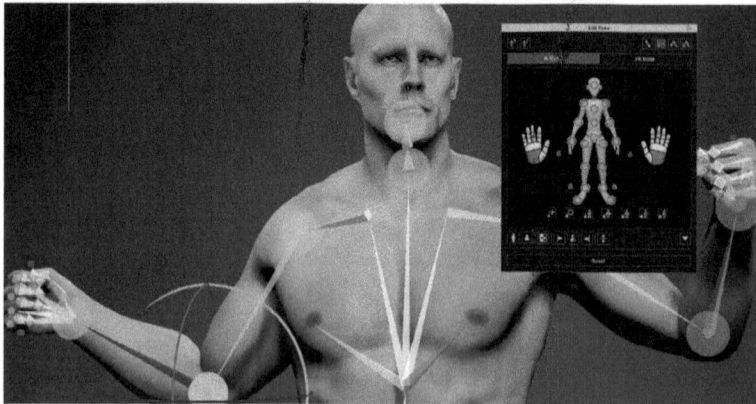

Figure 4.9: *Posing the right arm*

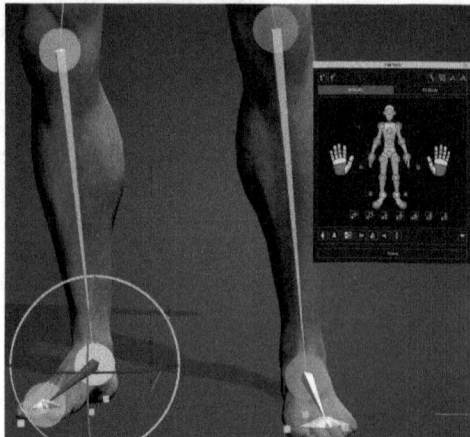

Figure 4.10: *Posing the legs*

7. Character Creator 4 shows us what the actual human character would look like, but since we are creating a statue, we are interested in geometry and not so much in the textures. Let us change the model's viewing mode to **Smooth** as shown in *Figure 4.11*, with the result of that being shown in *Figure 4.12*:

Figure 4.11: *Change view mode to Smooth/geometry only*

Figure 4.12: *The model posed, in smooth view*

8. We are ready to send our base model to ZBrush. With our base model selected on the main Viewport, we press the **GoZ** icon on the top left of the application, as seen in *Figure 4.13*:

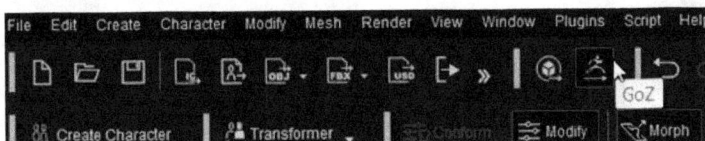

Figure 4.13: *Sending the base model to ZBrush*

9. Next, we need to modify some of the settings on the screen that pop up. More specifically, we want to create, rather than relink, an existing model, and we want to make sure we use the current pose. In other words, use the same settings as in *Figure 4.14*:

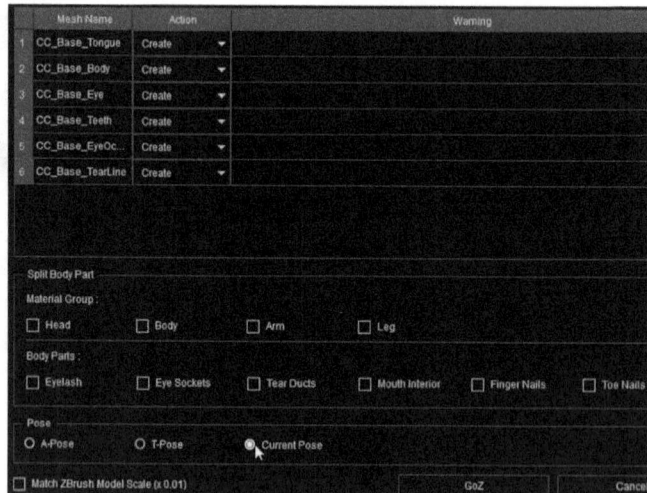

Figure 4.14: Settings to send the base model from Character Creator 4 to ZBrush

Using ZBrush to sculpt our statue

At this point we are done with using Character Creator 4 for this project's purposes, and now we focus on using ZBrush to sculpt our statue. By using the **GoZ** button in Character Creator 4, ZBrush has loaded, and now we need to draw the object in ZBrush's canvas, and then press *T* and *F*, to enter sculpting mode and focus on the object. Doing that will result in the base model being displayed in ZBrush's canvas, with the default red wax material, as seen in *Figure 4.15*:

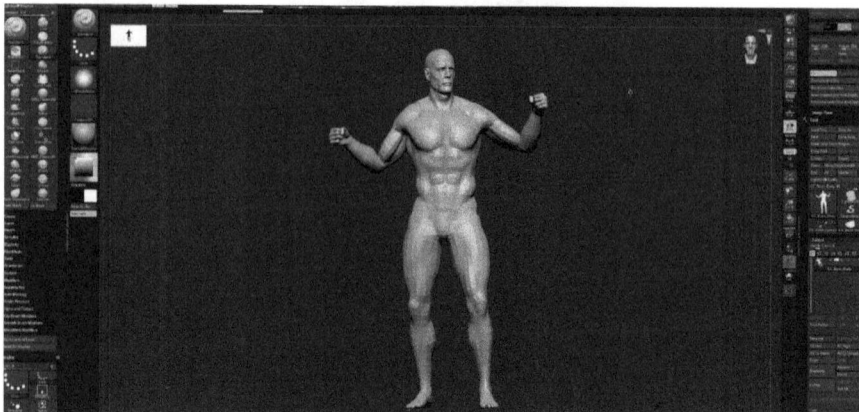

Figure 4.15: Our base model in ZBrush

Commencing the sculpting process in Zbrush, proceed with the following steps:

1. While this is a matter of personal preference, the author finds it easier to work with a gray material rather than the default red wax one. Unless you prefer the default or any other material, switch to the **MatCap Gray**, as shown in *Figure 4.16:*

Figure 4.16: Switching ZBrush Materials

2. For the next step, we want to divide our model and achieve a higher resolution geometry, as this will allow us to sculpt in more detail. Let us divide the model until we have reached 3 levels of subdivision, as shown in *Figure 4.17* and *Figure 4.18:*

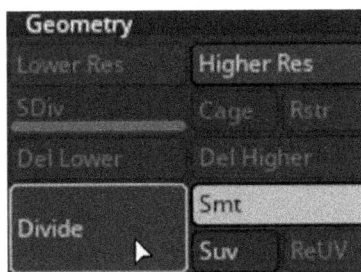

Figure 4.17: Divide the model

Figure 4.18: Reach 3 levels of subdivision

3. Next, we need to scale up our brush sizes, so navigate to **Preferences**, then **Draw** and set **Max Brush Size** to the max value, while also setting the **Dynamic Brush Scale** value to 10, as shown in *Figures 4.19* and *Figure 4.20*. This will allow us to comfortably work with the mesh's large scale, as exported by Character Creator 4.

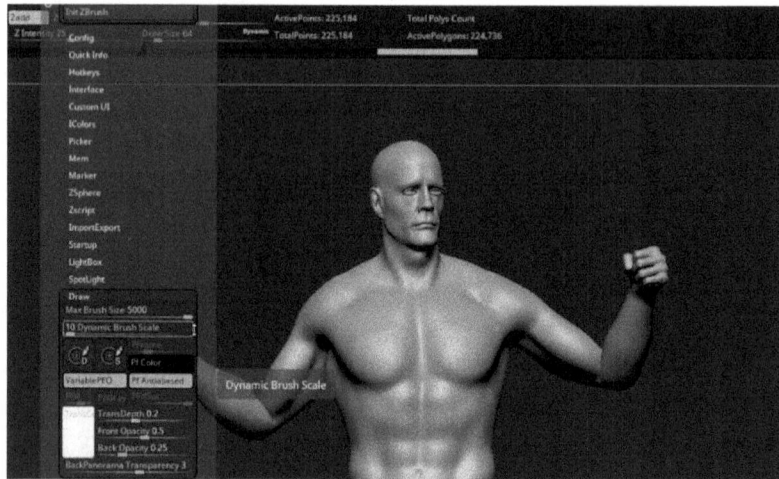

Figure 4.19: Adjusting brush scale settings

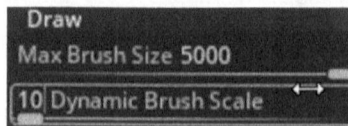

Figure 4.20: The desired settings for our brush scale

4. If you have used ZBrush before, then you know how integral masking is. Let us begin creating the statue's torso garment (part number 3 from *Figure 4.3* earlier in this chapter). Let us roughly mask the area we expect the garment to cover more or less, as seen in *Figure 4.21*:

Figure 4.21: Masking the area that will make up the torso's garment

5. With the torso masked, we navigate to Subtool, then **Extract** and click on the **Extract** button, as seen in *Figure 4.22*. You will notice that the extracted geometry appears too thick to be suitable for a garment; therefore, edit and change the **Thick** value from **0.02**, which is the default, to 0.00985, as seen in *Figure 4.23*:

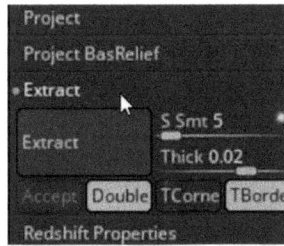

Figure 4.22: The UI for extracting a masked area

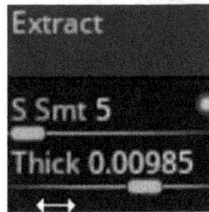

Figure 4.23: Adjust the thickness to this value

Hit the **Extract** button again, and this time, being happy with the extracted geometry's thickness, hit **Accept**, as shown in *Figure 4.24*. The end result should look much like in *Figure 4.25*:

Figure 4.24: Click accept once happy with the extracted geometry's thickness

Figure 4.25: The end result of our extraction

6. Next, while being masked, we smoothen out the extracted geometry, by holding *Shift* pressed while painting over it, and then we unmask it (*Ctrl+ Click* and drag anywhere in the canvas other than the geometry). The end result of this step should approximately resemble *Figure 4.26*:

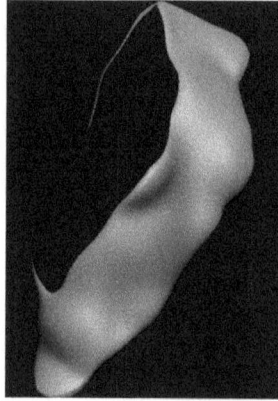

Figure 4.26: *Smoothened out extracted geometry*

While it is extremely admirable to sculpt every little detail by hand, in order to be efficient in a real life production environment, ZBrush artists often rely on a palette of tools they can either create themselves or purchase online, tools such as brushes, alpha maps, all intended to allow them to click add shapes, objects, and details on geometry they are working on. From here on, the author used several of the tools he has collected over the years, to achieve the details and ornaments featured on the model. Some of the best places for a 3D artist to purchase such tools are *ArtStation*, *GumRoad* and *FlippedNormals*, to name a few.

7. By using tools as just described, combined with a constant process of masking different surface areas of the geometry, we can start adding details to the main torso's garment, such as cloth creases, folds, etc., as depicted in *Figure 4.27*:

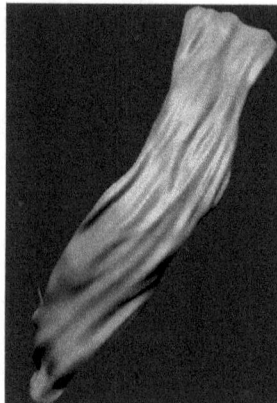

Figure 4.27: *A combination of masking and tool palette allows us to start adding details*

By further working in that manner, we finalize the cloth's details, as shown in *Figure 4.28*:

Figure 4.28: Finalized sculpt of the garment covering the torso

8. In a similar way, we proceed to model the rest of the parts shown earlier in this chapter in *Figure 4.3*. *Figures 4.29* and *Figure 4.30* show the progress achieved to finalize the sculpt:

Figure 4.29: Sculpting the belt

As can be observed by carefully examining *Figure 4.30*, most of the parts sculpted, begin as simple, basic shapes, lacking in detail and definition, yet slightly resembling the silhouette of the desired final result:

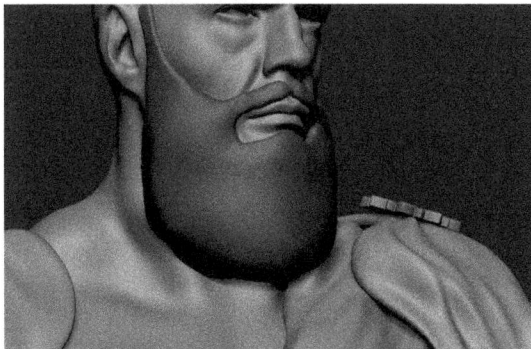

Figure 4.30: Preparing the geometry for the hair and beard

Observing *Figure 4.31*, one can note how sculpting the details on the basic geometry, can yield the desired results, with detail and defintion:

Figure 4.31: The head and beard finalized

Figure 4.32: The statue's final sculpt

9. Next, for each sub tool our sculpt has, we decimate its geometry to make it easier to work with while still retaining the level of detail we achieved. We will be using ZBrush's **Decimation Master**, where we will **Pre-process Current**, as shown in *Figure 4.33*, and then **Decimate Current** by setting the percentage of decimation desired, which varies for each sub tool. Overall, we will want to keep each and every tool in the neighborhood of 50k-300k **Polys**.

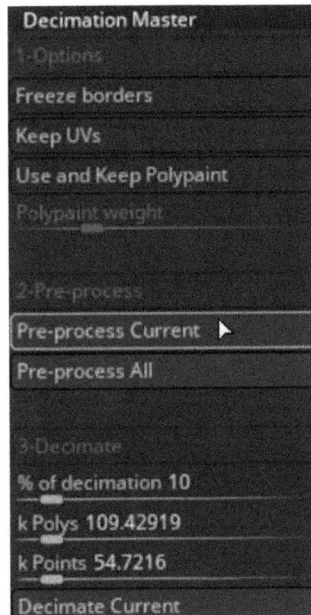

Figure 4.33: *Decimation Master*

10. Once we have decimated the geometry for each and every one of our sub tools, we can either choose to unwrap each of them within ZBrush with its UV Master plugin, or we can have the entire model unwrapped in Adobe Substance Painter. For this project's purpose, the author chose to go with the latter option; therefore, what remains for us to do in ZBrush now is to merge all the decimated tools and then finally export them in an FBX format. By going under Tool, select Export, select an FBX file format, and use the export settings depicted in *Figure 4.34*:

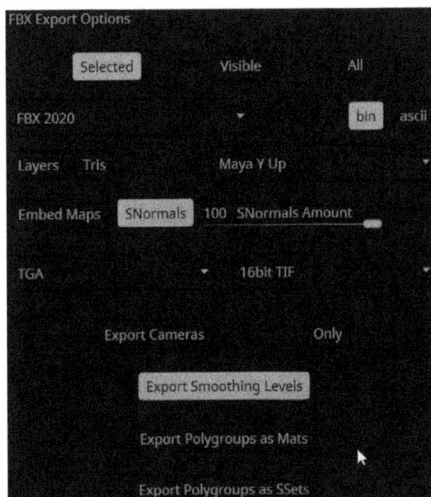

Figure 4.34: *ZBrush export settings*

Using Substance Painter to generate our textures

We are now ready to use the exported FBX in Substance Painter, where we will be generating the necessary texture maps, that will allow us to create our statue's material shaders in Unreal Engine 5. To begin, observe the steps as follows:

1. Hit *Ctrl+N* to start a **New project** in Substance Painter. Use the settings seen in *Figure 4.35* and click **Select**. From there, browse to the location of the FBX we just exported from ZBrush, and select it. Once that's done, click **OK** on the **New project** dialog box.

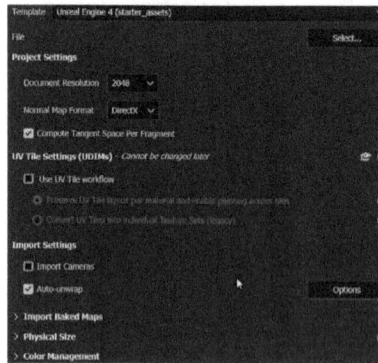

Figure 4.35: New project settings in Substance Painter

2. Once the application has finished unwrapping the model (it will take some time since this is a high poly model, so be patient with it, good opportunity to complete some other tasks or go for a walk instead), hit *F8* to enter the Baking Texture mode, as seen in *Figure 4.36*. There, use the settings provided in *Figure 4.37*, specifically **Output Size** set to **8192**, **Dilation Width** to **128**, **Max Frontal Distance** and **Max Rear Distance** set to **1**, and everything else as is by default. Then click **Bake selected textures**:

Figure 4.36: Texture Baking Mode in Substance Painter

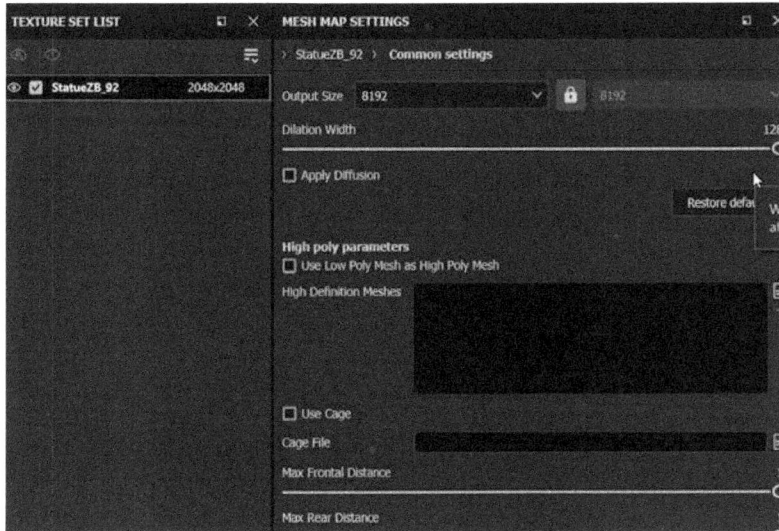

Figure 4.37: *Settings for Baking the textures*

3. Once baking is done (once again, be patient, it takes a while), click **Return to painting mode**.

4. Next, navigate to the **Smart Materials** found under the Asset Library, as shown in *Figure 4.38*, and look for **Gold Damaged** as shown in *Figure 4.39*:

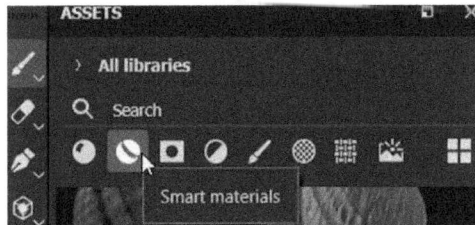

Figure 4.38: *Smart Materials*

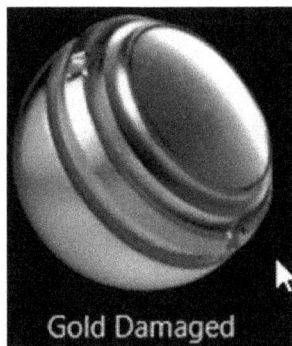

Figure 4.39: *Gold Damaged material*

5. Click and drag the **Gold Damaged** material over the goddess statue mesh in the main Viewport, as shown in *Figure 4.40*. This will result in what is depicted in *Figure 4.41*.

Figure 4.40: Clicking and dragging the gold material on the statue mesh

Figure 4.41: Final result of the textured mesh

6. Since we unwrapped/generated UV maps for the mesh within Substance Painter, we want to re-export the mesh, once again in an FBX format. Click **File**, and then **Export Mesh...**, as shown in *Figure 4.42*. Then, use the same settings as in *Figure 4.43* and click **Export**.

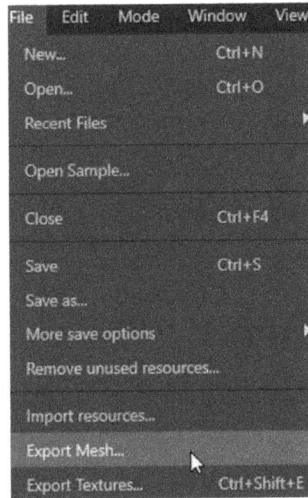

Figure 4.42: *Export Mesh*

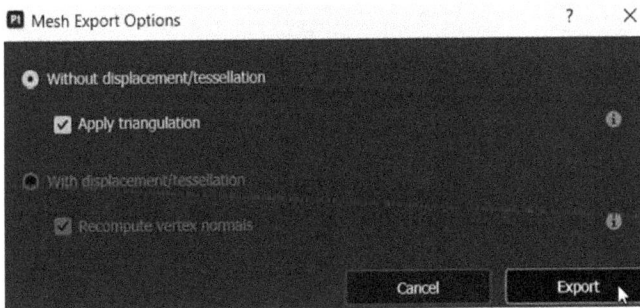

Figure 4.43: *Export Mesh Settings*

7. Much like with exporting the mesh, navigate to **File**, but this time select **Export Textures,** which is right under **Export Mesh…**. Once selected, click on the **Output directory** field, to choose your file destination, and use the export settings displayed in *Figure 4.44*. Then click **Export**.

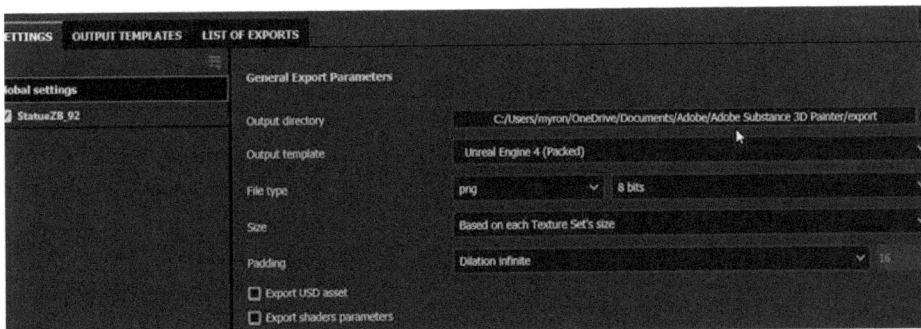

Figure 4.44: *Texture Export settings*

Conclusion

Now that we successfully created the asset from scratch and given it all the necessary details and textures, we are ready to import it into the Unreal Engine and work on it some more there.

In the next chapter, we will import the asset, create its Materials, and place it in a scene that we will build around it.

Points to remember

- Breaking down a concept into different manageable tasks.
- Brief, high level overview of Reallusion Character Creator 4.
- Brief, high level overview of the surface of ZBrush sculpting power.
- Brief, high level overview of the surface of Adobe Substance Painter.

Exercises

1. If you own any of the programs used in this chapter, you are encouraged to experiment with creating your own version of this or any other statue, or even any other mesh.

2. Attempt creating and posing a character in Character Creator.

3. Transfer your Character Creator mesh to Zbrush and practice sculpting until you create a form that matches your idea of a statue.

4. Practice material assignments in Substance Painter.

Join our book's Discord space

Join the book's Discord Workspace for Latest updates, Offers, Tech happenings around the world, New Release and Sessions with the Authors:

https://discord.bpbonline.com

CHAPTER 5

Importing Assets and Setting Up the Statue Scene

Introduction

Now that we are done with creating our main asset in *Chapter 4, Project Overview and Main Asset Creation for Statue Scene*, it is time to get back in Unreal.

In this chapter, we will better organize our project's folder structure import the statue Static Mesh and Texture assets in the engine, while we will be utilizing Unreal Engine's Nanite to ensure the statue asset is displayed in its most glorious level of detail. We will be creating Materials and Material Instances, while learning how to utilize their parameters and settings. We will also learn how to take full advantage of Quixel Bridge and Megascans, while we will use all that to set up a scene that resembles the concept we used in the previous chapter.

In case you skipped the previous chapter, we used an AI generated concept of a golden statue of a Greek God placed in a modern-day garden environment. In the beginning of the chapter, we learned how to identify the key elements of the concept.

Structure

The following are the topics covered in this chapter:

- Importing the statue in Unreal Engine 5
- Nanite

- Material parameters
- Material Instances
- Quixel Bridge and Megascans
- Setting up the Greek God Statue scene

Objectives

By the end of this chapter, we will learn how to import the created Greek God Statue asset. We will be creating some Materials and Material Instances within the Engine while we will also explore Quixel Bridge from within the Engine to find any freely available assets that can help us complete our scene. In the process, not only will you be utilizing everything learned in the previous chapters, but you will also have a better basic understanding of Unreal Engine 5's Nanite, while you will be improving and advancing your overall scene creation workflow.

Importing the Statue in Unreal Engine 5

If you feel that some of the following steps are going too fast or some terms sound unfamiliar, it is strongly encouraged you refer back to *Chapters 1 to 3*. Any other terms or features that have not been introduced in *Chapters 1 to 3* will be covered and explained. To begin with the project, follow the next steps:

1. Earlier, in *Chapter 2, Unreal Engine UI*, we created an Unreal Engine project titled *Greek God Statue*. Let us load it up by launching our Epic Games Launcher, and finding it under **Unreal Engine**, under **Library**, as shown in *Figure 5.1*:

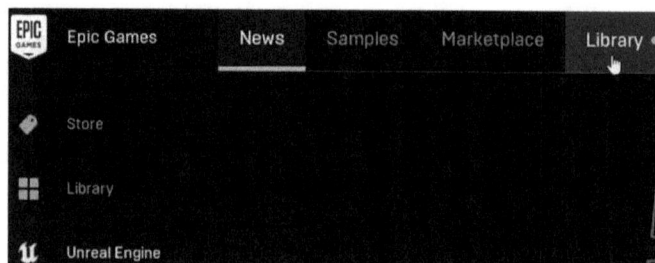

Figure 5.1: Epic Games Launcher

Either through the Content Drawer (*Ctrl + SpaceBar*) or by having a Content Browser open, we will start organizing our project's folder structure. The author's personal preference is to have 4 Content Browsers open on a secondary monitor while having the main Viewport on the main PC monitor. This allows the need to be constantly bringing up the Content Drawer, but it is left to the reader's discretion, as to the way they prefer working with content. To bring up one or more (up to four) Content Browser windows, navigate through **Window**, then **Content**

Browser, and from there, select any of the available 4 Content Browsers. If you are already using a Content Browser, it will be displayed with a small checkmark next to it. Please refer to *Figure 5.2*:

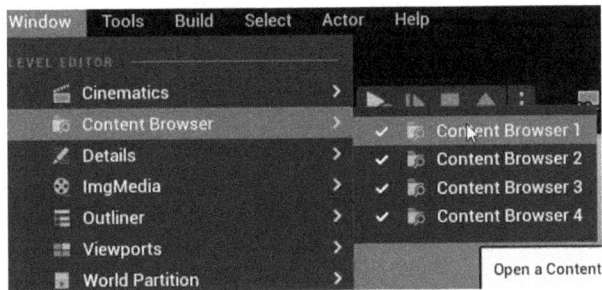

Figure 5.2: *Accessing the Content Browsers*

2. Now that we know two ways of accessing our **Content** folders, let us proceed with organizing our project's folder structure. Continuing from where we left off in *Chapter 3, Unreal Engine's Building Blocks*, your folder structure should look like the one shown in *Figure 5.3*:

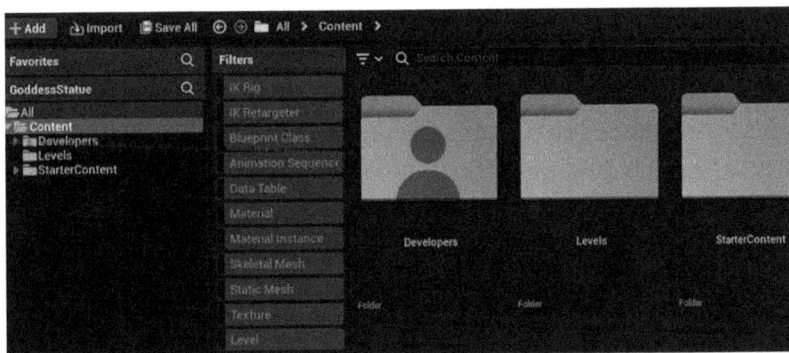

Figure 5.3: *Current folder structure*

3. While in the Content Browser or Drawer, click on the **+Add** button and select **New Folder** as depicted in *Figure 5.4*:

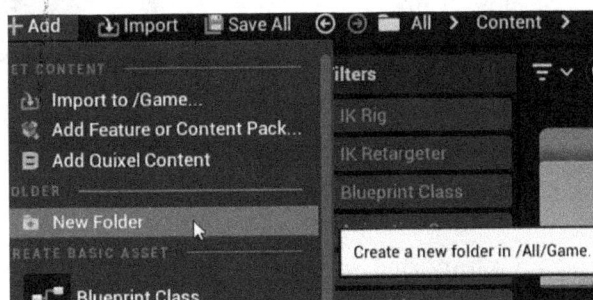

Figure 5.4: *Create a New Folder*

4. Name the new folder **StaticMeshes**, as shown in *Figure 5.5:*

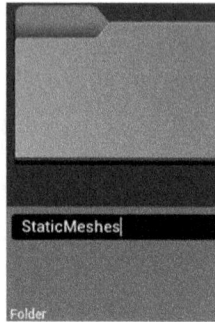

Figure 5.5: Name it StaticMeshes

5. In a similar way, create two more folders. One will be named **Materials** and the other one **Textures**.

6. Access the **Textures** folder you just created, and while in it, click the **Import** button on top of the Content Browser, as depicted in *Figure 5.6*. Browse to the location of the textures we exported from Substance Painter. If you skipped these steps, simply browse to the location of the textures you downloaded with the resources accompanying this book. Specifically, browse to the drive you saved and extracted the file and then navigate to **\Unreal Projects and Source Files\ Project1_GreekGodStatue\Assets\Textures** (similar to *Figure 5.7*) and select all the files in there to import them into the Unreal Engine.

Figure 5.6: Importing assets

Looking at *Figure 5.7*, observe browsing to the associated texture assets:

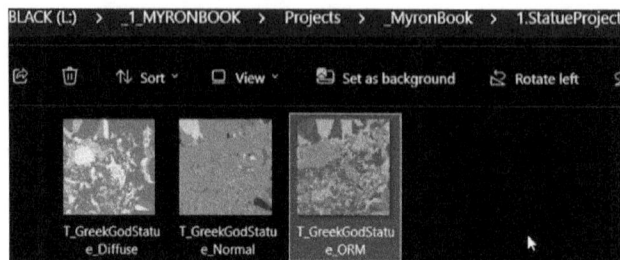

Figure 5.7: The textures found in the book's accompanying resources

7. Once the textures are imported, make sure you save them by having all three of them selected, right-clicking on any of them, and selecting **Save** (or *Ctrl+S*) as depicted in *Figure 5.8:*

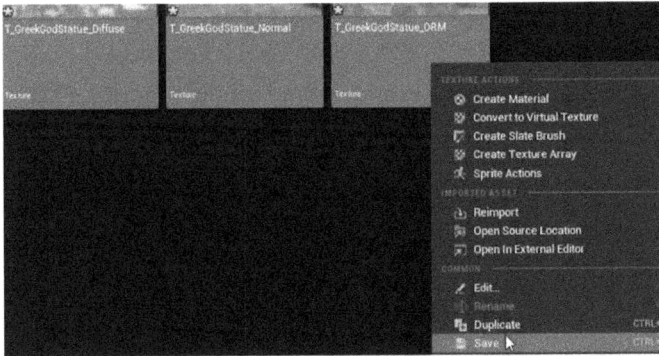

Figure 5.8: *Saving imported textures*

8. Next, within the Content Browser, navigate to the **StaticMeshes** folder we just created. Once more, click the **Import** button. This time, we are looking for the statue's FBX file we just exported from Substance Painter, or once again, if you downloaded the accompanying resources, found under \ **Unreal Projects and Source Files \Project1_GreekGodStatue\Assets\StaticMeshes\SM_ GreekGodStatue**

9. Upon selecting the **SM_GreekGodStatue.fbx** to import, you are prompted with a dialog box displaying different FBX Import Options, much like the one displayed in *Figure 5.9*. Use the exact same options seen in the same figure, and then click on the **Import** button at the bottom of the dialog box.

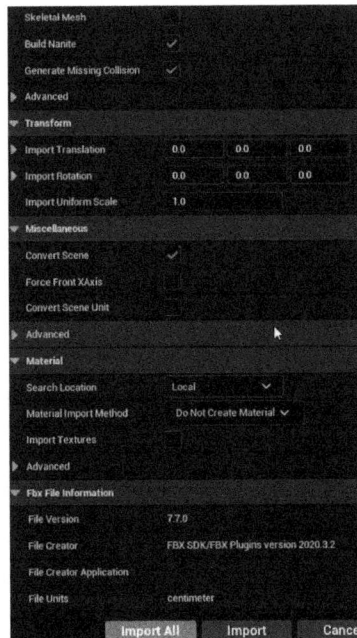

Figure 5.9: *FBX Import options*

Before proceeding to the next steps, it is an appropriate moment to consider the steps we just took. We organized our folder structure into different asset types, namely **Textures**, **Materials**, and **StaticMeshes**. If you pay close attention to the naming conventions of each and every asset, they are not random. In smaller projects, it is rather easy to keep track of the different assets, so naming conventions might not seem too important, but in larger projects, with hundreds and thousands of files and assets, things can get quite complicated. Therefore, it is good common practice to use proper naming conventions, regardless of a project's size.

Let us briefly analyze the naming conventions we used thus far:

- **T_GreekGodStatue_Diffuse**: T stands for Texture, Greek God Statue indicates the name of our asset or the asset we intend to use with, and Diffuse stands for the type of map used. This type of map might also be found named Color or Albedo, depending on an asset package you might be using in the future, but the function remains more or less the same, and we will be exploring that soon.

- **T_GreekGodStatue_Normal**: Same as above; however, this time, instead of Diffuse, we got the Normal suffix. This is because this texture map, is a normal map.

- **T_GreekGodStatue_ORM**: Same as above; however, ORM is an acronym for Occlusion, Roughness, and Metallic. All the values we will be needing when creating our asset's Materials.

- **SM_GreekGodStatue**: SM stands for StaticMesh.

Another excellent reference for naming conventions can be found on the official Unreal Engine documentation, specifically here: **https://dev.epicgames.com/documentation/en-us/unreal-engine/recommended-asset-naming-conventions-in-unreal-engine-projects** but if working in a team, it is best to ask the project lead about the preferred naming conventions.

By using proper naming conventions, it is a lot easier for a developer to find an asset they might be looking for. If, for example, a developer needs to find a texture, knowing there is a proper naming convention in place, they will begin by typing *T_* in the Content Browser's or drawer's search box. One could argue that there are filters for this, which we covered in *Chapters 2* and *3*; however, sometimes it is faster to just type the name of the asset needed, or there might even be situations in which one cannot use filters.

Prior to resuming our asset creation and management steps for this project, let us briefly analyze *Figure 5.9*, the FBX import options we just used when importing the statue asset:

- **Skeletal Mesh**: The type of mesh we imported is a Static; therefore, we unchecked Skeletal Mesh. A Skeletal Mesh would be the type of mesh used with animations, a fully rigged mesh, much like you would use for NPCs, characters, or even pre-animated assets, such as a weapon mesh that plays specific animations when being fired and so on.

- **Build Nanite**: We want to take advantage of the Unreal Engine 5's technical power, therefore since we are importing a Static Mesh that features high polygonal count, we are enabling Nanite. Will be explaining Nanite in greater detail shortly.

- **Generate missing collision**: Having this option enabled allows the Engine to create an invisible geometry surrounding our mesh, which will serve as the means to block cameras, players, or any other actor necessary (depending on collision settings), preventing them from going through the Static Mesh's geometry. While we could use the Static Mesh's actual geometry to achieve the same result, that would have a negative effect on performance since the more complex the collision geometry, the more performance is needed to calculate and enforce any collision between actors and the Static Mesh. Therefore, it is preferable to have a much simpler — in geometrical terms — shape for the collision, a shape which is also invisible, therefore not disrupting the visual representation of the mesh.

- **Material import method**: Generally, the author prefers to have this set to Do Not Create Material, as he finds it preferable to be manually creating Materials, when chosen to.

- **Import textures**: While the textures used, including their location, can be stored within the FBX file's information, the author once more prefers to manually import textures and manage them separately, thus leaving this option unchecked.

Further FBX import information can be found on the official Unreal Engine documentation, by following this link: **https://dev.epicgames.com/documentation/en-us/unreal-engine/fbx-import-options-reference-in-unreal-engine**.

Nanite

Probably, you have grown tired by now, counting the times Nanite has been mentioned so far in this book. But Nanite is one of the most important and powerful features Unreal Engine 5 specifically and exclusively has. Let us take a moment to better understand why Nanite is so important.

Up to very recently, game developers — mainly — had to maintain a polygonal budget for any 3D assets created. What this means is every 3D model is a geometrical shape, typically a rather complex geometrical shape. The more complex the geometrical shape is, the more detailed a model is. We can measure the complexity of a 3D model's geometrical shape in polygons, or triangles, generally referred to as polycount. The higher the polycount is, the better a 3D model looks. However, the higher the polycount is, the more performance-demanding the 3D model is, as it consumes more **Graphics Processing Unit (GPU)** power to properly calculate and render the 3D model's interaction with the conditions of its surrounding environment, specifically the lighting and the shadows.

To solve this problem, up to the point Unreal Engine 5 was released, developers would create extremely high polycount models, mainly in 3D applications such as ZBrush, reaching millions of polygonal counts, therefore achieving impressive levels of detail, but then would need to use a low poly counterpart, a 3D model with a considerably lower polycount, with a much simpler geometry, that still however overall resembles the desired and targeted shape. 3D artists would need to extract the geometrical information from the high poly model and apply it to the low poly model through texture maps holding that information, such as normal, bump, height, displacement maps, and more. While the end result was very good and highly resembled the high poly counterpart, all while maintaining the performance-friendly levels of the low poly counterpart, the production process was (still is to this day) very consuming and at times even tedious.

With Unreal Engine 5's Nanite, a 3D artist could export the high poly model from an application such as ZBrush and directly import it into the Unreal Engine, without needing to follow the processes mentioned in the previous paragraph. This is revolutionizing the production and development of 3D models not only from a technical perspective, but also from a creative perspective. 3D Artists now have more time to dedicate to building high poly models, and they are able to focus on the creative aspects without worrying too much about polycount budgets and lengthy tedious processes while achieving the best possible visual results.

To better understand it, let us use a very simple analogy. Imagine you have an object you need to place in a box and transport it from point A to point B, and this object weighs 500kgs. This is an impossible task because, simply put, there is no human that can carry that much weight. Now imagine that someone offers you a special box to put this object in, and once placed inside this special box, the object's weight decreases to 5kgs. The average human will have no problem transporting 5kgs from point A to point B. That special box is what Nanite is — in extremely simplistic terms.

In our project, we imported a Static Mesh that weighs at around 3 million triangles. Were we to import this in any other engine, including Unreal Engine 4, it would bring any average consumer-grade GPU to its knees if the application did not crash on the desktop first. Yet, bringing it in Unreal Engine 5, Nanite works its technological magic and treats it as a 21K triangle object instead! Refer to *Figure 5.10* and pay attention to the **Triangles** and **Nanite Triangles** numbers displayed in it, which can be obtained by hovering the mouse over the asset:

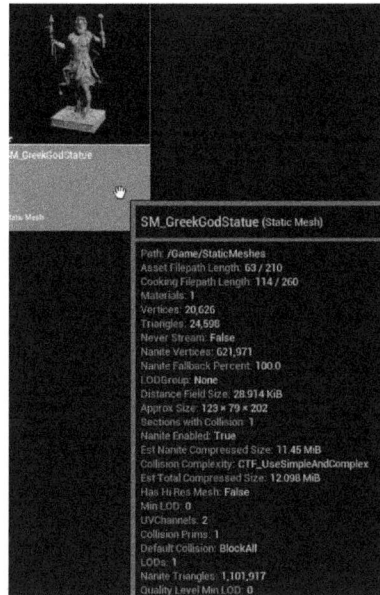

Figure 5.10: *Nanite's magic by the numbers*

Now, we will resume our step-by-step process of importing and creating assets for the Greek God Statue project:

10. Back in our Content Browser, we navigate to the **Materials** folder we created in step 5. We right-click anywhere in the empty browser and select **Material**, as shown in *Figure 5.11*. Let us name it **M_MasterMaterial** as shown in *Figure 5.12*. M stands for Material, and we name it MasterMaterial, because we will use it as a main Material to derive — if needed — any Material Instances that utilize the same properties as this Material.

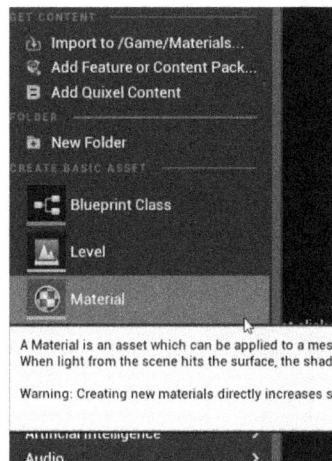

Figure 5.11: *Creating a new Material*

Observe the newly created Material in *Figure 5.12*:

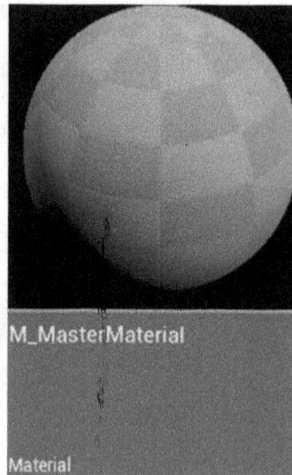

Figure 5.12: *Our newly created Material*

11. Double click the Material, and a new window will open, featuring the Material Editor and showing a preview of the Material on a sphere, as well as an empty **Material Graph**, much like the one shown in *Figure 5.13*:

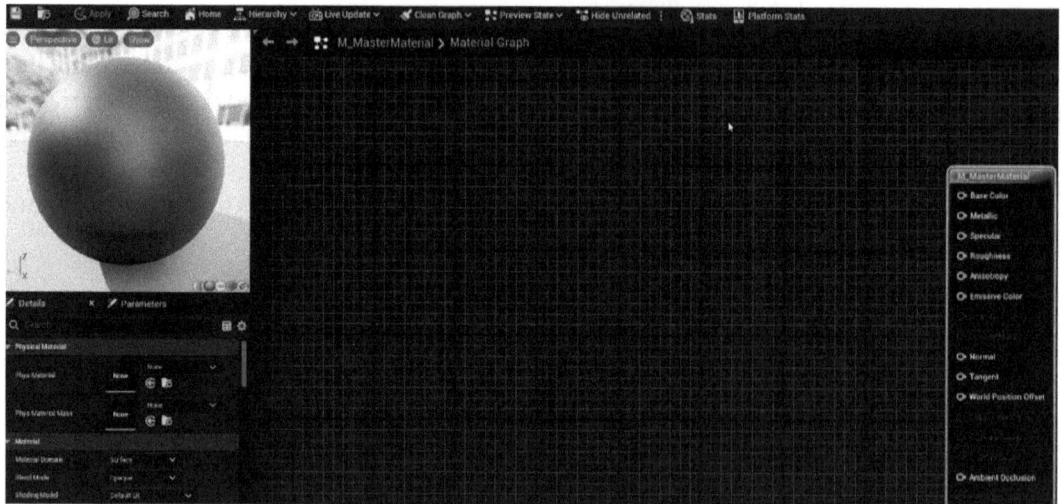

Figure 5.13: *Empty Material Graph of our new Material*

12. Back in the Content Browser, navigate to our **Textures** folder, select all three textures, and while having them selected, click and drag them into the **Material Graph**. Now arrange each **Texture Sample** node in a way similar to the one displayed in *Figure 5.14*:

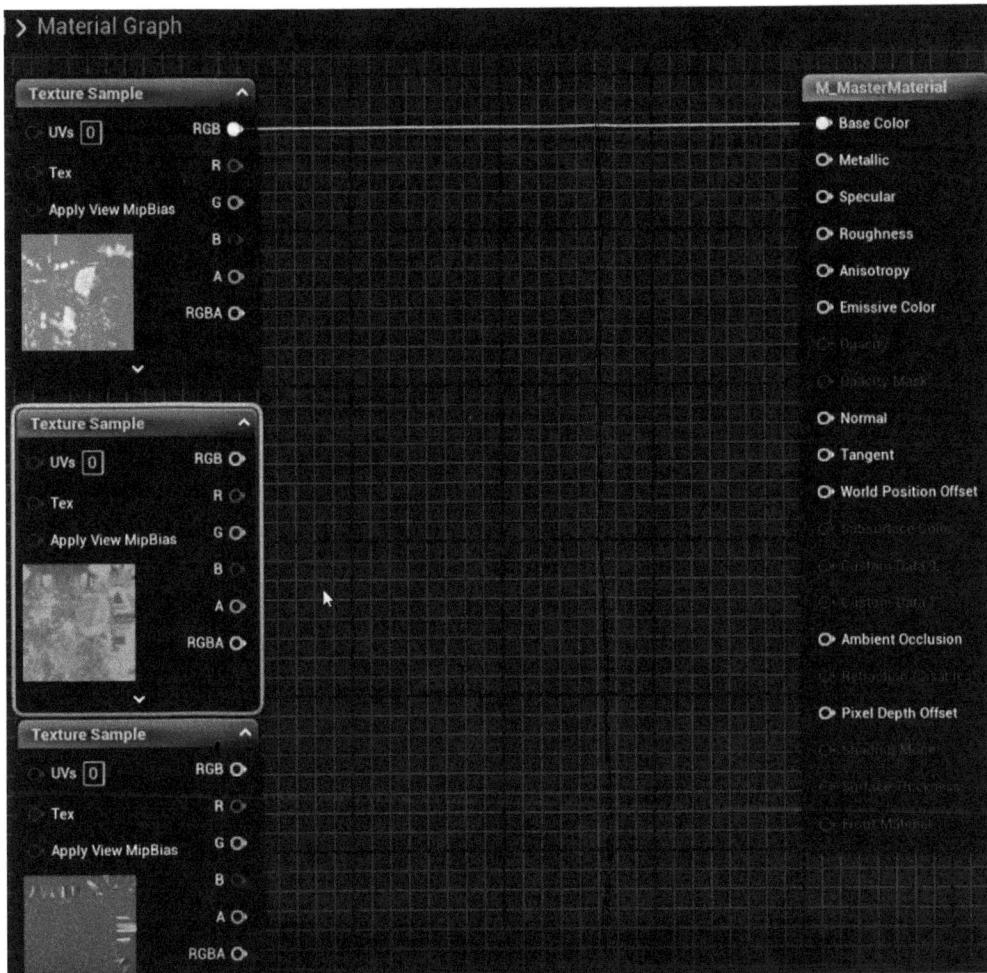

Figure 5.14: *Three textures placed into the Material Graph*

13. Click and drag from the **Red Green Blue (RGB)** output of the Diffuse texture sample node to drive a cable into the Base Color input of the **M_MasterMaterial/** Result Node, as shown in *Figure 5.15*.

14. Click and drag from the ORM texture sample node's red channel (**R**) to the **M_ MasterMaterial** node's **Ambient Occlusion**. Also depicted in *Figure 5.15*.

15. Next, click and drag from the ORM node's green channel (**G**) output to the result node's **Roughness** input, once more.

16. Click and drag from the ORM node's blue channel (**B**) output to the result node's **Metallic** input, again.

17. Lastly, click and dragon from the **Normal** texture sample node's **RGB** output into the result node's **Normal** input, also shown in *Figure 5.15*:

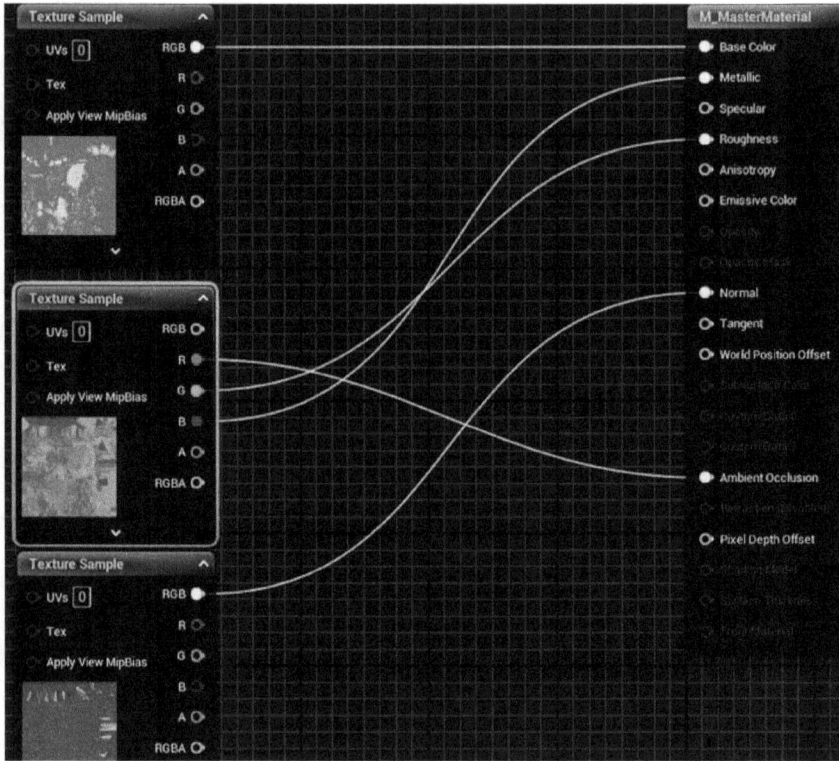

Figure 5.15: Connecting the texture sample nodes to the Material's Result node

18. While still in the Material Editor, click the **Apply** button found in the upper left corner of the Material Editor's window, as shown in *Figure 5.16*:

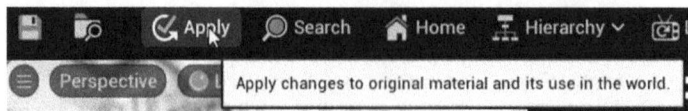

Figure 5.16: Applying our Material changes

19. Next, press *Ctrl+S* or click the Save button (as shown in *Figure 5.17)* to save your Material.

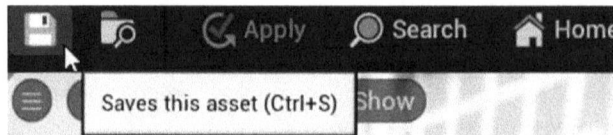

Figure 5.17: Saving the Material

20. Going back to our **StaticMeshes** folder, double click on the SM_GreekGodStatue Static Mesh. The Static Mesh browser opens up, appearing much like in *Figure 5.18*:

Figure 5.18: *Static Mesh browser*

21. Back again in the **Content Browser**, navigate to the **Materials** folder, and click on our newly created M_MasterMaterial to select it.

22. With the Material selected, go back to the Static Mesh browser, and under **Material Slots** click the small icon of a leftwards arrow in a circle, as shown in *Figure 5.19*. You have just applied the selected Material to the Static Mesh, and it should look much like *Figure 5.20*.

Figure 5.19: *Apply the selected Material to the Static Mesh*

Note *Figure 5.20*, where the Static Mesh has the Material applied to it.

Figure 5.20: *The Static Mesh with the applied Material*

Material parameters

While the Static Mesh certainly starts looking better, it is not perfect. As you can see, the Material we just applied looks highly reflective, which might be fine; however, we want to stay closer to our original concept, where the gold used on the statue was not as reflective. This presents us with the perfect opportunity to modify our M_MasterMaterial, in a way that not only can we derive Material Instances from it but also gives it the flexibility of using different diffuse, normal or ORM texture maps, as well as assign it parameters that determine some of the Material properties, such as in our case, the amount of reflection. Let us get started:

1. Open up M_MasterMaterial by double clicking it in the Content Browser. Once in the Material Editor, go to the Material Graph and right-click on the Diffuse map's **Texture Sample** node, and select **Convert to Parameter** as shown in *Figure 5.21*:

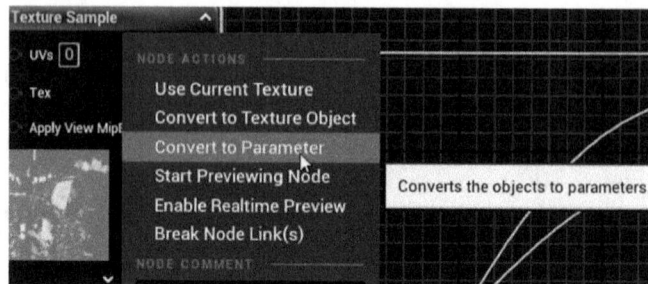

Figure 5.21: Converting a texture sample node to a parameter

2. Name it **Diffuse**, as shown in *Figure 5.22*:

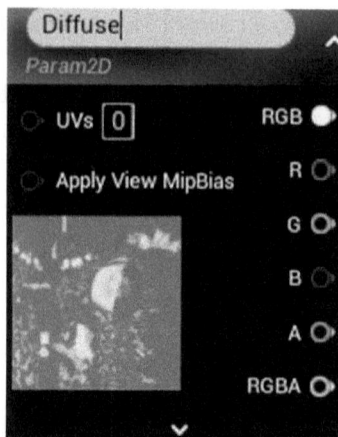

Figure 5.22: Assigning a name to the converted parameter texture sample

3. Repeat steps *1* and *2* for the ORM and Normal texture sample nodes by naming them **ORM** and **Normal**, respectively, as shown in *Figures 5.23* and *Figure 5.24*:

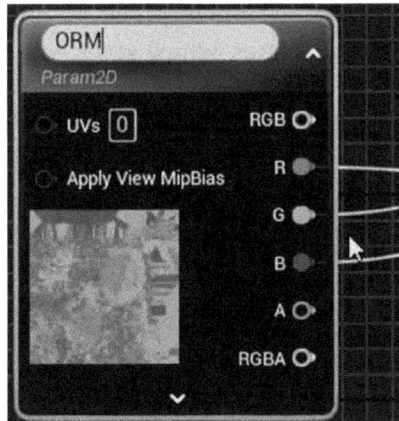

Figure 5.23: ORM node

Observe *Figure 5.24* and note how the **Normal** node and parameter are made:

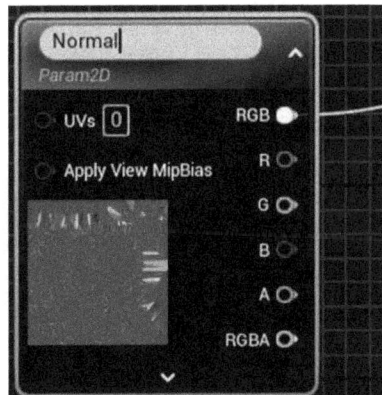

Figure 5.24: Normal node

4. Next, right-click anywhere on an empty spot in the Material Graph, and type in **multi** or **multiply**, and click on **Multiply** as shown in *Figure 5.25*:

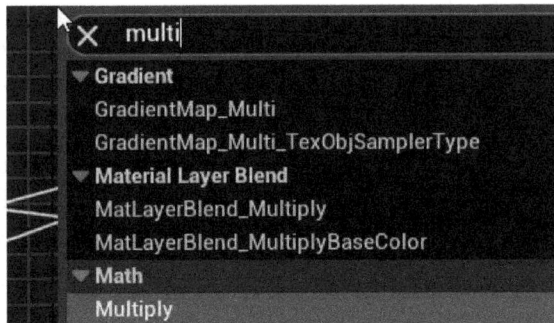

Figure 5.25: Looking for the multiply node

5. Alternatively, you can press and hold the *M* key and click anywhere in the Material Graph, it will yield the same result, which gives you a Multiply node as shown in *Figure 5.26*:

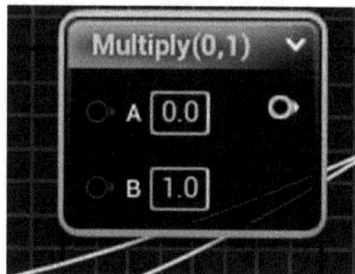

Figure 5.26: Behold the Multiply node

6. Create one more Multiply node, as described in the previous step.

7. In a similar way, either by right-clicking and typing in **Constant** or simply by pressing and holding 1 while clicking anywhere in the Material Graph, create a Constant node. Once that is created, right-click on it and Convert to Parameter which we will name **Roughness Multiplier**. Both the Constant node and its parameter name are shown in *Figure 5.27*:

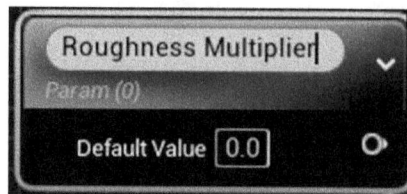

Figure 5.27: Constant node

8. Repeat the previous step and create a Constant node, which you will then convert to a parameter, but this time, you will name it **Metallic Mulitplier**.

9. For this step, disconnect the **ORM** node's green channel by pressing and holding *Alt* while clicking on the green circle/output found on the **ORM** node. Instead, connect this with our first **Multiply** node's input **B** while connecting the **Roughness Multiplier** node's output to the first multiply node's input **A**, as can be seen in *Figure 5.28*.

10. Similarly, disconnect the **ORM** node's blue channel, and connect it to the second **Multiply** node's input **A**, while connecting the **Metallic Multiplier** node's output to the second **Multiply** node's input **B**, once again seen in *Figure 5.28*.

Now connect the first **Multiply** node's output to the **Roughness** input of the result node while connecting the second **Multiply** node's output to the **Metallic** input of the result node, once more depicted in *Figure 5.28*:

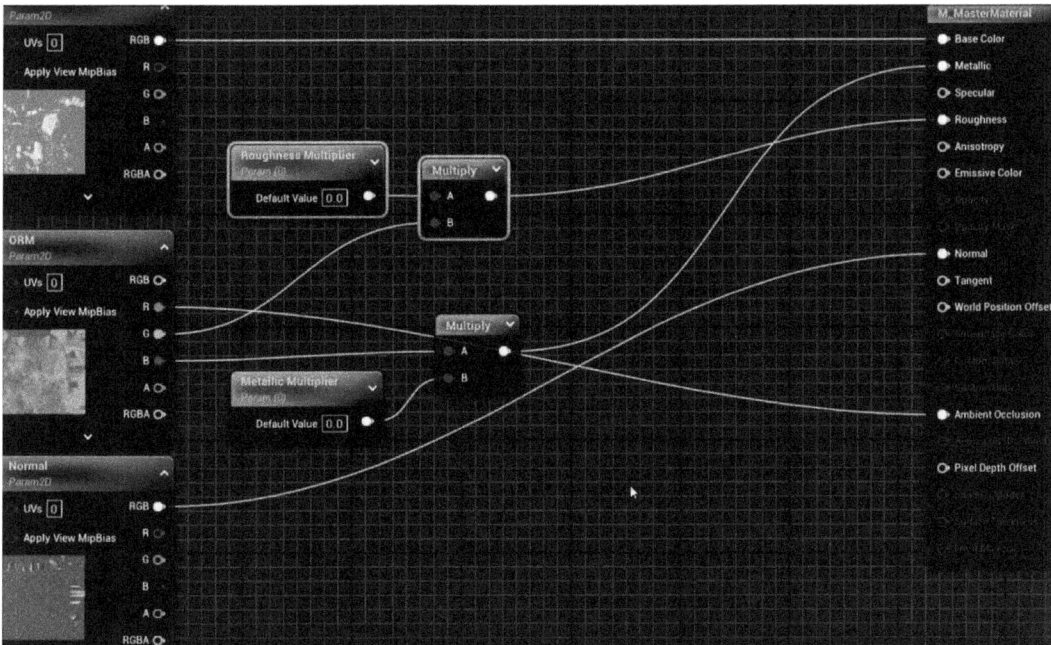

Figure 5.28: Connecting the constant and Multiply nodes

As you can see, our Material Graph starts looking slightly more complex and perhaps even a bit messy. Next, let us clean it up a bit.

11. Click and drag over to select the **Roughness Multiplier** and the first **Multiply** nodes. While having them selected (highlighted in yellow), press C to create a comment box that surrounds them, and name it **Roughness**, as shown in *Figure 5.29*:

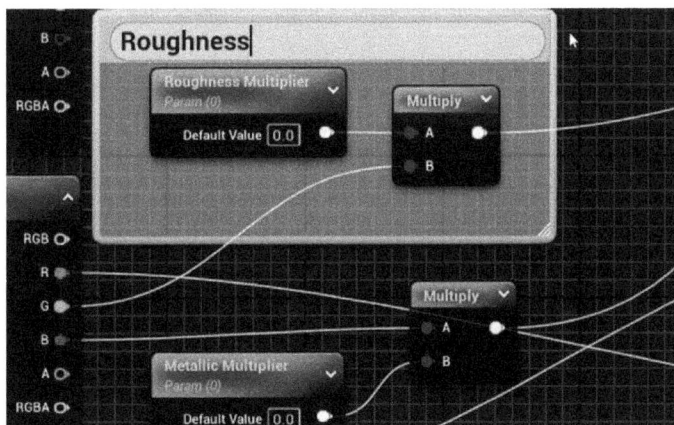

Figure 5.29: Creating a comment box

12. Repeat the same process by selecting the **Metallic Multiplier** and second **Multiply** nodes. Name this comment box `Metallic`.

13. You can change the color of the comment boxes to anything you prefer. In the author's case, working till late at night makes bright colors tiring to the eye, therefore usually resorting to changing the comment box colors to darker ones, such as black or dark gray. To do that, while having any of the comment boxes selected, double click on the white bar next to **Comment Color** found in the Material Editor's **Details** tab on the left side, as shown in *Figure 5.30*. Select the color you prefer.

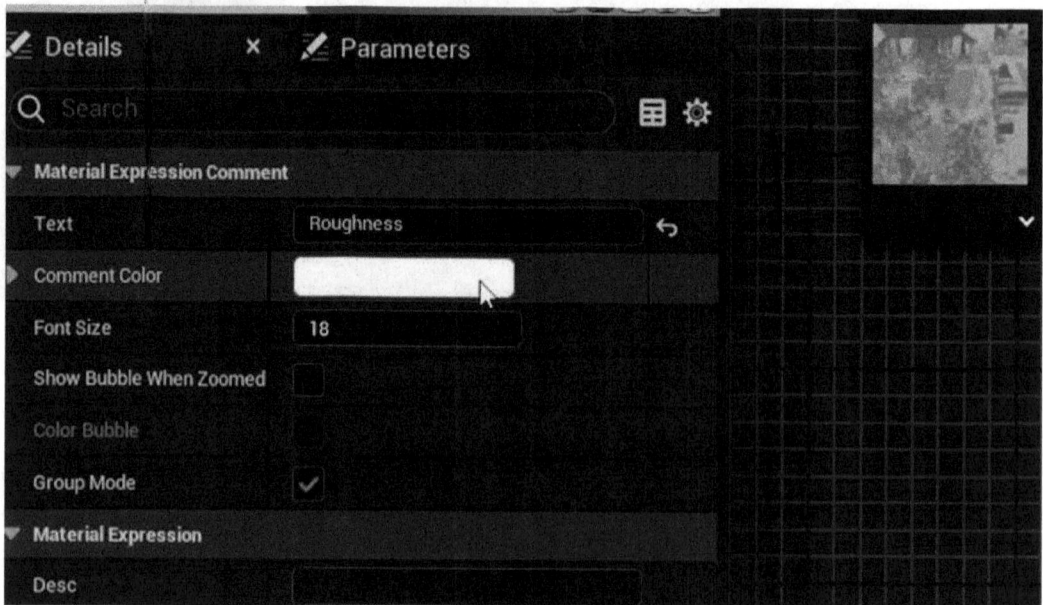

Figure 5.30: Changing the comment box color

14. As discussed in *Chapter 3, Unreal Engine's Building Blocks* when we were editing our very first Blueprint, let us organize the cables a bit better. Double click anywhere on any cable connecting two nodes, and then click and drag the newly created white dot to arrange the cables a bit better. Once you have done that, your **Material Graph** should look nice and tidy, much like in *Figure 5.31*:

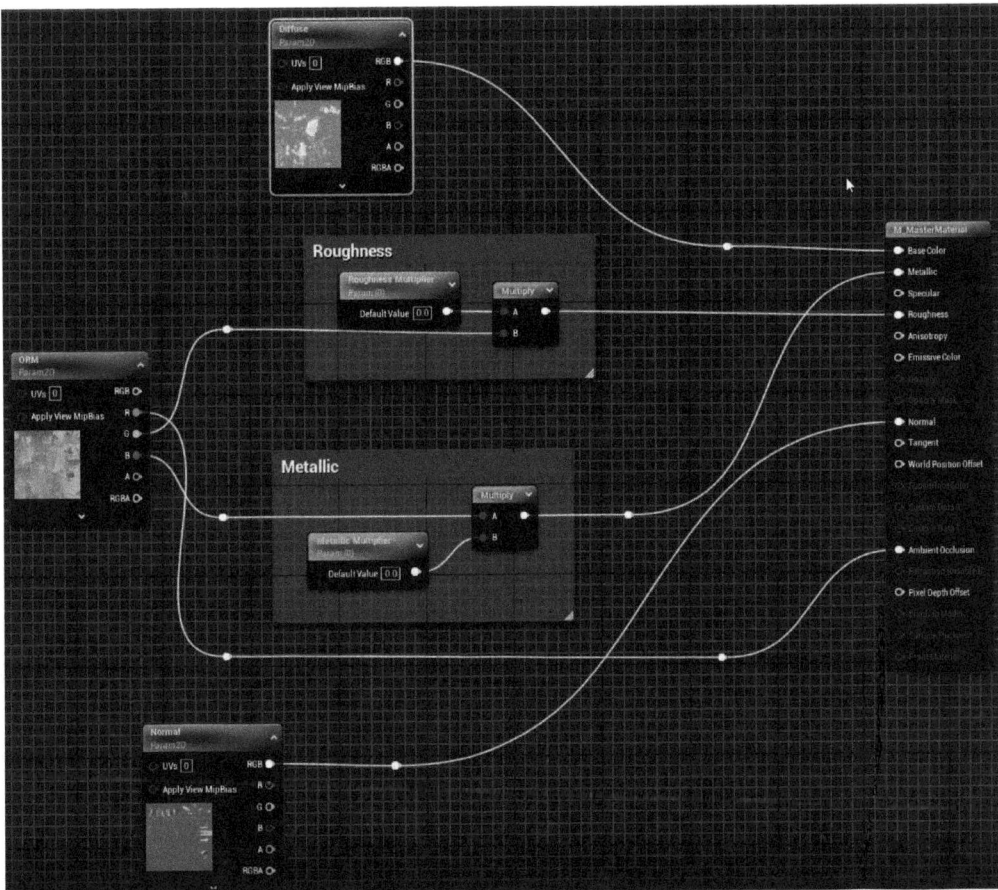

Figure 5.31: *A cleaned-up Material Graph*

15. Now, let us change the default values for both the **Roughness** and **Metallic Multiplier** nodes. Click on the **Roughness Multiplier** node and change the **Default Value** under **Material Expression Scalar Parameter**, found in the **Details** tab on the left-hand side of the Material Editor, from 0 to 1. Repeat that step for the **Metallic Multiplier** node, as seen in *Figure 5.32*:

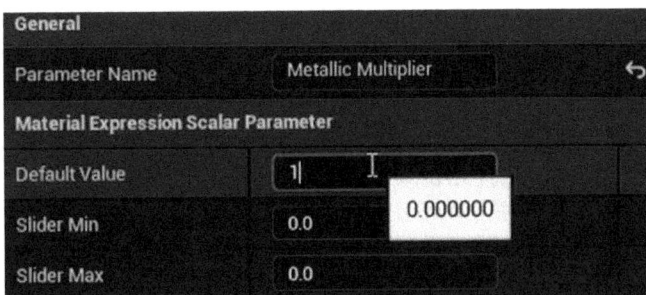

Figure 5.32: *Modifying the Default Value*

Material Instances

When having large projects with multiple assets, it is preferable to limit the number of master or parent Materials and use Material Instances instead. Not only does that give performance benefits due to not having to compile and render a new Material for each and every object, but it also makes working a lot easier and faster. The way we modified our master Material in the previous section, we prepared the ground for creating and easily working with Material Instances, in which we just need to plug different texture maps or modify the different parameter values, such as Roughness and Metallic. Recall how the statue looked highly reflective, whereas in the concept the gold Material was a bit more dull. To rectify that, all we need to do is create a Material Instance out of our master Material and play around with different Roughness values.

1. In the Content Browser, in the **Materials** folder, right-click on **M_MasterMaterial**, and select **Create Material Instance**, as shown in *Figure 5.33*:

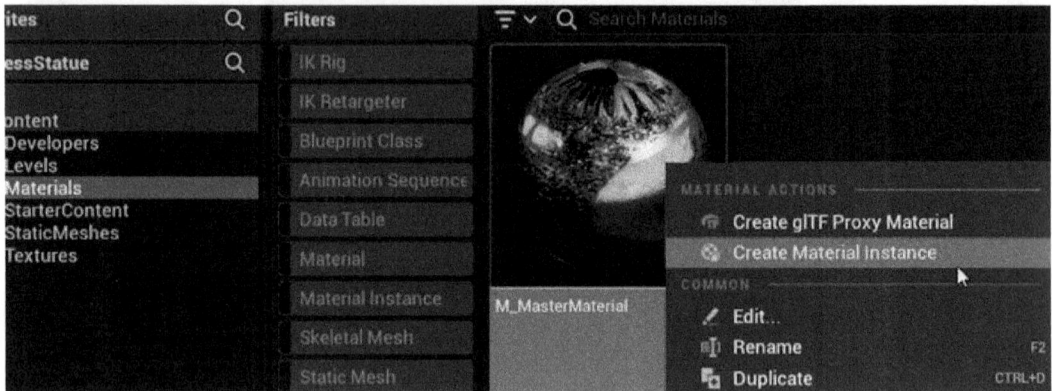

Figure 5.33: Creating a Material Instance

2. Name it MI_GreekGodStatue MI standing for Material Instance.

3. With MI_GreekGodStatue selected, go back to the Static Mesh browser with the Greek God Statue mesh. If you close it, you can open it by pressing *Ctrl+Spacebar* to bring up the Content Drawer, then navigate to the **StaticMeshes** folder and double click on the SM_GreekGodStatue asset. Once it opens up, while having MI_GreekGodStatue selected in your Content Browser, assign it to the statue mesh, as described earlier in *Figure 5.19*.

4. Double click on MI_GreekGodStatue to open it in a separate editor, where we can modify its different parameters. The new editor that popped up, should look identical to the one in *Figure 5.34*:

Figure 5.34: Material Instance Editor

5. Check the **Metallic Multiplier** and **Roughness Multiplier** boxes and assign them values of 1 and 40, respectively. Alternatively, you can leave the **Metallic Multiplier** unchecked, since 1 is its default value. Your settings should look identical to *Figure 5.35*:

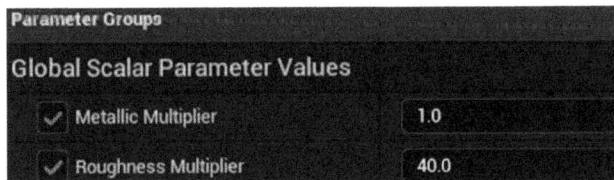

Figure 5.35: Metallic and Roughness Mutliplier values

Upon completing step 5, if you go back to the Static Mesh browser and look at our statue, you will notice that it has completely lost its reflectivity. That is because, generally speaking, the higher the roughness value in a Material shader is, the less reflective it becomes. Usually, these values range from 0, defining full reflective properties — mirror-like — to 1, defining no reflective properties at all. By assigning an absurdly high value (40) to our multiplier, we ensured that the end result reaches — if not surpasses — the overall roughness value of 1, therefore giving this non-reflective, dull appearance to our mesh, as you can see in *Figure 5.36*:

Figure 5.36: The Material's reflection is gone

6. However, if we scale down the **Roughness Multiplier** to a considerably lower value, like 7, as shown in *Figure 5.37*, we end up getting a nice, but not over the top, reflective surface, resembling the gold Material of our concept. You can see the result of our change in *Figure 5.38*:

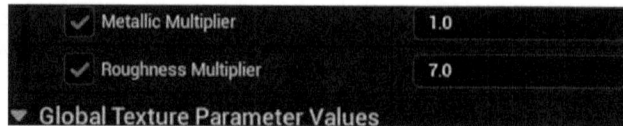

Figure 5.37: Scaling down the roughness multiplier to 7

Note the balanced Material reflections shown in *Figure 5.38*:

Figure 5.38: Reflections are back on, but not over the top

You might be wondering why we are using a value of 7, since earlier it is stated that Roughness typically ranges between 0 and 1. The reason we use 7 is because the ORM map's green channel, the one that gives us the Roughness we generated from Substance Painter, does not feature an absolute 0 or 1 value; instead, it has a variety of values across the texture map. Think of 0 as black, 1 as white, 0.5 as gray. The Roughness of our ORM map is a combination of a variety of decimal values other than absolute 0 or 1, mostly lower than 0.5 since the Substance Painter Material we use is meant to be gold, therefore having some reflectivity in it.

At the same time, when we were setting parameters in our master Material, we also connected them to the Multiplier node. So, in essence, we multiply our Roughness Multiplier value by whatever value is given by the ORM's green channel. If, for example, the ORM green channel gives us a value of 0.25, if we assign a value of 2 to our roughness multiplier, our end result is *0.25*2=0.5*, which is well within the 0-1 range.

Essentially, what we achieved with our changes above, is take a highly reflective Material, whose Roughness was approximating 0 (in other words it was almost as reflective as a mirror) and increasing it to a value closer to 0.3-0.5 which is ideal for the amount of reflectivity we want to achieve.

While this sorts out the statue's overall reflectivity, there is one remaining problem, at least when compared to the concept we use; our color or diffuse map, is a bit brighter than we would like it to be. One way to fix this would be to open up the diffuse texture map (T_GreekGodStatue_Diffuse) in an external application, such as *Photoshop*, and change its brightness and contrast settings. We could also do that within the Unreal Engine. However, we would then be essentially changing the default texture's values, and that is not something that is always desirable, as there might be settings or circumstances under which we prefer the texture map to be the way it is.

We could also duplicate it and perform these changes on the duplicate texture, but then we increase the number of textures used, and with that the space and memory needed to store and render these.

So instead, we can go back to our master Material and add one more parameter that will easily fix this problem for us.

7. In the Content Browser, under Materials, double click on M_MasterMaterial and once in the Material editor's Material Graph, press and hold *M* and click anywhere in the graph to create a new Multiply node. Next, right-click anywhere in the graph and type in **Constant 3**, or Alternatively, press and hold *3* and click anywhere in the graph. That will give you a Constant 3 node, which essentially is a node with 3 output values, which can be thought of as X, Y and Z, or as we prefer in our present case, as red, green, and blue.

8. Right-click on the newly created node, convert it to a parameter and name it **Brightness&Color**, as shown in *Figure 5.39*:

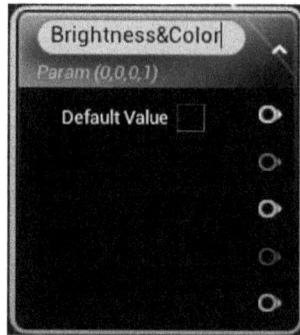

Figure 5.39: Constant 3 node converted into a parameter

9. On the Material Editor's **Details** tab on the left-hand side, change the **Material Expression Vector Parameter Default Value** to 1 for **R**, **G** and **B**, as shown in *Figure 5.40*:

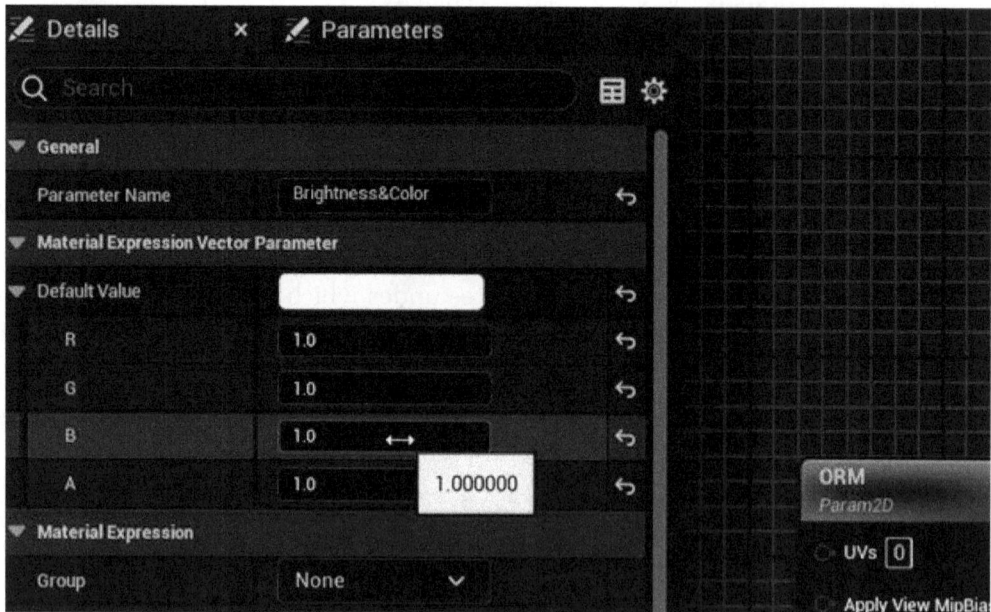

Figure 5.40: Setting default values to 1

10. Now, connect the Constant 3/Brightness & Color node's overall output (white output circle on the node's top, above the red output) to the last **Multiply** node's input **B**, while disconnecting the **Diffuse** node's output and reconnecting it to the last **Multiply** node's input **A**. Then connect the **Multiply** node's output to the Material's result node **Base Color**, all as depicted in *Figure 5.41*:

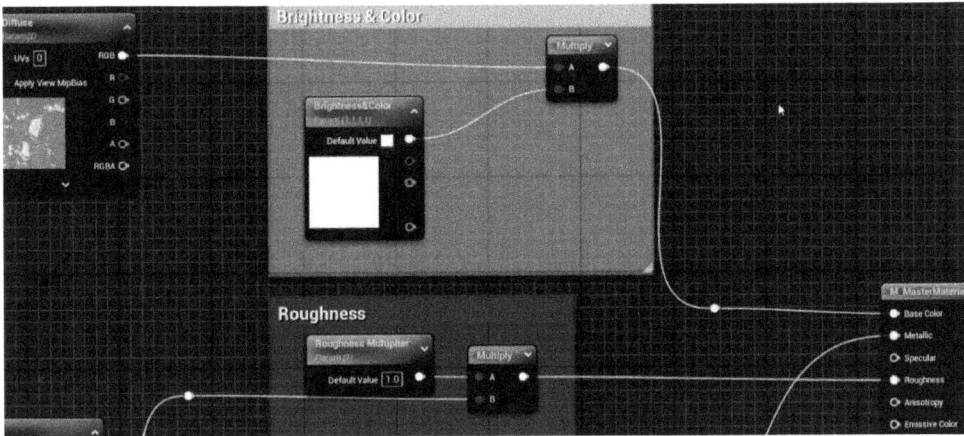

Figure 5.41: *Connecting all the nodes properly*

11. Back to the Content Browser, under Materials, double click on MI_GreekGodStatue, and now when it pops up in the Material Editor, you can see we have a new parameter to edit, found under **Global Vector Parameter Values,** and this parameter is none other than the **Brightness&Color** we just created. Check the box corresponding to it, as shown in *Figure 5.42*:

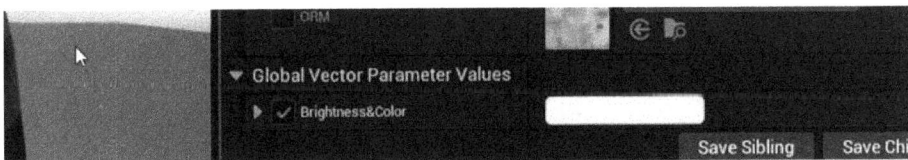

Figure 5.42: *Brightness & Color parameter is now available*

12. To demonstrate the power of our newly created parameter, let us expand the parameter by pressing the small arrow next to the parameter's check box. Set **R** (red) to 0, **G** (green) to 0 and leave **B** (blue) to 1, as shown in *Figure 5.43*. The result of our actions is what you can see in *Figure 5.44*:

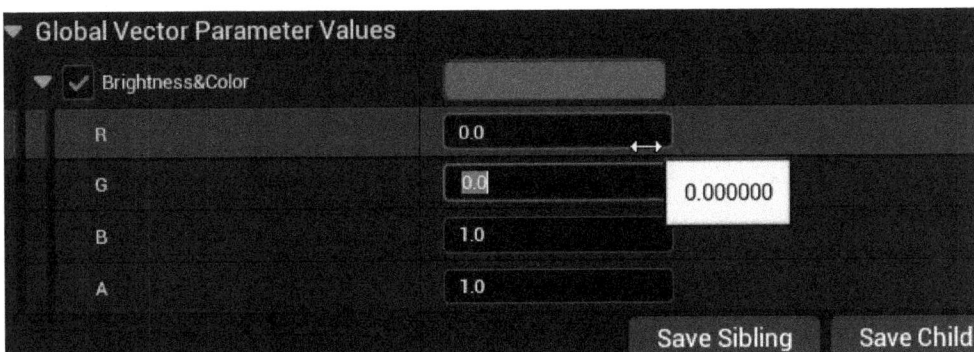

Figure 5.43: *Adjusting the values*

Figure 5.44: We have a blue statue

As you can see, we zeroed out the red and green values while leaving the blue value at 1, therefore, unsurprisingly, making our statue look blue! Now let us try a more moderate approach and finally match the Material we have in our concept reference.

13. Change the **Brightness&Color** parameter's RGB values to 0.5, as shown in *Figure 5.44*. That essentially tones down our original diffuse map by half. The end result is shown in *Figure 5.45*:

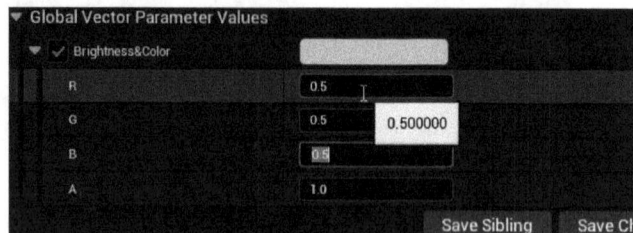

Figure 5.45: Adjusting our RGBs to 0.5

Figure 5.46 shows the end result:

Figure 5.46: The end result

At this point, it is highly advisable to save all your work by simply clicking the **Save All** button in your Content Browser, as depicted in *Figure 5.47*:

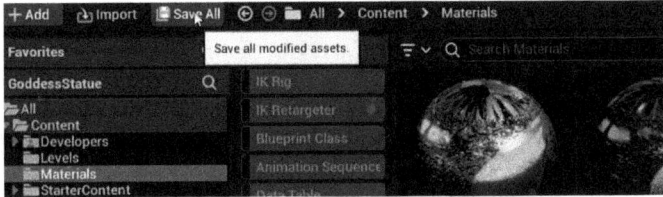

Figure 5.47: *It is good to Save All once in a while*

Quixel Bridge and Megascans

It is certainly fun creating one's own original assets and is most certainly a necessity if one wishes to stand out and be original. However, there is nothing wrong with being efficient, and that is where Quixel Bridge and, by extension, Quixel Megascans are most helpful. Sometimes, there are generic assets, such as rocks, trees, and walls, that do not necessarily need to be the most original ever, especially if they are used as a backdrop or as a filler. Yet it is important to have qualitative assets to work with, and not only do the Quixel assets ooze quality, but even more astonishingly, they are available for free!

We will be using such assets in our project to fill up the scene and make it resemble somewhat the environment of our concept:

1. To access Quixel Bridge, navigate to **Window** all the way on top of the main Unreal Engine window, and select **Quixel Bridge** as shown in *Figure 5.48*. That will pop up a new window. You might be required to sign in with the same credentials you used when you launched the Epic Games Launcher. Once you have signed it, the new window that pops up, looks much like the one in *Figure 5.49*:

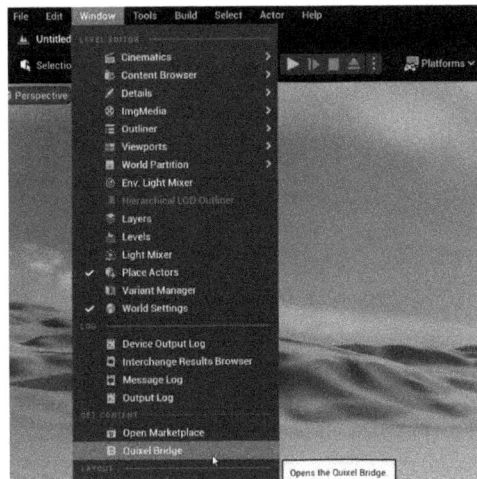

Figure 5.48: *Finding Quixel Bridge*

Figure 5.49: *Welcome to the Quixel Bridge*

2. We want to download some 3D assets from Quixel Bridge. Click on the sphere-like icon, and then click on **3D Assets**, as shown in *Figure 5.50*. In the search dialog box on the top, type in `Walls`, as depicted in *Figure 5.51*:

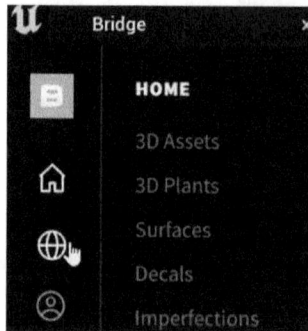

Figure 5.50: *Browsing asset categories*

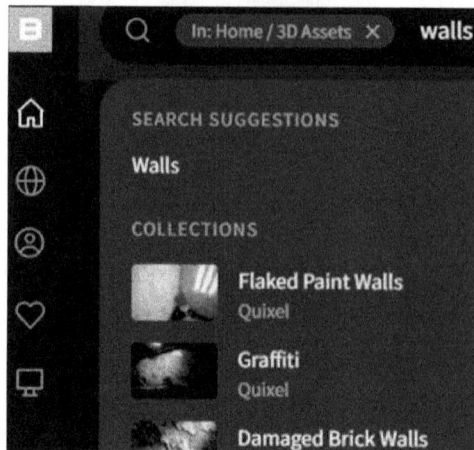

Figure 5.51: *Searching for wall assets*

3. Look for **Modular Building Base Wall Kit** that looks like the one in *Figure 5.52*.

4. Click on it, and on the right-hand side, click on the Quality drop down menu, and select **Nanite**, as shown, also in *Figure 5.52*. For this project's purposes, whatever assets you decide to download from Quixel Bridge, you always want to ensure the quality is set to **Nanite** or the highest possible if **Nanite** is not an option.

5. Next, click on the green arrow, as shown in *Figure 5.52*, to download the asset. Once the download is complete, click the blue + icon, as shown in *Figure 5.53* to add it to your asset library.

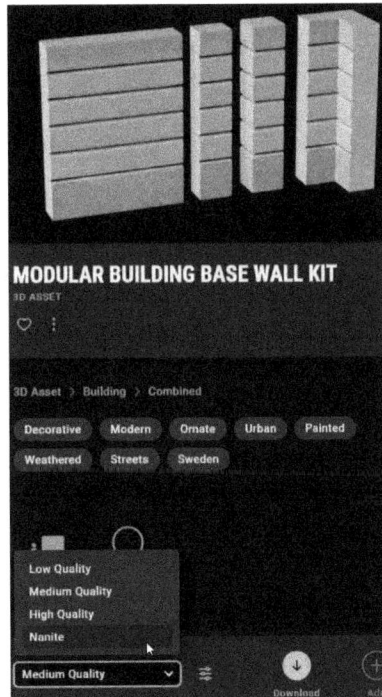

Figure 5.52: Changing asset quality settings and downloading the asset

Figure 5.53: Downloaded asset, ready to be added

6. Next, download some more assets either by searching them in the search bar, or by selecting the appropriate category. *Figures 5.54 and Figure 5.55* show you some assets you can download if you want. Feel free to download any other assets you prefer instead, as long as they can satisfy a similar function to the ones suggested in this book.

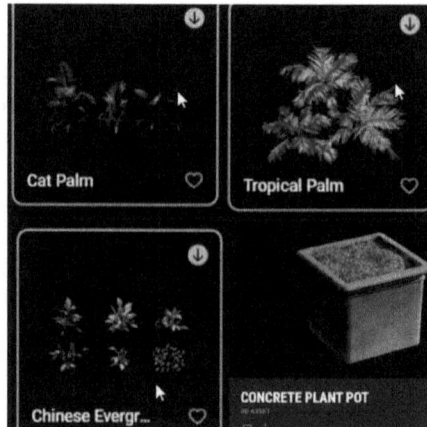

Figure 5.54: Some of the suggested assets

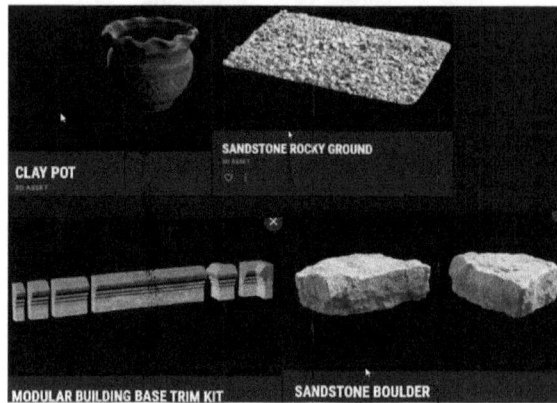

Figure 5.55: More suggested assets

7. Lastly, download two surfaces/Material assets, specifically the ones depicted in *Figure 5.56*:

Figure 5.56: Surface suggested assets

Once you have downloaded all these assets, you can easily find them in your **Content Browser** under the **Megascans** folder, as shown in *Figure 5.57*. Within this folder, there will be a **3D_Assets** folder, which contains the Static Meshes (and their Materials and textures) we just downloaded, a **3D_Plants** folder, which contains the Static Meshes of the plants (and their Materials and textures) we just downloaded, and a **Surfaces** folder, which contains all the Material Instances (and their parent Materials and textures) we just downloaded.

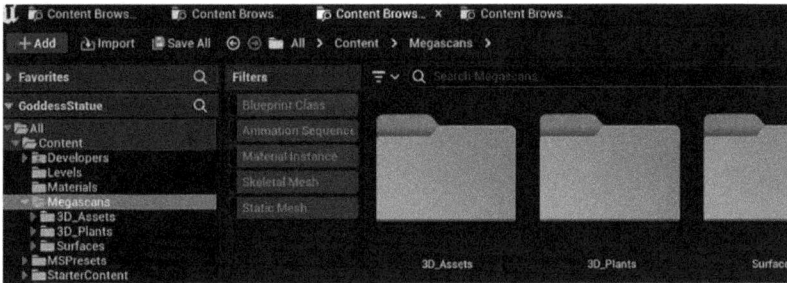

Figure 5.57: Megascans folder structure

Usually, when browsing through the Megascans asset library, it is useful to utilize the Content Browser's filters, specifically the Static Mesh filter for the **3D_Assets** and **3D_Plants** folders and the Material Instance filter for the **Surfaces** folder.

Now, we have all the assets we need, and we are finally ready to carry on with the creation of our project's scene!

Setting up the Greek God Statue scene

Much like we did in *Chapter 3, Unreal Engine's Building Blocks*, once again we will be using our assets to drop them in our scene, manage them by rotating them, placing them, scaling them, but this time, we will perform it with higher quality assets, while you should also be much more comfortable with the process than you were in *Chapter 3*. To begin with the process, follow the next steps.

1. In the main window of the Unreal Engine, press *Ctrl+N*, then select **Basic** and then click **Create**, as shown in *Figure 5.58*:

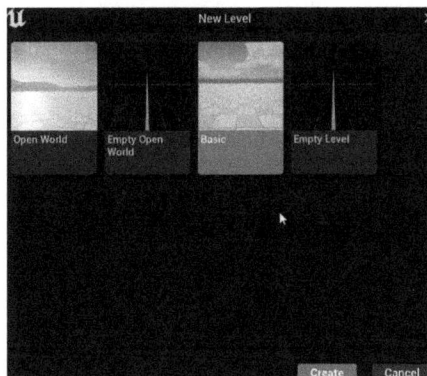

Figure 5.58: Creating a new level for our project

2. Once the level is created, bring the Greek God Statue mesh into the scene (you should know by now that the fastest way to do this is by finding it in the Content Browser, under Static Meshes, clicking and dragging it into the main Viewport), as shown in *Figure 5.59*:

Figure 5.59: The Greek God Statue is brought into the scene

3. It is a good time to save our level, so go to **File,** then **Save Current Level As…,** as shown in *Figure 5.60,* and name it **GreekGodStatueLevel** as shown in *Figure 5.61*:

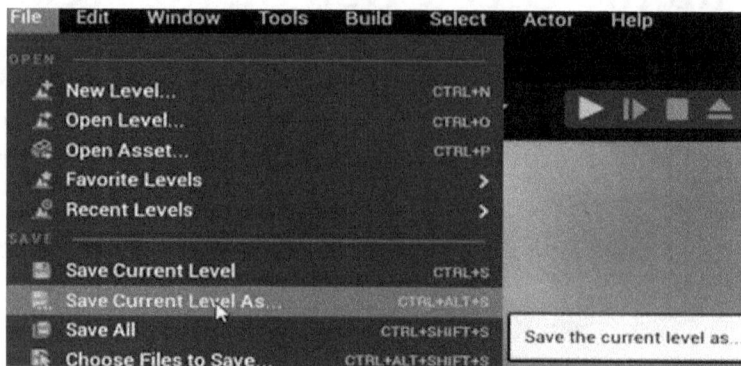

Figure 5.60: Saving the level

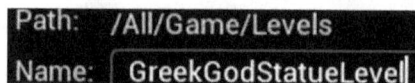

Figure 5.61: Save it as GreekGodStatueLevel

4. Bring in our scene the Megascans wall asset depicted in *Figure 5.62*:

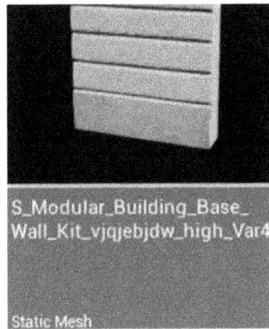

Figure 5.62: Admittedly Megascans naming is not the easiest to deal with

5. After having brought the wall Static Mesh into the scene, duplicate it and create 3 more, for a total of four wall meshes. Place them as depicted in *Figure 5.63*. Given all the steps we took in *Chapter 3, Unreal Engine's Building Blocks*, you should be comfortable with completing this step. If you are not, it is strongly recommended you go over *Chapter 3, Unreal Engine's Building Blocks* one more time.

Figure 5.63: Placement of the wall meshes in the scene

Next, let us bring in some of the plants we downloaded. If you downloaded the recommended assets, once having selected the **Megascans/3D_Plants/** folder with the **Static Mesh** filter applied, your Content Browser should give you a plentiful variety of plants to choose from, as shown in *Figure 5.64*. Strongly recommend using the ones seen in *Figures 5.65* to *Figure 5.67*:

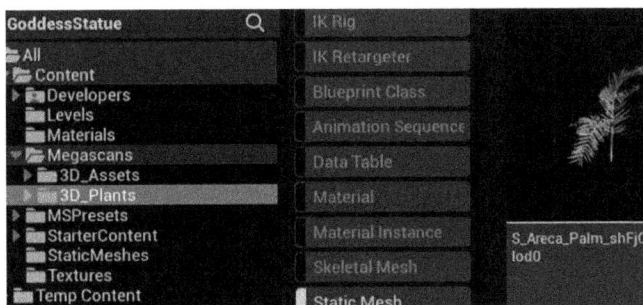

Figure 5.64: A plethora of Megascans plants to choose from

Figure 5.65 showcasing one of the plants that could potentially be used in the scene:

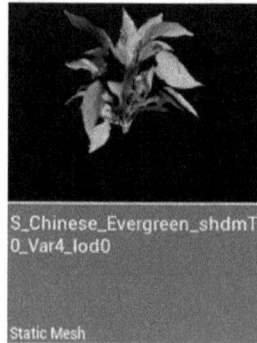

Figure 5.65: *A good choice of plant for our scene, as it fits the broad-leafed plant in the concept*

Figure 5.66 showcases another plant that could potentially be used in the scene:

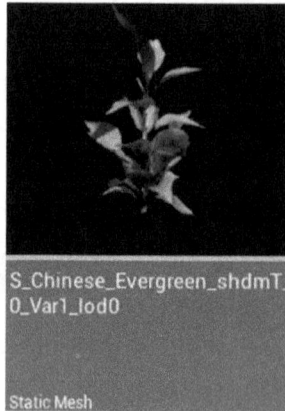

Figure 5.66: *A variety of the same plant we chose in the previous figure*

Figure 5.67 showcases yet another plant that could potentially be used in the scene:

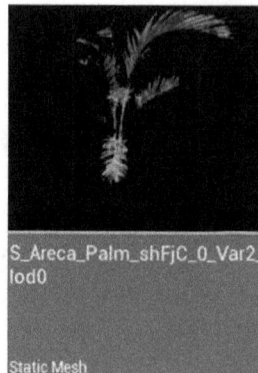

Figure 5.67: *A suitable choice matching the fern-like plant of our concept*

6. Place all these plant assets, duplicate them, move them, and scale them as you see fit until you get a result that resembles the scene in *Figure 5.68*:

Figure 5.68: *We are far from done, but it starts vaguely resembling our concept*

7. In *Figure 5.55* you can see we downloaded a 3D asset named **Sandstone Boulder**. Place that in the scene under the Greek God Statue mesh, as shown in *Figure 5.69*:

Figure 5.69: *Using the boulder asset as the statue's base*

The boulder resembles the rock that serves as a base for the golden statue in the concept, however there is one small problem; the one in the concept is golden. Now that we are familiar with the Material and Material Instance workflows, let us rectify the situation by creating a Material Instance based off the boulder's default Material.

8. With the boulder mesh selected, locate its Material, which is found under the **Materials** section in the Details tab, and click the little icon with the magnifying glass and the folder, to browse straight to the Material, as seen in *Figure 5.70*:

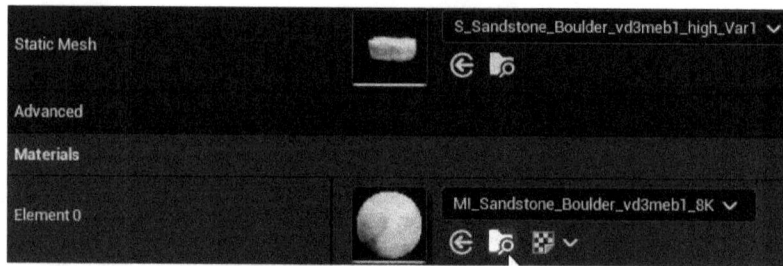

Figure 5.70: *Click the magnifying glass with the folder icon to find the Material (Alternatively can press Ctrl + B)*

9. Once in the Content Browser with the Material, right-click on it and select **Create Material Instance** as depicted in *Figure 5.71*:

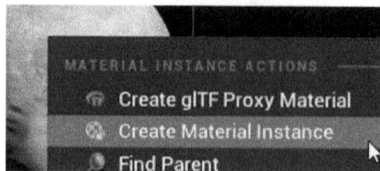

Figure 5.71: *Create a Material Instance of the boulder's Material*

10. Name the Material Instance MI_Sandstone_Boulder_GOLD.

11. Apply it on the boulder mesh in the scene.

12. Double click it to open and edit it in the Material Editor, and change its parameters to the same ones depicted in *Figure 5.72*:

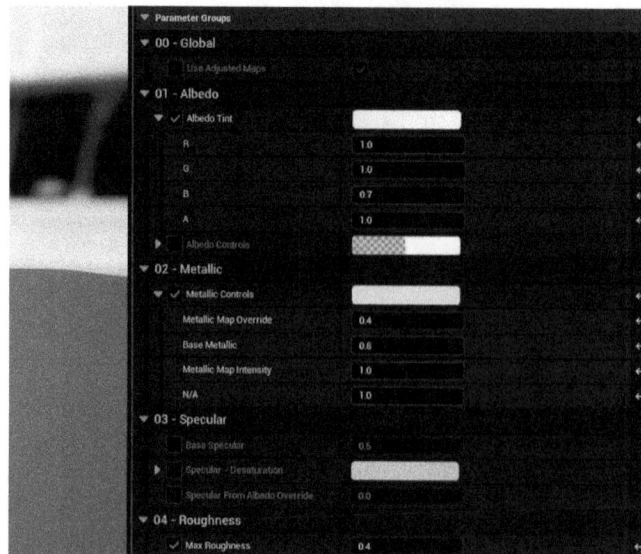

Figure 5.72: *Parameter settings to get the boulder MI (Material Instance) to look like gold*

Once successfully applied and saved, your Material Instance will make your scene's boulder look golden, matching the statue's Material, as depicted in *Figure 5.73*:

Figure 5.73: Boulder and statue Materials perfectly matching each other

13. Next add the following Megascans 3D asset, shown in *Figure 5.74*, which we will use as gravel and overall ground decoration for our scene:

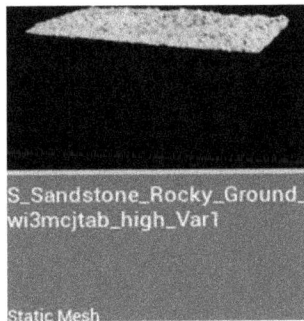

Figure 5.74: The perfect mesh for the ground in our scene

14. Once again, by utilizing everything you have learned so far, duplicate, place, rotate, and scale as you see fit until you achieve results similar to the ones shown in *Figure 5.75*:

Figure 5.75: Gravel starts making our scene more realistic and complete, but we still have some way to go

15. If you navigate around the Viewport, you might notice that some of the walls are letting light bleed through, even though their façade seems to be solid, this specific issue is clearly displayed in *Figure 5.76*. This happens due to the geometry being one sided, therefore not casting any shadows from the mesh's rear side. A quick and easy way to fix this, is to make the mesh's Material a two-sided one.

Figure 5.76: Light bleeding through a spot that is supposed to be shadowed

16. By selecting the wall mesh in the Viewport, double click its Material, once again found under the Materials section in the Details tab, and when it pops up in the Material Editor, scroll down until you find **Maerial Property Overrides"** which you then expand, to check **Two Sided**, as shown in *Figure 5.77*:

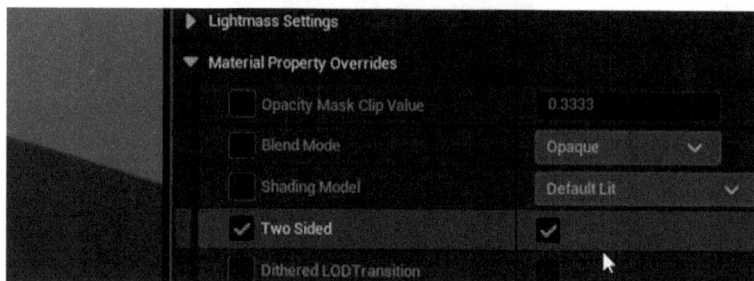

Figure 5.77: Converting the wall mesh's Material to two sided

As seen in *Figure 5.78*, now the wall mesh's shadows are being cast properly:

Figure 5.78: Shadows being cast the way they are meant to

17. While it is entirely optional and up to the reader, the author felt like making the gravel's Material a bit darker, matches the scene a bit better (seen in *Figure 5.79*). If you wish to replicate that effect, just select any of the gravel meshes, double click once again on its Material, and then under the **Albedo** section, check the box and expand **Albedo Tint** and set the RGB values to 0.3, as seen in *Figure 5.80*. This is essentially the same as the parameter Brightness & Color we created earlier on for our Materials.

Figure 5.79: Darker gravel

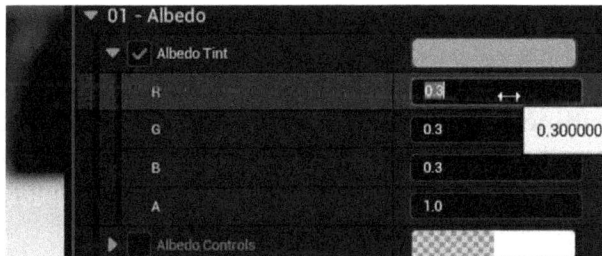

Figure 5.80: The parameters to change in the gravel's Material to get the darker color

18. At this point, you can either keep using the same wall mesh we have been using, or if you want to make things a little bit more interesting, you can download the Megascans asset shown in *Figure 5.81*, straight from Quixel Bridge, like before.

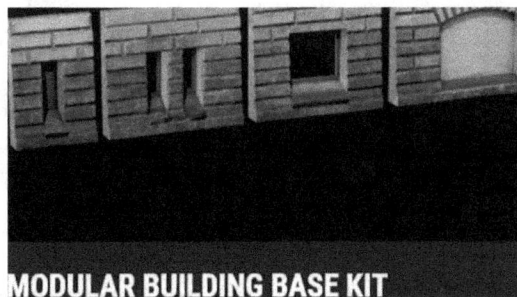

Figure 5.81: Another Megascans asset we could use

19. Be adventurous and creative, so feel free to add whatever assets you feel complete the look and match the concept, but in the meantime if you want to go with the author's approach, add the windowed wall from the asset pack we downloaded in the previous step. Place a whole row of them next to each other, right above the existing wall meshes occupying our scene, as shown in *Figure 5.82*.

20. In addition, click and drag a cube mesh, which you then stretch and use as a floor underneath the windowed wall meshes, we just placed, while applying the Megascans concrete surface (we downloaded earlier, as seen in *Figure 5.56*) to it, all to ultimately resemble what is depicted in *Figure 5.82*.

Figure 5.82: Almost done with our scene's building

Should you have forgotten how to bring a cube or any primitive actor into the scene — something we extensively did in *Chapter 3* when we added walls to our scene), remember you can access it by navigating to the **Place Actors** tab right next to the **Outliner** tab (if you followed this book's steps, this all should be on the upper right-hand corner of your main Unreal Engine window), then clicking the Shapes icon, as shown in *Figure 5.83*, and clicking and dragging the **Cube** into the scene:

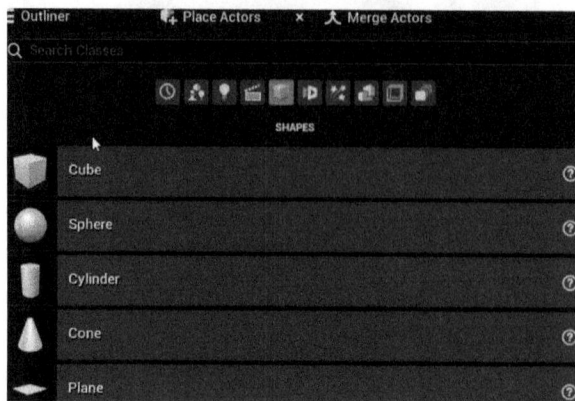

Figure 5.83: Place Actors tab from where you can get numerous actors, including primitive shapes and lights

21. If you used the windowed wall asset depicted in the previous step, you noticed it is missing glass, and we have no glass Material. So, let us create one! Back to your

`Materials` folder in the Content Browser, right-click and select Material, name it **M_MasterGlass**, save it, double click it to open it up in the Material Editor.

22. While in the M_MasterGlass's Material Graph, press and hold 3 and click anywhere in the empty graph, then convert the newly created Constant3 node to a parameter, which you will name **Color**. Plug the output into the Material's result node's **Base Color** input.

23. Press and hold *1* and click anywhere in the graph, convert the newly created constant node to a parameter, which you will name **Roughness**. Plug the output into the Material's result node's **Roughness** input.

The result should be a dark, highly reflective, mirror-like surface, emulating the effect of a tinted glass. Your Material Graph should look similar to the one in *Figure 5.84*:

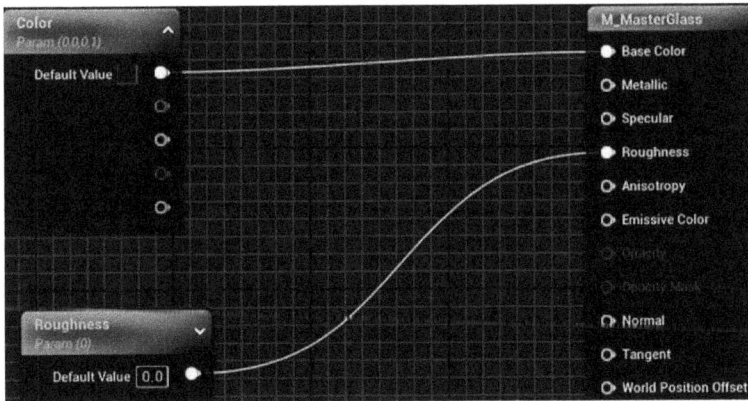

Figure 5.84: This will do well enough for a glass Material for now

Do not forget to make it **Two Sided**, as shown in *Figure 5.85*, so that it casts shadows properly should it be used on one sided geometry (which we will be doing in the next step by applying it on a plane):

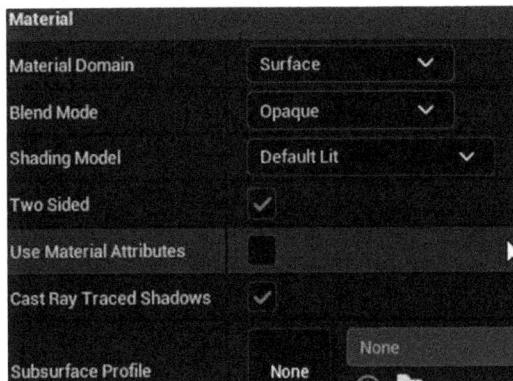

Figure 5.85: Setting the glass Material to Two Sided

24. Back to the **Place Actors** tab, much like we dragged the cube for the concrete floor a few steps earlier, now we drag a **Plane** into the scene, as shown in *Figure 5.86*, and place it, scale it, and apply the glass Material to it, to achieve the result shown in *Figure 5.87*:

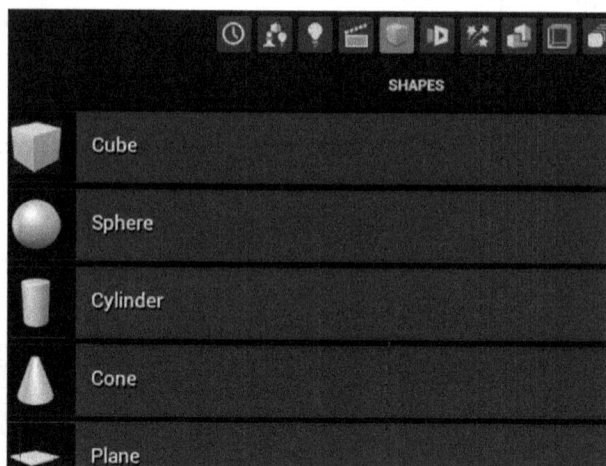

Figure 5.86: *Getting a Plane actor into our scene*

Figure 5.87: *Our building now has glass windows*

25. If you recall, we also downloaded some flower pot meshes, wall trims, and more, all using Quixel **Bridge**, so feel free to get creative and decorate the scene based on everything you have learned so far. *Figures 5.88* and *Figure 5.89* depict what the final scene looks like as per the author's setup:

Figure 5.88: Final scene

Figure 5.89: A different, zoomed out view of the final scene

At this point, you already have a complete scene; however, if you want some further inspiration and ideas, here is a simple variation the author made to further the scene a little bit more. Firstly, the concrete pavement was added around the garden, overlapping the gravel mesh, just to create walkways. This was achieved by placing cubes, scaling them, and applying a Megascans concrete Material we downloaded earlier. The result of this small addition is shown in *Figure 5.90*:

Figure 5.90: *A subtle addition can sometimes have a huge impact*

Next, the large grid-like floor mesh that was in the scene from the start was scaled down to reveal more of the sky backdrop, as shown in *Figure 5.91*:

Figure 5.91: *The initial floor mesh is scaled down*

Figure 5.92 shows what the final scene — with these subtle adjustments — looks like:

Figure 5.92: *Final scene, ready for lighting and cinematic!*

Do not forget to hit **Save All**!

Conclusion

You have successfully completed your first, real scene in Unreal by utilizing so many different techniques! The level we have now, is ready for lighting, Although truth be told already looks good, so there would not be too much to adjust in the next chapter.

Overall, this project prepared the ground for the third, biggest, and final project of this book, which starts from *Chapter 7, Fantasy Castle Project Breakdown and Planning* on.

In *Chapter 6, Lighting and Cinematic for the Statue Scene,* while a considerably shorter and easier chapter, we will be adjusting the lighting, learning a bit more about how lighting overall works, while creating a short cinematic that highlights all the hard work we have done so far in *Chapter 5, Importing Assets and Setting Up the Statue Scene.*

Points to remember

- Setting up the project's folder structure.
- Importing Static Meshes.
- Nanite's functions (on a high level), what it does, why it is important.
- Creating own Materials and Material Instances.
- Creating editable Material parameters and working with different nodes.
- Using proper naming conventions.
- Reapplying and furthering knowledge obtained in *Chapters 2* and *3*.
- Connecting into Quixel Bridge to browse useful, qualitative assets.
- Downloading Megascans assets from the Quixel Bridge and being able to find them through their different categories within our project's folder structure.
- Setting up a first complex scene in Unreal 5!!

Exercises

1. It is strongly recommended you go over key moments in the chapter, and try to create your own scene from scratch, utilizing everything you learned in this chapter. Set up your own scene, with your choice of Megascans assets taken from the Quixel Library, place the provided Greek God Statue within the new scenes and see what you come up with.

2. If you need a starting point, here is a challenge: find ancient/historical asset packs on Quixel Bridge and build a scene that takes place in an ancient temple, in which the Greek God Statue is the centerpiece!

Join our book's Discord space

Join the book's Discord Workspace for Latest updates, Offers, Tech happenings around the world, New Release and Sessions with the Authors:

https://discord.bpbonline.com

CHAPTER 6
Lighting and Cinematic for the Statue Scene

Introduction

In this chapter, we will be looking into lighting and cinematic sequences. We will look into Unreal's lighting basics in more detail than we did previously, preparing the ground for the next project, which will require a lot more lighting. We will also look into some lighting properties.

In addition, this chapter offers us an opportunity to introduce the Level Sequencer, cinematic cameras, and rendering cinematic scenes, as well as high resolution screenshots, all of which can be used as a great means to showcase one's Unreal work.

Structure

The following are the topics covered in this chapter:

- Playing with lights
- Introduction to Lumen
- Playing with cameras
- Using the Sequencer
- Rendering a cinematic scene
- Rendering high-resolution images

Objectives

In this chapter, we will use Light Actors, explore their properties, and gain a basic understanding of their functions. Will look into different lighting modes, such as static, stationary and movable, what they mean how they affect performance and lighting, and some other properties and details which can be adjusted. We will also learn the basics of Level Sequences, by setting up a Level Sequence, add some cinematic cameras to the scene, animate them and render a short but beautiful cinematic, showcasing the main theme of our scene, the Greek God Statue.

Lastly, we will learn how to take high resolution screenshots, which can be a qualitative way of showing one's Unreal Engine work, in portfolios, promotional Materials or anywhere else applicable.

Playing with lights

Continuing from where we left off in *Chapter 4, Project Overview and Main Asset Creation for Statue Scene,* let us save a new version of our **GreekGodStatueLevel**. If you do not have the level opened up already, load it, and then Save Current Level As and name the new level **GreekGodStatueLevel_CINEMATIC**, as shown in *Figure 6.1*:

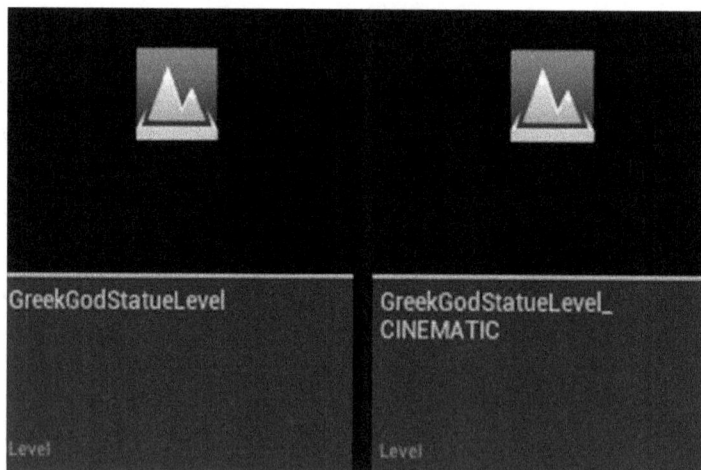

Figure 6.1: The previous chapter's level and this chapter's level, next to each other in our Content Browser

1. The first change we will make, is select the Directional Light, either through the Outliner or directly from the scene, and modify its rotation values, to match the ones in *Figure 6.2*:

Figure 6.2: Directional Light's new rotation values

You probably noticed that by modifying the Directional Light's rotation the environment color changes as well. Think of the Directional Light as the sun. The higher it is the brighter the day becomes, the brighter the environment becomes. The lower it is, the darker, more orange or even red it becomes, much like during the dawn or the sunset. However, this is not achieved by the Directional Light alone, the other actors that influence atmosphere, such as Exponential Height Fog, Sky Atmosphere, the Sky Light, all affect the lighting conditions, but nonetheless, the Directional Light is the main source of light in this scene.

2. Next, we modify the Directional Light's **Intensity**, we decrease it from 6.0 lux to 1.0 lux, as seen in *Figure 6.3*. This change makes the directional light a little bit darker, just enough to allow us to build an atmosphere that is perhaps a bit easier on the eyes.

Figure 6.3: Decreasing the Intensity

For this chapter's purposes we will not further edit the Directional Light. Now let us move on to Point Lights, which we briefly used in *Chapter 3, Unreal Engine's Building Blocks,* as well.

3. Click and drag into our scene a Point Light Actor from the **Place Actors** tab, under Lights as shown in *Figure 6.4*:

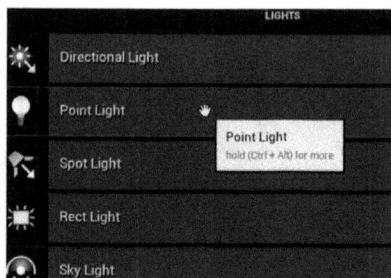

Figure 6.4: Point Light Actor

Note how the Point Light (and Light Actors in general, including the Directional Light) have three mobility settings, namely static, stationary and movable.

Let us look into these within a bit more detail:

- **Static**: Static lights are the most performance friendly lights, but they also look the worst. In essence, they are baked lighting, meaning the lighting does not have to be calculated in real time, but it does take quite some effort to make them look good. They are by far the fastest to render.

- **Stationary**: The stationary lights are somewhat performance friendly, since they are a hybrid between static and dynamic lights. They can have their color and intensity changed in real-time, but cannot be moved; imagine, for example, you have a flashlight actor the player in a game is using. This flashlight moves along with the player. Therefore, it could never be a stationary (nor static, for that matter) light. While stationary lights cannot be moved and have partially baked (not rendered in real time) shadows and bounced lighting coming from static geometry, they will also cast dynamic shadows from movable objects. In other words, if you have a playable character or even a physics-enabled ball bouncing right in front of a stationary light, then this shadow will be cast on the rest of the environment.

- **Movable**: Movable lights look the best, because they are fully dynamic, performing all lighting functions in real time. However, they are quite heavy on performance and need to be used carefully. There are ways to optimize them, such as disabling their ability to cast shadows, but they still need to be used in moderation.

Next, follow the steps below:

1. For this project's needs, we will convert the Point Light we just dropped in the scene into a movable light. While having the Point Light selected in the scene and click on the movable setting, as shown in *Figure 6.5*:

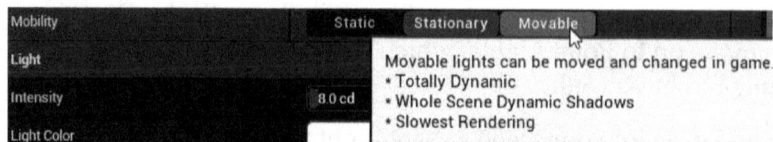

Figure 6.5: Setting the Point Light to movable

2. Now let us change the Point Light's color. Click on the color right next to the **Light Color**, as shown in *Figure 6.6*, in the Point Light's details, and pick a value similar to the one depicted in *Figure 6.7*.

Figure 6.6: *Change the Light Color*

Picking a **Light Color** can be seen in *Figure 6.7*:

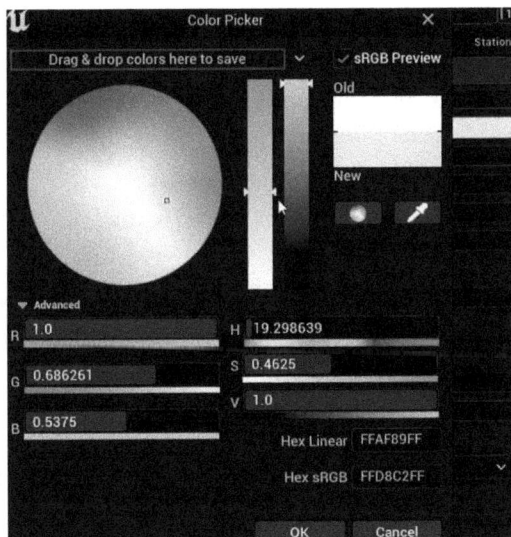

Figure 6.7: *So many colors to choose from*

3. Now let us modify the Point Light's **Attenuation Radius** from 1000 units, which is the default, to 100 units as seen in *Figure 6.8*. Note how the **Attenuation Radius** is represented by a white wireframe sphere around the Point Light Actor in the Viewport. By changing the value this sphere got noticeably smaller, as seen in *Figure 6.9*.

Figure 6.8: *Changing the Attenuation Radius*

Figure 6.9: *The attenuation radius is represented by the white wireframe sphere surrounding the Point Light*

If you want to notice the difference even more, change the value down to 20 and pay attention to how small that sphere gets (as shown in *Figure 6.10*). Ultimately, change the value up to 250, and leave it at that.

Figure 6.10: *The sphere got significantly smaller with the attenuation radius set to 20*

4. Next, you can uncheck and then check back again Affects World. It is self-explanatory, but just so there is no doubt, unchecking this value, switches off the light completely, in other words it does not affect the world, it does not cast light, it does not cast, shadows.

5. You can uncheck and then check back again the Cast Shadows value. Also self-explanatory, this value determines whether this Light Actor can cast shadows or not. If it is disabled, the light will still be shedding light, but would not be rendering any shadows; however, this is not entirely true, as some very basic and simplistic form of shadowing will still be noticeable, but in essence, it can change a light to performance friendly. Generally, it is best to avoid placing lights that do not cast shadows next to architectural geometry, or you will end up having light bleeding through walls and other such elements. You can compare the difference between the shadows being turned on and off, in *Figures 6.11* and *Figure 6.12* respectively.

Figure 6.11: Cast Shadows is disabled

Figure 6.12: Cast Shadows is enabled

6. Next, we will use another trick, to use a light to affect a specific set of actors and not all of them. Since the statue is our main theme, we want this point of light to be affecting only the statue and no other actor. To achieve that, we will be modifying both the Point Light's and the statue's **Lighting Channels**. First, with the Point Light selected, let us change its **Lighting Channel** to 1, by clicking Channel 0 to toggle it off and Channel 1 to toggle it on, as depicted in *Figure 6.13*. You will have to scroll down to find the **Lighting Channels**, or you can simply type in **Lighting Channels** in the search field.

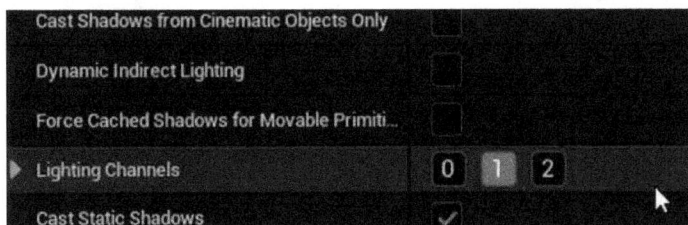

Figure 6.13: Changing the light's Lighting Channel to 1

7. Now, let us modify the statue's Lighting Channels. With the statue, we will not toggle Channel 0 off because that is the default channel, and we want the statue to still be affected by the environment and the surrounding lighting conditions. So, click on the statue, and with the statue selected, type in the details' search field **Lighting Channels** and now leave the Channel 0 toggled on, while also enabling Channel 1, as depicted in *Figure 6.14*. Overall, this is a technique that can be used when you want to turn the end user's attention to something. You could, for example, have a quest item you want to highlight without messing up the rest of the environment's lighting conditions. That is one way to do it.

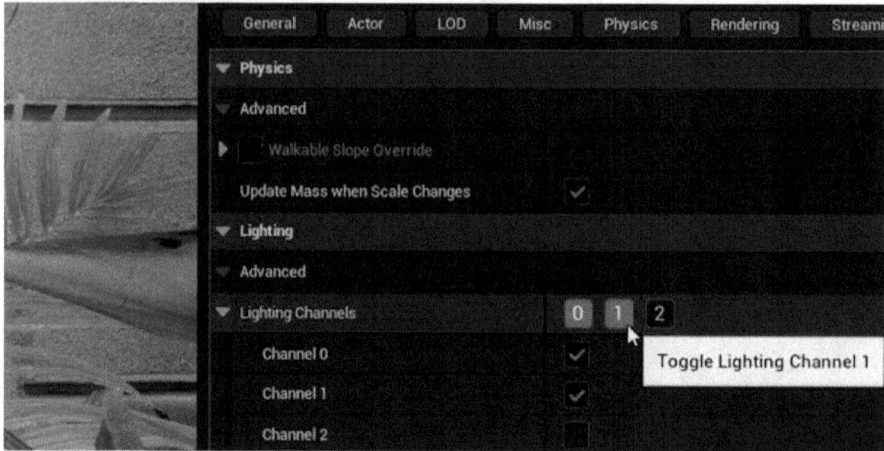

Figure 6.14: Enabling the statue's Lighting Channel 1, while leaving channel 0 toggled as well

8. Lastly, let us modify the Point Lights intensity. Just to see how it affects the environment, and how channels also influence what gets affected by a light, increase the Point Lights intensity all the way to 60, as depicted in *Figure 6.15*:

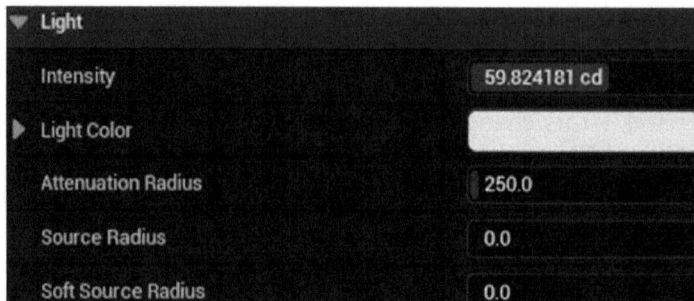

Figure 6.15: Making the light's intensity as bright as almost 60

Note in *Figure 6.16* how bright the statue looks, while the rest of the environment is unaffected by this change, thanks to the Lighting Channel settings:

Figure 6.16: Note how the statue glows, while the rest of the environment remains unaffected by the light

9. Now, let us tone down the light's intensity value to a very subtle 0.2, as seen in *Figure 6.17*:

Figure 6.17: Dropping the light's intensity down to 0.2

The effect of that change can be seen in *Figure 6.18*:

Figure 6.18: The light affects only the statue, and it is effect is very subtle, just enough to emphasize some of the details

10. Note how the Point Light's position has changed in *Figure 6.18*; for this project's purposes, that is a good position to move the Point Light to; the coordinates can be seen in *Figure 6.19*; however, you are more than welcome to play around with the light's positioning. Keep in mind that your positioning of the scene's actors might be slightly different than the author's. Therefore, the suggested light coordinates might not work the best in your scene's setup.

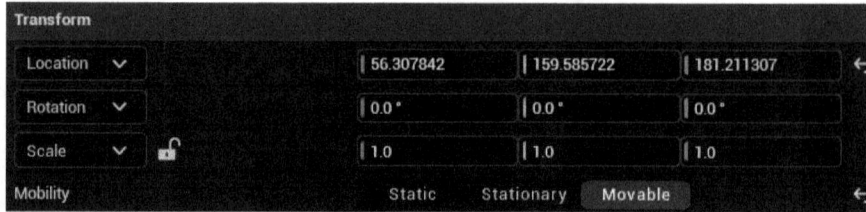

Figure 6.19: The final coordinates of this Point Light for the project. You do not need to follow them, as your coordinates for all other actors may vary

At this point it is worth mentioning that there are more light types to work with, including spotlights, rectangular lights and sky lights, as well as additional ways to light up a scene, by taking advantage of Unreal Engine 5's Lumen technology, however most of these will be covered in the next project. But first, let us take a closer — and high level — look at Lumen.

Introduction to Lumen

Lumen is Unreal Engine 5's lighting system, more specifically, the system that focuses on global illumination and reflections. It is the technology that affects how light is cast as well as reflected in the 3d space, how it affects objects, and how it bounces back from them.

Lumen is handling both direct and indirect lighting efficiently and realistically. Imagine you have a room where sunlight comes through the window and it hits directly a wall. In older gaming engines, that light would not bounce off the wall, therefore indirect lighting had to be achieved through different means.

In addition, Lumen is perfectly capable of generating illumination out of emissive Materials. To demonstrate this, refer to *Figure 6.20* which is taken directly from a game the author is working on at the time of this writing. In *Figure 6.20*, note how an entire space is illuminated, all light generated from the emissive Material used as a sky, placed atop the structure's opening on the ceiling:

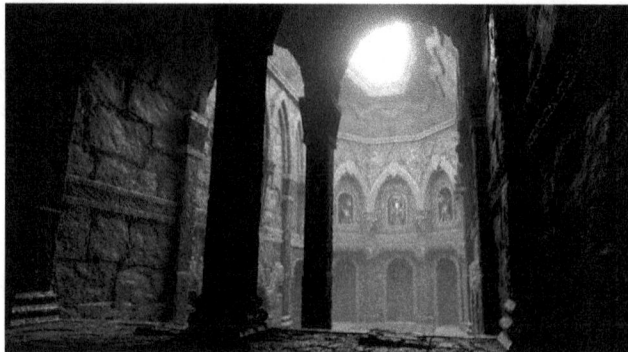

Figure 6.20: Emissive Material used as the sky, illuminating the entire space with 0 Light Actors thanks to Lumen

To better understand Lumen, while optional, it is strongly recommended you try the following exercise:

- Create a new level (*Ctrl +N*), choose the Empty Level.
- Place a cube in it and stretch it enough to look like a floor.
- Then duplicate it and place it high enough to emulate a ceiling.
- Then duplicate it again and rotate it 90 degrees on either X or Y axis so that you have a standing wall, repeat these two more times so that you have built a room with 3 walls, a floor, and a ceiling.
- Place a Directional Light (you can place it in the center of the room, Directional Light location does not matter as it affects the entire level however rotation makes all the difference).
- Rotate it around and see how it affects the room you just created.

Figures 6.21 to *Figure 6.23* show this exercise and the results of rotating the Directional Light at different angles:

Figure 6.21: *The lighting exercise, with the Directional Light coming through from the right*

Figure 6.22: *Now the Directional Light hits the room from the top, and slightly from the front*

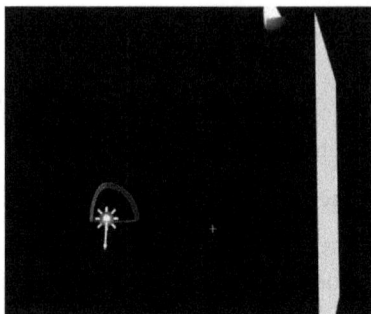

Figure 6.23: Light hitting the room from the top and behind

If you want to further expand the exercise, create an emissive Material and place a small cube in the room, then apply the emissive Material to the cube.

1. Create a new Material in your **Materials** folder, name it M_EmissiveTest.

2. Double click it to open it up in the Material Editor.

3. Create a Constant 3 node (press and hold 3 and click in the Material Graph).

4. Convert the Constant 3 node to a parameter, named **Brightness&Color**.

5. Change the default RGB values to R:30, G:10, B:0, and connect the overall output pin to the result node's **Emissive Color** input pin.

6. Save the Material.

Your M_EmissiveTest Material's Graph should look exactly like the one in *Figure 6.24*:

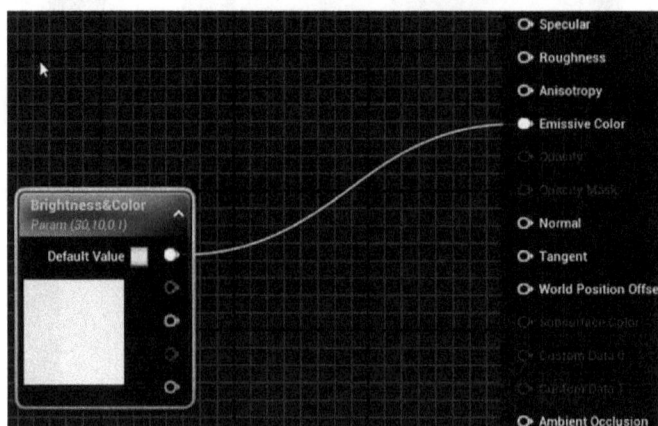

Figure 6.24: M_EmissiveTest Material Graph

7. Now place a cube in the room, preferably somewhere in the back near a corner.

8. Apply the emissive Material you just created to it.

Your results should look like *Figure 6.25*:

Figure 6.25: *The emissive Material applied to the cube in the room*

You are encouraged to create Material Instances of the emissive Material you just created and adjust the RGB values however you want. Be adventurous and try something crazy, like a B value of 100, or something along these lines.

If you downloaded the resource Materials that come with this book, you also have the entire project, so in case you did not perform the exercise you can load up the level from the **Levels** folder, LightingExercise.

Playing with cameras

Open our level GreekGodStatueLevel_CINEMATIC and now let us start preparing the ground for our short cinematic cutscene.

1. Let us grab and place a **Cine Camera Actor** on our map. You can find it under the **Place Actors** tab, under the Cinematic section, as shown in *Figure 6.26*:

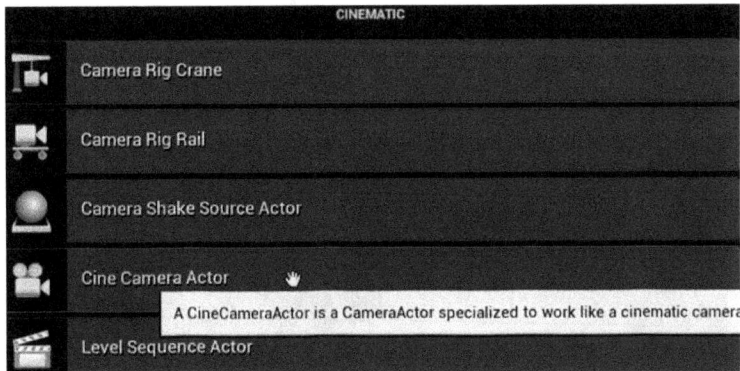

Figure 6.26: *Cine Camera Actor*

2. As soon as you place it in the scene, you can see a small preview window popping up within the main Viewport, much like in *Figure 6.27*. This will be visible every time you select the camera. You could also pin it so that it shows whenever you deselect the camera, however for this project's purposes this is not necessary.

Figure 6.27: Small camera preview window

3. Next let us move the camera to a more dramatic angle, with the statue being the main focal point. Your camera positioning should resemble the one in *Figure 6.28*:

Figure 6.28: That is how the camera positioning should be more or less

If it helps, here are the exact coordinates and rotation values the author used for his camera, do remember that these coordinates might not work perfectly with your setting, depending on where the rest of the actors are placed.

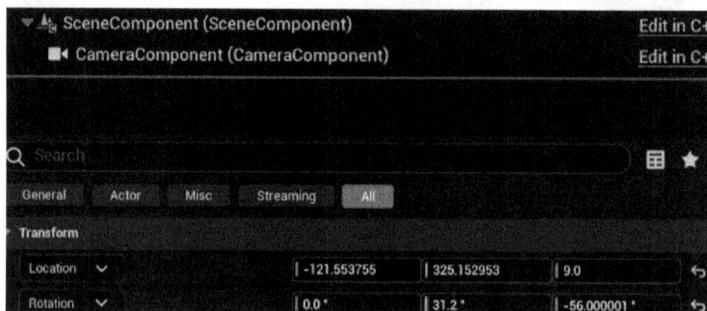

Figure 6.29: Camera coordinates and rotation in the author's setup

4. Next, let us change some of the camera's settings. Ensure you have the same ones as in *Figure 6.30*:

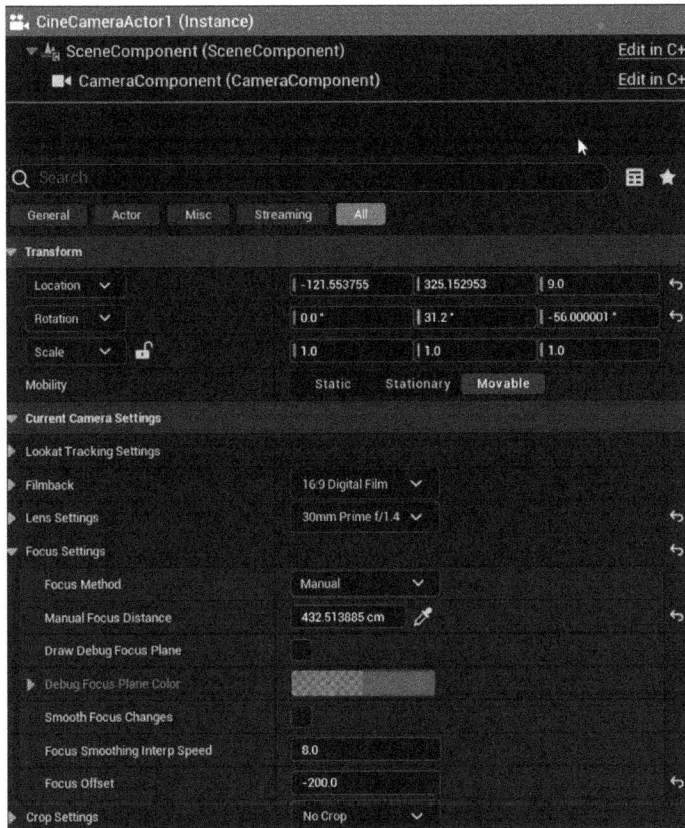

Figure 6.30: Camera settings

5. If you want to finetune the camera's position and get a better understanding of what the camera sees there is a better way to control and move around the camera. By simply becoming it! To do that, click on **Perspective** in the upper left-hand corner of your Viewport, and then select **CineCameraActor1**, as shown in *Figure 6.31*:

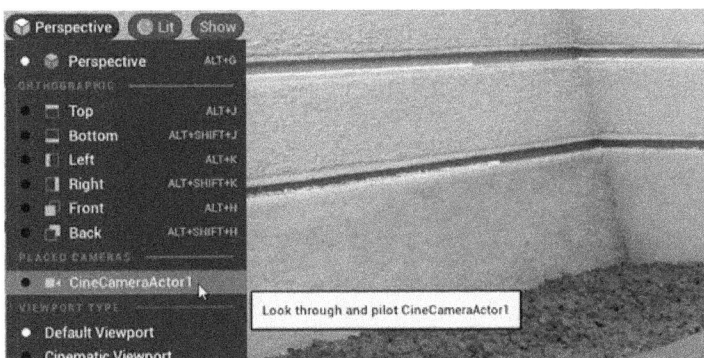

Figure 6.31: Assuming control of the camera actor

This results in a much more cinematic point of view, and any navigation you perform within the Viewport, is where the camera will be left at. So essentially, you see exactly from the camera's point of view, as seen in *Figure 6.32*:

Figure 6.32: Seeing things from the camera's perspective

6. To exit this perspective, you just need to click the eject button on the upper right-hand corner in your main Viewport, as shown in *Figure 6.33*:

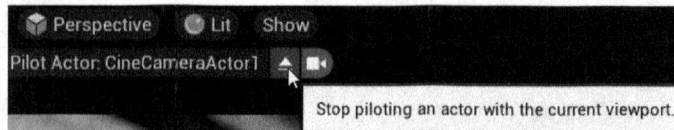

Figure 6.33: Ejecting from the camera's point of view

Once you eject, you no longer control and therefore no longer affect the camera's position. Now that we have placed our first camera and are happy with its current position, which will also serve as our short cinematic's initial camera position, we can proceed with placing a Sequencer in our scene.

What we want to do is add a Level Sequence anywhere in our level. To do that, press the cinematic button on the top right-hand side and then select **Add Level Sequence,** as shown in *Figure 6.34*:

Figure 6.34: Adding a Level Sequence in our level

As soon as you have added the Level Sequence, Unreal will ask you to save it somewhere. For this project's purposes, save it in the **Levels** folder and name it **LS_GreekGodStatueCinematic**, LS standing for Level Sequence. Please refer to *Figures 6.35* and *Figure 6.36* for the saving steps.

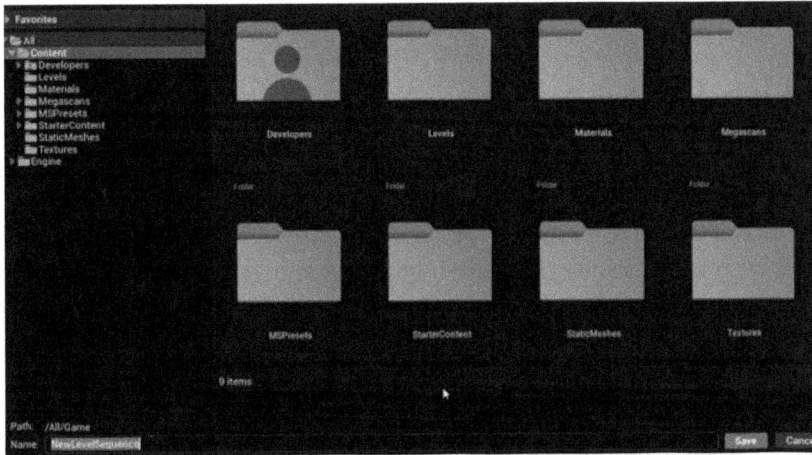

Figure 6.35: Unreal asking you to save the new Level Sequence

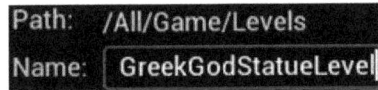

Figure 6.36: Recommended save location and name

Next, make sure your Level Sequence actor is selected, if you are uncertain, just pick it from the **Outliner**, by typing **sequence** in the Outliner's search box and selecting it from the results there, as shown in *Figure 6.37*:

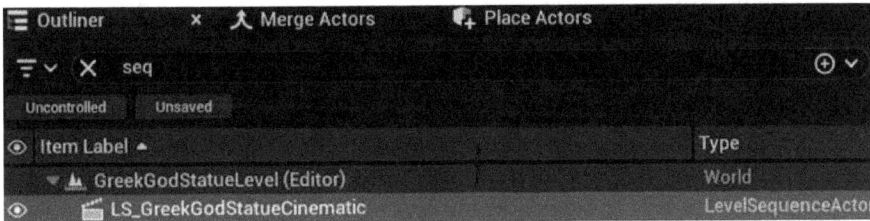

Figure 6.37: Selecting the sequence actor from the outliner

Now, with the Level Sequence actor being selected, just drag it somewhere you can easily find it in your scene, much like the author did in *Figure 6.38*:

Figure 6.38: Placing the Level Sequence actor somewhere easily found

At this point, it is a good time to Save All, and we are ready to move on to the next part.

Using the Sequencer

Undoubtedly, the first thing that got your attention when you added the Level Sequence actor in the level was the UI that popped up, specifically the Sequencer's timeline, as shown in *Figure 6.39*:

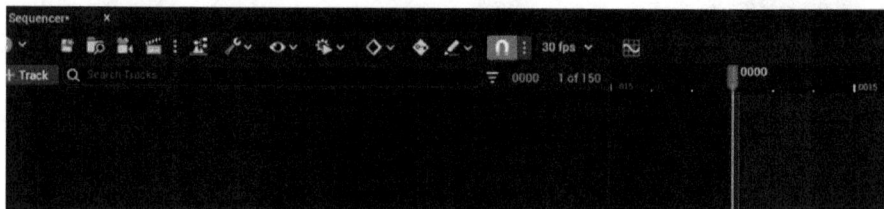

Figure 6.39: The Sequencer timeline UI

If you have ever used a video editing program such as *Adobe Premiere Pro* or similar, you are familiar with the overall layout and timeline functionalities. But regardless of previous experience, we will approach this in a very basic and easy-to-follow way:

1. The first thing we need to do, is allow the Sequencer to be aware of our Cine Camera Actor's existence. While having the Sequencer open, select your CineCameraActor1. If, for some reason, you closed the Sequencer UI, simply click on the Level Sequence Actor, and then select Open Level Sequence from the details tab, as shown in *Figure 6.40*:

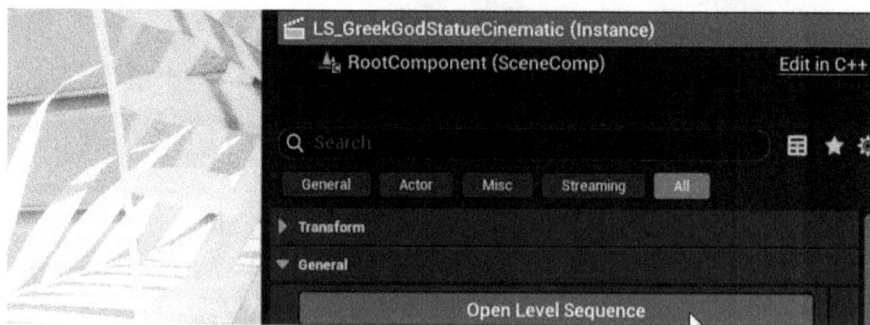

Figure 6.40: Opening the Level Sequence

2. Now that we are certain you have the Sequencer UI opened, let us make sure we have CineCameraActor1 selected. Either click it in your main Viewport, or click it through the list under your **Outliner** tab.

3. While having CineCameraActor1 selected, either press the **+Track** button or right-click in the empty space underneath, and select **Actor to Sequencer,** and then click **Add 'CineCameraActor1'** , as shown in *Figure 6.41*:

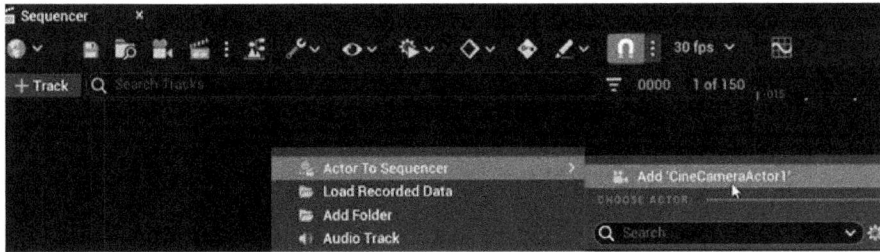

Figure 6.41: *Adding the camera actor to the Sequencer*

4. Once that is added, your Sequencer should look exactly like the one in *Figure 6.42*:

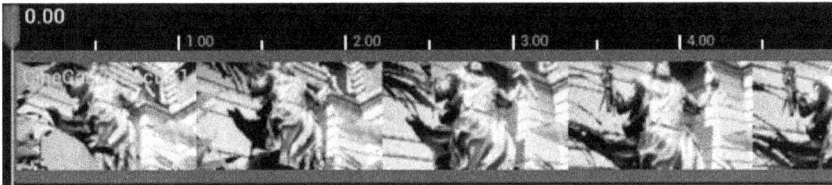

Figure 6.42: *The Sequencer with the camera actor*

5. While many developers and artists prefer displaying the Sequencer's time in frames, the author often resorts to using seconds. It is a matter of the reader's personal preference; however, if you have never worked with animation or similar fields before, it is recommended to use seconds, as it is a concept we all understand and use daily. To do that, click on the **30 fps** drop down menu, then select **Show Time As**, and then select **Seconds**, as shown in *Figure 6.43*:

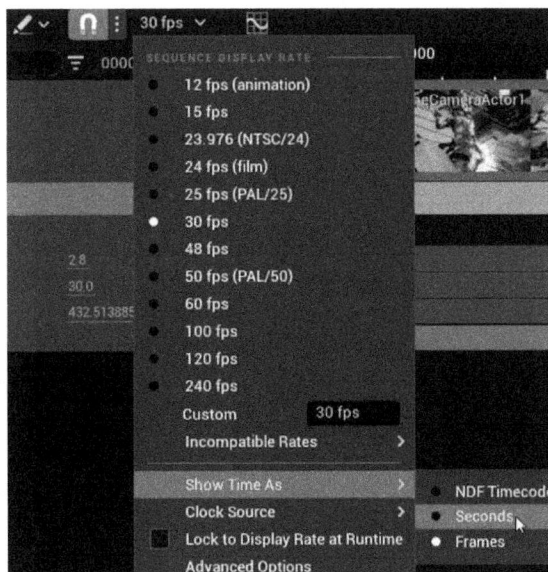

Figure 6.43: *Changing the Sequencer's timing from frames to seconds*

6. Since we now know how to access this drop-down menu, let us also change the project from 30 **fps (frames per second)** to 60 fps, as shown in *Figure 6.44*:

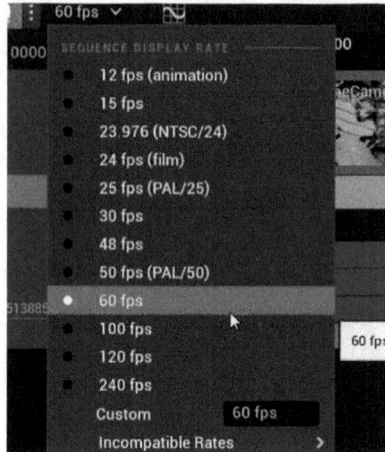

Figure 6.44: Changing from 30 to 60 fps

7. Now, let us define how the camera moves around for the duration of our short cinematic sequence. Under **CineCameraActor1's** track on the Sequencer's UI, you will notice there is a **Transform** section. This defines the overall positioning of the camera anywhere in the timeline. On the right side of this section, you will notice there is a + sign, two arrows, and a small circular icon with a plus (almost impossible to see) sign it in. Press that small circular icon, as shown in *Figure 6.45*:

Figure 6.45: Adding a key to the timeline

What we just did, is add a key to the Sequencer's timeline. Think of a key as the point in time during which we indicate to the Sequencer we want to change something. So, by adding a key on the **Transform** section of the **CineCameraActor1's** track in the Sequencer, essentially, we informed the Sequencer that at this specific time, which is 0.0 seconds, we want the camera to be at this specific location, with the rotation it has. If we add no more keys to this track, then our camera will remain there for the duration of the entire cinematic sequence. However, we want our short cinematic sequence to show some movement; therefore, we will want to make sure our camera actor does not remain fixed in one position but move around, making our scene look more dynamic.

Let us Shift our attention to the timeline. As it stands now, we have a total of 5 seconds, as indicated by the Sequencer and as shown in *Figure 6.46*:

Figure 6.46: Our Sequencer timeline is currently 5 seconds long

8. Let us make our sequence a bit longer than 5 seconds. Let us extend it to 10. To do that, place your mouse cursor over the red line right above number .00 (indicating the seconds on the timeline), as shown in *Figure 6.47*:

Figure 6.47: See how your mouse cursor changes to this double arrow icon

9. As you have probably noticed, your mouse cursor's icon has changed into a double arrow one. Now click and drag the red line towards the right until you reach 10.00 seconds, as indicated in *Figure 6.48*. We have just extended our timeline from 5 to 10 seconds. Therefore, we also extended our cinematic sequence's duration to 10 seconds.

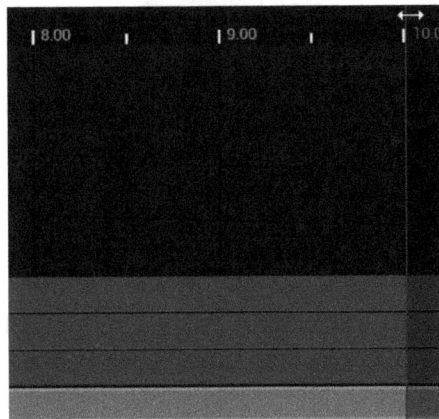

Figure 6.48: Extending the timeline to 10 seconds

10. While having our CineCameraActor1's Transform track selected/highlighted, let us click on the 5.00 seconds on our timeline. Click on 5.00. Now you can see you

moved the playback marker to 5 seconds, in other words, we are presently at the fifth second of our sequence, as shown in *Figure 6.49*:

Figure 6.49: Presently previewing the fifth second of our sequence

11. Without closing any of the UI or changing anything in the Sequencer, click on CineCameraActor1, either through the Outliner or through the Viewport. Assume control of it, like we did earlier in the *Playing with cameras* section of this chapter, specifically step 5, or refer to *Figure 6.31*. As you have assumed control of the camera's view, navigate in your Viewport higher and a bit closer to the statue, much like in *Figure 6.50*:

Figure 6.50: Moving Camera Actor 1 a bit closer to the statue

12. Back to the Level Sequencer's UI, click the small circular icon (same as in *Figure 6.45*) in the Transform section of the CineCameraActor1's track. Your timeline now should look exactly like it does in *Figure 6.51*. What you just did is inform the Sequencer that you want the CineCameraActor1 to be at these coordinates, with this rotation at the fifth second of our timeline.

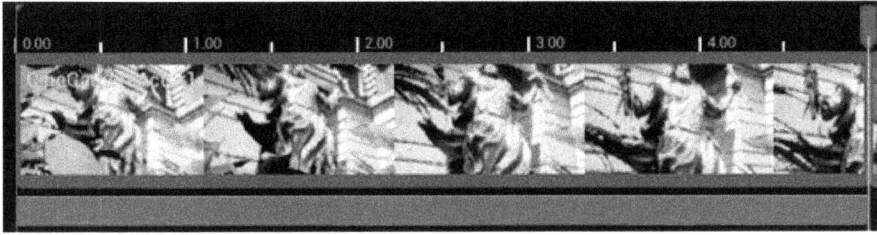

Figure 6.51: *A complete track for CineCameraActor1*

So, based on our timeline, at 0.00 seconds (the beginning) of our cinematic sequence, the camera will be at the location we had it right before we started the whole Sequencer affair. At 5.00 seconds our camera will be at the location we just placed it now.

However, that raises the question; what happens to the camera between 0.00 and 5.00 seconds? And that is the beauty of it, because the Unreal Engine smoothly interpolates the actor between the two points. In other words, it ensures that the camera smoothly moves from its initial position at 0.00 seconds, to its final position at 5.00 seconds, without us needing to do anything.

Of course, if you wanted to, you could certainly go to any time in between (say 3.25 seconds) and, while having the timeline's playback marker there, move the camera around in the Viewport, then add a key to that timestamp, and once again, between 0.00 seconds and 3.25 seconds, as well as between 3.25 and 5.00 seconds, Unreal will smoothen out the transitions. At the end of this chapter, you are more than welcome to experiment with such actions, but for now, let us resume working on our short cinematic sequence:

1. Since our playback marker is currently at 5.00 seconds, let us go back to the beginning at 0.00 seconds. One fast and easy way to do that is to click the **To Front** icon, in the Sequencer's bottom left corner, as shown in *Figure 6.52*:

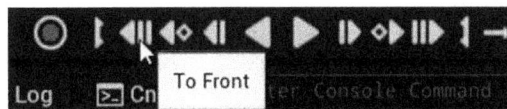

Figure 6.52: *Taking our playback marker to the beginning of our Sequencer timeline*

2. Make sure your CineCameraActor1 is still selected and that you are in piloting mode in your Viewport (once again, *Figure 6.31*), but do not move it around.

3. Now hit the **Play** button in your Sequencer, as shown in *Figure 6.53*, and watch your camera move!

Figure 6.53: *Hitting the Play button of the Sequencer*

4. We have covered our cinematic sequence from 0 to 5 seconds, but we have nothing interesting happening between 5 and 10 seconds. Let us change that by adding one more camera. Much like before, add a new CineCameraActor into our scene. If you have already forgotten how to do that, re-read the *Playing with cameras* section of this chapter.

5. Let us pilot through the second camera and place it in a nice but significantly different spot than the first camera. To pilot the second camera, please refer to *Figure 6.54*:

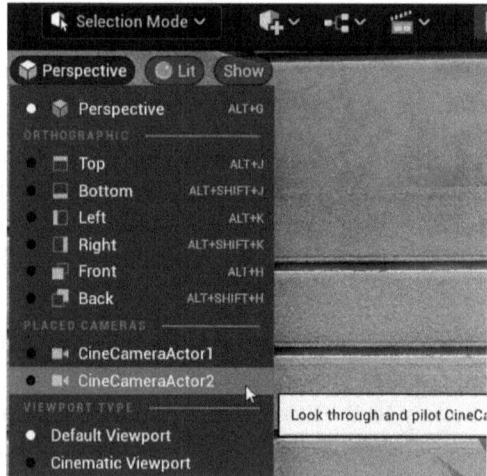

Figure 6.54: Piloting the second camera

6. For this camera, let us use slightly different settings. Let us change its **Focus Method** under **Focus Settings** to **Manual**, and **Manual Focus Distance** to **Tracking**, as shown in *Figure 6.55*:

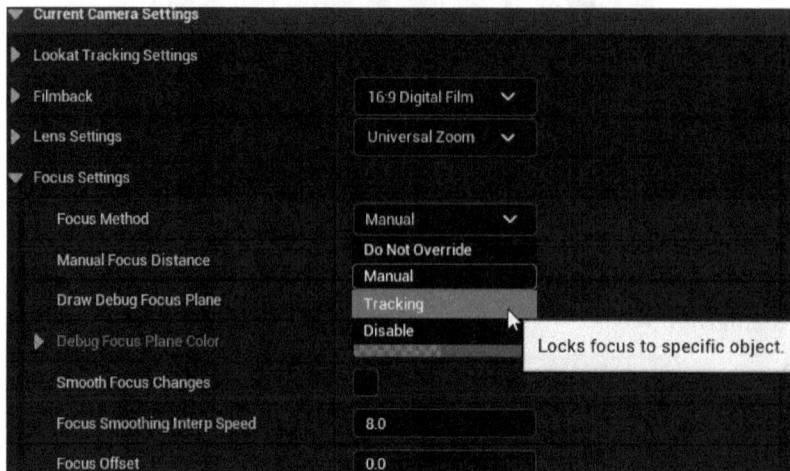

Figure 6.55: Changing the focus settings

7. Next, let us select the actor we are going to track, which is none other than the statue. Click on the pipette-like icon next to **Actor to Track,** as shown in *Figure 6.56,* and after that click on the statue in the Viewport, as shown in *Figure 6.57*:

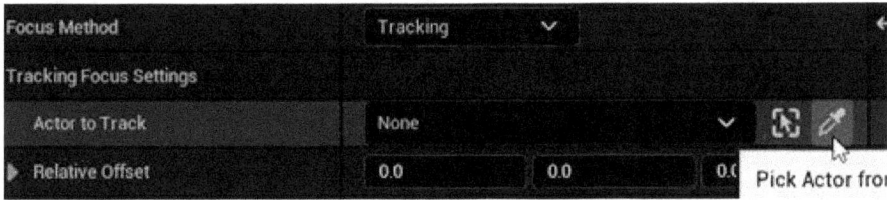

Figure 6.56: Picking an actor to track

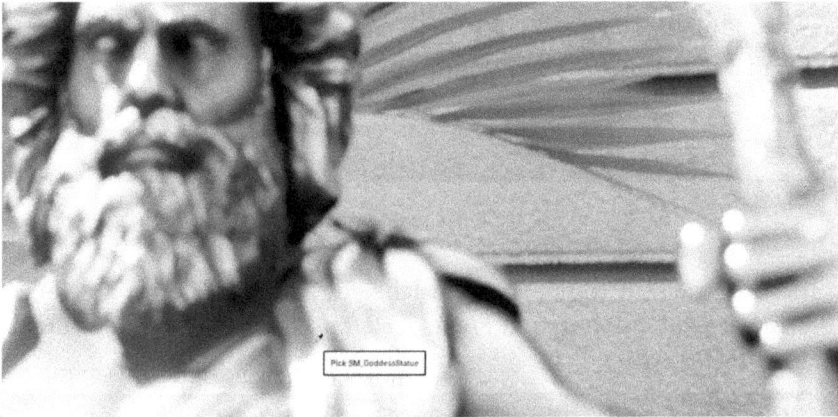

Figure 6.57: Picking the Greek God Statue

8. Maintain **CineCameraActor2** selected, and back to our Sequencer, add a track for it, as shown in *Figure 6.58*, much like we did for the first camera in *Figure 6.41*:

Figure 6.58: Adding a track for the second camera to our Sequencer

9. Move the playback marker in the Sequencer to the 6.00 seconds of our timeline, and with the **CineCameraActor2** still selected, add a new key in its **Transform**, as shown in *Figure 6.59*:

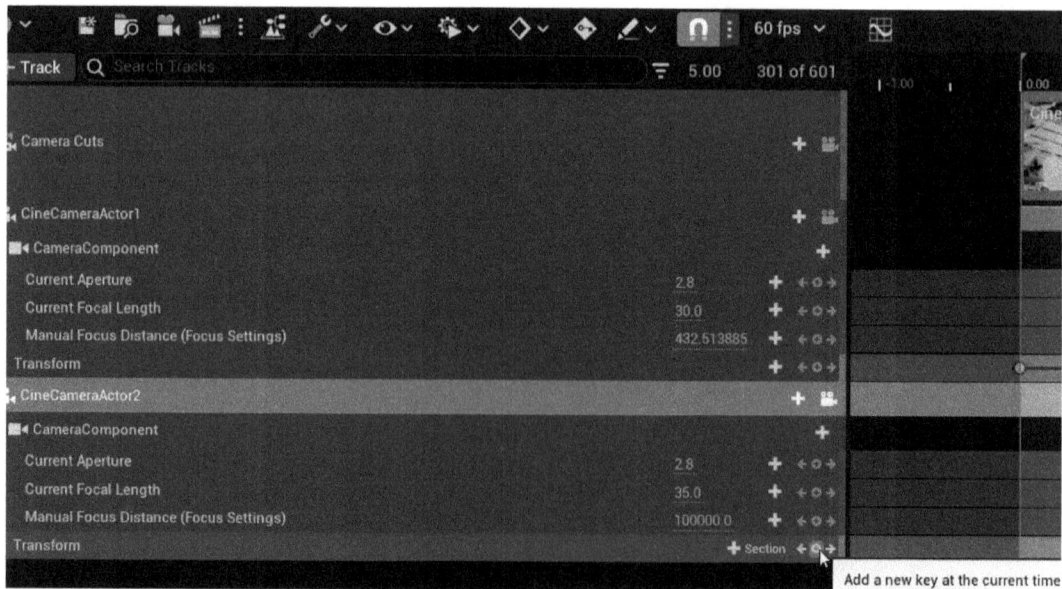

Figure 6.59: *Adding a key to the second camera's transform section*

10. On the first track of the Sequencer, labeled **Camera Cuts** press the + button to add a camera cut, as shown in *Figure 6.60*, and then select **CineCameraActor2**, as shown in *Figure 6.61*:

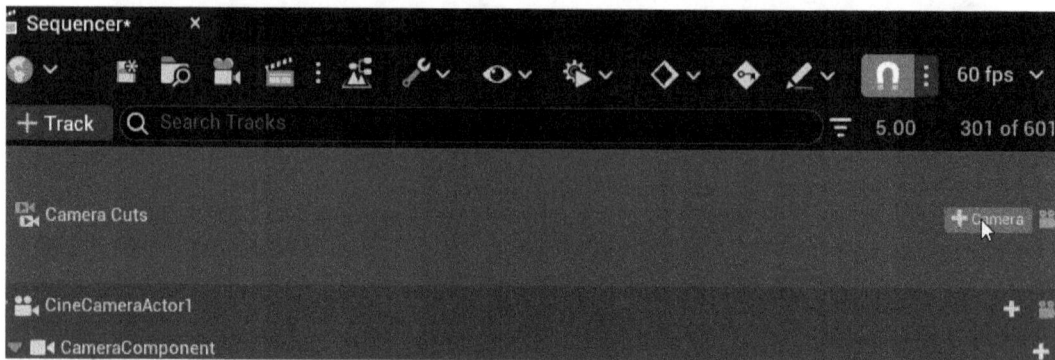

Figure 6.60: *Adding a camera cut*

Figure 6.61: *Selecting Camera Actor 2 for the Camera Cut*

Your timeline should resemble the one shown in *Figure 6.62*:

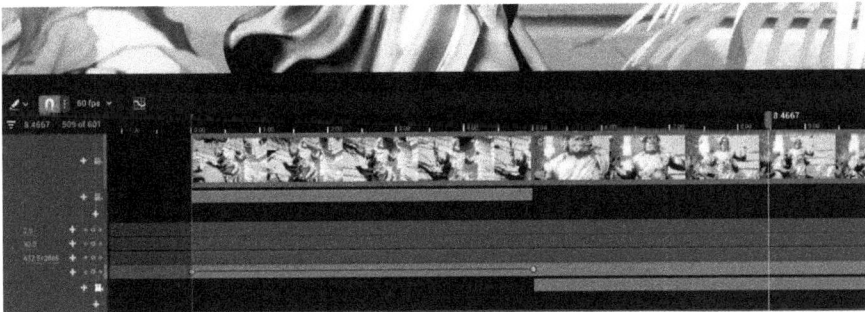

Figure 6.62: *Our updated timeline*

11. Press the **To End** button in the Sequencer, as shown in *Figure 6.63*:

Figure 6.63: *Forward the playback marker to the end of the timeline*

12. Ensure CineCameraActor2 is still selected. Pilot it to a new location, slightly going further away from the statue, as shown in *Figure 6.64*:

Figure 6.64: Moving the second camera a bit further away from the statue

13. Back in the Sequencer, under CineCameraActor2's track, add another key to its Transform section, as shown earlier in *Figure 6.59*.

14. At this point, make sure you save our sequence's progress, as shown in *Figure 6.65*

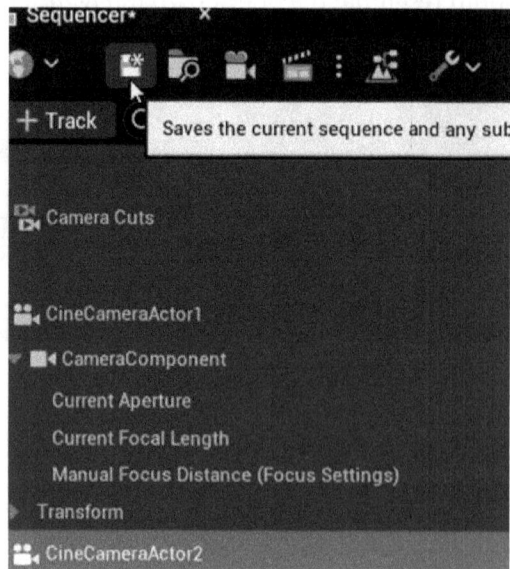

Figure 6.65: Saving our sequence

15. Just to be on the safe side, also hit Save All in your Content Browser.

Rendering a cinematic scene

Now, it is time for us to render our short cinematic sequence.

1. Press the Render button in the **Sequencer**, as shown in *Figure 6.66*:

Figure 6.66: Rendering a sequence

2. The **Render Movie Settings** dialog box pops up. Use the same settings as shown in *Figure 6.67*:

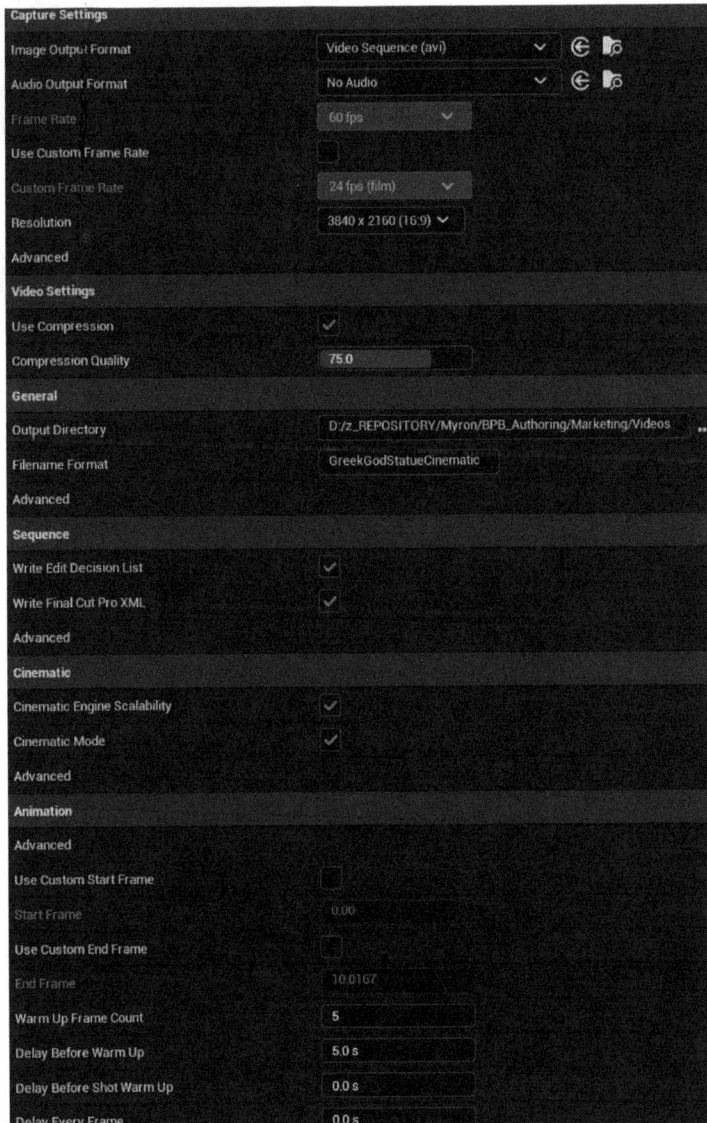

Figure 6.67: The rendering settings you want to be using

3. It will start rendering, give it a little bit of a time. You will be seeing a preview window much like in *Figure 6.68,* while on the lower right corner of your screen, you will have an indication that the video is being captured, as shown in *Figure 6.69*:

Figure 6.68: Rendering preview screen on the upper left corner

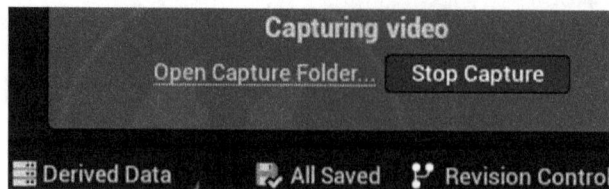

Figure 6.69: Capturing video indication on the lower right corner

4. Once your video finishes, you will get a brief notification on the lower right corner, as shown in *Figure 6.70,* you can also click on **Open Capture Folder** to be taken straight to the folder where your rendered video is at, as shown in *Figure 6.71*:

Figure 6.70: Capture finished, Open Capture Folder

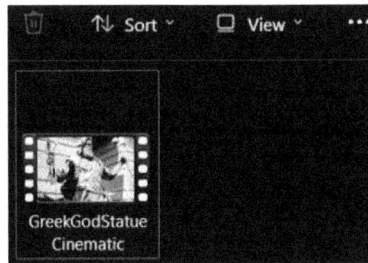

Figure 6.71: Our rendered video, as seen in Windows Explorer

Alternatively, you can also select the Level Sequence actor, and under its Details tab, enable its **Auto Play**, as shown in *Figure 6.72*. Once you play the level, the Level Sequence will be the first thing to play, and once it finishes, then you will be given control of the camera to fly around the environment.

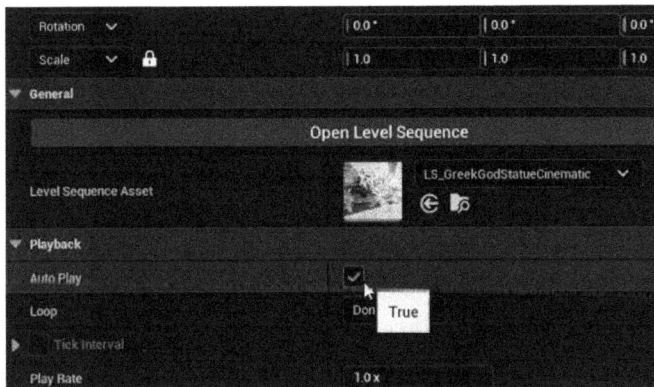

Figure 6.72: Enabling the Sequencer's autoplay

Rendering high-resolution images

While navigating anywhere in the main Viewport, press G to hide all actors, such as light icons, Sequencer icons, etc., in essence simulating what you would see in-game. Right after that, if you pilot any of the existing cameras (or add a new one), positioning it at any angle you want, and then press ` to bring up the command console, and type **HighResShot 2** or type it in straight in the command console prompt in the lower left corner of your Unreal Engine's main window, as shown in *Figure 6.73*. This will render a high-resolution screenshot of what you currently see, and 2 indicates that it will be at twice the resolution you are currently using.

Figure 6.73: HighResShot command in the command prompt

As soon as Unreal is done taking the high-resolution screenshot, it will briefly prompt you at the lower right hand corner of your screen, while providing you a clickable link that will lead you to the location of the saved screenshot, as shown in *Figure 6.74*:

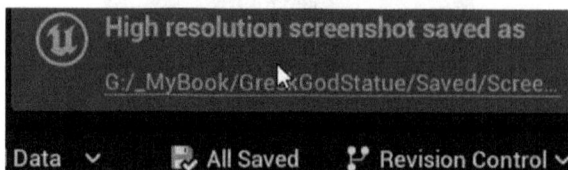

Figure 6.74: Prompting you that the high res shot has been rendered

Generally speaking, high-resolution shots are saved **ProjectName/Saved/Screenshots/** where **ProjectName** is the name of any project you are working on in Unreal.

Figure 6.75 shows one such screenshot the author took in the process of writing this book:

Figure 6.75: A high-resolution screenshot with the end result

Conclusion

This chapter allows us to take a closer look at Unreal's lighting options, methodologies as well as examine a bit more what Lumen is and why it is important.

We also had the opportunity to render a short cinematic sequence, and better understand how to use cinematic cameras, the Sequencer and overall produce some Materials that are great for showcasing in portfolios, or situations that require promotional imagery.

Most importantly, we further prepared the ground for the third, final, and most challenging project of this book, which will feature an entire castle, with both outdoor and indoor areas, with more complex lighting, with a lot more creation, importation, and management of assets, while it will also push us towards creating Blueprint Actors, using particle FX (effects) and more.

Points to remember

- The different types of lighting (static, stationary, movable).
- The application of a Directional Light.
- The application of a Point Light Actor.
- Light intensity values and how they affect a Light Actor's brightness.
- Light attenuation radius and how it affects a Light Actor's range of influence.
- Assigning a light color to achieve different colors of lighting for a Light Actor.
- The light channels of a Light Actor and how they can be used to affect specific scene actors.
- The basics of the Lumen technology.
- The significant of emissive Materials and how they can be used for lighting.
- Cinematic camera actors and their applications.
- Piloting a cinematic camera in the Viewport.
- Using Level Sequences to create a cinematic of a scene.
- Using the Sequencer to create cinematics.
- Using Sequencer tracks and camera cuts within the Sequencer tool.
- Rendering a move in Sequencer.
- Taking high-resolution screenshots by using the command prompt.

Exercises

1. You are encouraged to further explore lighting, use different types of lights, such as spotlights, different settings and values.

2. It would also be a great exercise to try completely changing the lighting environment of the statue level. Try making it look like it is taking place late in the evening, and there are lights across the garden, which you could use emissive Materials to make them more believable.

3. Finally, do experiment with your movie making skills, by placing cameras around and moving them around at different points in the Sequencer's timeline, you might be surprised to find you always had a film maker somewhere inside you!

Join our book's Discord space

Join the book's Discord Workspace for Latest updates, Offers, Tech happenings around the world, New Release and Sessions with the Authors:

https://discord.bpbonline.com

CHAPTER 7

Fantasy Castle Project Breakdown and Planning

Introduction

In this chapter we are beginning this book's biggest and most ambitious project. Specifically, in this chapter, we will analyze our concept image, break it down into manageable parts, and discuss the approach and strategy we will use to easily tackle an otherwise massively daunting — with a first look at least — task.

Chapters 8, Fantasy Castle Base Mesh Modeling, Chapter 9, Fantasy Castle High Poly Mesh Sculpting, and *Chapter 10, Fantasy Castle Texturing and Materials* are optional, as we will be covering the creation of the assets needed to create the level for this project. If the reader wishes to continue with the Unreal Engine parts of this project and use the assets created and provided by the author, then they can skip *Chapters 8, 9,* and *10* and proceed instead with *Chapter 11,Fantasy Castle – Bringing it all in Unreal.* However, while this chapter prepares the ground and the roadmap for the asset creation, it is still a necessary chapter for the reader who decides to skip to *Chapter 11,* as the current chapter provides necessary information on efficiently dividing the project into smaller segments, which can be easily managed later on.

Structure

The topics covered in this chapter:

- Overview of the project's concept
- Breaking down the project's concept

Objectives

The objective of this chapter is to effectively break down what appears to be a massive task at first into smaller manageable tasks while analyzing and planning our overall project workflow.

The reader will learn to think and plan in an efficient and effective manner, which can be applied virtually to any other project in the future as well.

Overview of the project's concept

For this project, we have an AI generated concept depicting a fantastical themed castle in a beautiful, lush landscape that appears to be a beautiful sunny day. Since this is a fantasy themed subject, the author created a prompt that requested a fantasy themed castle, with influences drawn from Indian and medieval European, as well as general fantasy architectures. The result of the prompt is depicted in *Figure 7.1*:

Figure 7.1: The AI generated concept

With a first look, the reader might presume this is a rather complex project, and to be honest, this is a fair and true assessment. However, as complex as creating this environment might be, there are techniques and ways to break it down into smaller and easier to manage tasks. Earlier, in *Chapter 4, Project Overview and Main Asset Creation for Statue Scene,* we used a similar approach to tackle the Greek God Statue project; we analyzed the concept image and identified key elements, which then were broken down into smaller tasks.

In a very similar fashion, we will now analyze our Fantasy Castle concept, identify key elements in our scene composition, and then produce a plan of breaking down the overall composition into multiple, but also smaller and easier individual tasks, that collectively will compose the entire — and very complex — end result.

Once we are done with analyzing, identifying, and breaking down our concept, we will proceed to the next couple of chapters to create the architectural elements that compose our scene, while in the chapters following the asset creation, we will get deeper into Unreal Engine's Blueprints, to add a playable character to our project successfully, and most importantly interactable actors which make our environment fully interactive and fun! Additionally, we will work on the terrain and natural environment surrounding the castle while also working on both exterior and interior lighting.

Finally, once we have completed all these tasks and achieved our goals, we will optimize our project and prepare it for packaging and distribution.

However, let us not get too ahead of ourselves just yet, let us focus on this chapter's goal, which is to plan the project in an efficient manner.

Breaking down the project's concept

Looking at our concept, the first and perhaps easiest observation we can almost immediately identify is that the castle is placed in the middle of a landscape featuring lush vegetation, with mountains seen in the distant background, all taking place during daytime, on a rather sunny and possibly warm day. Therefore, it is easy for us to identify four major areas we will need to be focusing during the creative process:

- The architecture/building
- Landscape
- Vegetation
- Sky

The second observation we can make is that while our architecture is complex, it is also symmetrical. Therefore, it can already reduce our architectural asset creation workload by at least half. To effectively demonstrate this point, the author cut the image in half, and then mirrored it, as shown in *Figures 7.2* and *Figure 7.3*:

Figure 7.2: The concept cut in half

Observe how the concept's half has been copy, pasted and mirrored to create a complete image in *Figure 7.3*:

Figure 7.3: The concept's half, pasted and mirrored next to the original half

Going back to the half version (*Figure 7.2*) we can identify so many different elements to work on, but at the same time we need to strike a balance between being extremely — and perhaps unnecessarily — detailed, and being efficient and minimize our workload, as much as possible, without sacrificing the quality or level of detail we want to achieve.

If you are building up a portfolio by working on personal projects that do not necessarily have any time restrictions or requirements, then by all means, go as detailed and thorough as you can, as the end result can be nothing short of stunning. However, in most professional settings, there will be deadlines and milestones to be met, therefore being able to effectively balance between the time and effort you need to invest and at the same time maintain a level of quality and detail that achieves the wow factor for the end result, is as important a skill as any. And let us not forget that more often than not, extreme levels of detail could lead to more demanding performance requirements, Although, as we saw earlier, Unreal Engine 5, along with its Nanite and Lument technologies, makes these concerns a lot easier to deal with than they have been in the past.

So, with all of the above in mind, let us together identify the elements we can work on, in a way that will allow us to achieve the coveted balance mentioned in the previous two paragraphs. We can easily see that the environment is one large section set apart from the architecture. But the architecture itself appears quite overwhelming and detailed at first look. We have arches, pillars, walls, railings, domes, staircases, doorways, and flooring, all in a variety of styles and in different iterations.

Refer to *Figure 7.4* for a numbered overview of our concept's breakdown, which we will then proceed to analyze in full detail:

Figure 7.4: *The concept's half, pasted and mirrored next to the original half*

By looking at *Figure 7.4*, what we have is several asset sets, numbered and detailed as:

1. A gigantic, and perhaps the main dome, supported by a circular structure composed of archways.

2. A set of cylindrical towers, which appears to be having different dome formats.

3. Another set of towers, which appears to be similar to each other but with different scaling.

4. Another cylindrical tower, composed of multiple cylindrical stories featuring curved archways.

5. A set of archways that appear to be composing a central grand entrance to the castle.

6. A set of supporting, smaller archways that appear to be supporting the building, more specifically, the towers above them.

7. Similar to 6, but even smaller.

8. Yet another cylindrical tower, which seems to be quite ornate when compared to the rest.

9. Large outdoor platform, complete with floor, support walls, connecting different towers to each other, and all to the main building's core.

10. Both a large outdoor platform serving as a floor to the upper levels of the building, as well as a main entrance, with archways and supportive walls, leading in to the lower levels of the building.

11. A decorative, rectangular tower, or perhaps even a guardhouse or gazebo, depending on how you visualize its utilization.

12. Ground level watchtower, with quite a complex and beautifully detailed ornamentation.

13. Supportive walls that appear to be the entire building's main supporting foundation while also connecting to *12*.

14. Some ground level staircases, that is used to break the flatness of the ground level, while also seemingly facilitating access to the higher levels.

15. A ground level fountain area, surrounded by nicely decorated pathways that connect the castle to the surrounding environment.

16. This all falls under the landscape and overall environment, which will include terrain, Foliage, and sky.

At first, we want to focus all our attention and effort on *1* to *15*. Let us look into each of them in greater detail and see how we can find elements that can be reused in multiple of these assets, and if not necessarily reused, at least slightly modified to meet the aesthetic criteria of each asset we will be creating.

Asset set #1

Let us start with a larger view of asset set #1 and analyze it in greater detail. Please refer to *Figure 7.5* first before reading any further:

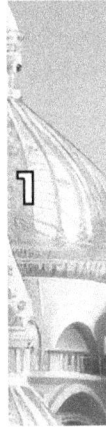

Figure 7.5: A larger view of the first asset set

The first and most obvious element we can reuse is the dome. The dome in the rear and the dome in the front both look identical, the only difference between them being the scale. In addition, the same dome could be reused, or slightly modified and reused with other assets, such as some of the cylindrical towers for example.

Then we have the rounded, walled, archways, which technically repeat themselves on both levels under the dome, just the lower one being much larger in scale.

In front of the top level's curved archways, we also have some sort of railing. This railing can be reused wherever else we need railing in the rest of the castle.

While in the half image it is harder to see, if you refer to both the mirrored full image (*Figure 7.3*) and the initial concept (*Figure 7.1*), you will see that atop of each dome, we got a much smaller, but also elongated done, supported by a cylindrical wall that also seemingly features pillar support structures.

To summarize then, for asset set#1 we will be creating:

- A large dome.
- A modular, straight archway, that will then be rounded via modifiers, to allow us to align several such archways in a way that they make up a full circle.
- A modular straight railing asset, which can be reused wherever else needed, as well as rounded through modifiers -wherever needed.
- An elongated dome, supported by a cylindrical wall, decorated with pillar-like support structures.

Asset set #2

Let us start with a larger view of asset set #2 and analyze it in greater detail. Please refer to *Figure 7.6* first before reading any further:

Figure 7.6: A larger view of the second asset set

Once again, we have several domes, four in total, as a matter of fact, three of which are identical. To make things even easier on ourselves, note how the three elongated domes (or rooftops perhaps) are very similar — if not identical — to asset set #1's fourth asset. Therefore, to save us time and maintain efficiency, we will be reusing that asset to achieve this result.

Similarly, we can reuse the cylindrical support for the two smaller domes. However, we will need to create a new one for the upper leftmost tower.

Next, we have the upper rightmost tower, which seems to be deviating from the overall pattern the rest of the towers follow, going with a more spherical approach (almost spaceship-like). Therefore, we will be creating this as a separate asset.

To summarize, we will be creating only two assets for this asset set, more specifically:

- A support structure for the upper leftmost tower will be placed underneath the dome/rooftop.

- An entire piece for the upper rightmost tower.

Asset set #3

Referring to *Figure 7.7*, we can see an enlarged view of asset set #3's elements:

Figure 7.7: A larger view of the third asset set

Domes appear to be a predominant element throughout the concept, which makes sense considering that the multitude of towers gives a sense of elevated presence and magnificence to the overall structure. The best part is that both domes depicted in *Figure 7.7* are identical to the ones we found in the previous two sets. Therefore, we will not have to build them again. Same with any support structures they feature. At this point, it is worth noting that Unreal Engine's transform tools (found in the details panel of a selected asset, as shown multiple times in previous chapters), will help us reuse assets in ways that do not appear repetitive. More about this in later chapters, when we will be importing and placing the castle's modular assets into the Unreal Engine project.

Asset set #4

Referring to *Figure 7.8*, we can see an enlarged view of asset set #4's elements:

Figure 7.8: A larger view of the fourth asset set

As you might have guessed by now, asset set #4 is helping us maintain efficiency since all its elements, such as the dome, the support structure etc. are identical to the ones we found in previous asset sets. Once again, the scaling and placement of the assets within the Unreal Engine is what will diversify this asset set from the rest.

Asset set #5

Unlike asset sets #3 and #4, this asset set has quite a few new and unique looking elements we will need to carefully consider and create. Refer to *Figure 7.9* for an enlarged view of the fifth asset set:

Figure 7.9: A larger view of the fifth asset set

While we have pillars and archways from previous asset sets, the ones found in this fifth asset set are quite large, distinctive, and, most importantly, placed centrally. Therefore, they are meant to catch the viewer's attention, and thus, we want them to stand out from the rest, not only in terms of uniqueness but also in terms of detail. We need to put some extra effort and time into detailing them.

Given the importance of this asset set, we want to refer back to the original concept, isolate the corresponding part, and enlarge it so we can study it more thoroughly and plan it out accordingly. Refer to *Figure 7.10* for an enlarged view:

Figure 7.10: *An enlarged view of the fifth asset set's elements, as seen in the initial concept*

Much like we broke down the overall concept, now we can break down this set into smaller, easier to identify pieces.

Firstly, we have the bottom layer, with a focus on its center, which can be considered as the main grand entrance to the castle. Refer to *Figure 7.11* for a clearer, isolated view:

Figure 7.11: *An isolated view of the grand entrance*

We can clearly see an archway to the front, followed by a staircase leading to second row of arches, with one of them featuring the door that leads into the castle. So, we need to create the front archway, the rear arches, the staircase, the wall, and the ceiling connecting the two rows of arches.

Then, to the left and to the right of the central grand entrance, we have two identical towers, as shown in *Figure 7.12*:

Figure 7.12: Tower next to the grand entrance

Given that the elongated dome of this tower is very similar to ones found in previous asset sets, we can at least reuse the base mesh we will be creating for them, but since it is also part of the central grand gate, we can differentiate it by sculpting it differently and assigning it different Materials than the ones we will be using in the other asset sets. This way, we are still efficient in our workflow but also effective in achieving an impressive visual result that breaks any repetitive patterns. The rest of the tower is rectangular, and while we could build it modularly, with every single piece being reusable, since we will not be doing any additional levels for this project, we might as well just create this element as one larger piece.

Next, we have the upper section, which features another row of arches in the front, as seen in *Figure 7.13*:

Figure 7.13: Top row of arches and another gate in the background

In this case, we can see that this row of arches is rounded and rests upon a rounded wall, also featuring a rounded floor — which we cannot see in the concept — while in the background, we have what appears to be a straight wall with a gate at its center. In addition, we need to consider there is a ceiling piece we cannot see, which also will have to follow the rounded or curved if you prefer, shape. Then, there is also a central archway protruding from the center of the rounded wall supporting the curved arches, which can be interpreted in many ways (such as a set of windows, for example). However, for this project, we will interpret it as a collection of decorative panels.

Lastly, we have another pair of towers, as seen in *Figure 7.14*:

Figure 7.14: *Another tower, larger than the previous one, found to the left and to the right of the grand entrance*

Once more, we have a dome to work on, an oval shaped one this time, and a rectangular support structure, which again for this project's purposes we will create as one piece instead of multiple modular ones.

To summarize the rather loaded asset set #5, we will need to create several assets for this set, more specifically:

- Bottom front archway
- Staircase
- Rear wall with arches and central gate
- Ceiling between front archway and rear wall
- Smaller tower dome/rooftop
- Smaller tower rectangular support structure
- Top, rounder row of arches
- Rounded wall supporting row of arches
- Floor layered over the rounded wall

- Rear wall with central gate
- Ceiling within rounded row of arches
- Central piece protruding from rounded wall, featuring decorative panels
- Larger tower dome
- Larger tower rectangular support structure

Asset set #6

Referring to *Figure 7.15*, we can see an enlarged view of the sixth asset set elements:

Figure 7.15: A larger view of the sixth asset set

Sometimes, concept artwork can be a bit vague or somewhat harder to interpret. While one might be inclined to think this is a bad thing, in fact, it can be creatively freeing and sometimes even a bit relieving as it can help expedite the workflow by assuming a simpler interpretation. Such is the case with the sixth asset set, as we can see a simple rectangular structure comprised of archways. We will be able to choose from plenty of similar assets from the previous sets, therefore making our workload a little bit easier and allowing us to move on to the seventh set.

Asset set #7

Referring to *Figure 7.16*, we can see an enlarged view of the elements found in the seventh asset set:

Figure 7.16: A larger view of the seventh asset set

Yet again another row of arches, plenty to choose from previous asset sets, thus saving us a bit of time and effort.

Asset set #8

Referring to *Figure 7.17*, one more tower appears in the enlarged view of asset set eight:

Figure 7.17: A larger view of the eighth asset set

While the reader might be tempted to presume we will reuse assets from other sets, and rightly so, in this case, we can see that this tower stands out more than others in the overall composition of the concept image. Therefore, we will need to give it the attention to detail it needs, both to more accurately represent the concept and to break repetition and achieve an overall qualitative and visually superior result.

Firstly, we have the elongated, slightly oval-shaped dome, which we can sculpt from a previous asset's dome base mesh. This way, we save a little bit of time and effort with the basics but still need to spend time detailing the mesh when sculpting its high poly counterpart.

The same holds true for the cylindrical support structure underneath the dome.

As such, to summarize, we have two main parts to create:

- Dome/rooftop
- Cylindrical archway/support structure of the tower

Proceeding on to the ninth asset set.

Asset set #9

Looking at the enlarged image of the ninth set, as seen in *Figure 7.18*, this set should be relatively easy and quick:

Figure 7.18: A larger view of the ninth asset set

We have some flooring to create, as well as a wall asset. Both will be tileable and modular; this way, we can easily repeat them where and when needed. It certainly works to our advantage that they do not appear to be anything special in the sense of detail and uniqueness because these are usually the best assets to fill in any missing gaps without destroying an overall composition or attracting too much attention from other assets that require it.

Thus, to summarize, we have two main parts to create:

- Tileable floor
- Tileable wall

Asset set #10

As seen in *Figure 7.19*, this set could reuse a lot of assets from previous sets:

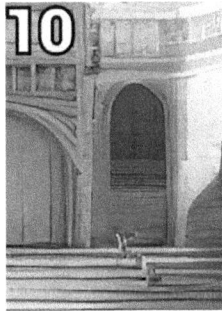

Figure 7.19: A larger view of the tenth asset set

At this point, it is fairly easy to predict the approach we will use for this set. There are so many assets we can reuse from previous sets, such as the tileable floor, the stairs, the railings, the archways, and the walls. The hard work we will perform to complete the other sets will pay off by saving us time with sets such as the tenth one thus allowing us to proceed on to the eleventh.

Asset set #11

Figure 7.20 displays a larger view of the eleventh asset set:

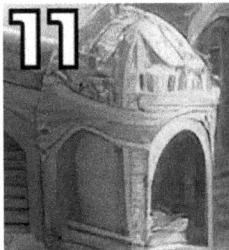

Figure 7.20: A larger view of the eleventh asset set

While we can reuse assets, such as the dome and the arches, in this case, we will sculpt the entire asset as one piece to set it a little bit more apart from the rest of the repeated assets. We will, however, use some of the base (foundation, if you prefer) meshes from other sets in order to sculpt this one. More on this in the next couple of chapters.

To summarize and itemize for easier task related reference purposes, the entire small tower structure is in one asset.

Asset set #12

Figure 7.21 displays a larger view of the twelfth asset set, which features yet another tower, however, this one is quite detailed and unique when compared to the others from the concept:

Figure 7.21: A larger view of the twelfth asset set, featuring a beautiful tower

We can most certainly reuse the dome from another set; however, the rest of the tower is quite distinct from the others in the concept; therefore, we will need to create it. We can break it down into two octagonal support structures.

To summarize:

- Upper and smaller octagonal shaped tower structure
- Lower and larger octagonal shaped tower structure

Asset set #13

In *Figure 7.22*, we can see a larger view of the thirteenth asset set:

Figure 7.22: A larger view of the thirteenth asset set

We can and most certainly will reuse the railing, archway, and wall from previous sets. However, there is one specific support pillar (in the center of *Figure 7.22*) that we will need to create to match the concept. The vegetation is a separate topic all together, which we will cover in a much later chapter.

To summarize, there is only one asset we need to create for this set which is a support pillar, as seen in the center of *Figure 7.22*.

Asset set #14

In *Figure 7.23*, we can see a larger view of the fourteenth asset set, the focus of our attention being the stairs:

Figure 7.23: A larger view of the fourteenth asset set

We only need to focus on the stairs seen in *Figure 7.23*. In theory, we could reuse stairs found in the other sets. However, the ones in the fourteenth set differ visually, and thus we need to accurately represent the concept and create the assets anew.

To summarize, there is only one asset we need to create for this set specifically the stairs seen in *Figure 7.23*.

The remaining assets seen in *Figure 7.23* can technically be considered part of the next asset set, the fifteenth, to be specific. Let us take a look at that one next!

Asset set #15

In *Figure 7.24*, we can see a larger view of the fifteenth asset set, which continues with assets briefly seen in asset set number fourteen as well:

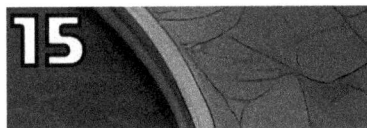

Figure 7.24: A larger view of the fifteenth asset set

As can be seen in *Figure 7.24*, there is a curved path, seemingly made out of stone, a curved wall — or trim if you prefer — separating the path from a large fountain's basin.

To summarize, there are two assets we need to create for this set:

- Curved stone-based path/floor
- Curved wall/trim with fountain basin

Asset set #16

As seen in *Figure 7.25*, there are no architectural elements in this set. Instead, we have vegetation, landscaping, and the sky, all of which will be done with assets freely available by *Epic Games* with the Unreal Engine:

Figure 7.25: *A larger view of the sixteenth asset set, featuring all the landscaping, vegetation, and sky elements of the concept*

Other assets

While we broke down the overall concept into smaller, manageable segments, while creating the assets, as well as while putting the level together in the Unreal Engine, we will be often going back and forth between our creative process and the original concept to ensure we stayed true, or at least close enough, to the concept, and add or adjust assets and elements as needed.

Two such examples are the fountain on the ground floor, seen in the lower center of *Figure 7.1,* and the pool on the second level, once again seen in *Figure 7.1*, both of which can also be seen in *Figure 7.26* for easier reference:

Figure 7.26: *A larger view of the concept's ground-level fountain and second floor pool*

Conclusion

We successfully took a very complex and overwhelming concept and broke it down into much smaller and easier to complete segments. While the number of assets we still need to create remains daunting, one technique to not allow it to overwhelm you is to focus on each segment separately instead of thinking about the entirety of the project, especially with the first couple of asset sets. Think of it as a journey with several stops in between, while the journey might be long, each stop serves as an immediate destination and thus the focus of our attention, allowing us to steadily cover smaller distances that quickly accumulate into a rather large distance, bringing us closer to the final destination, without feeling overwhelmed and stressed, instead learning and picking up new experiences along the journey itself.

In *Chapter 8, Fantasy Castle Base Mesh Modeling*, we will use *Chapter 7's* breakdown and lists as our guide to create the base meshes. If the reader decides to attempt modeling the base meshes themselves, they can use any 3D modeling application they feel comfortable with, but for this book's purposes, the author will be using *Autodesk 3ds Max*. In *Chapter 9, Fantasy Castle High Poly Mesh Sculpting*, the author will proceed with sculpting the base meshes in ZBrush, but the reader can — once again, if they decide to attempt high poly modeling and sculpting themselves — do the same in any 3D sculpting application they feel comfortable with.

Points to remember

- Learned how to properly break a complex environment concept down into different manageable segments and asset sets.

- Reusing assets is not lazy; it is efficient if done properly.

- The concept artwork is your guide; you should often refer back to it.

Exercises

1. Find an environment themed image on the internet, or even in printed media (a poster, a book, a photograph even) that triggers your interest, and try to break it down into segments by finding repeating patterns and assets that could be reused throughout, if you were to build said environment in the Unreal Engine.

2. Identify and isolate the key architectural elements and divide them into repeated and unique.

3. Look for any patterns or elements that are not only repeated but also mirrored and identify them.

Join our book's Discord space

Join the book's Discord Workspace for Latest updates, Offers, Tech happenings around the world, New Release and Sessions with the Authors:

https://discord.bpbonline.com

Chapter 8

Fantasy Castle Base Mesh Modeling

Introduction

Working with the Unreal Engine will resume in *Chapter 11Fantasy Castle - Character and Interaction Blueprints*, whereas between *Chapter 8, Fantasy Castle Base Mesh Modeling*, and *Chapter 10, Fantasy Castle Bringing it All in Unreal*, the focus will Shift to external workflows and processes.

In this chapter, we will be briefly showing the process of modeling the base meshes of the previous chapter's breakdown of asset sets. The author used Autodesk's 3ds Max to create the base meshes, and while we will be mentioning some of the application's functions and tools, this chapter — or this book — is not meant to teach you 3ds Max. If you are comfortable (intermediate to advanced levels) with 3ds Max or with similar 3D modeling applications, you should have no issues following through. If you have no experience with any 3D modeling applications, you can still read through the chapter, mainly to get a better understanding of the processes and overall workflow that is followed to create a Static Mesh from scratch.

Structure

The topics covered in this chapter:

- Base mesh modeling of asset set #1
- Base mesh modeling of asset set #2

- Base mesh modeling of asset set #3
- Base mesh modeling of asset set #4
- Base mesh modeling of asset set #5
- Base mesh modeling of asset set #6
- Base mesh modeling of asset set #7
- Base mesh modeling of asset set #8
- Base mesh modeling of asset set #9
- Base mesh modeling of asset set #10
- Base mesh modeling of asset set #11
- Base mesh modeling of asset set #12
- Base mesh modeling of asset set #13
- Base mesh modeling of asset set #14
- Base mesh modeling of asset set #15

Objectives

In this chapter, we will briefly showcase the process followed to model through the modular base meshes, focusing mainly on the logic behind the workflow rather than a strict step-by-step tutorial. We will go through the thinking process of giving our base meshes enough detail to vaguely resemble the concept's intended assets while ensuring they will be easy to work with in our sculpting application later on when we are creating the high poly and highly detailed versions of them.

Base mesh modeling of asset set #1

We begin creating the meshes we discussed in *Chapter 7, Fantasy Castle Project Breakdown and Planning,* specifically the first set of assets. For quick reference and as a reminder, *Figure 8.1* shows the assets we identified from the concept for this first set:

Figure 8.1: The first set of assets we need to create base meshes for

The most obvious asset, to begin with, is the dome. It is not a primitive shape, such as a cylinder, a pyramid, or a cube, for instance, so the best approach will be to use a line or a spline shape that resembles the outer silhouette and, from there, generate the rest of the geometry. Therefore, we create a line shape, much like the one in *Figure 8.2*:

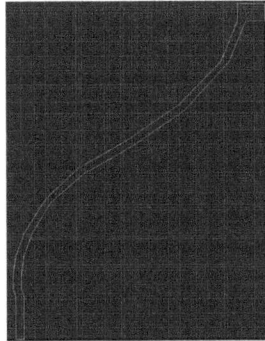

Figure 8.2: *We create a line loop that resembles the dome's outer silhouette*

Next, it is best we ensure that its pivot point is located at X,Y,Z coordinates set to 0. Next, with our line shape selected, we want to apply the **Lathe** Modifier, as shown in *Figure 8.3*:

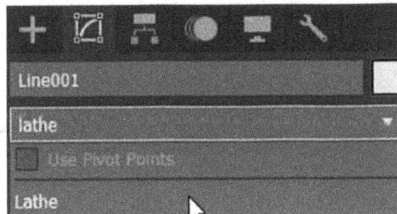

Figure 8.3: *The Lathe Modifier will help us get a nice, rounded shape that resembles the dome*

Once the modifier is active, ensure you have set the **Degrees** value to 360 under the modifier's parameters, ensuring the shape rotates around the three-dimensional Z axis to create a nice, rounded shape that resembles the dome from the concept, as shown in *Figure 8.4*:

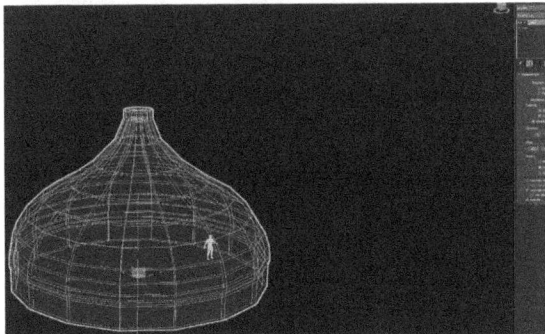

Figure 8.4: *The Lathe Modifier in effect*

Traditionally, we would want our base meshes to be as economical as possible in terms of polygonal count, but thanks to Unreal Engine 5's Nanite, we do not need to worry about that right now; instead, we want to create as detailed a geometry, which in turn will make our life easier when sculpting the highly detailed, high poly counterpart of each mesh. However, we want to ensure we do not spend too much time adding too much detail in the base mesh modeling stages since that can be time consuming in an application such as 3ds Max; instead, we can go in full detail mode in our sculpting application later on (ZBrush is the sculpting application the author uses). With that said, we can increase the number of **Segments** we use under the Lathe Modifier's parameters, so for this instance, the author set the **Segments** value to 32. The higher this value, the smoother and the more rounded the onion-like shape of the dome will be however, as we can see in the concept, it is not perfectly rounded, so we still want to retain a somewhat polygonal aesthetic to it, as shown in *Figure 8.5*:

Figure 8.5: *Segments value set to 32*

At this point, it is a good time to right click on our mesh and convert it to an Editable Poly, as shown in *Figure 8.6*:

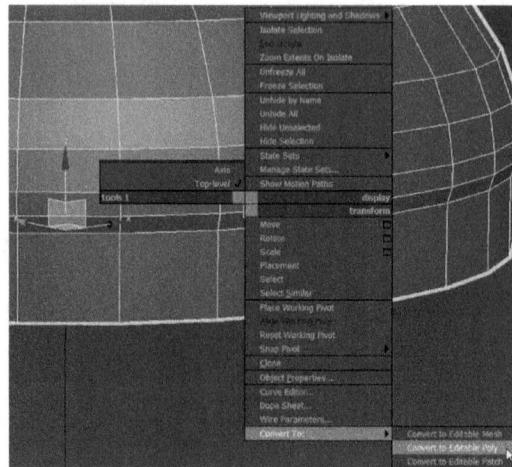

Figure 8.6: *The Lathe Modifier in effect*

Next, we want to start adding a bit more detail to the mesh. We achieve that by strategically selecting some of the mesh's polygons, other times the edges and vertices, and moving them around, extruding them, beveling them, chamfering them, until we have achieved a shape or geometry, we are content enough with. *Figures 8.7* to *Figure 8.12* briefly demonstrate part of that process:

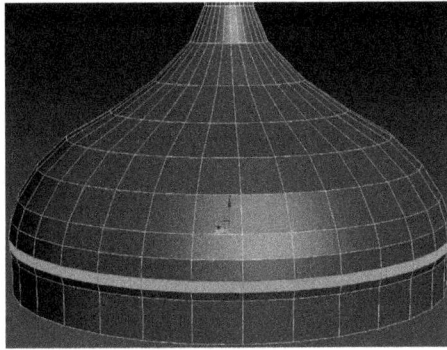

Figure 8.7: *Selecting some of the polygons to create a trim around the dome*

We proceed with extruding the selected polygons to achieve a circular trim around the dome mesh, giving it more depth, as shown in *Figure 8.8*:

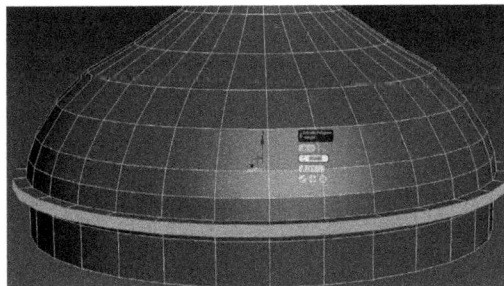

Figure 8.8: *Extruding the selected polygons to achieve more depth*

Chamfering is a rather useful function when it comes to geometrical edge manipulation, as depicted in *Figure 8.9*:

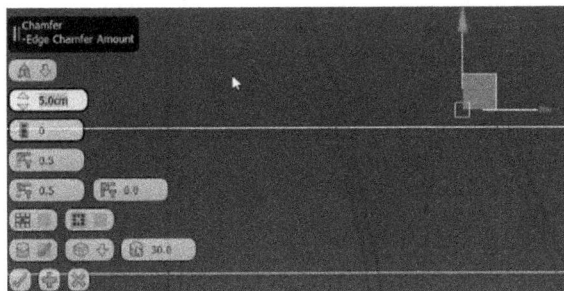

Figure 8.9: *Selecting and chamfering some of the edges*

To give the dome some further definition, we will continue using a combination of previous techniques, on different parts of its geometry, as demonstrated in *Figure 8.10*:

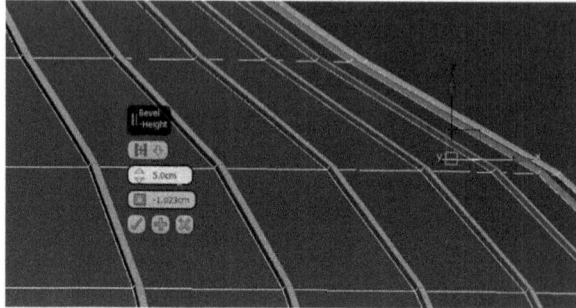

Figure 8.10: *Selecting and extruding the polygons that resulted from the chamfered edges*

To further modify the overall shape of the dome and better define it, we will next apply the FFD modifier, as shown in *Figure 8.11*:

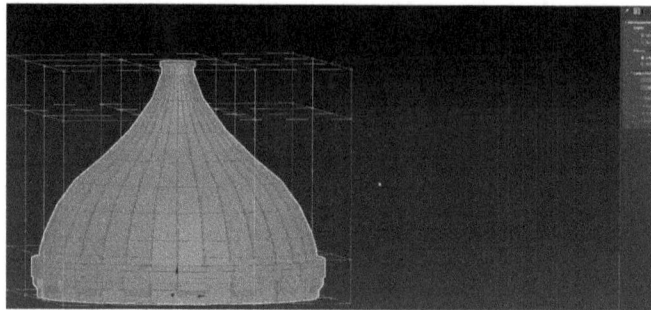

Figure 8.11: *After many polygons were selected and modified, we also utilized the FFD modifier to shape up the dome closer to the concept*

After much geometrical manipulation of the dome mesh, we conclude with the results shown in *Figure 8.12*:

Figure 8.12: *Much better, much closer to the concept*

Next, we need to focus on the details of the meshes around the main dome. We proceed by creating simple cylindrical shapes, which then, once again, by selecting surfaces or polygons and extruding them, we achieve shapes that resemble pillars or anything else that the concept, combined with our imagination and interpretation of the concept's details, allow us to express. *Figures 8.13* and *Figure 8.14* briefly demonstrate the dome's evolution through such steps. While we evolve the dome mesh, we also work on separate meshes, allowing us to take advantage of their modular nature later on. The different colored geometry indicates separate, different meshes.

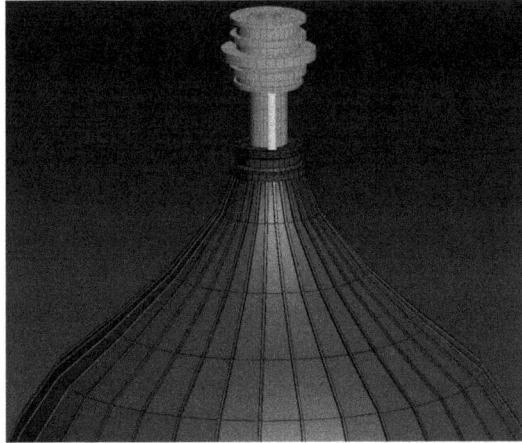

Figure 8.13: *Working on separate meshes, above the dome*

Figure 8.14 gives a better understanding of how varying geometrical shapes and meshes can be combined with each other to start creating a more complete picture of the desired end result:

Figure 8.14: *The more meshes we add, the more detail we have and the closer we get to the concept*

Another function that will really help us with the base mesh modeling is the Boolean approach applied to multiple meshes. For example, we will need to have archways, which in essence are a flat wall or solid rectangular shape, which is then having an archway's shape cut out from its geometry. To demonstrate this, we start with a rectangular, wall-like shape, as shown in *Figure 8.15*:

Figure 8.15: The rectangular geometry represents a wall

Next, we need to create the shape of the archway. In essence, a rounded archway is a combination of a rectangle and half a cylinder. To expedite the process, we can use a full cylinder as well and use the cylinder and the rectangle to merge them with each other. *Figure 8.16* shows the two geometrical shapes positioned in a way, ready to be merged into one:

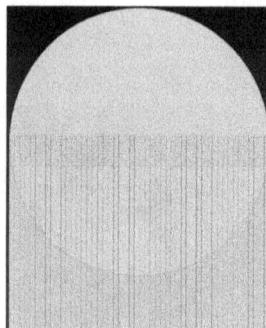

Figure 8.16: A rectangle and a cylinder positioned together in a way that will allow us to create an archway's basic shape

In 3ds Max we can merge the two by selecting **Boolean** under the Create tab, specifically under the **Compound Objects** category, while having the cylinder selected, and then clicking **Add Operands** and selecting the rectangle. Lastly, since we want to combine the two, we will select **Union**. In this case, you could also have chosen **Merge** or **Attach** and you would still achieve the desired result. Detailing the difference between the operand parameters, or any other parameters and functions within 3ds Max, would be beyond this book's scope and purpose, so there would not be any detailed explanation, but purely for reference purposes, *Figure 8.17* demonstrates the settings used to derive a single mesh out of the two separate ones:

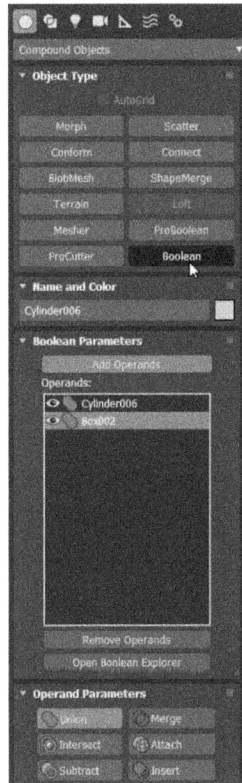

Figure 8.17: *The Lathe modifier in effect*

The end result is depicted in *Figure 8.18*:

Figure 8.18: *The basic archway shape, in one mesh*

Now that we have the basic archway shape, we can line up several instances of it in front and intersecting with the rectangular wall mesh, as shown in *Figure 8.19*:

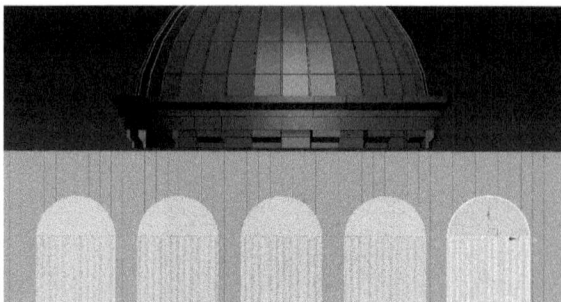

Figure 8.19: It starts resembling a row of archways

Now that we have all the shapes in place, we resort once again to using the Boolean operation while having the wall selected and then picking the archway shapes as our secondary operands. This time, however, the operand parameter we need to use is **Subtract**, as shown in *Figure 8.20*:

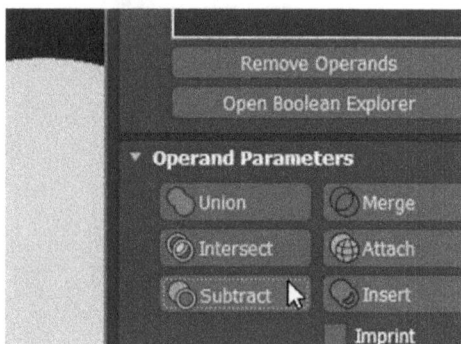

Figure 8.20: Subtract is the operand parameter we need to create a hole in the geometry

This will allow us to punch holes in the wall in the shape of the archways, as demonstrated in *Figure 8.21*:

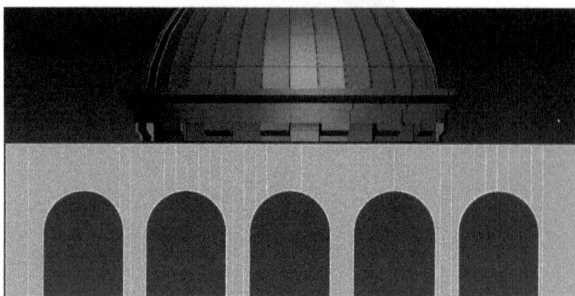

Figure 8.21: A simple but effective archway

The next step to follow is to bend the archway around the dome's circular shape. The initial state of the archway row is depicted in *Figure 8.22*:

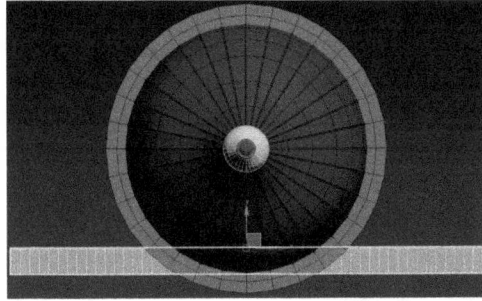

Figure 8.22: *The archways are straight*

To bend it, we will select it and use the **Bend** modifier, with the parameters and effect shown in *Figure 8.23*:

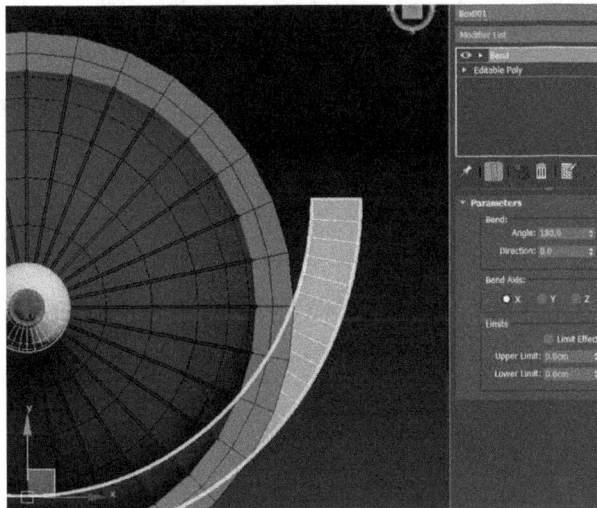

Figure 8.23: *The Bend modifier in effect*

Next, we need to scale the curved archway just enough to match the dome's circumference, as shown in *Figure 8.24*:

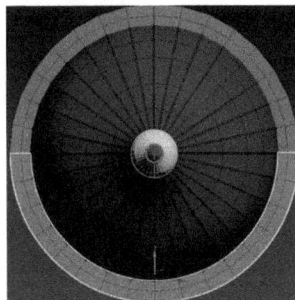

Figure 8.24: *The archway now perfectly matches the dome's circumference*

If our archway was longer and featured more arches, we could have achieved a full circle with the bend modifier, but in this example, we had enough arches to make it presentable with half a circular bend, in other words, we bent it by 180 degrees instead of 360 degrees, because had we done a full circle, the archways would look stretched and exaggerated. With our bent archway selected, we can simply mirror it and create a copy towards the Y-axis (in top view), as shown in *Figure 8.25*, and then merge the two bent archways into one fully circular mesh, as shown in *Figure 8.26*:

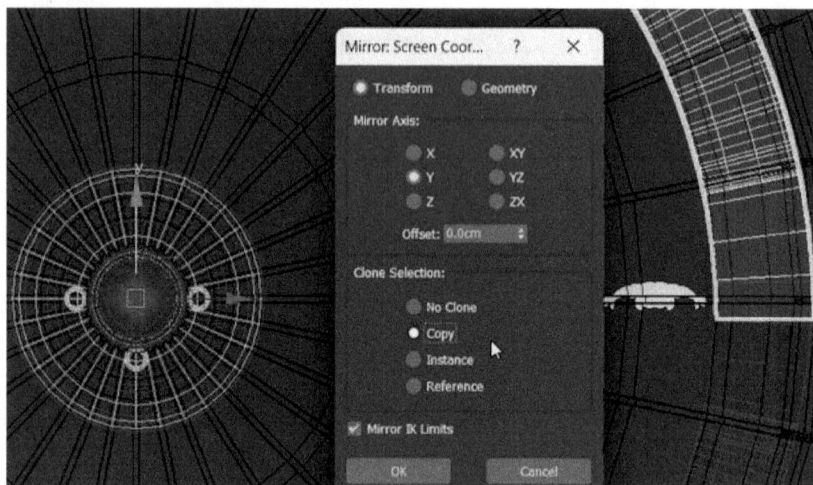

Figure 8.25: Creating a mirrored copy of our bent archway

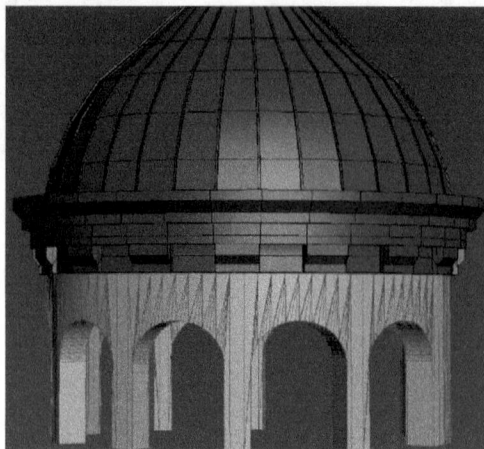

Figure 8.26: A fully circular archway supporting the entire dome

To give an additional sense of magnitude, we will now duplicate the circular archway and place it right under the first one, and next, we will work on some polygonal extractions to give it a more refined and detailed shape, as shown in *Figure 8.27*:

Figure 8.27: Steadily expanding asset set 1

For our next step, we create the railing mesh, which we will need to reuse several times throughout the base mesh modeling creative process. For a start, we will draw a line of the rail support shape we want, only to apply Lathe later to give it a complete geometrical shape, much like we did with the dome at the beginning of this chapter. Once we have created the railing support, we will create several copies of it, much like we did with the archway shapes. *Figures 8.28* to *Figure 8.30* depict all the steps just described:

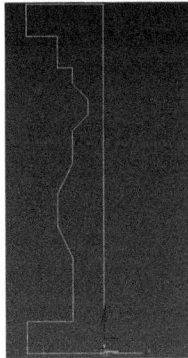

Figure 8.28: The railing's support column, starting with a line

The previous steps help transform a collection of 2D lines into an actual 3D object, as seen in *Figure 8.29*:

Figure 8.29: The Lathe modifier gives us the full geometry

If one creates multiple instances of the 3D object, it is easy to visualize the desired end result of a railing mesh, note the instanced meshes in *Figure 8.30*:

Figure 8.30: *Lining up several copies of the railing support*

To complete the railing, next, we will create two rectangular boxes, above and below the support columns, and then with edge selection and chamfering, smoothen them out, to achieve the result shown in *Figure 8.31*:

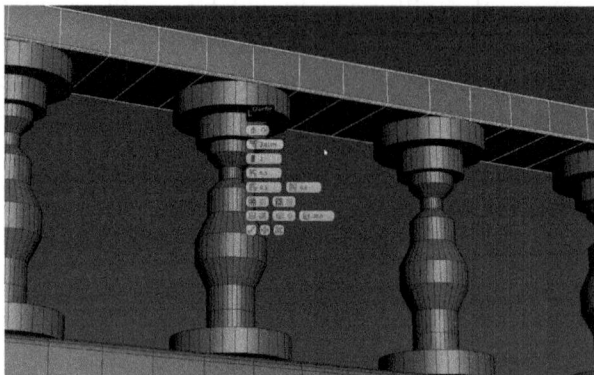

Figure 8.31: *The railing base mesh*

To close up the gap between the circular archways supporting the dome, we will place a basic cylinder with a radius wide enough to close any gaps, as shown in *Figure 8.32*:

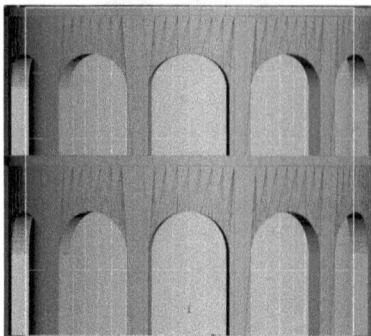

Figure 8.32: *The primitive and basic cylinder serves great as a wall behind the circular archways*

Now, by using the Bend modifier and mirroring steps described earlier, we will surround our cylindrical wall with curved copies of our freshly created railing, as shown in *Figures 8.33* and *Figure 8.34*:

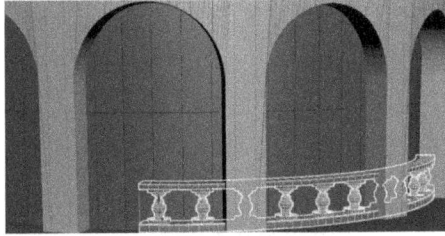

Figure 8.33: A curved copy of the railing mesh

Figure 8.34: Another view of the curved copy of the railing mesh

Having curved the railing mesh, we simply need to create multiple instances and place them around the architectural geometry, as seen in *Figure 8.35*:

Figure 8.35: Curved railing complete

As such, we have completed our first asset set, as shown in *Figure 8.36*. In a similar fashion, with the same techniques, we will create more base meshes, or use and modify copies of the existing ones, to fully complete all the other asset sets.

Figure 8.36: The first asset set is complete

As a brief reminder, this chapter's (and, extension, this book's) purpose is not to teach you 3ds Max or any similar application. However, the author deems the inclusion of this chapter as a good addition that can easily be followed and replicated by someone familiar with such applications or as an additional piece of information that provides a deeper insight and better understanding as per the processes and workflows utilized when creating assets for use with the Unreal Engine.

Chapter 11, Fantasy Castle Bringing it All in Unreal is where the book resumes detailed, step by step tutoring within the Unreal Engine.

To keep *Chapter 8, Fantasy Castle Base Mesh Modeling* relatively brief, yet informative, the author will provide only brief descriptions of the steps followed, along with imagery that helps all readers understand the basic principles of the processes conducted for the purpose of creating the complete asset pack that will be later used in *Chapter 11, Fantasy Castle Bringing it All in Unreal* to import and use to create our Fantasy Castle level, and in extension project.

Base mesh modeling of asset set #2

Moving on to creating the second set of base meshes, as discussed in *Chapter 7, Fantasy Castle Project Breakdown and Planning*. For quick reference and as a reminder, *Figure 8.37* shows the assets we identified from the concept for this second set:

Figure 8.37: The second set of assets we need to create base meshes for

With the same combination of techniques, tools, and functions used previously, we create the modular meshes that together create each of the towers seen in *Figure 8.37*. To begin with, we create a chamfered rectangular shape, long enough to begin resembling a tower. Then, we duplicate it, and scale it up in all directions while making it a bit shorter on the Z-axis (vertically). We then proceed to use a copy of the merged geometry that represented the archway's shape earlier in this chapter, only to proceed with applying the Boolean operation between this and the second (duplicated) chamfered rectangle, mentioned only a couple of lines above. All these steps and the end result of these steps are briefly displayed in *Figures 8.38* and *8.39*:

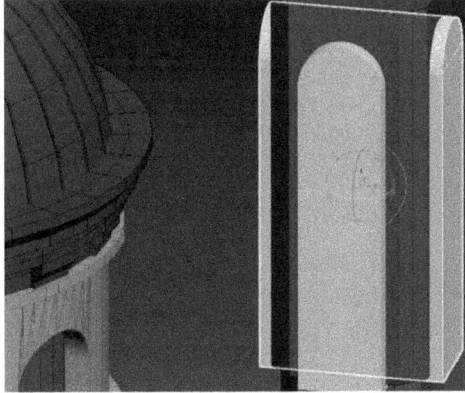

Figure 8.38: The beginning of the tower

Figure 8.39 depicts how the different geometry helps create the desired end result:

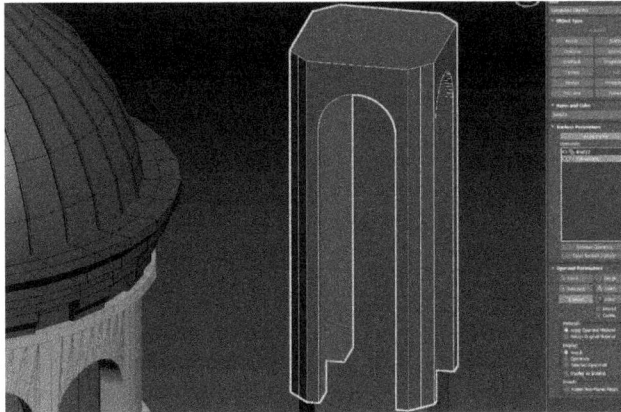

Figure 8.39: Creating arches that surround the tower

We proceed with making holes in the tower's walls, while we make its trim a bit more detailed and elaborate. We also duplicate some of the meshes previously created for asset set one, with the purpose of completing the tower's roof. The end result is depicted in *Figure 8.40*:

Figure 8.40: The first tower's base mesh is ready

In the same way, we create two more towers, therefore completing asset set #2. *Figure 8.41* shows the base meshes for both asset set 1 and 2:

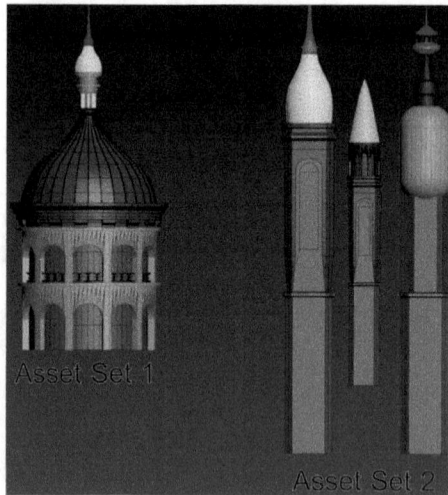

Figure 8.41: Overview for asset sets 1 and 2

At this point, it is worth noting that throughout this process, we keep visiting not only the broken-down parts of the concept or the list of assets found in *Chapter 7, Fantasy Castle Project Breakdown and Planning* but also the complete concept, as it is rather easy to have overlooked some details that become obvious only after creating the base meshes. The same will hold true in *Chapter 9, Fantasy Castle High Poly Mesh Sculpting*, when we will be sculpting the high poly, detailed versions of the meshes. In addition, it is equally important to remember that the concept leaves a lot to the 3D modeler's imagination and interpretation, so generally speaking, it is encouraged to apply your personal version of the concept's creative interpretation.

Another thing to consider is that throughout the base mesh and sculpting steps of the creative process, we would not worry too much about scaling dimensions, as we just aim for a relative scale approximation for the time being, since we will spend a lot of time finetuning scaling, mesh positioning and combining in the actual level design process, in the Unreal Engine.

Base mesh modeling of asset set #3

What follows next is the creation of the third set of base meshes, as discussed in *Chapter 7, Fantasy Castle Project Breakdown and Planning*. For quick reference and as a reminder, *Figure 8.42* shows the assets we identified from the concept for this third set:

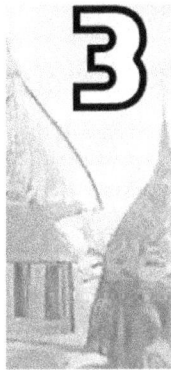

Figure 8.42: The third set of assets we need to create base meshes for

After much meddling with primitive shapes, polygonal manipulation, extraction, and scaling, the first tower of the third asset set is complete and can be seen in *Figure 8.43*:

Figure 8.43: The first tower of the third set

Similarly, we complete the second tower of this set as well, completing the entire third set as shown in *Figure 8.44*:

Figure 8.44: The third base mesh set is now complete

Base mesh modeling of asset set #4

Moving on, we proceed with the creation of the fourth set of base meshes. For quick reference and as a reminder, *Figure 8.45* shows the assets we identified from the concept for this fourth set:

Figure 8.45: The fourth set of assets we need to create base meshes for

From here on, the functions, techniques, and overall processes followed and applied are mostly the same as before, so after much work, *Figure 8.46* depicts the end result we get for asset set 4:

Figure 8.46: *The fourth set of base mesh assets*

Figure 8.47 shows a summary of the four asset sets created so far:

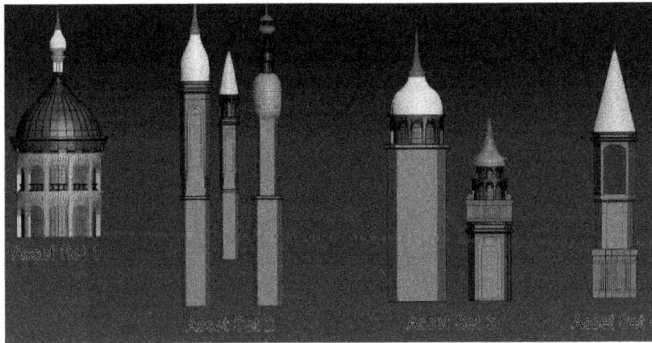

Figure 8.47: *The first four asset sets, summarized*

Base mesh modeling of asset set #5

Next up is the fifth set. *Figure 8.48* serves as a quick reminder of the assets we identified from the concept for this set:

Figure 8.48: *The fifth set of assets we need to create base meshes for*

The fifth set of assets was a lot more complicated to create than the rest due to the number of assets featured and the level of detail it needed due to being quite central in the overall composition. *Figures 8.49* to *Figure 8.61* depict several of the steps it took to create different modular meshes and finally complete the overall set:

Figure 8.49: Creating another arch

After all these steps, the desired end result for this archway can be seen in *Figure 8.50:*

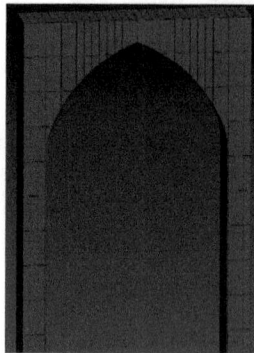

Figure 8.50: Arch complete

In the next figure, we will see the creation of a door frame for the archway:

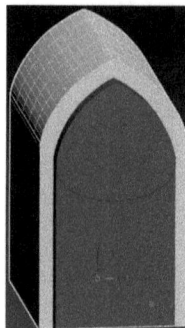

Figure 8.51: Creating a door frame for the archway

In the next figure, we will place the doorframe:

Figure 8.52: *Placing the doorframe*

The following figure shows how we can create different sized archways:

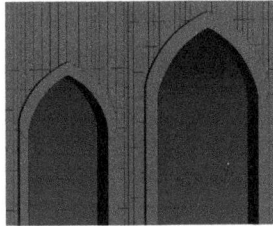

Figure 8.53: *Creating different sized archways*

In the next figure, a complete and symmetrical row of archways is shown:

Figure 8.54: *Creating a complete and symmetrical row of archways*

The next figure shows the creation of the central part:

Figure 8.55: *Creating the central part*

The next figure will show the trimming of some parts:

Figure 8.56: *Trimming some unnecessary parts*

In the next figure, we can see a more complete vision of the desired outcome:

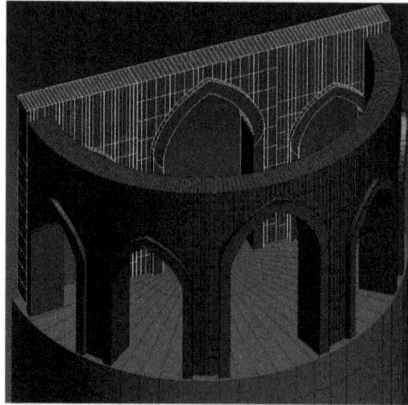

Figure 8.57: *Getting closer to a complete picture of the desired end result*

In *Figure 8.58*, it becomes easier to see the intended end result:

Figure 8.58: *The central part is now almost complete*

We carry on with more architectural geometry in *Figure 8.59*:

Figure 8.59: More archways for the central part

The following figure shows some columns that will support the central arch:

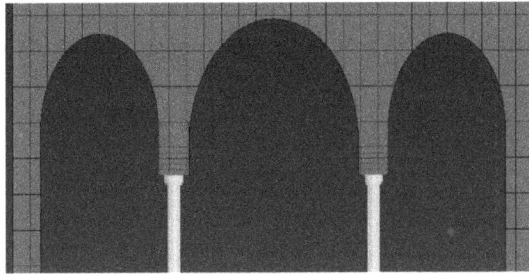

Figure 8.60: This time, we need some columns to support the central arch

Figure 8.61 demonstrates several architectural elements, composites of smaller geometrical parts, combined together to create a larger, intricate piece:

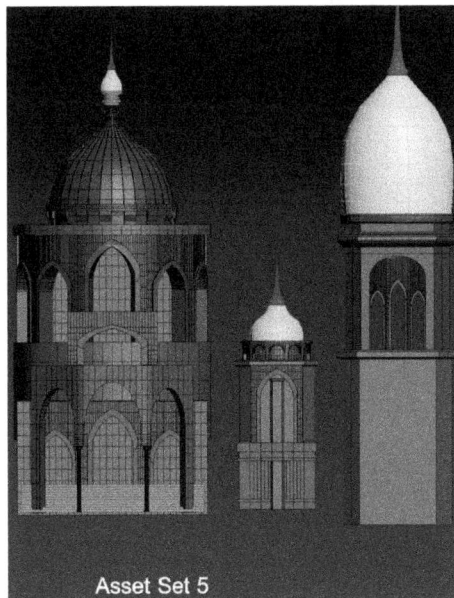

Figure 8.61: After much work, the fifth base mesh set is finally complete

Base mesh modeling of asset set #6

The sixth set is much easier than the fifth set. *Figure 8.62* shows the assets we identified from the concept for this set:

Figure 8.62: The sixth set of assets we need to create base meshes for

By reusing copies of previously created meshes, we quickly derive the sixth set, as seen in *Figure 8.63*:

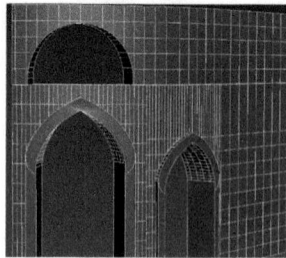

Figure 8.63: The sixth set of base mesh assets

Base mesh modeling of asset set #7

On to the seventh, *Figure 8.64* shows the assets we identified from the concept for this set:

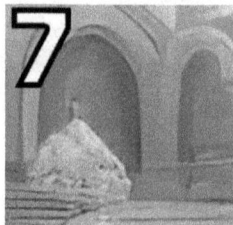

Figure 8.64: The seventh set of assets we need to create base meshes for

In *Chapter 7, Fantasy Castle Project Breakdown and Planning,* we did not include one of the towers that could be included in the seventh set, which is why it is important to keep going back and forth between the concept and any work in progress. *Figure 8.65* shows the final result for the entire seventh set, including the additional tower:

Figure 8.65: The seventh set of base mesh assets

Base mesh modeling of asset set #8

By now, the process followed is pretty easy to predict and follow. *Figure 8.66* shows the assets we identified from the concept for the eighth set, and *Figure 8.67* shows the end result:

Figure 8.66: The eighth set of assets we need to create base meshes for

Compare *Figure 8.66* with *Figure 8.67* and note how the 3D geometry resembles our initial concept:

Figure 8.67: The eighth set of base mesh assets

Base mesh modeling of asset set #9

Figure 8.68 serves as a reminder of the concept for the ninth set, while *Figure 8.69* shows the final result:

Figure 8.68: The ninth set of assets we need to create base meshes for

For this set, we have basic walls and floors, which, in essence, are easier to work with since we need to build them in a way that makes them tileable. Therefore, we did not need to replicate the exact structure we see in the concept. Instead, we will tile these modular pieces within the Unreal Engine in a way that resembles the concept. *Figure 8.69* shows the modular base meshes created for the ninth set:

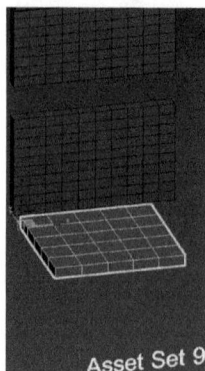

Figure 8.69: The fourth set of base mesh assets

Base mesh modeling of asset set #10

Figure 8.70 shows the assets we identified from the concept for the tenth set, which is another central set. *Figure 8.71* shows the end result:

Figure 8.70: The tenth set of assets we need to create base meshes for

The following figure shows the tenth set of base mesh assets:

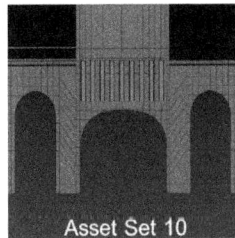

Figure 8.71: The tenth set of base mesh assets

Base mesh modeling of asset set #11

The concept reference for the eleventh set can be seen in *Figure 8.72*, while the end result is displayed in *Figure 8.73*:

Figure 8.72: The eleventh set of assets we need to create base meshes for

Once again, a comparison between *Figures 8.72* and *8.73* demonstrates how the resulting 3D geometry compares to the 2D concept, even with the creative liberties taken during the 3D modeling process:

Figure 8.73: The eleventh set of base mesh assets

Base mesh modeling of asset set #12

The twelfth set needed some additional meshes; *Figure 8.74* shows the assets we identified from the concept for this set, while *Figure 8.75* shows the resulting base mesh assets:

Figure 8.74: The twelfth set of assets we need to create base meshes for

Yet another side-by-side comparison, between 2D concept and resulting 3D object, as shown in *Figure 8.75*:

Figure 8.75: The twelfth set of base mesh assets

Base mesh modeling of asset set # 13

The thirteenth asset set also required several new meshes. *Figure 8.76* shows the assets we identified from the concept for this set:

Figure 8.76: The thirteenth set of assets we need to create base meshes for

Figures 8.77 and *Figure 8.78* show some of the assets created in the process:

Figure 8.77: A support pillar

The following figure shows another support pillar:

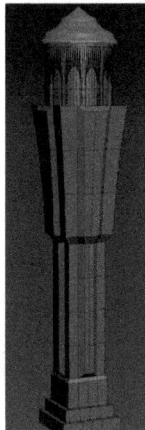

Figure 8.78: Another support pillar

Figure 8.79 shows the final result:

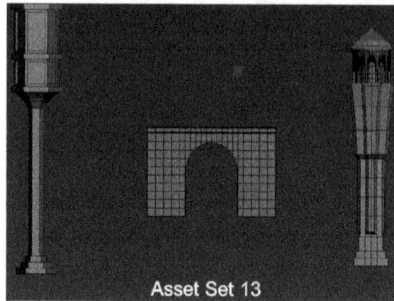

Figure 8.79: *The thirteenth set of base mesh assets*

Base mesh modeling of asset set #14

Figure 8.80 shows the assets we identified from the concept for the fourteenth set, which features some oddly shaped stairs.

Figure 8.80: *The fourteenth set of assets we need to create base meshes for*

Figure 8.81 shows the final result:

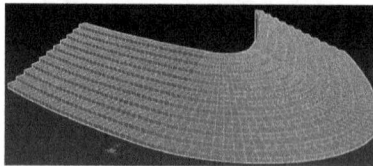

Figure 8.81: *The fourteenth set of base mesh assets, an oddly shaped staircase*

Base mesh modeling of asset set #15

Finally, *Figure 8.82* shows the assets we identified from the concept for this fifteenth and final base mesh asset set, which features floors and trims:

Figure 8.82: *The fifteenth set of assets we need to create base meshes for*

While the shape of the final base meshes does not entirely match the shapes seen in the concept, with the help of Foliage and vegetation, combined with modular mesh placement, we will achieve an identical appearance within the Unreal Engine when designing our level for the Fantasy Castle Project. *Figure 8.83* depicts the final result of this base mesh asset set:

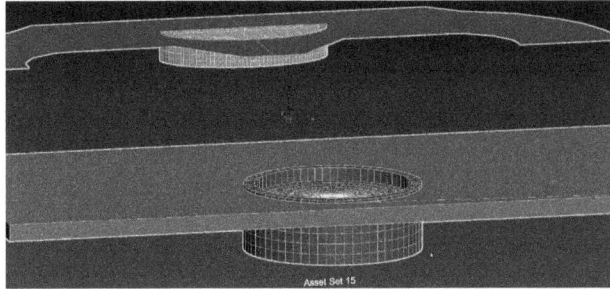

Figure 8.83: The fifteenth and final set of base mesh assets

Figure 8.84 shows the entire collection of modular base mesh assets created for the Fantasy Castle Project:

Figure 8.84: A plethora of modular base meshes!

Conclusion

While we barely went into any detail, *Chapter 8, Fantasy Castle Base Mesh Modeling,* still gives a good understanding of the logic and some of the techniques and processes an environment 3D modeler would use to create base meshes that will serve as the foundation for the higher poly and significantly more detailed versions of these meshes. Given that we are preparing these meshes for usage with Unreal Engine 5's Nanite, we did not need to be too careful with the topology and overall structure of the base meshes. Instead, we focused on getting close enough to the shapes identified (or sometimes interpreted) in the concept.

In the next chapter, *Chapter 9, Fantasy Castle High Poly Mesh Sculpting,* we will export these meshes from 3ds Max and import them into ZBrush, where we will sculpt all the details and reach millions upon millions of polygons, which then will be prepared for exporting as well as material and texture assignment, which we will perform in *Chapter 10, Fantasy Castle Texturing and Materials,* so that we can finally go back to the Unreal Engine 5 in *Chapter 11, Fantasy Castle Bringing it All in Unreal,* where we will be importing all these assets, and get to designing our level for the Fantasy Castle Project!

Points to remember

- Modularity is key when creating base meshes
- Reusing assets is important and expedites the process
- With slight modifications, reused assets will not look repetitive
- Do not get more detailed than you have to, sculpting the high poly geometry will take care of the extreme levels of detail and realism

Exercise

1. Find environment concept artwork or even photographs that inspire you, and break down the structures depicted into different asset sets, which you then proceed to create 3D base meshes for each asset set.

Join our book's Discord space

Join the book's Discord Workspace for Latest updates, Offers, Tech happenings around the world, New Release and Sessions with the Authors:

https://discord.bpbonline.com

CHAPTER 9

Fantasy Castle High Poly Mesh Sculpting

Introduction

In this chapter, we will export the basic meshes we created in *Chapter 8, Fantasy Castle Base Modeling*, and import them into ZBrush, where we will proceed with increasing their polygonal count and sculpting details onto them. This chapter is not a step-by-step tutorial for ZBrush beginners. Instead, it serves as an overview that allows readers unfamiliar with ZBrush to get a better understanding of the processes and steps taken in between an asset's concept and its realization within the Unreal Engine. For readers familiar with ZBrush, this chapter serves as a general suggested guideline to quickly yield the results needed for this project.

ZBrush is a complex and advanced application with multiple methodologies and techniques, and entire books can be written about it. Therefore, this chapter aims to only cover rather basic notions and concepts.

Structure

The format followed in this chapter:

- Exporting the base meshes
- Importing the meshes to ZBrush
- Prepping the meshes for high poly sculpting

- Prepping the meshes for symmetrical sculpting
- Ready to sculpt
- Some optimization before exporting
- Exporting from ZBrush
- Points worth noting

Objectives

By the end of this chapter, we will learn how to export base meshes and import them into ZBrush, where we will prepare them for detailed sculpting. Once sculpted, we will slightly optimize them to be able to slightly expedite our workflow and file sizes without sacrificing details and visual quality, and we will then export them for using them with Substance 3D Painter in the next chapter.

Exporting the base meshes

Continuing from where we left off in the previous chapter, now that we have all our base meshes ready, we need to prepare them and export them. Since in the previous chapter we separated our meshes into different asset sets, ideally, we want to collectively export all the assets from each set together, and sculpt them all in one file, basically treating every asset set's sculpting as a mini project.

Ideally, we want every individual asset to have a pivot point that is located at the asset center, at least in terms of X and Y coordinates (width and depth), as this will allow us to easily work with symmetry later on.

To modify the pivot point in 3ds Max, simply select the mesh you want to modify, and then select the **Hierarchy** tab (upper right corner), then select **Pivot**, as shown in *Figure 9.1*:

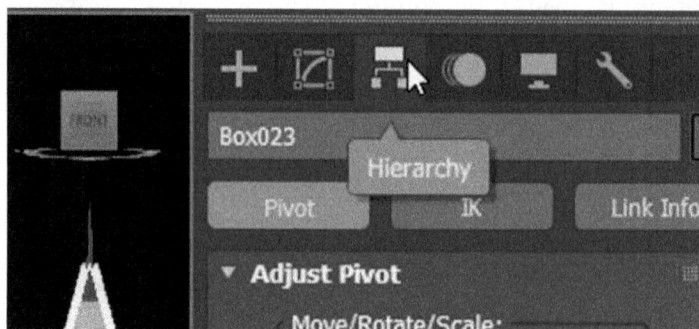

Figure 9.1: Modifying the pivot point in 3ds Max

Next, under **Adjust Pivot**, select **Affect Pivot Only** and after that, select **Center to Object**, as shown in *Figure 9.2*:

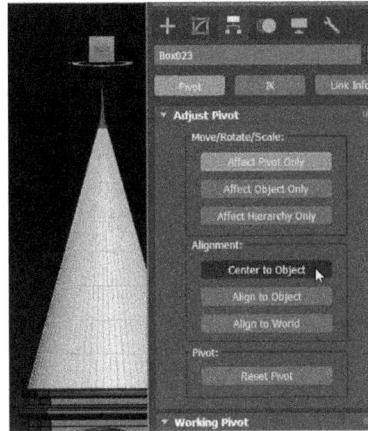

Figure 9.2: Centering the pivot point to the selected mesh's center

Then click **Affect Pivot Only** again to deselect it, and go back to the Modify tab, which is to the left of the **Hierarchy** tab.

Repeat the process for each and every mesh that belongs to an asset set until all the meshes of the asset set have their pivot points centered. Then select all of your asset sets meshes, as shown in *Figure 9.3*, and with them selected, press *W* on your keyboard to ensure you are in the move mode.

Figure 9.3: Asset set 3's meshes are all selected

At the bottom right of your screen, locate the XYZ coordinates, as shown in *Figure 9.4*, where you will set each to 0:

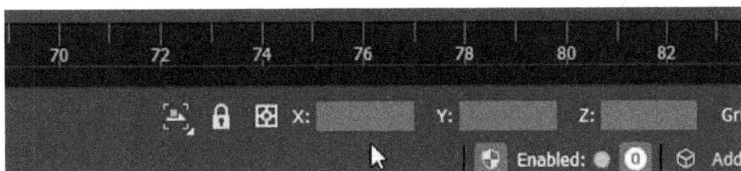

Figure 9.4: Set XYZ to 0

This results in all of the asset set's meshes being centered at the world space's origin, so now these meshes are ready to be worked in a symmetrical way. If you activate wireframe view, you can see that all of the meshes are overlapping each other, as shown in *Figure 9.5*:

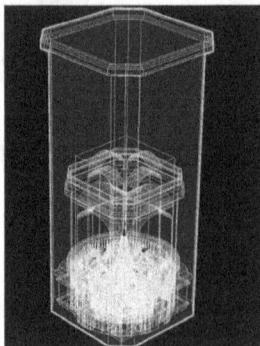

Figure 9.5: *Asset set 3's meshes are all centered and overlapping each other*

With your asset sets meshes still selected, navigate to **File**, hover over **Export,** and then click on **Export Selected**, as shown in *Figure 9.6*:

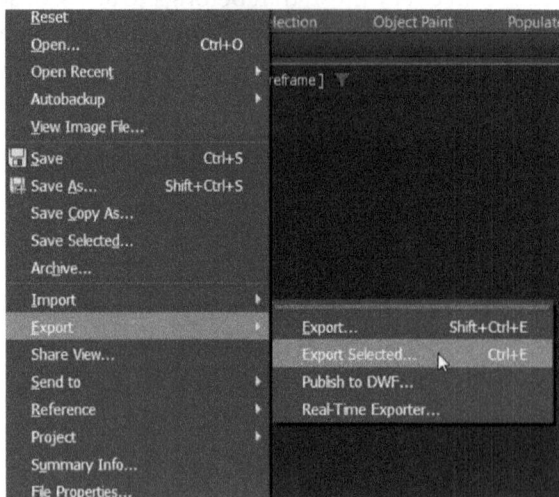

Figure 9.6: *Exporting all of the asset set's meshes*

This will result in a pop-up window, prompting you to select the location, the filename and the filetype you prefer. Choose a location easy to remember, under a folder that represents this stage of the process (e.g. **BaseMeshes** or **BaseMeshesForZBrush**) and use a name that indicates the asset set, (e.g. **AssetSet3** or **AssetPack3**), while selecting FBX as the file type to export in.

Next, you are prompted with a plethora of different export options to choose from. For this book's and project's purposes, just leave the default settings, as shown in *Figure 9.7*. Press OK:

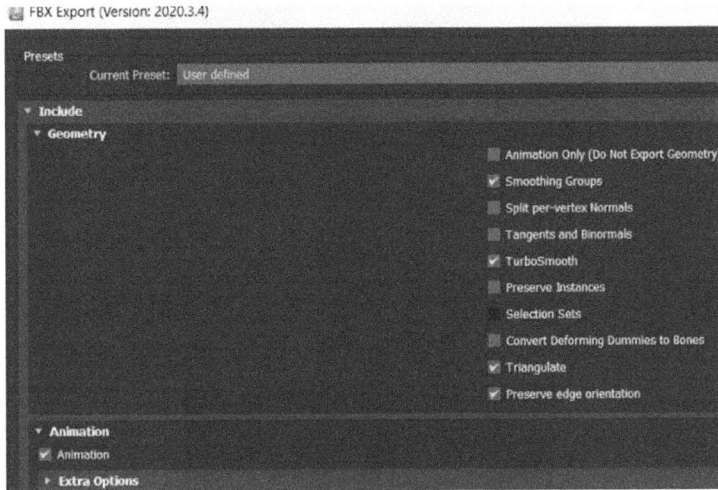

Figure 9.7: Use the default export settings

Importing the meshes to ZBrush

Next, load up ZBrush, and under **Tool** select **Import** to import the files you just exported, as shown in *Figure 9.8*. Use the default import options.

Figure 9.8: Importing into ZBrush

Once imported, click and drag/draw anywhere in the Viewport, press *T* on your keyboard to enable Edit mode, and *F* on the keyboard, to focus on the object in the Viewport.

You will notice how the assets are imported overlapped, just the way we had them in Max. But if you browse under subtool you will notice each mesh listed as an individual subtool, which is what we need for the occasion.

With any of the subtools selected (preferably the first), click on the **Solo** button, as shown in *Figure 9.9*, as this will make the selected subtool the only visible tool in your Viewport:

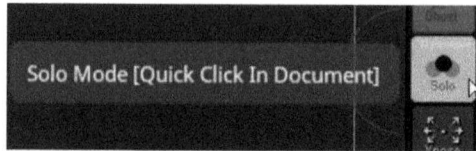

Figure 9.9: Solo Mode in ZBrush

Prepping the meshes for high poly sculpting

Next, press *Shift+F* or click the **Draw Polyframe** icon, as shown in *Figure 9.10*:

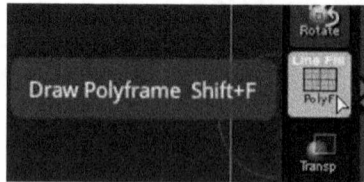

Figure 9.10: Set XYZ to 0

This will allow us to view the mesh's geometry in terms of polygons, as shown in *Figure 9.11*:

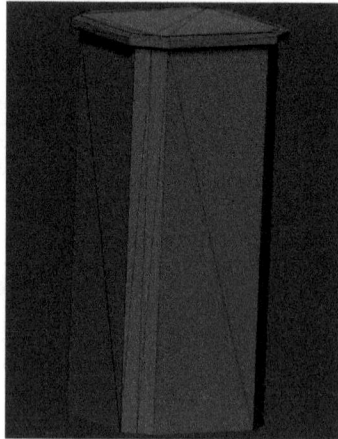

Figure 9.11: Geometry in Polyframe view mode

If we were to sculpt on this geometry as is, not only would everything look low res (low resolution), but it would also be nearly impossible since our brush would jump from one vertex to another, and there are not that many of them at this stage. That is where increasing the subdivision levels of our mesh would help, as we would increase the polycount and the number of vertices, thus allowing us to draw in more detail, yet our mesh is not ready to be divided yet. If we were to divide our mesh as is, the result would be a deformed geometry that no longer represents the shape we want, much like shown in *Figure 9.12*:

Figure 9.12: *This geometry might feature multiple subdivision levels,*
yet it is deformed and therefore unusable

So, before dividing our geometry, we will need to either **DynaMesh** it or **ZRemesh** it.
Figure 9.13 displays what happens when we **DynaMesh** our mesh at a resolution of 128:

Figure 9.13: *Our meshed DynaMeshed at a resolution of 128*

Figure 9.14 shows the same mesh **ZRemeshed** with a **Target Polygon Count 5**, with
ZRemesher Adapt mode enabled:

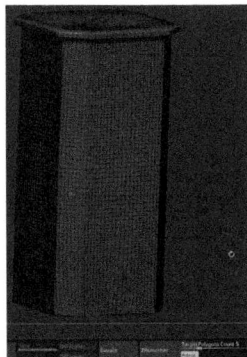

Figure 9.14: *Our mesh ZRemeshed at a target polycount of 5 with Adapt mode enabled*

As you can see, in both cases, we have a resulting geometry that is identical to what we intended, yet it features a lot more vertices and polygons, all of which are more or less uniformly distributed across the geometry, making for a good topology to work with. In this specific example, the DynaMeshed result looks better organized than the ZRemeshed result, which appears to have a few areas that stretch and slightly break off any uniformity, yet they are both workable from here on. As to which method you should use overall, it depends on the mesh you are working on, some complex geometries are responding better to one or the other, so it usually depends on each geometry. At the same time, it might be worth noting that the geometry can already be high enough before you export it from your 3D modeling application.

Traditionally, you would want a low poly, highly optimized — in terms of poly count and topology — base mesh in your 3D modeling application, one which you would already unwrap within the application (*Chapter 10, Fantasy Castle Texturing and Materials* covers the basic concept of unwrapping/UV mapping), then transfer it over to ZBrush or any other 3D sculpting application, increase its poly count to millions of polygons, sculpt it, and then export it and use the high poly mesh to derive geometrical and spatial information which is stored in flat texture maps, such as a normal map (*Chapter 10, Fantasy Castle Texturing and Materials* briefly cover those as well) and then apply those texture maps on the optimized, low poly, base mesh, which would look similar to its high poly counterpart, yet perform at considerably better framerates. With Unreal Engine 5's Nanite technology, all these time-consuming processes are beginning to change — if not even entirely eliminated — and while we still need to optimize our geometry, we do it for entirely different purposes, and in less time and effort consuming ways.

Essentially, we primarily focus on the shape of our base mesh, bring it into our sculpting application, such as ZBrush, where we modify its topology and polycount to allow us to sculpt in greater detail, only to finally export a version of the high poly mesh, that is still detailed enough, geometrically speaking, yet a bit lighter — in terms of polycount — than the ultimate version, not because Nanite has any problems handling that, but because it will be easier for us to work with. Export and import times will be shorter, file sizes will be smaller, and even Nanite's reduction methods can be very effective and result in better performing meshes. So, there are still optimizations to consider, but they are not as demanding or time-consuming as they used to be.

Back to ZBrush's DynaMesh and ZRemesh, if you wish to DynaMesh your mesh, you can find that function under **Tool**, then expand **Geometry**, expand **DynaMesh** and set the **Resolution** you want (default value is 128). The higher the resolution, the higher the polycount of the DynaMeshed geometry will be. *Figure 9.15* shows you where to find the DynaMesh function:

Figure 9.15: DynaMesh

Much like DynaMesh, the ZRemesher can also be accessed by expanding **Tool**, then expanding **Geometry**, then expanding **ZRemesher**, where you can set the desired **Target Polygon Count**. The maximum value you can enter there is 100, which indicates 100 thousand polygons are your target polycount; the default value is 5, which indicates 5 thousand polygons are your target polycount. If **Adapt** is disabled, ZBrush will try to stay as close as possible to the targeted polycount, if **Adapt** is enabled, it will interpret it as having more room to increase the polycount. *Figure 9.16* shows you where to access ZRemesher:

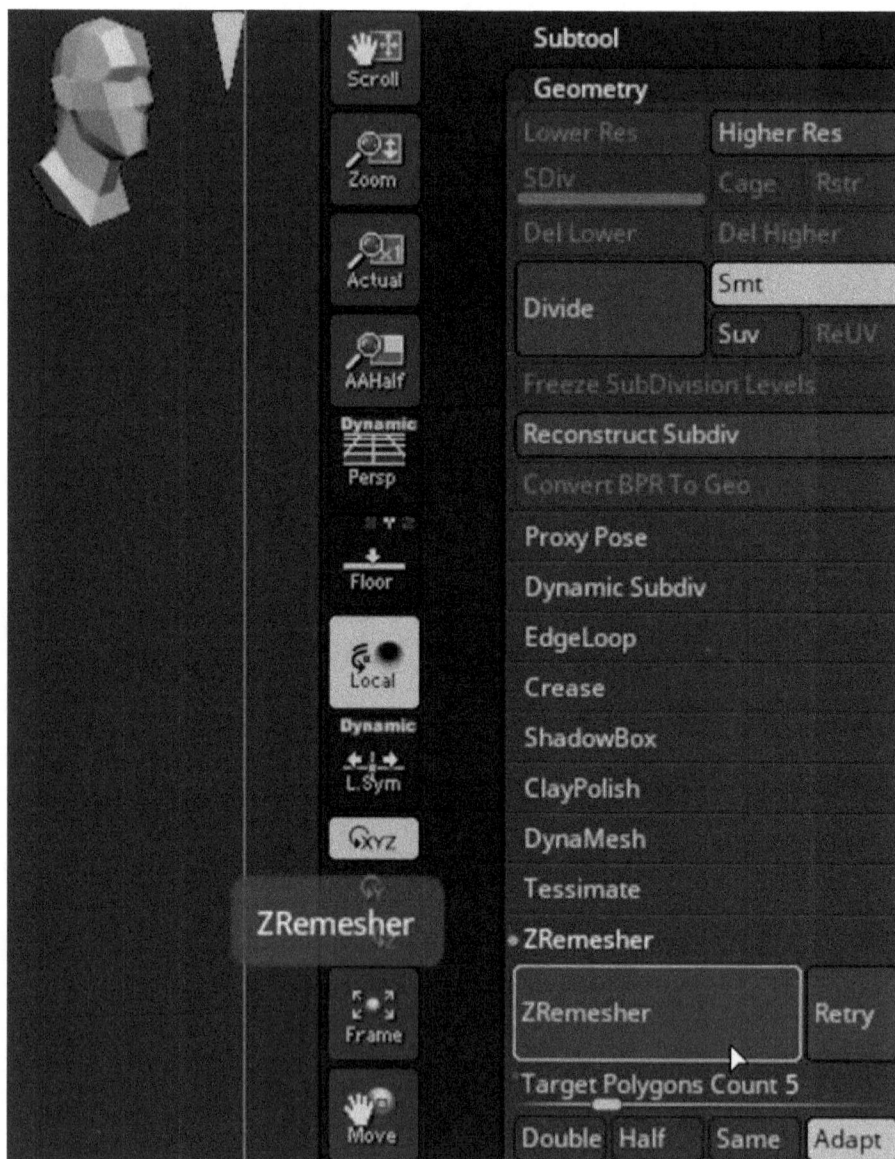

Figure 9.16: ZRemesher

Regardless of the method you choose, now you are ready to divide your mesh several times to reach millions of polygons and begin sculpting it in full detail.

To divide your mesh, navigate under **Tool**, expand **Geometry**, and click **Divide** several times till your poly count reaches at least a million polygons. You can view the poly count on the top center of your screen. Accessing **Divide** is shown in *Figure 9.17*:

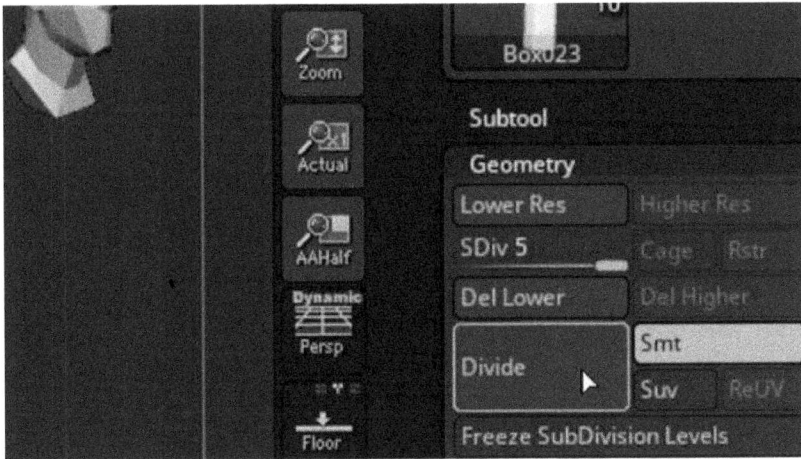

Figure 9.17: *Dividing our mesh*

Figure 9.18 shows you the polycount we reached by having divided our mesh 5 times:

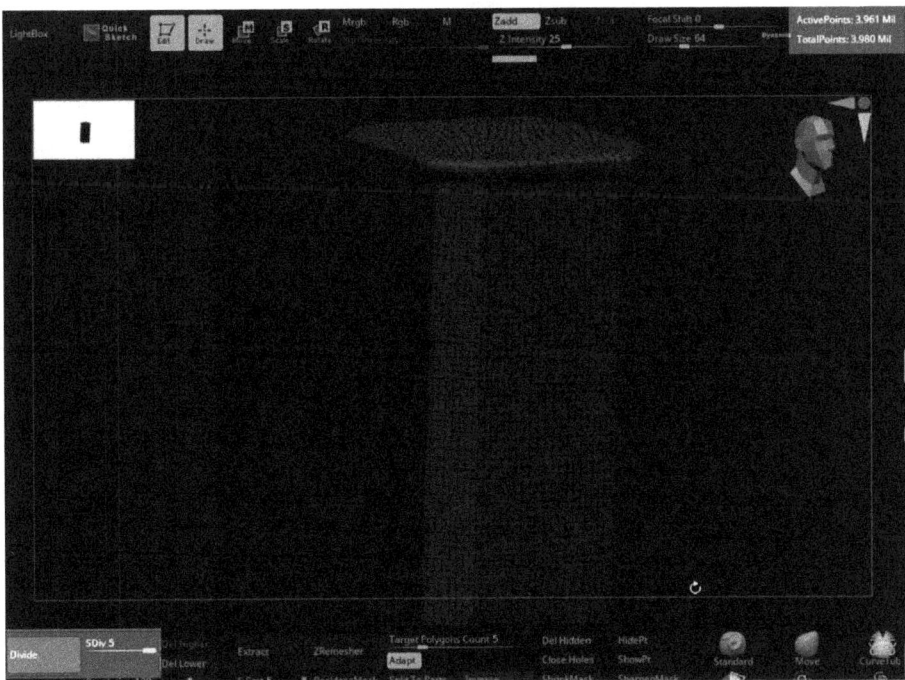

Figure 9.18: *Our mesh reached 3.9 million points (also approximately 3.9M polygons) with 5 subdivision levels (we clicked Divide five times)*

While in theory we are ready to start sculpting, there is one more little detail we need to address, which is symmetry, as symmetrical sculpting can save a lot of time and effort when sculpting.

Prepping the meshes for symmetrical sculpting

It is important to ensure we have a good symmetrical workflow, that is one of the reasons we modified pivot points in Max. With that end in mind, we want to ensure our meshes have their XYZ coordinates set to 0 in ZBrush as well, so navigate under **Tool**, then expand **Geometry**, expand **Position**, as shown in *Figure 9.19,* and set X, Y, and Z to 0:

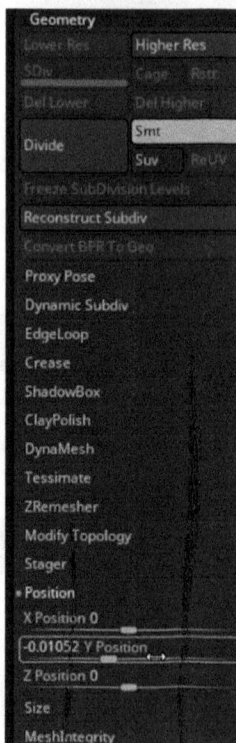

Figure 9.19: Setting XYZ coordinates to 0 in ZBrush

Next, you want to activate symmetry, either by pressing X on your keyboard or navigating under Transform to **Activate Symmetry**, as shown in *Figure 9.20:*

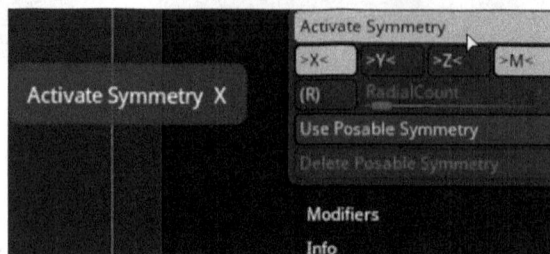

Figure 9.20: Activating Symmetry

Most of the shapes our base meshes have are symmetrical not only from left to right, but also from back to front. In this case we want to enable symmetry for both the X and the Z-axis. In ZBrush, X symmetry will enable symmetry on left and right, Y on top and bottom, Z back and front. Most of the shapes in this project can use X and Z symmetries, some only X and a few no symmetry at all.

In the example shown right now, we need X and Z activated. You will know your symmetry is enabled, by hovering over your mesh. If there is a single red dot appearing at any of the mesh's vertices, then symmetry is not enabled. If you see two dots, as shown in *Figure 9.21*, then you have enabled symmetry for one of the axis, in this case, we are looking at the X axis symmetry being active.

Figure 9.21: *Symmetry activated for X-axis*

If you add the Z-axis symmetry, then you will see four red dots, much like in *Figure 9.22:*

Figure 9.22: *Symmetry activated for X and Z-axis*

Ready to sculpt

You will need to repeat the prior steps for each subtool, for each asset set you import.

With our mesh DynaMeshed or ZRemeshed, with our subdivision levels being high enough for our geometry to range in the millions of polygons, and with our symmetry being taken care of, we are not ready to sculpt. While ZBrush, by default, comes equipped with more than enough brushes and alpha maps to allow you to sculpt virtually anything, it is also worth noting that it is a highly customizable application with a vibrant and active community, which will often release plugins, alphas, brushes and overall tools that can be downloaded for free or purchased, and incorporated in your ZBrush workflow. This will result in easier, faster and equally impressive workflows, but if you like a challenge and you have the time for it, it is always fun to perform all your sculpting with the default brushes and tools ZBrush provides. However, should you be interested in such plugins and addons, you can find them on creative websites such as *ArtStation Marketplace*, *Gumroad*, *FlippedNormals*, and more.

We briefly went over some sculpting in *Chapter 4, Project Overview and Main Asset Creation for Statue Scene*, when we worked on the Greek God Statue project. In a similar fashion, by combining different brushes, alphas, enabling/disabling symmetry, we sculpt each and every single base mesh we created in *Chapter 8, Fantasy Castle Base Mesh Modeling*. The author ended up having a total of 95 sculpted meshes for this project, which you are able to download in their final FBX format, as well as the entire Fantasy Castle Unreal Engine project, by accessing this book's resource links.

In the meantime, *Figures 9.23* to *Figure 9.29* showcase some of the sculpting work that was done by the author:

Figure 9.23: *A sculpted roof*

A sculpt of a foundation mesh can be seen in *Figure 9.24:*

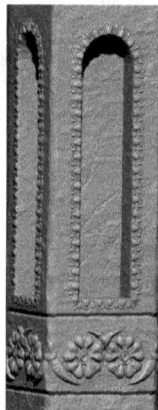

Figure 9.24: *Sculpted foundation mesh*

Figure 9.25 shows the finished sculpt of the archway mesh:

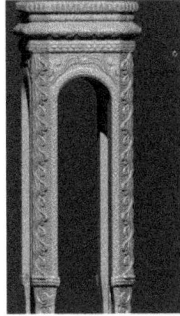

Figure 9.25: *Sculpted archway*

Figure 9.26 demonstrates the finished sculpt of the entire central dome mesh:

Figure 9.26: *The first asset set's subtools, all sculpted
and positioned to resemble the desired end result*

In *Figure 9.27*, the finished sculpt of one of the tower meshes is shown:

Figure 9.27: *Yet another asset set's subtools all sculpted and positioned in a
way that allows us to visualize the end result*

As shown in *Figure 9.28*, yet another tower mesh sculpt is completed:

Figure 9.28: Another completely sculpted asset set

Figure 9.29 showcasing the finished sculpt of one more architectural section:

Figure 9.29: Set completely sculpted

Some optimization before exporting

Once all subtools of all asset sets have been sculpted, in theory, we are ready to export them as they are, with their millions of polygons, and there is no doubt that the Unreal Engine's Nanite will be able to handle them just fine, reducing them to assets that look as good, but perform much better than one would expect. However, there are more reasons to consider besides real time performance; one of the most valuable commodities any developer has — one can argue any person has — is time!

We need to consider the time it takes to export a multimillion polycount mesh, the time it takes to import it to any other applications, as well as the time it takes for these applications to process it and perform any additional actions we might need (in *Chapter 10, Fantasy Castle Texturing and Materials* we will use Substance Painter to auto-unwrap our meshes for us) and then the time it will take these applications to re-export that mesh, just so we can ultimately import it the Unreal Engine. Multiply that by 95 times (these are the number of meshes the author sculpted for this project), and you can see why this might start becoming an issue.

At the same time, we went through all the trouble of successfully increasing our polycounts to the millions, just so we can have all this detail, so it might feel like a step back to even be discussing any polycount reduction at this point. Yet our work was not wasted. Our higher polycounts allowed us to be detailed at higher resolutions, and now we can maintain that level of detail (or close enough to it), while also reducing — not too much — our polycounts. The result will be files that are faster to work with yet detailed enough and still — by traditional game engine standards — extremely high in terms of polycounts.

To achieve this, take any subtool that is completely sculpted, and you consider finished and duplicate it. Make sure you save a backup version. For example, *Figure 9.30* shows a selected subtool from a finished asset set (specifically the same one as in *Figure 9.29*). Specifically, we selected the archway found in that set:

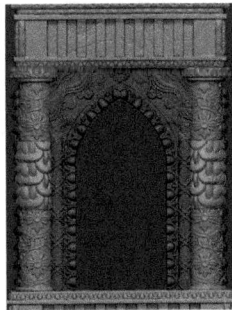

Figure 9.30: *The archway in Polyframe mode is the selected subtool from this finished asset pack or asset set if you prefer*

As we can see in *Figure 9.31*, this subtool alone clocks in at 5.2 million polygons:

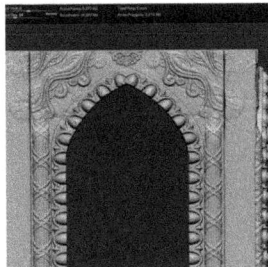

Figure 9.31: *That is a lot of polygons!*

As it stands, this subtool has three subdivision levels. The easiest way for us to reduce the polycount, would be to reduce the subdivision level. Let us take a closer look at each subdivision level's numbers:

- **Subdivision level 3**: 5.2 million polygons
- **Subdivision level 2**: 1.3 million polygons
- **Subdivision level 1**: 325 thousand polygons

Great, you might be tempted to just reduce the subdivision level and proceed with exporting the mesh, yet let us take a closer look at how the mesh looks at each subdivision level. *Figure 9.32* shows a closeup of the mesh at subdivision level 3. Looks as good as in *Figure 9.31*:

Figure 9.32: Closeup of the mesh in subdivision level 3

Figure 9.33 is a closeup of the same mesh in subdivision level 2. Note how the resolution of the details drops significantly.

Figure 9.33: Closeup of the mesh in subdivision level 2

While the point is proven and we can already see that subdivision level 2 would not look any good, let us just take a look at subdivision level 1 as well, as seen in *Figure 9.34*:

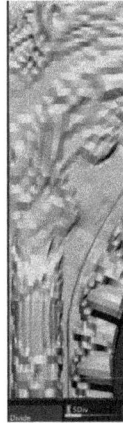

Figure 9.34: Closeup of the mesh in subdivision level 1

Clearly, dropping the subdivision level alone would not be enough. Theoretically, we could duplicate the subtool (which we did), drop the subdivision layer, and then use a function ZBrush has to transfer details from a higher poly mesh to a lower one. This function is the Project All function, but in this case, this would not make much of a difference. We could also use DynaMesh and drop the resolution or ZRemesher, which will give us significantly fewer polycounts, but again, all that at the cost of the level of detail.

Instead, we will take advantage of ZBrush's powerful **Decimation Master** plugin! You can access the **Decimation Master** under **Zplugin**, expand **Decimation Master**, and with the subtool we want to optimize selected, click on **Pre-process Current**, as shown in *Figure 9.35*:

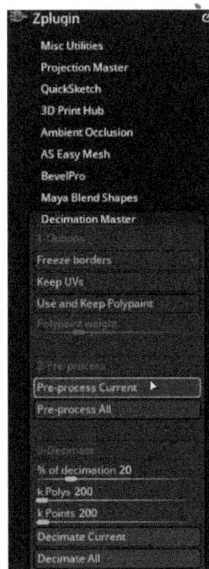

Figure 9.35: Click Pre-process Current under the Decimation Master plugin

After you have pressed Pre-process Current, be patient and give ZBrush some time to perform its calculations. You can see its progress on the top of your screen, as shown in *Figure 9.36*:

Figure 9.36: The Decimation Master pre-processing your current mesh, evidently at 5% at the time this screenshot was taken

Once it is complete, once again, on top of your screen you will be able to see a notification, as shown in *Figure 9.37*:

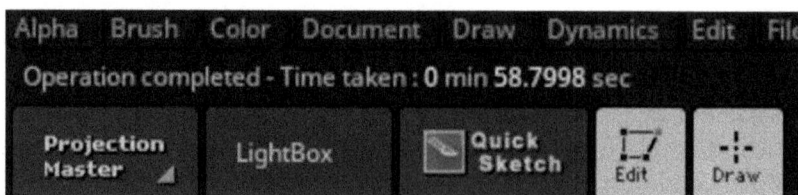

Figure 9.37: The Decimation Master pre-processing is complete, and in this case ZBrush informs us it took almost a minute

Once the pre-processing is done, let us set the % **of decimation** to **10**. That means we will reduce the total polycount to approximately 10% of the current polycount. So, if the original high poly mesh was at 100 polygons, the resulting mesh would be reduced to a total of 10 polygons! Once you have set the percentage to 10, click **Decimate Current** as shown in *Figure 9.38*:

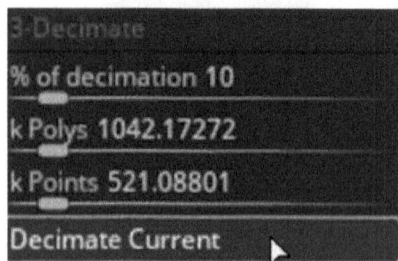

Figure 9.38: Decimating the current mesh to 10% of its total polycount

This should be a much faster process than **Pre-process Current** was. We started with a 5.2 million polycount mesh, and now we reduced it to 1 million polygons (which is not exactly tenth of our original count, but the reduction has been achieved), and the end result can be seen in *Figure 9.39*:

Figure 9.39: Dropping from 5.2M to 1M polygons, yet it looks identical to the higher poly version

As it can be seen, the decimation master successfully reduced the polycount — significantly, one might add — and yet retained the same level of detail. Let us repeat the process and try to reduce it a bit further. After all, as long as we retain the visual detail, we should not mind further polygon reductions. We **Pre-process Current** again, and once more, we decimate the current mesh to 10% of its value. The resulting mesh is indeed in the 100K poly range, which is a tenth of what we started with, yet, upon closer inspection, it looks like we lost a lot of detail, as seen in *Figure 9.40*:

Figure 9.40: Dropping from 1M to 104K polygons, this time, we can see the quality drop as our triangulated polygons stick out more

The Decimation Master triangulates the mesh, meaning instead, it changes it from a quad-based polygonal mesh to a triangle-based mesh (*Figure 9.41* shows the difference between the two), and we can see that the triangles are looking ugly with this last decimation.

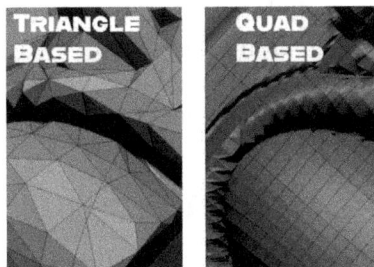

Figure 9.41: On the left side, you can see the triangulated version of a mesh, on the right side, the quad based version of the same mesh

Let us undo the last decimation, and instead of decimating it to 10%, let us try a higher value, like 50%, for example. *Figure 9.42* shows the result of that reduction:

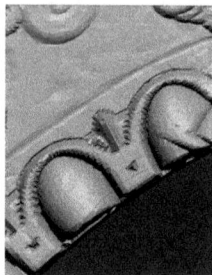

Figure 9.42: Dropping from 1M to 500K polygons, the quality drop is still noticeable from up close

If we zoom in close enough, we can see that the quality has been reduced — when compared to the high poly version we started with — however, it is considerably better than the last attempt we had a few pages earlier. Most of these meshes will be seen at a distance, so zooming out might give us a better perspective and allow us to make a more objective decision as to whether it is worth saving a bit of time and exporting this version or investing more time and exporting the higher quality version. *Figure 9.43* shows the zoomed-out version of the decimated mesh:

Figure 9.43: Zoomed out screenshot of the 500K polygon version of this mesh

From a distance, it looks like it might be serving the intents and purposes we have in mind. Ultimately, it is entirely up to the artist, or the reader in this case, to decide how much they wish to compromise quality in favor of time or the other way around. For what it is worth, the author tried to keep all meshes within — approximately — the 400K-1M polycount range, with some exceptions being considerably lower since, ultimately, it all depends on each individual mesh and the level of complexity it comes with.

Exporting from ZBrush

Once you are happy with your polygonal optimization's results, you are ready to export each subtool. With the finalized subtool selected, navigate to **Tool** and then select **Export**, as shown in *Figure 9.44*:

Figure 9.44: Exporting from ZBrush

You will want to export in FBX format, without overwriting any existing FBX files that we originally imported in ZBrush. Save it in an appropriately named folder, such as **/HighPoly/AssetPack1/**, for example, or anything else that will facilitate your workflow, and use a filename that allows you to easily keep track of the assets in each asset pack. For this stage, the author's naming convention was simple, such as **AP1_1.fbx**, where AP1 stands for asset pack 1, and _1 stands for the first subtool of the first asset pack. Once you have selected the location you want to export to, the filename you want, and the FBX filetype, you will be prompted with a window that looks like the one in *Figure 9.45*. Use the same settings as in *Figure 9.45*:

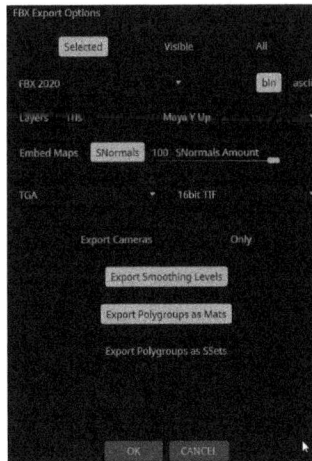

Figure 9.45: Use these export settings for this project

Repeat this process for all of the meshes (again, in the author's case, there were 95 total meshes), and you are ready to proceed to *Chapter 10*, where we will be texturing these assets, among other things.

Points worth noting

For the purposes of this book, the author tried to keep the workflow as simple as possible while still getting great visual results in the end. As stated often in various parts of this book, the book's main focus is the Unreal Engine, specifically the 5th generation, but due to the nature of the workflow, the author deemed it necessary to include some chapters, such as this one, that serve as a brief overview to the readers unfamiliar with some of these applications and methodologies mentioned in here, or as a quick suggestion to readers who are familiar with these applications. With that said, there are more advanced ways to get even more detailed and thorough and further optimize all assets, for example, using polygroups to assign multiple Materials to one mesh, or ensuring a near-perfect topology that makes high-resolution sculpting very smooth and very efficient, among many, many other techniques, which one could write books upon books on them. Doing that would go beyond this book's scope.

Hopefully, all the chapters that are not strictly related to the Unreal Engine, have, at the very least, stimulated your interest in these other applications, helped you polish up some old and possibly forgotten skills or processes, or at least given you a better understanding of the amount of work it takes to create even a single asset from nothing to a fully realized product within a gaming engine, specifically the Unreal Engine 5 in this case.

Conclusion

We modified our base meshes' pivot points, by placing them to each mesh's center, allowing us to easily move these meshes in 3D space, but most importantly, allowing us to prepare the ground for symmetrical sculpting. We then proceeded to export the base meshes from our 3D modeling application and import them into ZBrush, where we optimized them and prepared them for high poly sculpting. After that, we focused on optimizing the sculpted mesh, by decimating its polycounts while still retaining a close enough level of detail for the purpose of expediting our workflow. Lastly, we exported these files, and now we are ready to move on to the next chapter.

In *Chapter 10, Fantasy Castle Texturing and Materials*, we will be importing the meshes we just exported into Adobe's Substance Painter, where we will have the application unwrap them for us, and then we will play around with the application's existing Materials, modify them and achieve a visual result that resembles our concept, only to finally export it all and allow us to proceed to *Chapter 11, Fantasy Castle Bringing it All in Unreal*, where we will finally resume our workflow in the Unreal Engine!

Once again, the files to be imported to the Unreal Engine, as well as the Unreal Engine project itself (with all its files) are available through this book's accompanying, downloadable resources.

Points to remember

- Address a mesh's pivot point early on, it will help with symmetrical sculpting, as well as mesh manipulation later on, in the Unreal Engine.

- When importing the base mesh in ZBrush, we first need to make some optimizations before we can begin sculpting, such as:

  o Modify its topology

  o Divide it and get multiple subdivision levels, ensuring we have a polygonal count that ranges in the millions

  o Ensuring the mesh is positioned at XYZ coordinates set to 0, allowing us a smooth symmetrical sculpting experience

- External plugins, brushes, alpha masks and other tools can significantly improve your ZBrush experience and overall workflow, they can be purchased or sometimes downloaded freely at websites such as:

  o Artstation

  o Gumroad

  o FlippedNormals

- Using ZBrush's Decimation Master plugin can help significantly reduced final polycount, while retaining same level of detail.

- Reducing the final polycount, without sacrificing much of the quality leads to saving a lot of time between file exports, imports and other processes, which counts more when one needs to work with a large number of assets.

Exercise

1. Sculpt your own meshes, or import existing ones, and try modifying their topology with either DynaMesh or ZRemesher, then increase they subdivision levels, sculpt them to your liking, and finally experiment with the Decimation Master, to get the lowest possible polygon count, while retaining the level of detail, to the highest polycount version of your mesh.

Join our book's Discord space

Join the book's Discord Workspace for Latest updates, Offers, Tech happenings around the world, New Release and Sessions with the Authors:

https://discord.bpbonline.com

CHAPTER 10

Fantasy Castle Texturing and Materials

Introduction

In this chapter, we go through the texturing process. We take the high poly meshes we sculpted and exported from ZBrush in *Chapter 9, Fantasy Castle High Poly Mesh Sculpting*, import them in Substance Painter, and quickly assign textures and Materials while modifying them to resemble our concept.

Substance Painter is an advanced tool, belonging to *Adobe* and part of a complete toolset that overall focuses on material shader development. While it significantly makes material shader creation easier and better, it is also a rather advanced and complex tool for which an entire book — or even a series of books could be written. As such this chapter's intention is not to teach you Substance Painter but instead give you a very brief overview that barely scratches the surface.

If you have used Substance Painter before, the processes described in this chapter will be familiar and easy to follow. If you have not used the application before, treat this chapter as an informative overview instead that gives you a deeper insight into the overall asset production pipeline, from concept to realization. As a reminder, we followed a similar workflow in this book's earlier Greek God Statue project.

Additionally, in this chapter, we will take a brief look at different options for unwrapping our meshes, and finally, we will discuss the file organization and preparation prior to transferring all the resulting resources to the Unreal Engine.

Structure

The topics covered in this chapter:

- UV mapping and unwrapping
- Importing the high poly meshes in Substance Painter
- Baking the mesh
- Applying Materials and smart Materials
- Beige stone-like material
- Wear and tear/dirt material
- Gold material
- Rooftop material
- Exporting and organizing your files
- 3D model in FBX format

Objectives

By the end of this chapter, we will understand the basic concepts of generating the textures and geometry needed for finally importing to the Unreal Engine, specifically through the usage of Adobe's Substance Painter.

UV mapping and unwrapping

Before getting into creating the texture assets we will need for the material shaders for our assets, we need to get a basic understanding of the notion of UV mapping. In essence, UV mapping is the flattened, 2D version of a 3D object. Imagine you have a primitive cylindrical shape, for example, and you want to flatten it so you can easily write or paint on it. Ideally, you would want to cut the cylinder's top and bottom circular surfaces — provided the cylinder is closed — and then cut a vertical line in the remaining geometry, allowing you to unfold it or, more precisely, unwrap it. The end result would be two flat circles and a flat rectangle. *Figure 10.1* successfully demonstrates this example:

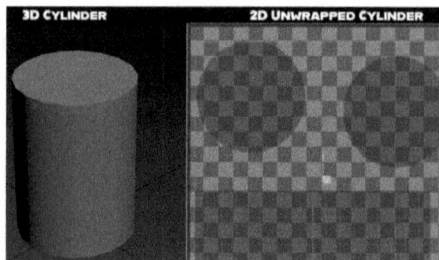

Figure 10.1: On the left side, there is a 3D cylinder, on the right side there is an unwrapped, 2D representation of the same object

The process of flattening a 3D object to a 2D representation is, in essence, the process of unwrapping, and the flat representation is our UV map. U and V represent the two-dimensional coordinates of the object's 2D map. The purpose of this process is to allow an artist to draw or create textures that will then be used in a material shader that is applied to the 3D object. While the concept is simple, unwrapping a 3D object can be quite complex, and there are several factors to consider, such as the resolution of the resulting map, the pixel density and distribution over the flat surface, ensuring that textures do not apply too stretched or compressed, or pixelated and blurred. At the same time, the more complex the 3D object, the more complex the unwrapping and resulting maps will be, often requiring several maps for one object, depending on the level of detail desired.

In addition to the above factors, generally speaking, we want UV maps to be densely populated with the 2D representations of the 3D object's surfaces (these 2D representations are referred to as UV islands within the map, in *Figure 10.1* the red circles and rectangle are our UV islands). It is also important to keep UV islands as seamless as possible to ensure better continuity of the 3D object's overall visual appearance.

There are many ways and tools to unwrap a 3D object, and ultimately it is up to the artist's discretion to use a tool and method they are most comfortable with, as long as they adhere to the general conditions that make for a good quality UV map.

In this book's project's alone, with the tools utilized within, we have four different ways to unwrap our 3D assets. More specifically:

- Unwrapping the base mesh in a 3D modelling application (3ds Max in this book's case)
- Unwrapping the 3D mesh in ZBrush
- Unwrapping the 3D mesh in Substance Painter
- Unwrapping the 3D mesh in the Unreal Engine

The first option would require a lot more manual contribution from the artist, while the latter three allow for fully automated solutions. By bearing that in mind, automated solutions are excellent for expediency purposes, yet they can yield errors and undesirable artifacts. Therefore, they are generally best combined with at least a partial manual contribution in the overall unwrapping process. However, as technologies advance, automated unwrapping tools are becoming increasingly good and efficient, and undoubtedly, with AI's introduction in the production pipeline, manual unwrapping will — most likely — soon become an obsolete process.

For this book's purposes, given the large number of assets needed for the project, the author needed to prioritize expediency. Therefore, all unwrapping was done automatically in Substance Painter.

Importing the high poly meshes in Substance Painter

In the previous chapter, we went over the steps of preparing and exporting our sculpted meshes from ZBrush. We will now import them in Adobe's Substance Painter, and we will ensure that while the mesh imports, Painter also unwraps it for us. We will be following the same process for each and every 3D model we created in the previous two chapters.

While in Substance Painter, we start a new project (*Ctrl + N*), and we are greeted with a **New project** dialogue with several options within. The first item we need to address is the **Template** we want to use, which is none other than the one that corresponds to Unreal Engine projects, as seen in *Figure 10.2*. Press and select **Unreal Engine 4 (starter_ assets)** from the available drop-down menu. Do not let the template's name confuse you; it simply ensures that the resulting textures are compatible with the desired platform's overall material shader options; in this case, Unreal Engine 4 and Unreal Engine 5 can use the same texture types, to the same end. More specifically, we will be generating 3 texture maps per object, which are:

- **Base color**: This texture map features the basic color information of our object.

- **Normal**: this texture map features any bump and dent information that is not part of the actual 3D geometry, instead it is faked through the 2D map. Since we will be using the Unreal Engine 5's Nanite in combination with highly detailed 3D meshes, we do not necessarily need to fake any geometry. However, some of the Materials we are using might have details, such as pores or perforations which we did not originally sculpt, yet we might still want to have them in the final product.

- **Occlusion, roughness, metallic (ORM) map**: essentially this is three different maps condensed into one. Each of our texture maps features an RGB channel structure, more specifically, a red channel, a green channel, and a blue channel. With ORM maps, we take advantage of the 3 different channels to store three maps into one, which allows us to save performance, since we reduce three texture maps into a single one, resulting not only in better rendering performance, but also smaller overall file size. As a result, the red channel features the map's occlusion map, which represents the amount of exposure a surface has to ambient lighting. The green channel features the roughness map, which, in simple words, defines how reflective our material will be. The roughness values can range from 0 to 1, or black to white, with 0/black resulting in a mirror-like reflection of our surface, 1/white resulting in a non-reflective, opaque material. As a reminder, we discussed this concept in this book's earlier chapters, when we were creating material shaders within the Unreal Engine. Lastly, the blue channel stores the metallic map, which dictates how metallic our material shader is. A value of 0 will result in a material that does not have any metallic appearance at all, while a value of 1 will result in a material that features a full metallic appearance.

Back to Substance Painter's New Project dialogue, now that we set our desired template let us ensure we also have the desired project settings.

Firstly, click the **Select…** button, and locate the FBX file of the asset you wish to import (in this case, we want to import an asset we just exported from ZBrush in *Chapter 9, Fantasy Castle High Poly Mesh Sculpting*).

For this book's purposes, we will set the **Document Resolution** to **2048**, as shown in *Figure 10.2*; however, the higher the resolution, the better the visual quality will be, but also, the more performance will be demanded from our hardware. We leave the rest of the project settings as shown in *Figure 10.2*.

Next, we ensure that in the **Import Settings**, **Auto-unwrap** is checked, as shown in *Figure 10.2*.

We are ready to press **OK**.

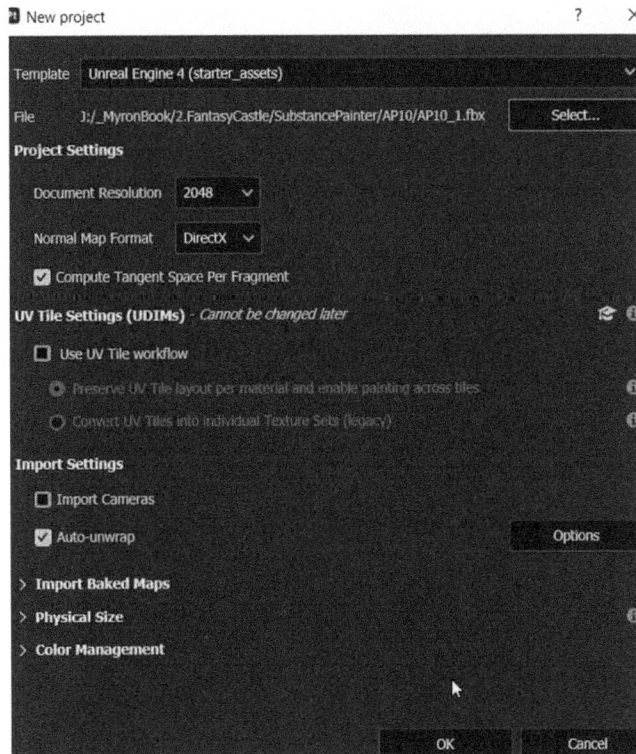

Figure 10.2: *Substance Painter's New project dialogue box*

Since the geometry we are importing is tens and hundreds of thousands of polygons, be patient and give Substance Painter plenty of time to unwrap it.

Once the model is done being imported, you will see it in your Viewport, untextured and plain, as shown in *Figure 10.3*:

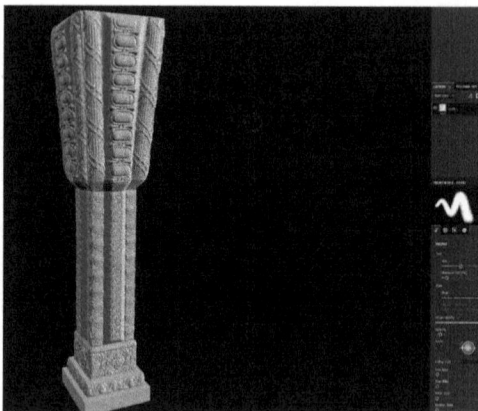

Figure 10.3: An example of a freshly imported mesh

Baking the mesh

Before applying any Materials to our freshly imported mesh, we first need to ensure it is baked, which basically allows Substance Painter to calculate the mesh's geometry so that the Materials applied to it are fully taking advantage of it, as well as its interaction with ambient light. This process will result in a much better end product, visually speaking. To bake the mesh, press *F8*, which will take you to a screen similar to the one seen in *Figure 10.4*:

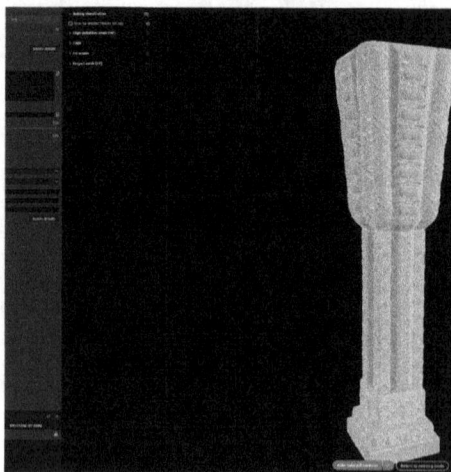

Figure 10.4: The baking screen we got here by pressing F8

There are a lot of different settings to be tinkered with here, but we will keep it simple for this book's scope. Leave everything at default, instead focus on the **Output Size**, which we will be setting to 4096, as shown in *Figure 10.5*. We will do the same for every time we repeat this process, for every single mesh we export from ZBrush.

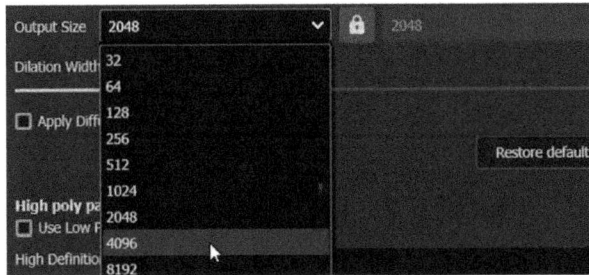

Figure 10.5: *Setting the output size to 4096*

Ready to bake the mesh now, press the **Bake selected textures** button at the bottom center of the screen, as shown in *Figure 10.6*:

Figure 10.6: *Bake selected textures button*

Once you have pressed the bake button, give the application some time to conduct the process. Once it is complete, you can press the **Return to painting mode** button, which is located right next to the **Bake selected textures** button. You will now notice that your 3D model has stronger accents in the shadows it casts upon itself, accentuating its crevices significantly more than before.

Applying Materials and smart Materials

Now, we can begin applying Materials to our model. We can use the application's included Materials. However, if you happen to be a Substance Painter user who is also proficient with Substance Designer, or you have acquired custom Materials, by all means, do not restrict yourself to the default ones. The most important aspect of the material assignment process is to use Materials or manipulate Materials that ultimately will somewhat resemble the ones our concept art features. It is not necessary to be extremely strict with this process. Sometimes, while assigning Materials, one might accidentally achieve a visual result that is far more interesting than the original concept, other times, the concept itself can be too vague about the Materials found throughout its depicted objects, therefore allowing plenty of room for creative interpretation. Yet there are times, more often than not, when a concept is highly detailed, with the concept artists going as far as specifically describing Materials and elements used in different objects within their art, thus not leaving much room for creative freedom or interpretation. For this project, we do not need to be too strict with ourselves, there is plenty of room for creative freedom and interpretation, but we will still try to adhere to the concept closely enough.

Prior to experimenting with different Materials, it is a good idea to look once again at the concept and identify repeating Materials, much like we did for the geometry in *Chapters 7"Fantasy Castle Project Breakdown and Planning"* and *Chapter 8" Fantasy Castle Base Mesh Modeling.*

By looking at the concept, we can identify the following four repeating Materials:

- A seemingly beige, stone-like material, available in different shades, appearing to be the foundation of the entire structure.

- A touch of wear and tear to make the structure's Materials more realistic.

- Gold or copper is used throughout the structure's decorative elements and ornamentation.

- A blue/light blue, almost topaz-like material, scarcely seen, mainly found on rooftop elements.

Now that we have identified the four main Materials we will be reusing, we simply need to find a way to achieve them within the application.

Beige stone-like material

By default, on the left upper-hand side of your screen, you can see the application's asset library. Navigate to the **Materials** tab, and in the search dialogue box, type in **concrete**, as shown in *Figure 10.7*, then press the *Enter* key:

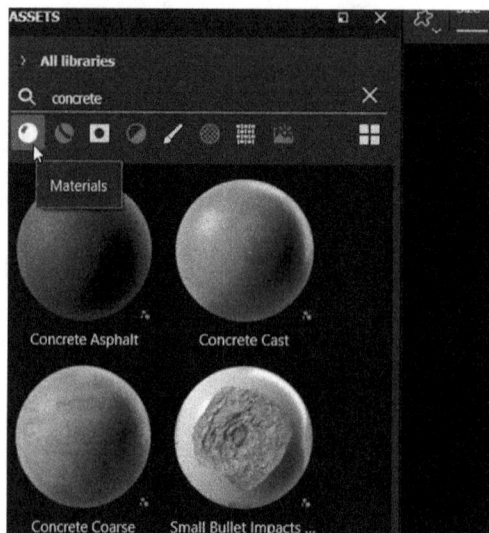

Figure 10.7: Searching for concrete in the Materials tab of Substance Painter's asset library

Click and drag the **Concrete Cast** material onto the 3D model in the Viewport, as shown in *Figure 10.8*:

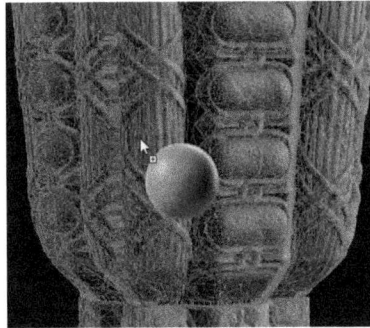

Figure 10.8: Click and dragging Concrete Cast onto our mesh

The first thing to notice is that the mesh indeed looks like it has concrete, which is normally gray, and not beige as we need it to be. That can be changed by navigating to the right-hand side of the screen, under the **LAYERS** tab, and selecting the layer with the **Concrete Cast** material, as shown in *Figure 10.9*:

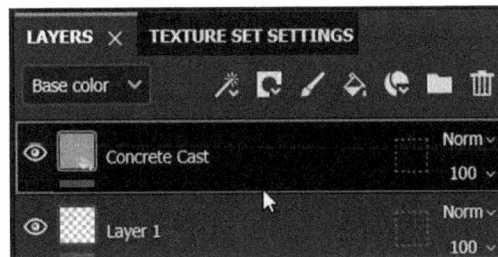

Figure 10.9: Ensure the Concrete Cast layer is selected

With the **Concrete Cast** layer selected, scroll down its properties, and under **Parameters** find the **Concrete Color** parameter, as shown in *Figure 10.10*:

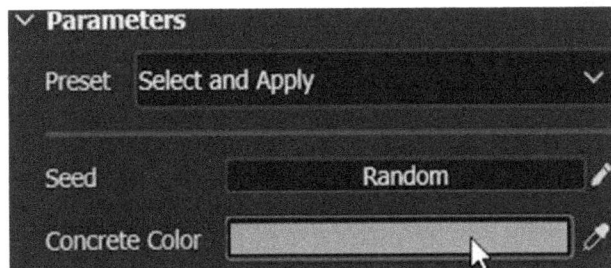

Figure 10.10: The Concrete Color parameter

Click on the color within the rectangular box, and a new window pops up, much like in *Figure 10.11*:

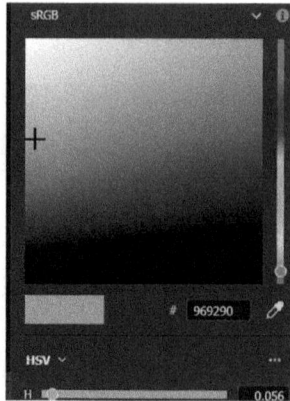

Figure 10.11: *A new window pops up, allowing us to select a new color*

You can now select any color you want, but if you desire to use the same color the author used, simply type this value in the # box: **AA917B**, as shown in *Figure 10.12*, which results in a shade of beige:

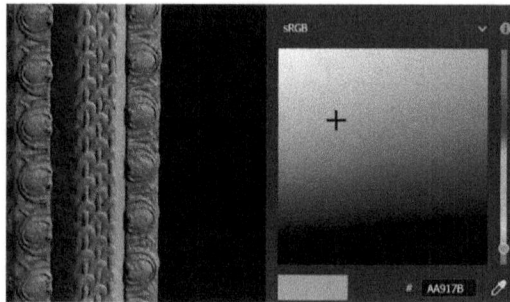

Figure 10.12: *AA917B is the hexadecimal value that can give us a shade of beige for the concrete material*

Going back to the left-hand side, under the Smart Materials tab in the asset library, we search for **jade** in the search box, as shown in *Figure 10.13*, and once more, click and drag this material on the 3D model in the Viewport:

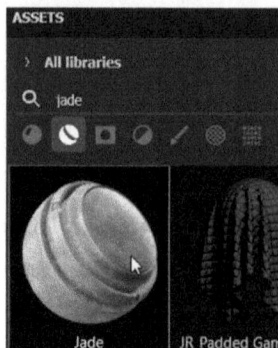

Figure 10.13: *Searching for a jade material under the Smart Materials tab*

Like before, on the right-hand side, under the **LAYERS** tab, ensure your **Jade** material layer is selected. This time, you will notice there is a small icon folder on the material layer name's left side, as shown in *Figure 10.14*, click on it to expand the layer:

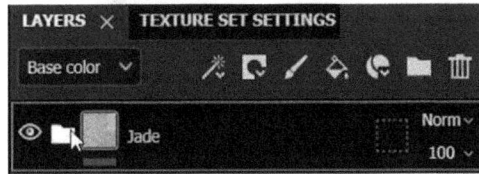

Figure 10.14: Click on the little folder icon to expand the Jade layer

Next, scroll all the way down to this layer's expanded folder until you find **Base**, as shown in *Figure 10.15*:

Figure 10.15: Scroll all the way down till you find and click on Base under the expanded jade material layer

By clicking on **Base** you can now access its properties, where you can find the **Base color** parameter, as shown in *Figure 10.16*, and click on the green (which is the default color for this material) rectangular to change the color once again, by using the hexadecimal value of AA917B:

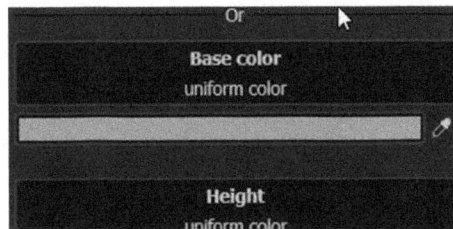

Figure 10.16: Click the green colored rectangle under Base color and modify its hexadecimal value to AA917B, as previously shown in Figure 10.12

Next, scroll up in the **LAYERS** tab, and click once again on the little folder icon next to the **Jade** layer, to collapse the layer. To the layer name's right, you will notice the word **Norm** and the value **100**, as shown in *Figure 10.17*. The numerical value represents the layer's opacity, which is by default set to 100.

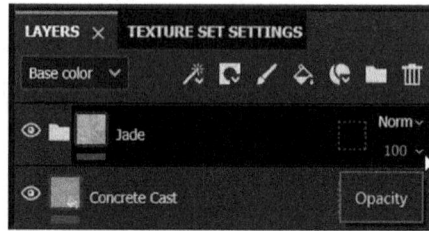

Figure 10.17: Click on the 100 under Norm in the Jade layer

Click on it and set it to 50, as shown in *Figure 10.18*:

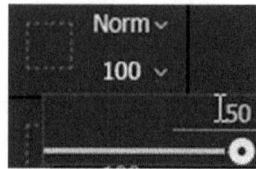

Figure 10.18: Set the opacity layer to 50

That concludes the steps we will be taking to assign the base foundation material to all the structural meshes that need this type of material. Meshes such as walls, archways, pillars, essentially all of them except the rooftops, and any meshes we decide we want to be fully golden, are all going to be using this material combination.

Wear and tear/dirt material

Back to the asset library's smart material tab, we type **dirt** in the search box and click and drag onto the 3D mesh. The dirt material shown in *Figure 10.19*:

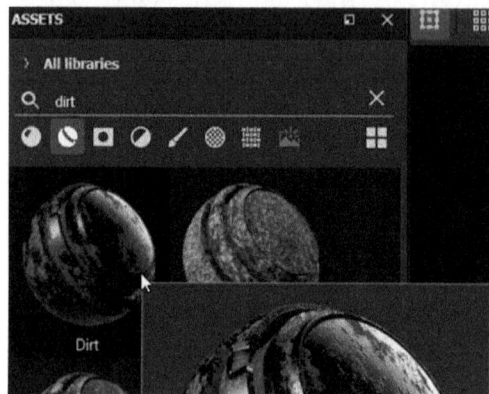

Figure 10.19: Adding dirt

The 3D model looks quite dirty now, a bit more than we would like it to. What we want to achieve with this layer is to have it behave realistically. Preferably, we want it to be found in the geometry's crevices, occasionally bleeding through to more surfaces without being overdone. To achieve this, navigate back to the asset library's **Smart masks** tab while still having `dirt` in the search box, as shown in *Figure 10.20*:

Figure 10.20: Navigating to Smart masks

Now select, click, and drag the **Dirt Cavities** smart mask shown in *Figure 10.21*:

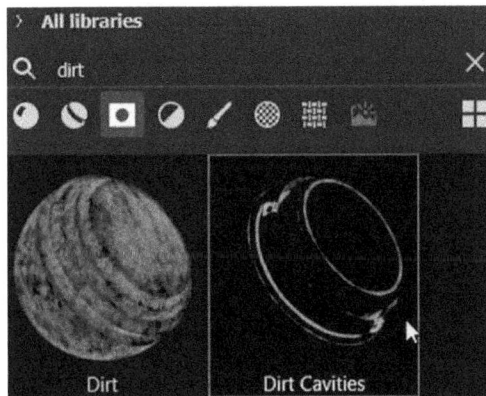

Figure 10.21: Selecting the Dirt Cavities smart mask

Place it on the little empty square that appears in the **Dirt** layer in the **LAYERS** tab, as shown in *Figure 10.22*:

Figure 10.22: Applying the Dirt Cavities smart mask to the Dirt layer

Click on the **Mask Builder** row that appears under the dirt layer, as shown in *Figure 10.23*:

Figure 10.23: Clicking the Mask Builder under the dirt layer

Scroll down its properties, and under **Parameters** adjust the values of **Level** and **Contrast**, as shown in *Figure 10.24*. Adjust the **Level** value to 0.68 and the **Contrast** value to 0.34:

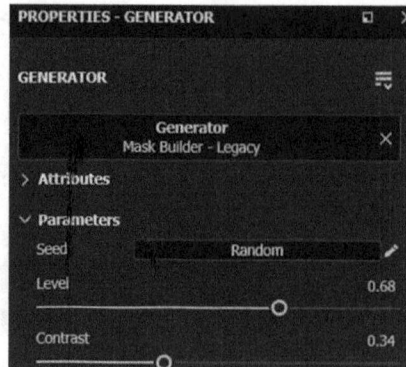

Figure 10.24: Set Level to 0.68 and Contrast to 0.34

This action will ensure the dirt looks more realistic; example shown in *Figure 10.25*:

Figure 10.25: Dirt now looks more realistic

Figure 10.26 shows how over the top dirt filters can sometimes appear on a mesh:

Figure 10.26: *Dirt overpowering the material before applying the smart mask*

The values we set for Level and Contrast do not necessarily have to be the same for every mesh. Every mesh's geometry will react differently to the smart layers and the smart masks, so adjust according to the visual results that best appeal to your creative vision.

Gold material

Many of the 3D models we created, will be needing a slight touch of gold. Others will be entirely made out of gold. In either case, gold seems to be a rather present material in the overall composition, mostly without overpowering the other Materials.

Like earlier before, navigate back to the smart Materials tab under the asset library, and this time type **gold damaged** in the search box. We want the gold to be shiny, but not too shiny, as it needs to appear used. *Figure 10.27* shows the smart material we want to be using next:

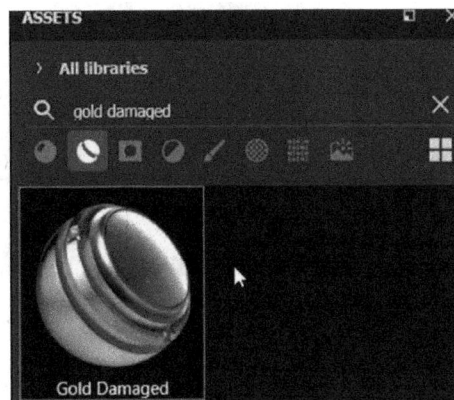

Figure 10.27: *The Gold Damaged smart material*

As before, click and drag it onto the 3D model in the Viewport. By default, it will overpower all the other Materials, as shown in *Figure 10.28*:

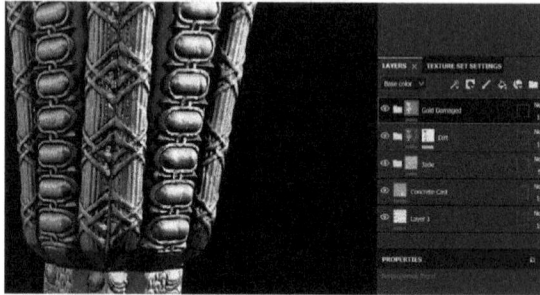

Figure 10.28: The gold material overpowering the other Materials

Much like before, a smart mask can help us tame the overpowering gold material. Back in the asset library's smart mask tab, search for **edges uber**, as shown in *Figure 10.29*:

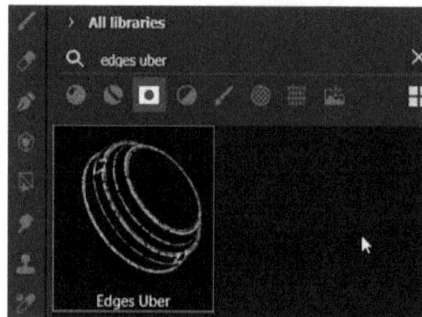

Figure 10.29: Edges Uber is the smart mask that will tame the gold material

Click and drag the **Edges Uber** smart mask onto the gold material's layer, as shown in *Figure 10.30*:

Figure 10.30: Applying the edges uber smart mask onto the gold material's layer

Select the **Mask Editor** row under the gold material's layer, as shown in *Figure 10.31,* and then adjust the **Global Blur**, **Global Balance,** and **Global Contrast** parameters, as shown in *Figure 10.32*:

Figure 10.31: *Clicking the Mask Editor under the gold material layer*

The following figure shows adjusting the three global values:

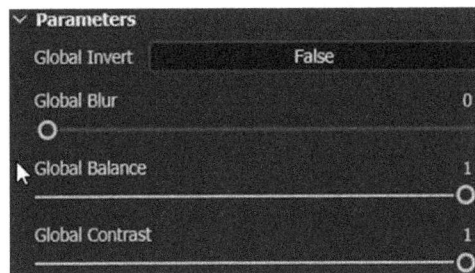

Figure 10.32: *Adjust the three global values to 0, 1 and 1 respectively*

This results in a nicely applied, balanced golden material, as shown in *Figure 10.33*, where only certain elements are highlighted by the gold, rather than the entire mesh being overtaken by it:

Figure 10.33: *The gold is in harmony with the other Materials*

As before, the values just used for **Global Blur** (0), **Global Balance** (1), and **Global Contrast** (1) work for this particular mesh. To ensure the gold material works well with the geometry and in harmony with the other Materials, these values would need to be adjusted depending on the visual results each individual mesh produces.

Rooftop material

The last type of material we need to address is the blueish material found on rooftops in the concept.

The process to be followed is identical to the ones followed for all other Materials, only a bit easier. While the gold will be applied in the exact same way as described previously, the base material will be a blue-based smart material, specifically the **Sapphire Corundum**, as shown in *Figure 10.34*:

Figure 10.34: Sapphire Corundum is the smart material to use for rooftops

You first apply this material on a freshly imported rooftop mesh, and then you repeat the same steps we took for the gold material and its smart mask, getting a result similar to the one shown in *Figure 10.35*:

Figure 10.35: A finished rooftop

Figures 10.36 to *Figure 10.38* showcase some of the finished meshes the author created for this project. The finished assets, as well as the Unreal Engine project are available for download at the provided links associated with this book's assets.

Figure 10.36: A finished pillar

Figure 10.37 shows one of the many archways for this project, fully finished:

Figure 10.37: A finished archway

Figure 10.38 shows yet another asset required for this project, fully finished:

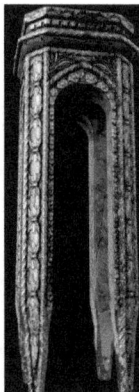

Figure 10.38: A finished support trim

Exporting and organizing your files

When working with asset packs, it is important to be organized. In this project's case, there are 3D models in an FBX format, three texture files per model, in PNG format, all of which will have to be matched once imported into the Unreal Engine project, in the next chapter. Therefore, it is important to be able to locate the files that correspond to each asset easily, and accordingly assign them where they need to be assigned.

This is an important process in every step of an asset's production cycle, from its initial concept to its basic creation, to its advanced sculpting, to its texturing, all the way to its inclusion and application within an Unreal Engine project. However, it is even more important to properly organize our files now that we will be exporting them from Substance Painter, due to the number of files associated with each asset.

To summarize, here are the files we will be exporting from Substance Painter, for every single asset:

- 3D model in FBX format
- Texture set associated with each 3D model:
  - Basic color map
  - Normal map
  - ORM map

3D model in FBX format

As described earlier in this chapter, when importing our 3D model in Substance Painter, we auto unwrapped it, therefore we changed its UV mapping, and thus we need to export it once more, before finally importing it in the Unreal Engine. By doing so, we ensure that the textures we export for this specific model, will be mapped correctly onto the geometry.

To export the mesh, while in Substance Painter, navigate to **File,** then select **Export Mesh…,** as shown in *Figure 10.39*:

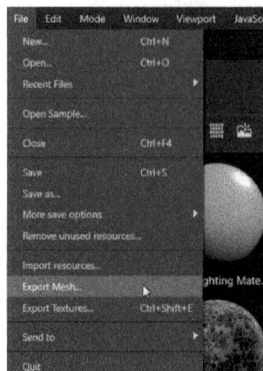

Figure 10.39: Exporting a mesh from Substance Painter

Use the default export options and simply click **Export**, as shown in *Figure 10.40*:

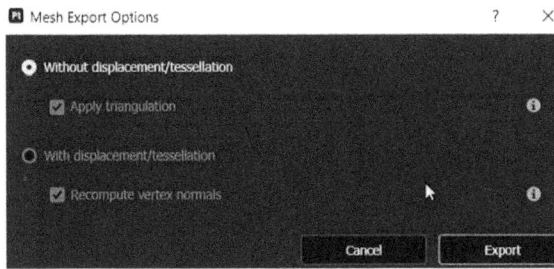

Figure 10.40: Export with the default options

While optional, it is strongly suggested you dedicate a folder for every asset pack's assets. If, for example, there is an asset pack that features a wall mesh, a door mesh, and a floor mesh, then you might want to export it in a folder named **Asset Pack 1** or any naming convention that is easily identified when it will be necessary to import these files into the Unreal Engine. In addition, it is strongly recommended that you use a naming convention that will also be easily identifiable in later stages. The naming convention format, recommended by the author, for the 3D meshes that will, in essence, be our Static Meshes in the next chapter is as follows:

- FileType_AssetPack#_NameRelatingToTheMesh

An example, taken from the files created for this project:

SM_AP1_Rooftop, which is explained as:

- **SM**: Static Mesh
- **AP1**: Asset pack 1
- **Rooftop**: This mesh is a rooftop that can be placed atop a structure

Once you have exported your first 3D mesh, you need to export its textures. To do that, simply navigate to **File** and then select **Export Textures...** as shown in *Figure 10.41*:

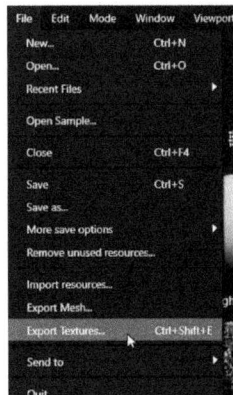

Figure 10.41: Exporting textures from Substance Painter

A new window pops up, prompting you to select the export options you want, as shown in *Figure 10.42*:

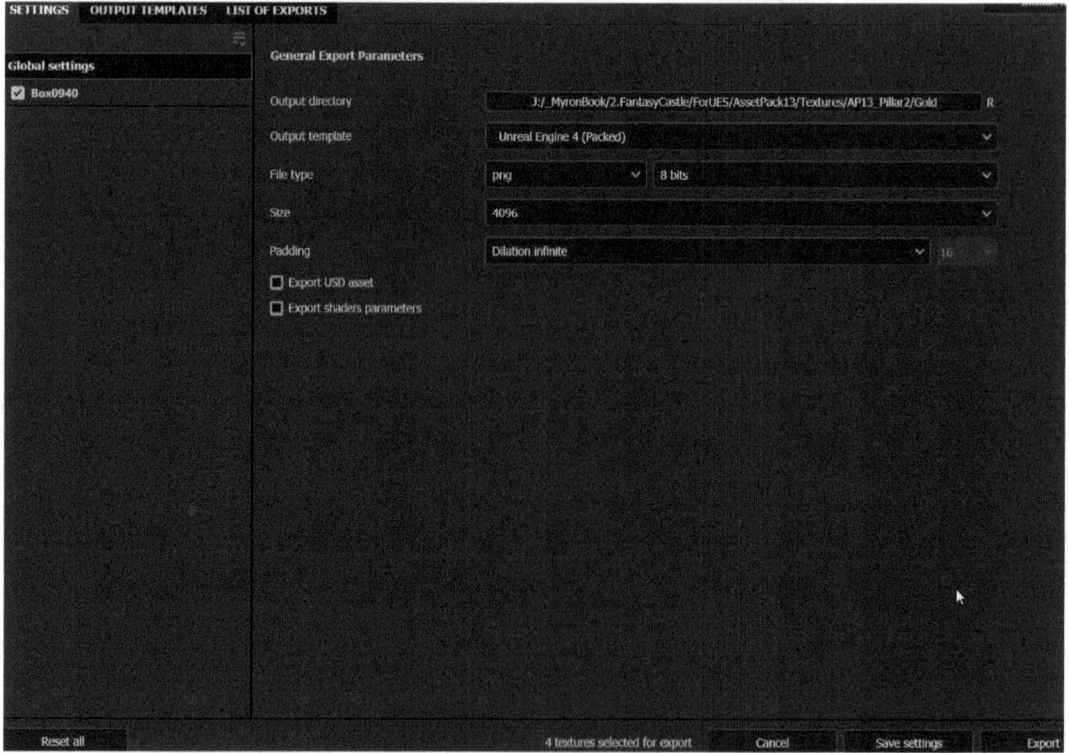

Figure 10.42: *Texture export options*

For this project's purposes, we will proceed with the options shown in *Figure 10.43*:

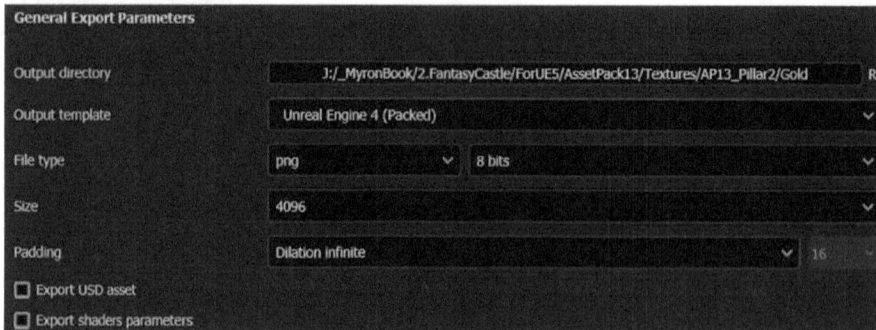

Figure 10.43: *Texture export options preferred for this project*

In more detail:

- **Output directory**: Select a directory that best works for your needs and will be easy to locate when you will need to import all these assets in the Unreal Engine.

- **Output template:** Unreal Engine 4 (Packed), this template will give us the texture maps we discussed earlier in this chapter.

- **File type:** **.png** 8 bits

- **Size:** 4096 is a good resolution for this project, not as qualitative as 8192, but still very detailed and current-gen-appopriate, while a bit friendlier on the performance demands, Although still on the heavier side of the performance spectrum.

- Everything else can be left to its default values.

Repeat all the above steps for every single mesh and its associated textures, and ultimately, you will find yourself with a large asset library. For the record, the author ended up having 14 asset pack folders featuring 95 FBX files and 306 PNG files. In the next chapter, all these files will be imported into the Unreal Engine. Should you want to manually import these files, they are available for download via the links associated with this book's resources.

Conclusion

This chapter was not meant to be a detailed Substance Painter tutorial, especially if you have never used Substance Painter before, however, to the reader who is familiar with Substance Painter, it offers a couple of quick suggestions on getting the results needed for this project, while to the reader unfamiliar with Substance Painter, gives a very brief overview of the steps that precede importing assets to the Unreal Engine.

In summary, we imported the detailed meshes we exported from ZBrush in *Chapter 9, Fantasy Castle High Poly Mesh Sculpting*, and had Substance Painter unwrap them for us. Next, we identified the Materials that appear to be repeated throughout the entire scene depicted in our concept and found ways to quickly emulate them with what is available in Adobe's Substance Painter. Then we proceeded with balancing the Materials' coexistence with each other, while finally we exported the 3D mesh (to ensure we have the correct UV map data associated with the 3D model) and the textures associated with the 3D mesh.

Next, in *Chapter 11, Fantasy Castle Bringing it All in Unreal* we will return to the Unreal Engine, where we will create a new project, import the files we just exported in *Chapter 10, Fantasy Castle Texturing and Materials*, create material shaders using the imported textures and assign these Materials to the imported meshes so that we can design our Fantasy Castle level!

Points to remember

- Basic concept of unwrapping/UV mapping for a 3D model
- Importing 3D models in Substance Painter
- Allowing Substance Painter to auto-unwrap the models

- Baking the model in Substance Painter
- Identifying repeating Materials in a concept
- Using Materials and smart Materials in Substance Painter
- Using smart masks to tame some of these Materials
- Exporting meshes from Substance Painter
- Exporting textures from Substance Painter specifically for Unreal Engine usage

Exercises

1. Import the FBX files you obtained from this book's resources into Substance Painter and try out different Materials than the ones used here. Try using silver or copper instead of gold, clay or stone instead of concrete, or maybe even plastic or metal!

2. Alternatively, you can also try creating your own sculpts and meshes, which you then import in Substance Painter and assign Materials to them.

3. As a third option, you can also use third-party meshes from different marketplaces or online sources and import them into Substance Painter, where you can assign different Materials to them.

Join our book's Discord space

Join the book's Discord Workspace for Latest updates, Offers, Tech happenings around the world, New Release and Sessions with the Authors:

https://discord.bpbonline.com

CHAPTER 11

Fantasy Castle Bringing It All in Unreal

Introduction

In this chapter, we resume using the Unreal Engine. Since, many of the steps discussed in this chapter were covered in great detail in earlier chapters, specifically *Chapters 1, Unleashing the Unreal Engine* to *Chapter 6, Lighting and Cinematic for the Statue Scene*. In this chapter, many of the steps revisiting workflows and processes covered in the earlier chapters, would not be as descriptive or detailed as earlier, as we will be trying to cover a lot more ground from this chapter on.

More specifically, in this chapter as well as *Chapter 12, Fantasy Castle Character and Interaction Blueprints* and *Chapter 13, Fantasy Castle Interactive Blueprint Actors*, we will work on and complete the Fantasy Castle Project, and then package it up in *Chapter 14, Fantasy Castle MiniGame Blueprints*.

In this chapter, we will quickly set up the project, import all the previously created assets, categorize them, create and assign Materials to any assets that need them. Then we will design our level with some placeholders for lighting, landscaping and more.

Structure

The following topics are discussed in this chapter:

- Creating the Fantasy Castle Project in Unreal

- Importing our previously created assets
- Creating the Materials for the project
- Assigning the Materials to their respective meshes
- Starting the level design
- Combining multiple meshes into a group
- Combining multiple meshes by merging them
- Combining multiple meshes by creating packed level actors
- Level designing is a creative process
- Modifying the atmospheric conditions
- Landscaping
- Combining the above techniques

Objectives

This chapter's objectives are to utilize everything learned in *Chapters 1* to *6* while, in addition, learning some new tools and workflows, such as the landscape and Foliage editing tools.

Creating the Fantasy Castle Project in Unreal

Firstly, let us create a new Unreal project by using the Epic Games Launcher, as described in the earliest chapters of this book. Load the Unreal Engine launcher, preferably with the latest Engine version (at the time of this writing the latest Engine version is **5.3.2** and this is the one the author used for this project), as shown in *Figure 11.1*:

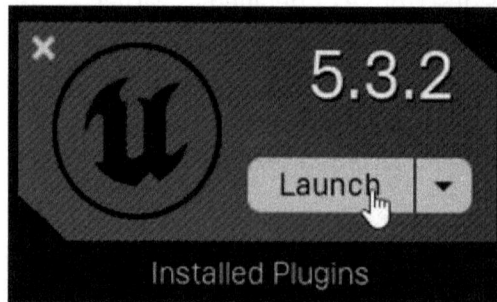

Figure 11.1: Launching the latest Unreal Engine version

Next, select the **Games** category on the left, and then select the **Third Person** project. Ensure you have selected a **Blueprint** setup, **Raytracing** is enabled, select the desired location for the project — you will need to have at least 50 GB of free space, and use **FantasyCastle** as the **Project Name**. All of these settings are shown in *Figure 11.2*:

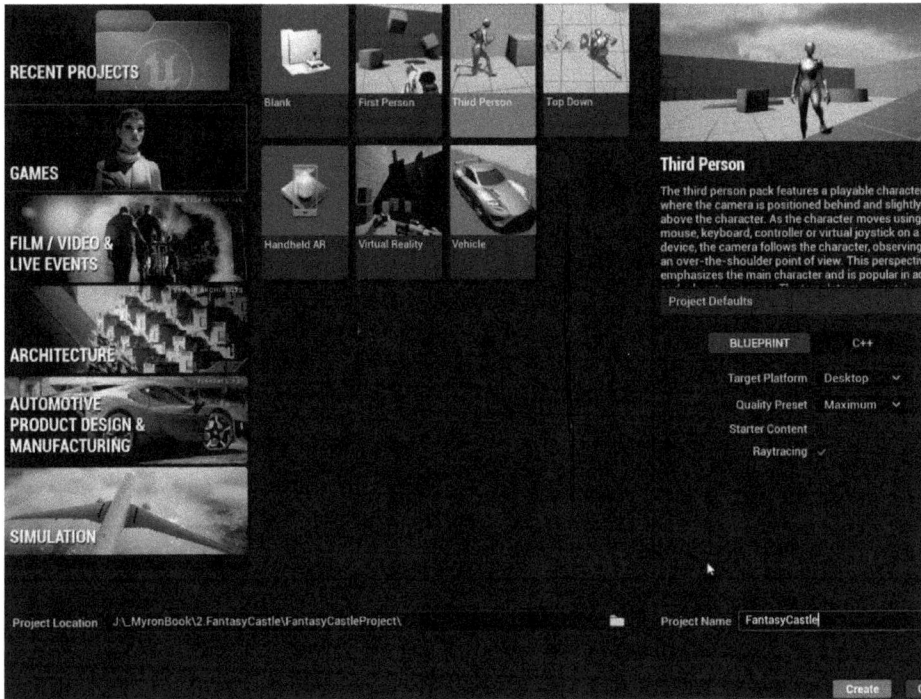

Figure 11.2: *Creating the Fantasy Castle Project*

Importing our previously created assets

Now that we have a blank project, we can begin setting up the desired folder structure and then proceed with importing all the assets we created in the previous couple of chapters. As a reminder, the author provides both the assets in their source format, ready to import, as well as the project, should you wish to skip or repeat any of the steps. All the resources related to this book can be accessed through the links provided at the start of this book.

By going to a Content Browser window, or by accessing the Content Drawer, under **Content** we create a folder named **AssetPacks**. In this folder, we will import all the asset packs and their associated files from the previous chapters. At this point, it is a good moment to mention that there are many ways to approach a project folder structure. For example, we could have instead created **Static Meshes**, **Textures and Materials** folders, like it was done in the Statue project. However, the Fantasy Castle Project is a considerably larger project, with a lot more files to manage; therefore, it will be a lot easier to navigate through the different assets by categorizing each asset pack into a folder of its own and within each pack's folder have folders specifically referring to any asset types associated (Materials, textures, etc.).

Due to the large number of assets this project uses, the author organized the source file folders in a way that can be easily clicked and dragged from Windows Explorer straight into the Unreal Engine Content Browser, specifically under the folder we just created (**Content/AssetPacks/**). *Figure 11.3* shows the source file structure in Windows Explorer:

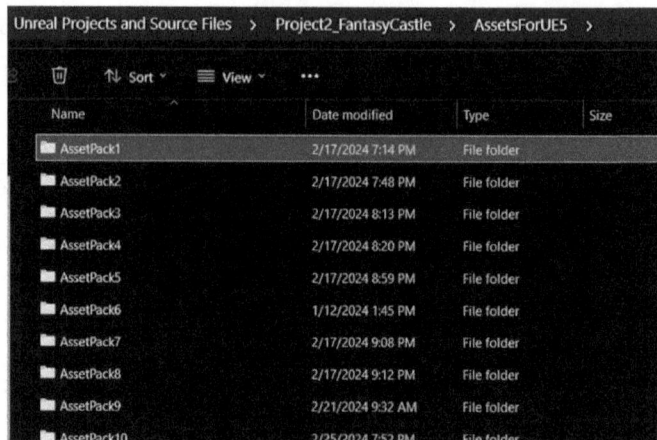

Figure 11.3: Source files for the Fantasy Castle Project, as seen in Windows Explorer

Figure 11.4 shows an example of what each **AssetPack** folder contains, once again displayed in Windows Explorer. You can see there are several FBX files, representing the Static Meshes/3D models we will import, as well as a **Textures** folder, which contains all the textures associated with each one of these 3D models. In this example, **AssetPack2** is what is shown:

Figure 11.4: Source files within an AssetPack folder, as seen in Windows Explorer

We could theoretically click and drag all of the **AssetPack** folders at once, but due to the amount of files, in addition to the fact that the Engine will need to perform some calculations in order to process the high poly meshes and apply Nanite to them, it is best we click and drag few files at a time, depending on your PC's system specs. In the author's case, first, he opened each asset pack's folder, selected all the contained FBX files (as shown in *Figure 11.4*), and dragged them into the corresponding **AssetPack** folder within the Unreal project. The import settings in Unreal used for the FBX files, are shown in *Figure 11.5*. It is very important you ensure **Build Nanite** is checked:

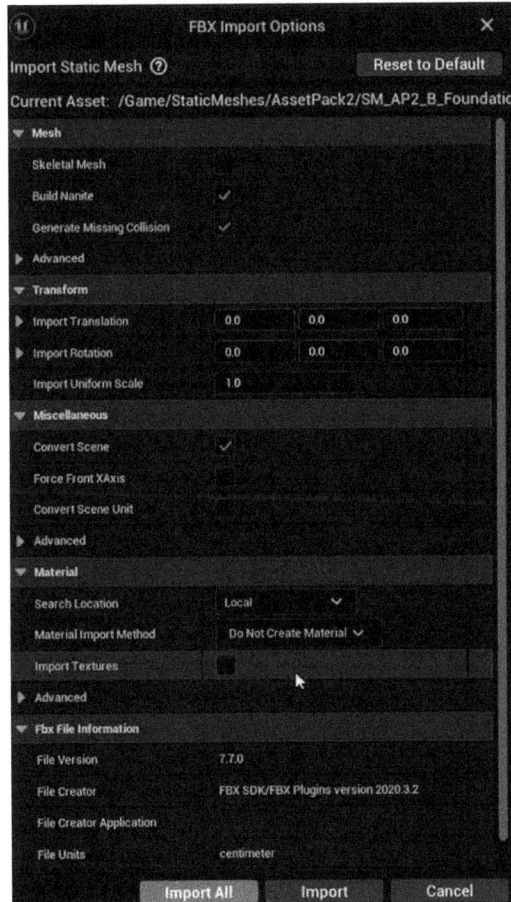

Figure 11.5: FBX import settings in Unreal

Once an asset pack's FBX files have been imported, next select the same asset pack's **Textures** folder in Windows Explorer, and drag it into the same asset pack's folder in Unreal's Content Browser. Once all of the files have been imported, do not forget to click Save All on Content Browser's upper left corner inside the Unreal Engine.

Repeat the above steps for all of the asset packs, and once again, ensure you have saved all your work. From here on, all steps and work will be done in the Unreal Engine.

Next, create a **Materials** folder inside each asset pack's folder, as shown in *Figure 11.6*:

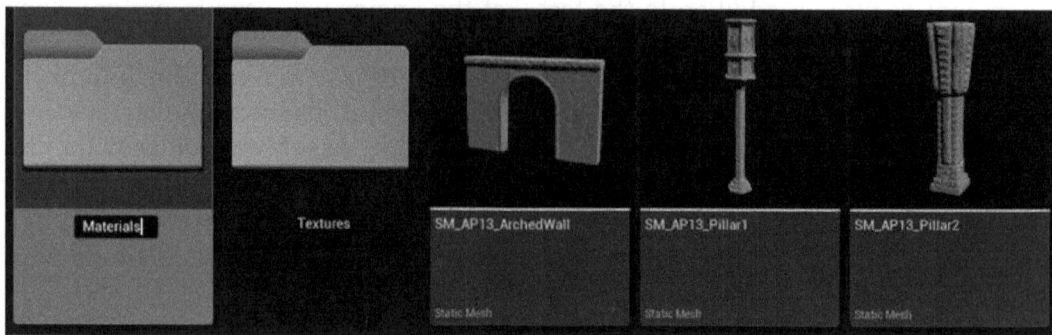

Figure 11.6: Creating a Materials folder for AssetPack13

Repeat the same process for all of the asset packs. *Figure 11.7* shows what your folder structure should approximately look like at this point in the project:

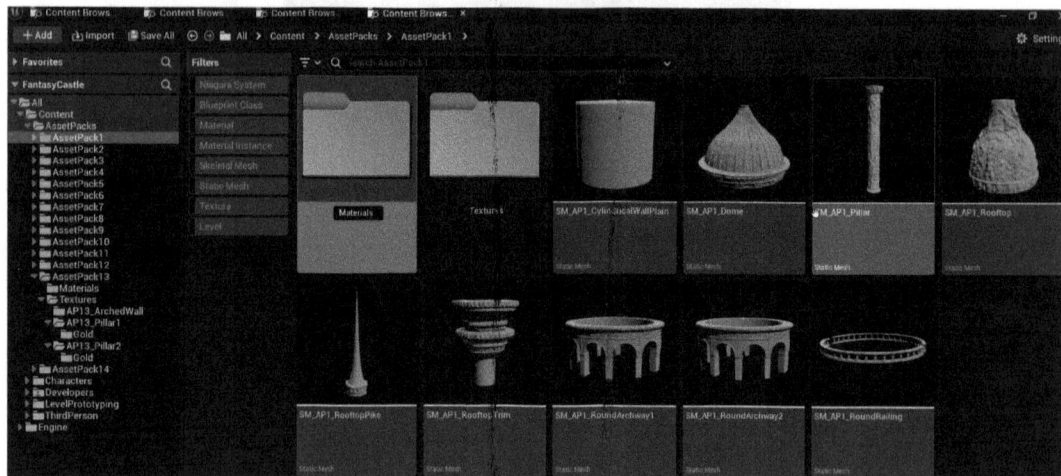

Figure 11.7: Project folder structure as seen in Unreal's Content Browser after repeating all of the previous steps

Creating the Materials for the project

There are an estimated 100 meshes and 330 texture assets that just got imported into the project. That allows us to estimate the need for approximately 100 Materials, each of these Materials using 3 textures. As discussed in *Chapter 10, Fantasy Castle Texturing and Materials*, we created three types of texture maps for each Static Mesh, specifically the color map, the ORM map and the normal map.

The color map will define the basic colors each Static Mesh uses, the ORM map will be defining how shiny as well as reflective our Material will look, while the normal map will assign any details that were not sculpted on the mesh but are instead part of the detail of the Material presets used in Substance Painter (*Chapter 10*).

Since all of the meshes will use the same type of maps, instead of creating one hundred individual Materials, we can create a Master Material that defines the pattern, and from there on simply create instances of that one Material, that still allow us not only to replace the texture maps used, but also Alter some parameters, therefore allowing us to finetune each Material Instance according to the Static Mesh it needs to be applied to.

Based on everything you learned previously in this book, you should be able to create your own Material, along with converting its texture maps to parameters, as well as by utilizing nodes that are also converted into parameters. More specifically, our Master Material needs to resemble the one depicted in *Figure 11.8*. To create the Master Material, first navigate to **Content/AssetPacks/AssetPack1/Materials/** in the Content Browser, and in there right click and create a new Material, which you can name M_MasterMaterial.

Next, navigate to **Content/AssetPacks/AssetPack1/Textures/AP1_ CylindricalWallPlain/** and select all three textures, click and drag them into the Material editor for the M_MasterMaterial you just created.

Convert the color map to a parameter named **Color**, the ORM map to a parameter named **ORM**, and the normal texture map to a parameter named **Normal**.

Create a vector 3 node, which you then convert to a parameter named **Color&Brightness**. Connect its first output pin (white) to a **Multiply** node's input pin, while connecting the **Color** map's output pin to the other input pin on the **Multiply** node. Now, connect the **Multiply** output pin to the **Base Color** input pin on the **M_MasterMaterial** result node.

Next, create two multiply nodes. Then, create two constant nodes, convert them to parameters, one named **MetallicMultiplier** and the other **RoughnessMultiplier**, and connect each one's output to the **B** input pin of a **Multiply** node. Drag a cable from the **ORM** map's red output pin and plug it into the result node's **Ambient Occlusion** pin. Drag a cable from the **ORM** green output pin to the **A** input pin of the multiply node connected to the **Roughness Multiplier**. Then, connect the **Multiply** node's output pin to the result node's **Roughness** input pin. Next, drag a cable from the **ORM** node's blue output pin and connect it to the **A** input pin on the **Multiply** node connected to the **Metallic Multiplier** node. Then, connect the **Multiply** node's output pin to the result node's **Metallic** input pin.

Lastly, connect the **Normal** map node's RGB (white) output pin to the result node's **Normal** input.

Hit Apply (Material editor's upper left corner) and save. Your **M_MasterMaterial** node structure when viewed in the Material Editor, should resemble *Figure 11.8*:

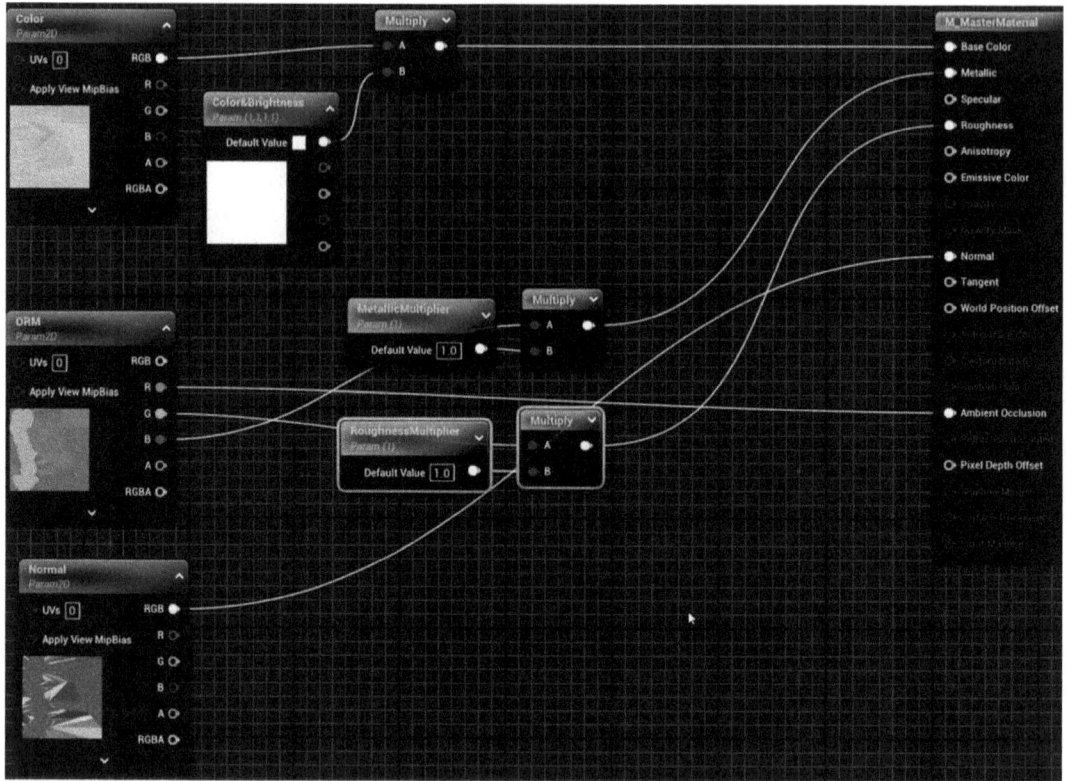

Figure 11.8: The Master Material's node and parameter structure

With the Master Material complete with parameters; we can now proceed with creating our first Material Instance. While in the Content Browser, right click on the M_MasterMaterial and select **Create Material Instance** (*Figure 11.9*):

Figure 11.9: Create a Material Instance out of the M_MasterMaterial

Name each Material Instance in a manner that you can easily identify the Static Mesh (or any other asset) it needs to be applied on. For example, the very first Material Instance is named **MI_AP1_CylindricalWallPlain** as shown in *Figure 11.10*:

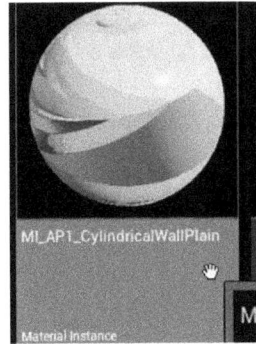

Figure 11.10: *The first Material Instance for this project*

More specifically, MI stands for Material Instance, AP1 stands for AssetPack1, and CylindricalWallPlain is the name of the asset it will be applied to (specifically SM_AP1_CylindricalWallPlain with SM being the prefix for Static Mesh). In a similar fashion, repeat the Material Instance creation steps for all the asset packs. *Figure 11.11* shows the resulting Material Instances for **AssetPack1**:

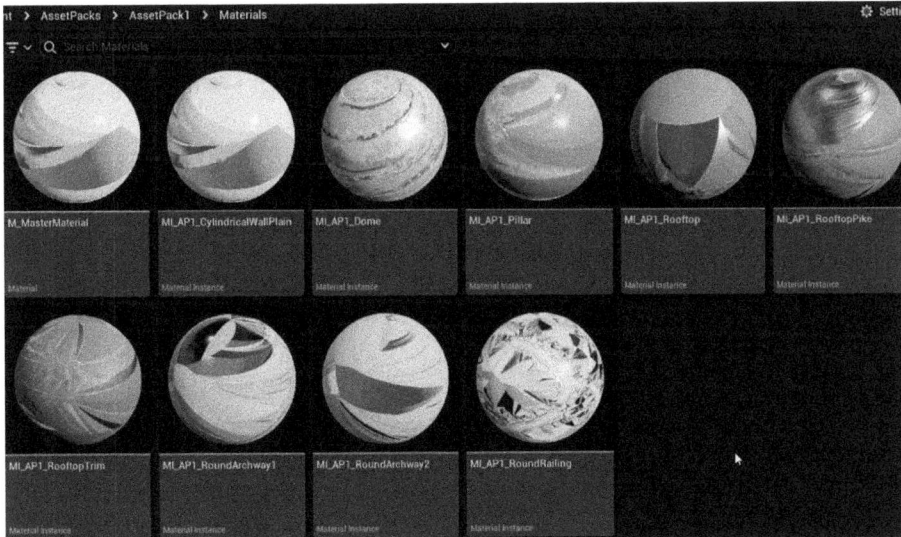

Figure 11.11: *AssetPack1's Material Instances*

Assigning the Materials to their respective meshes

Next, simply double click on a Static Mesh and apply its appropriate Material Instance to it, as shown in *Figure 11.12*. Do not forget to save the asset once the Material Instance is applied.

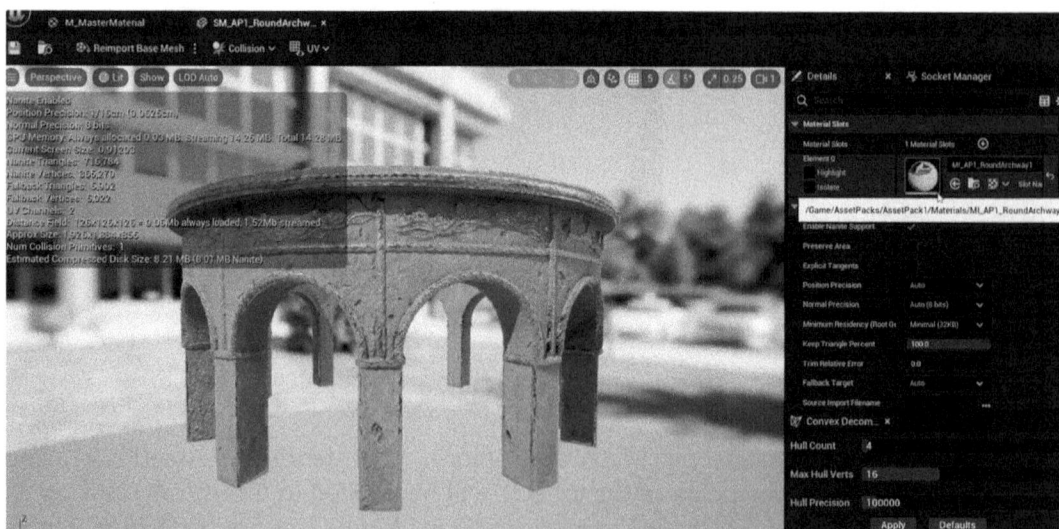

Figure 11.12: *MI_AP1_RoundArchway1 Material Instance,
applied to SM_AP1_RoundArchway1 as its default Material*

Repeat the process for all the Static Meshes. As you apply Material Instances to Static Meshes, you might notice that you want to finetune some of the visuals, such as the shine or the reflection amounts, or perhaps even the brightness and the color. That is where the parameters we created in the Master Material come to our aid. Feel free to play around with these values. *Figure 11.13* shows all the parameters checked and ready for adjustment in one of the Material Instances:

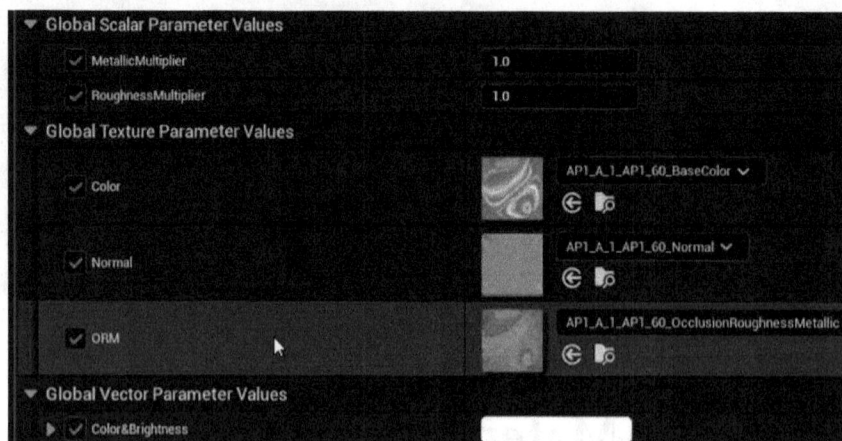

Figure 11.13: *A Material Instance ready to be fine tuned*

Figure 11.14 shows what the default settings for a Static Meshe's Material Instance originally looked like:

Figure 11.14: Gold surface being highly reflective with the default Material Instance parameters

Figure 11.15 shows the end-result after the Material Instance was adjusted to make the gold surface a bit less reflective:

Figure 11.15: Gold surface being slightly less reflective with the modified Material Instance parameters

Starting the level design

Now that all our assets are complete with Materials assigned to them, let us start building our modular pieces, slowly building our way to the castle depicted in the concept in *Chapter 7, Fantasy Castle Project Breakdownd and Planning*. It is best to approach this stage one asset pack at a time, Although the more you progress with building the modular pieces, the more you will find yourself relying on multiple asset packs.

Firstly, create a new basic clean map, (*Ctrl+N*) as shown in *Figure 11.16*:

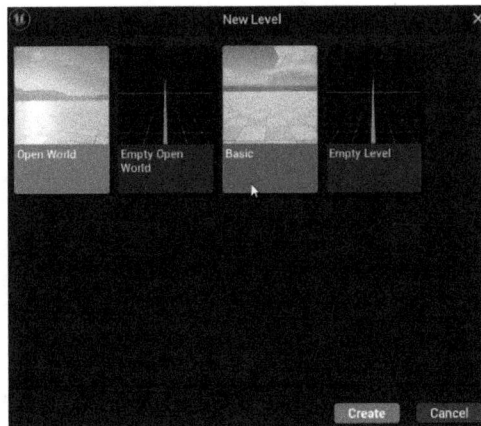

Figure 11.16: Create a new basic level

Save this level as **FantasyCastle**, under **Content/Levels/**. Select the floor, and scale it up considerably (default is 8, you might want to set it to 20 or more).

Since we are using Unreal's Third Person template, we can also bring in Skeletal Mesh, that will help us get a better sense of scale as we build our modular pieces. You can either navigate to **Content/Characters/Mannequins/Meshes** in your Content Browser, or while being in the **Content** root, search for **SKM_Quinn**, shown in *Figure 11.17*:

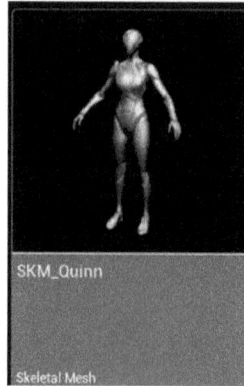

Figure 11.17: SKM_Quinn

Select **SKM_Quinn** and drag it into our scene, as shown in *Figure 11.18*:

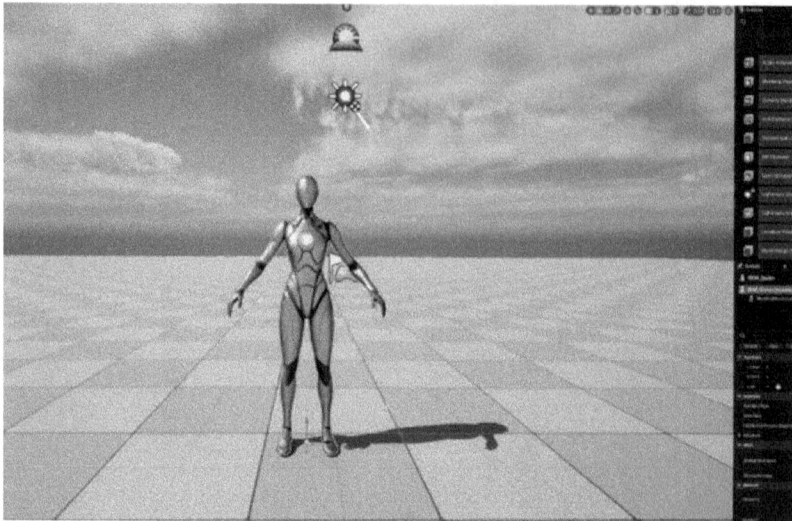

Figure 11.18: SKM_Quinn in the level

Save the level and proceed with bringing in Static Meshes from the first asset pack. The author started with the main tower; by placing and scaling different assets from the first asset pack, he created the main tower as shown in *Figure 11.19*:

Figure 11.19: *Playing through the map, with the main tower in the distance, built with different pieces from the first asset pack*

You can constantly monitor the sense of scale, not only by comparing it to Quinn's mesh, but also by playing the level. Since we are using the Third Person template, by default, you will be playing as Quinn, in Third Person mode, thus allowing you to navigate through the world in Third Person, being able to compare the environment's scaling in relation to your character's size.

Combining multiple meshes into a group

Throughout the level design process, you will most certainly need to move around the modular pieces you create, as well as scale them. One approach would be to group multiple meshes together. You select the meshes you want to group together by clicking one and then *Ctrl+click* to include more meshes or actors in your selection, ultimately right clicking on any of them, while they are all highlighted and selecting **Group**, as shown in *Figure 11.20*:

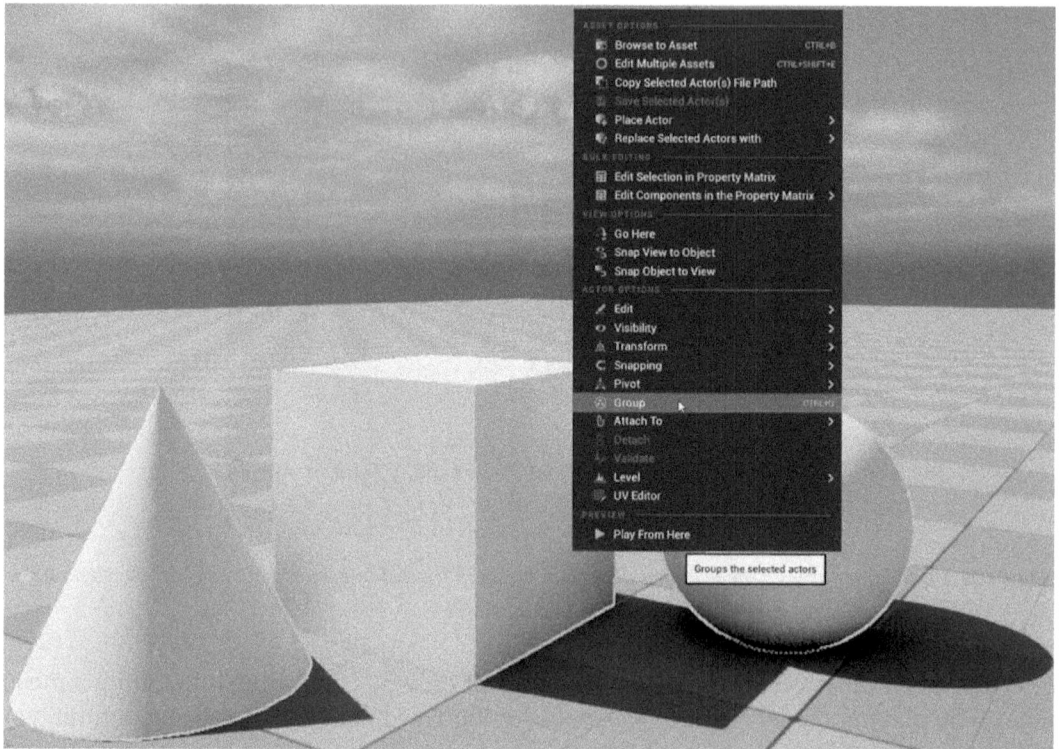

Figure 11.20: *Grouping the cone, cube and sphere together, while they are all selected*

Alternatively, while having all the actors you want to group together selected, you can press *Ctrl+G*. Grouping them together will result in a larger highlighter every time the group is selected, as shown in *Figure 11.21*:

Figure 11.21: *Moving the transform gizmo now, will move all grouped actors, which are all highlighted by a large rectangular boundary*

The disadvantage of using the grouping method is that if you decide you want to modify the scaling of the entire group uniformly, it is now possible. Note how after scaling up the previous example's group, all meshes ended up overlapping with each other, as shown in *Figure 11.22*:

Figure 11.22: Scaling up the group did not go as intended, the meshes did not scale uniformly

However, grouping can be very helpful when needing to quickly duplicate a selection of multiple meshes, move them around, or mirror them. Therefore, it is very common to use it, and can be an extremely reliable and helpful tool, expediting the level design process.

Sometimes, while working with a group of actors, you might want to scale or even move one of them, instead of the entire group. In this case, select the group, right click on it, navigate to **Groups** and click **Unlock**. Then, click the individual mesh from the group that you wish to modify. Alternatively, you can also select **Ungroup** which then dissolves the group, freeing up any dependencies each member of the group has to each other. *Figure 11.23* shows these options:

Figure 11.23: Unlocking and ungrouping

While having a group unlocked, right clicking on any of its members and navigating to **Groups** will present you with the options to ungroup, remove the selected member(s) from the group — thus once you lock the group back again, the removed members will not be part of the group any longer — and locking the group, all options shown in *Figure 11.24*:

Figure 11.24: Group options for an unlocked group

Combining multiple meshes by merging them

In Unreal, it is possible to select multiple Static Meshes in a scene and merge them into one single mesh. This is great, because it eliminates the need to perform such solutions in external applications, while ensuring that the resulting mesh can be uniformly scaled and modified. Let us look at the example shown in *Figure 11.25*. We have three separate meshes we want to combine into one. More specifically, we have a mesh for the roof, a mesh for the supporting arches, and a mesh for the base.

Figure 11.25: Three separate meshes we wish to combine into one

Ultimately, what we want to achieve is a mesh that resembles *Figure 11.26*:

Figure 11.26: The desired outcome

Firstly, we need to scale and move the meshes in the desired position. What you see in *Figure 11.26* is still three separate meshes, but they are scaled and positioned in the desired manner. Now that they are positioned as desired, we need to select all three of them, and while they are selected, navigate to the top of our Unreal window, to **Tools** then **Merge Actors**, as shown in *Figure 11.27*:

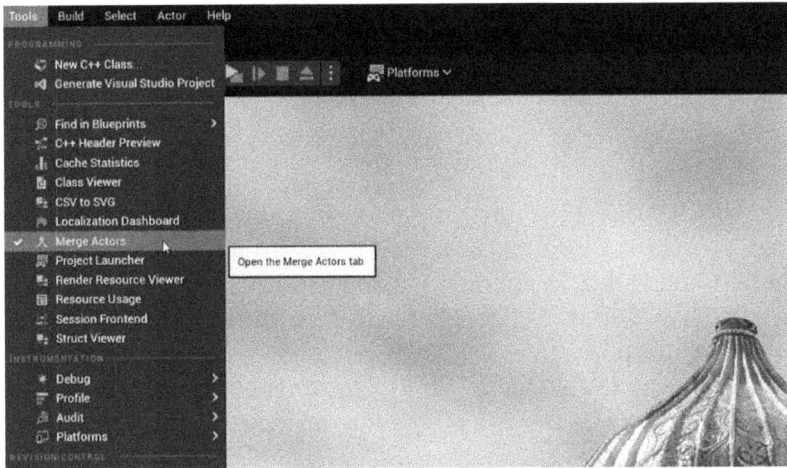

Figure 11.27: *Navigating to Tools | Merge Actors*

This action results in a new window popping up, similar to the one in *Figure 11.28:*

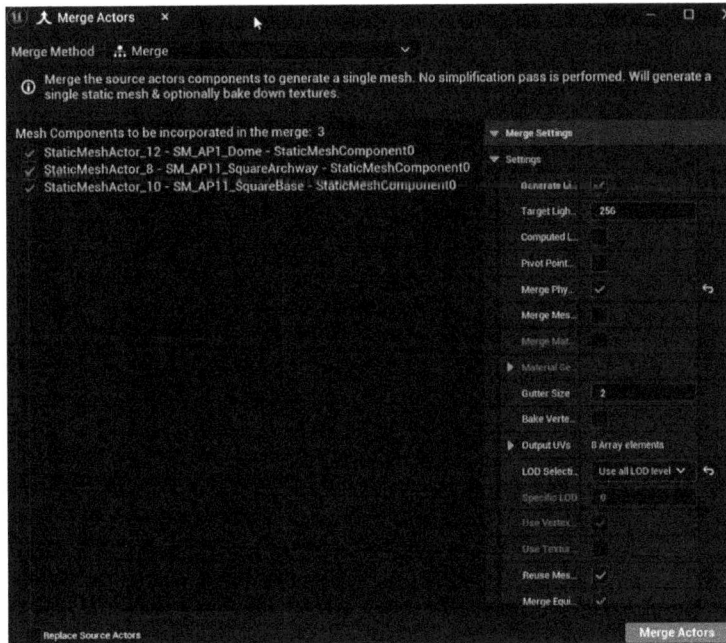

Figure 11.28: *The Merge Actors window*

With the **Merge Method** being **Merge**, we can see the names of the selected actors, while also having access to a plethora of settings for the merge. Usually, it is best to leave the default settings, however in this case, since all of our meshes are utilizing Nanite, we want to ensure that we scroll down in the **Merge Settings**, and have **Nanite Settings** set to **Enabled** as shown in *Figure 11.29:*

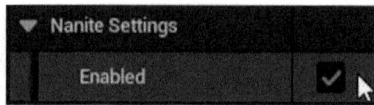

Figure 11.29: Enabling Nanite Settings for merging actors

Then, you can click on the blue **Merge Actors** button, which will result in a popup window, asking you for the location you wish to save the new mesh into. If you decide to use this method, the author recommends you create and save merged meshes under a **MergedMeshes** folder within each asset pack folder or under **Content** if you wish to have all your merged meshes in one location. Then, once you have selected the location, make sure you right-click on the resulting mesh in the **Content** folder and select save. *Figure 11.30* shows the three separate meshes on the left, and the resulting merged mesh on the right:

Figure 11.30: Three meshes on the left, one single merged on the right

Figure 11.31 shows the result of scaling up the three separate meshes as a group, and the single merged mesh. In both instances, the meshes were scaled up to double the original scale.

Figure 11.31: The difference between scaling up a group of meshes (left) and a merged mesh (right)

While this is an excellent solution, it does have some disadvantages, such as the resulting merged mesh being slightly inferior to the original meshes. There is a multitude of options to modify when merging meshes, including several Nanite related options, but it is not the easiest of endeavors, and certainly beyond this book's scope. It is up to the reader's discretion whether and when to use this method while designing the level for this project.

There are more **Merge Method** (*Figure 11.32*) such as **Simplify**, which we will not be using for this project, **Batch** which we will be using later for level optimization purposes and **Approximate** which we will not be using for this project:

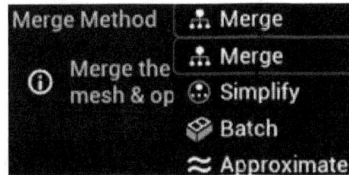

Figure 11.32: Different Merge Methods

Combining multiple meshes by creating packed level actors

Unreal Engine 5 has introduced a very interesting method of merging various actors into one, especially when one wants to do so for the purpose of creating buildings for cities or town types of environments. It is called **Create Packed Level Actor**, with which Unreal packages all the selected actors into a single Blueprint actor that utilizes performance friendly instances, and also saves these instances into level files, which can be used in conjunction with the larger world partition system, which is typically used for rather large environments (a good example would be any open world **Role Playing Game (RPG)** type of environment). In our project, while our world would not necessarily be open world, we want to give the impression of a grand scale, and while we would not need to dive into the World Partition tools for this book's purposes, we can still take advantage of the performance friendly Blueprints this method provides us with. Most importantly, we can place, move, rotate and scale the end result, as if it were a single mesh, without sacrificing any of the detail quality, fully preserving all the original mesh's settings (Nanite and otherwise).

To create a packed level actor, select all the meshes you wish to combine. While having them all selected, right-click on any of them, navigate to **Level** and then select **Create Packed Level Actor...** as shown in *Figure 11.33*:

Figure 11.33: Creating a Packed Level Actor

Next, a window pops up, presenting you with a couple of options. Leave them to their default values, but double check and ensure that you have **Pivot Type** set to `Center Min Z` as shown in *Figure 11.34*. Essentially, this ensures that the resulting actor, has a pivot point at the bottom center of the resulting geometry, which is ideal for building related actors.

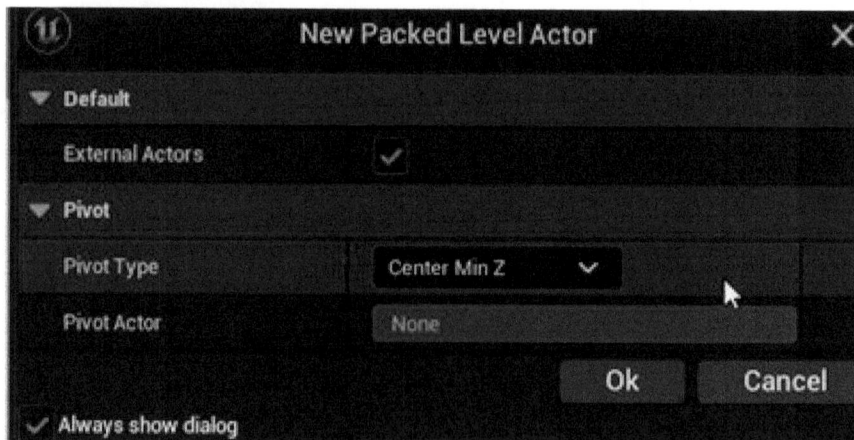

Figure 11.34: Packed Level Actor options

Next, you will be asked to choose a location to save a level file to a location of your choice. In truth we would not be using these levels, but we want to preserve the references associated between them and the resulting Blueprint actor — which is what we will be actually using in the level design process. As before, it is recommended you do so in either `Content/MergedMeshes/` or `Content/AssetPack/MergedMeshes/` folders, that the reader needs to create. Once you have selected the location, a new window will pop up, to which you want to check **Apply to All** and click **Yes** as shown in *Figure 11.35*:

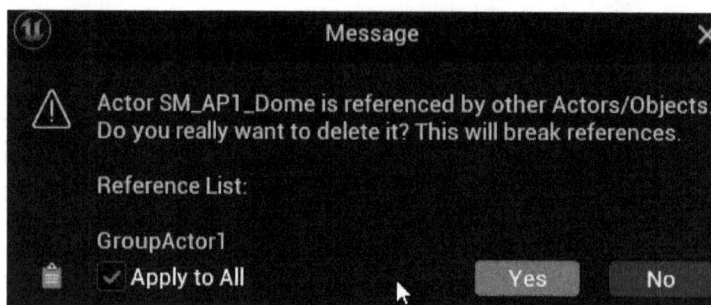

Figure 11.35: Apply to All and Yes

Immediately after, you will be asked to save the resulting Blueprint actor with the same name to a location of your choice. Use the same location as before. *Figure 11.36* shows the resulting Blueprint actor:

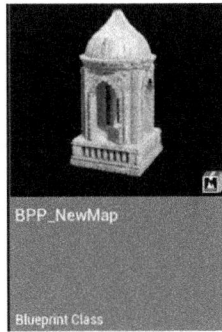

Figure 11.36: *Our newly created Packed Level Actor*

It is recommended that you follow this process for every structural set you complete, as they were defined in *Chapter 7's, Fantasy Castle Project Breakdownd and Planning* concept breakdown. However, it is entirely up to the reader's discretion when to utilize the **Packed Level Actor** method. *Figure 11.37* shows several such Packed Level Actors the author created in the process of building this project:

Figure 11.37: *Our newly created Packed Level Actor*

From here on, we continue building following the above-mentioned processes, until we can start placing the different assets together in a way that starts resembling the concept, or the desired end result. *Figures 11.38* to *Figure 11.40* show several steps of that process the author took during building this project:

Figure 11.38: *A collection of Packed Level Actors being placed in ways that resemble the end goal*

In the following figure, it starts looking like a castle:

Figure 11.39: *Starts looking like a proper castle*

The following figure shows the castle:

Figure 11.40: *Very close to the concept!*

Figure 11.41 shows the author playtesting the work-in-progress, in Third Person mode, to get a better sense of the scale as the environment is designed:

Figure 11.41: *This picture does not do the grand scale of the structure any justice*

Level designing is a creative process

At this point, the reader is encouraged to use their creativity and ingenuity, to not only replicate what is in the concept, but to also expand it further. If there is an asset missing for something you want to create, you can use the existing modular ones in combination with each other, while modifying their scaling as well as intended use. You will be amazed at the number of interesting combinations one can achieve with only a few assets. An arch duplicated and mirrored while laying flat, can become an interesting floor trim for example. The floors you see in *Figures 11.39* to *Figure 11.41*, were all created by combining simple cube geometry, by duplicating it, scaling it, rotating it and so on. Unlock your imagination!

At this point, it is also a good time to visit Quixel Bridge and consider whether there are some 3D assets — or most importantly — 2D/surface assets you can download and use. Quixel Bridge was covered extensively in *Chapter 5, Importing Assets and Setting Up the Statue Scene*, during the Statue Project.

Figure 11.42 shows some of the floor surface Materials the author downloaded from Quixel Bridge:

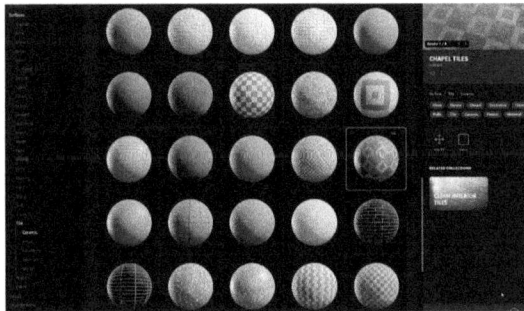

Figure 11.42: Excellent floor surface Materials can be found on Quixel Bridge

Figure 11.43 shows one of these tile Materials applied on the floors:

Figure 11.43: A Quixel Bridge floor Material applied on the floor's surface

Lighting the scene

While we are still in the earlier stages of the level design process, it does not hurt to slightly modify the overall lighting, just enough to resemble our concept reference. In *Chapter 6, Lighting and Cinematic for the Statue Scene* we went over lighting in quite some detail. For now, for this project, all the reader needs to do is modify the color and perhaps the rotation of the Directional Light (aka the sun). In the concept image, we can see the sun hitting the castle from the right, and it appears to be either closer to sunset or dawn, as there is a golden overall hue to the atmosphere. *Figure 11.43* already demonstrates the modified lighting (noticeable in the PDF version of this book), while *Figure 11.44* does the same, while playtesting the level with Quinn:

Figure 11.44: Playtesting with Quinn

Adding Foliage

Typically, Foliage is added in a level after the landscape has been created; however, in our case at present, we need to place some trees, so we can better visualize the castle's courtyard, which will later help us shape the landscape.

To start adding Foliage, the author downloaded one the permanently freely available packs from the Unreal Engine marketplace, more specifically *SilverTM's* **City Park Environment Collection** which features some excellent and highly optimized Foliage, including trees, grass, bushes and more. *Figure 11.45* shows the City Park collection as shown on the Unreal Engine marketplace:

Figure 11.45: City Park Environment Collection is an excellent pack for free Foliage

Upon adding the asset package to your project — unless using the project files provided by the author, then all these assets are included in the project — you will need to access the Foliage toolset. To do that, navigate to the upper left corner of your Unreal main window, click on **Selection Mode** to expand the drop-down menu and select **Foliage** as shown in *Figure 11.46*. Alternatively, you can also press *Shift+3*:

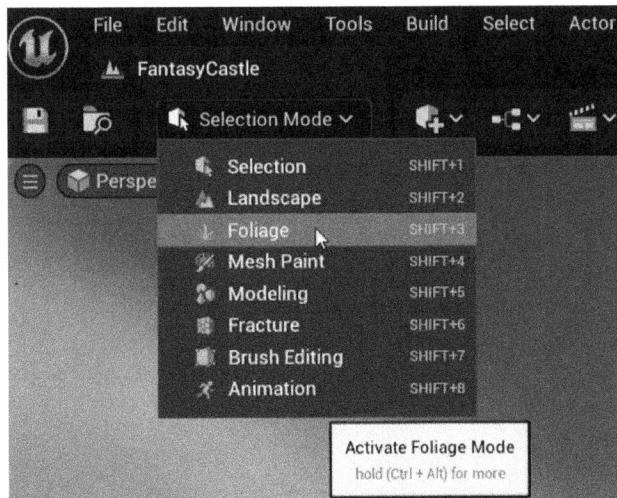

Figure 11.46: Accessing the Foliage tools

Next, you will see a new tab opening up, identical to the one in *Figure 11.47*:

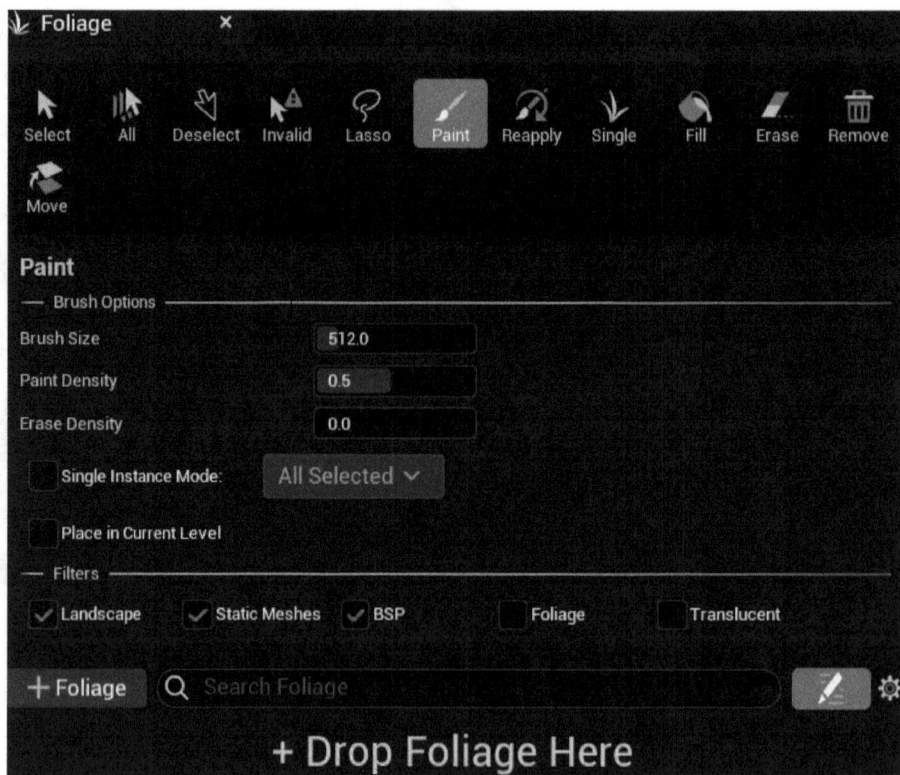

Figure 11.47: The Foliage tab

Back to the Content Browser (or the Content Drawer if you prefer it – *Ctrl+Spacebar*) navigate and select to a Static Mesh of a tree (any will do). If you have added the City Park collection to your project, or are using the author's provided project, search for **SM_Elm16** and click and drag it into +Drop Foliage Here in the Foliage tab, as shown in *Figure 11.48*:

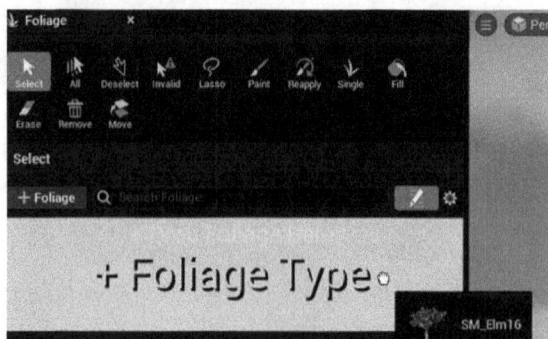

Figure 11.48: Adding SM_Elm16 to the Foliage tab

Next, click on the small elm thumbnail in the Foliage tab, which will then give you a multitude of options, all specific to this mesh, as shown in *Figure 11.49*:

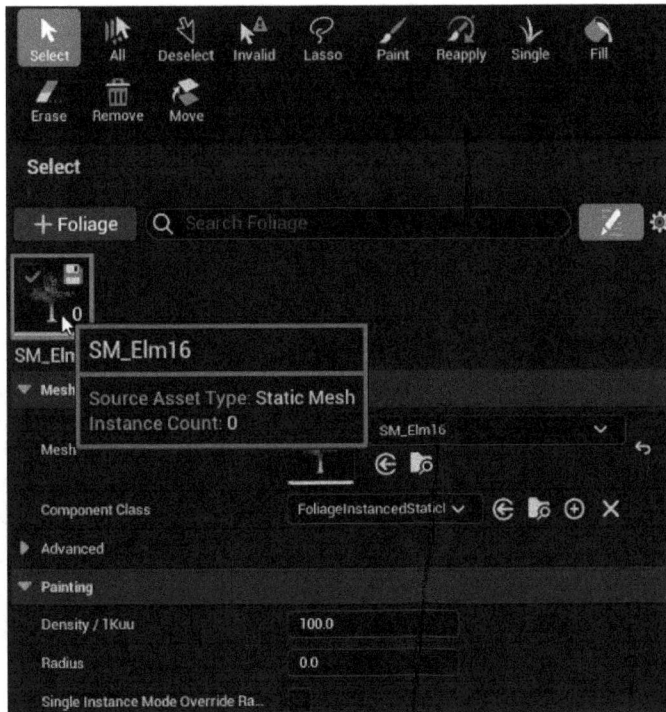

Figure 11.49: Options for the elm mesh as a Foliage actor

Now click on the **Paint** icon on the top, as shown in *Figure 11.50*. Paint will essentially allow us to paint or plant Foliage in the scene:

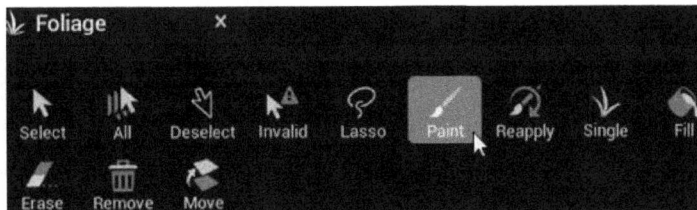

Figure 11.50: Paint will allow us to plant Foliage in the scene

Prior to painting anything, though, we need to take a closer look at the paint settings. Through the settings we can control the scale, or even the scale ranged each instance of Foliage is painted in, the surface angle threshold upon which we can paint, the distance at which we can cull the mesh for performance optimization purposes, whether it has collision enabled or not, whether it casts dynamic shadows or not and much more. For now, let us focus on only few of these settings, as we will be revisiting Foliage for the final version of the level in *Chapter 13, Fantasy Castle Interactive Blueprint Actors*.

For now, use the same settings as shown in *Figures 11.51, 11.52* and *11.53*:

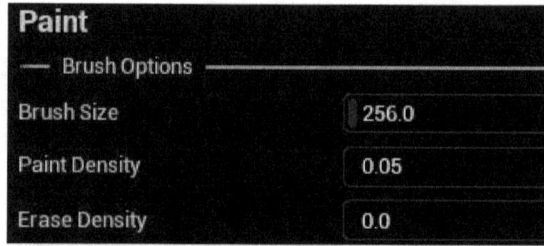

Figure 11.51: *Set Brush Size to 256 and Paint Density to 0.05*

Ensure you are using the settings depicted in *Figure 11.52*:

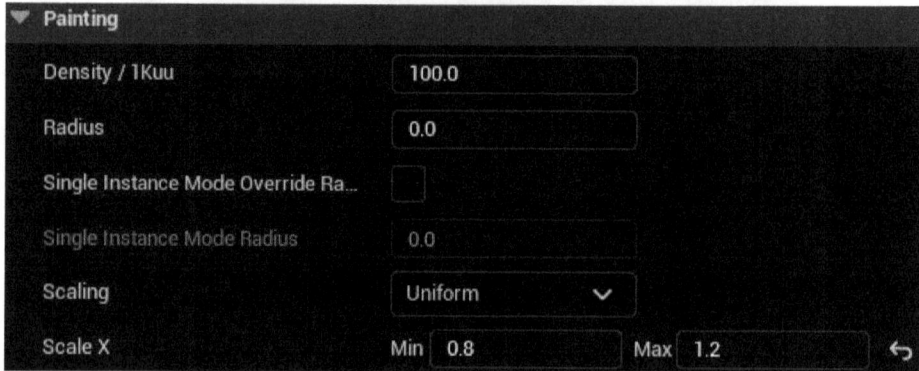

Figure 11.52: *Under Painting, set Scale X Min to 0.8 and Max to 1.2*

Also, ensure you are using the settings depicted in *Figure 11.53*:

Figure 11.53: *Under Instance Settings, set Cull Distance Max to 8000*

Now you can move your mouse cursor to the main Viewport, and you will notice there is a semitransparent, blue shaded dome following your mouse, as shown in *Figure 11.54*. Click somewhere on the floor, and you will start placing individual trees.

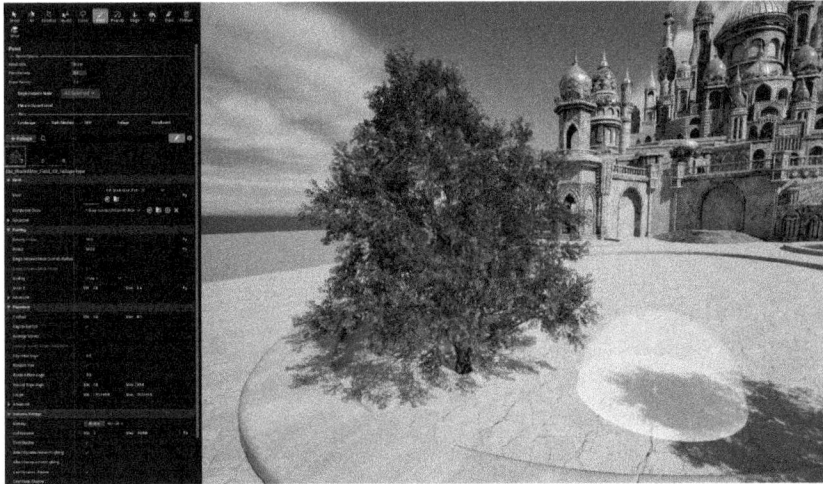

Figure 11.54: Not a spaceship, instead it is the radius within which you can paint Foliage with

This dome indicates the area in which you can paint Foliage. To expand it further, you just need to modify the **Brush Size** under **Paint** (as shown in *Figure 11.51*). If you click and drag the value, the maximum value it will accept is 8192. However, if you manually input the value, you can set some rather large values (e.g. 32000 units).

Overall, the Foliage tool is very powerful, but also needs to be properly set up before usage, or you could end up having a rather large number of densely and unnecessarily populated Foliage, which if not optimized, can drain hardware performance quite considerably.

Keep painting some trees; they do not need to be perfect as we will completely remove them and repaint them in *Chapter 13, Fantasy Castle Interactive Blueprint Actors*, but the process not only helps the reader familiarize themselves with the Foliage tools and processes but most importantly helps visualize the end result.

Figure 11.55 shows the result of this step when the author was busy developing this project:

Figure 11.55: The placeholder Foliage helps visualize the end result and enables the scene to resemble the concept more and more

Modifying the atmospheric conditions

To exit the Foliage mode and go back to the regular Selection mode press *Shift+1* or navigate to the same drop-down menu as in *Figure 11.46*. In the Outliner tab, look for the **ExponentialHeightFog** actor, select it, and then modify its color as shown in *Figure 11.56*:

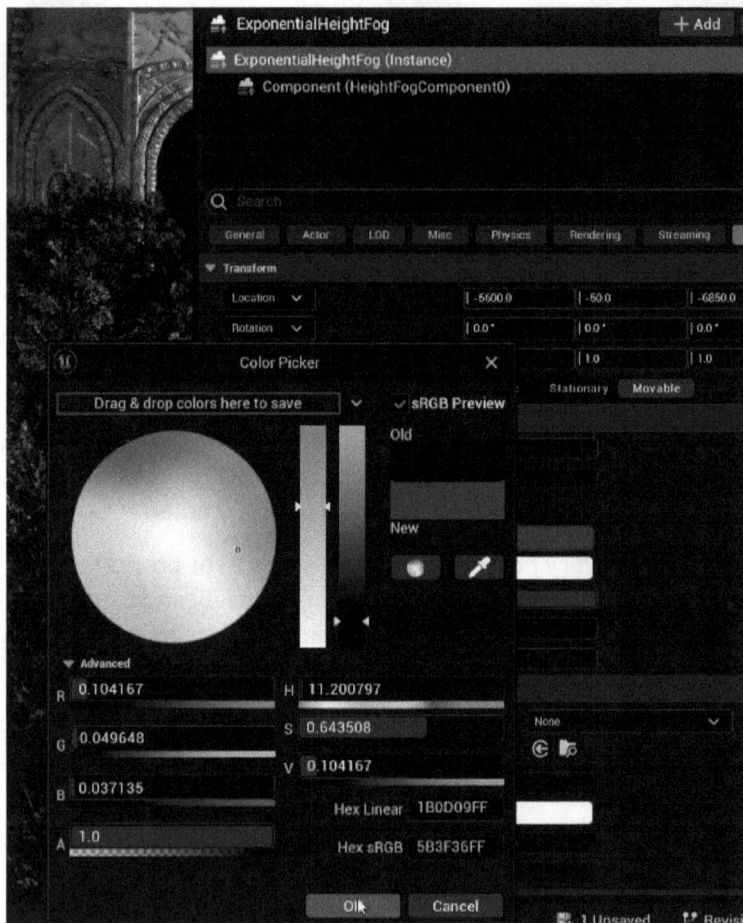

Figure 11.56: Getting the golden haze seen in the reference concept image in Chapter 7

Landscaping

There are two approaches for creating and completing a landscape in Unreal. One can either utilize the Landscape toolset (*Shift +2*), with which can create a grid-based terrain, assign it a specific Material — preferably a landscape Material, meaning a Material specially created for landscapes, featuring layers that can be used while painting the landscape (e.g. snow and grass, or grass and mud etc.), and of course sculpt it or use height maps to shape the terrain, and more.

The other approach is to use Static Meshes which contain terrain, rocks, mountains and other geological features. Usually, such Static Meshes are built with the help of 3D scanning processes, in order to achieve best results. Quixel Bridge is a fine place for such examples.

Ideally, most of the time a project will use a combination of both of the above-mentioned methods. For this project, truth is we can simply use the second method, and we mostly will, by downloading some qualitative Quixel Bridge assets, but just for the purpose of briefly introducing the landscape tool, we will shape some terrain on and around the castle grounds.

As a first step of giving some form and shape to the landscape, we can download the Quixel Bridge asset displayed in *Figure 11.57*:

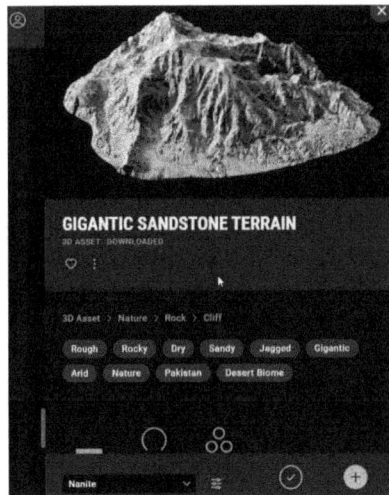

Figure 11.57: An excellent asset that can be used as a mountain backdrop

By scaling the mountain mesh considerably (set X,Y,Z scale values to 20) and placing it far in the back, then duplicating it a couple of times, rotating the duplicates, and slightly modifying their scales on different axis values, one can get a result similar to the one in *Figure 11.58*:

Figure 11.58: Mountain backdrops can add a lot to a scene

In *Chapter 15, Level Finalization and Packaging*, we will be adding more meshes, to complete the terrain surrounding the castle. For this next step, let us just create a simple terrain, which will serve as the foundation for some of the Foliage, mainly within the castle grounds (the courtyard).

Shift+1 or selecting **Landscape Mode** (*Figure 11.46*) opens up the **Landscape** tab, as shown in *Figure 11.59*. For the time being, we will create a landscape larger than we actually need because, once again, *Chapter 13, Fantasy Castle Interactive Blueprint Actors*, is where we will be optimizing the level.

Figure 11.59: The green grid represents the area the landscape will cover

Use the same settings as displayed in *Figure 11.60*:

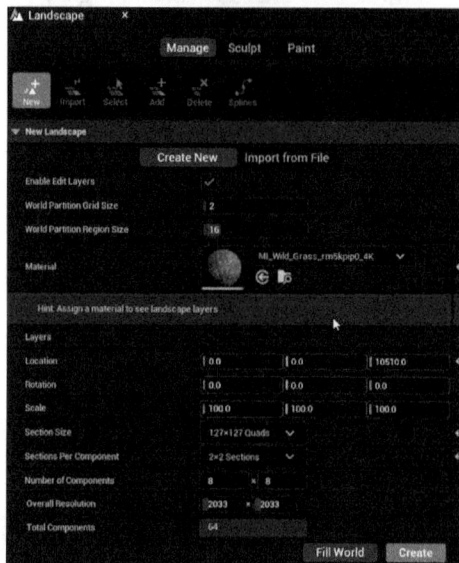

Figure 11.60: Use the above settings when creating the landscape

Once you have created the landscape with the settings displayed in *Figure 11.60*, you will get a flat terrain as the one depicted in *Figure 11.61*. From a distance, it looks like we used a single color-based Material, but upon closer inspection, we can see the detail of the Material used, as seen in *Figure 11.61*. This Material is rather simple, not necessarily the best option for a landscape, but it certainly covers the needs of this project. It is a Material borrowed from the freely available City Park collection, discussed earlier in this chapter.

Figure 11.61: The newly created landscape

Figure 11.62: A closer look at the landscape's Material reveals there's more detail

Next, while in the **Sculpt** mode of the **Landscape** tab, set the **Brush Size** to around 1024 (*Figure, 11.63*), leave everything else at default.

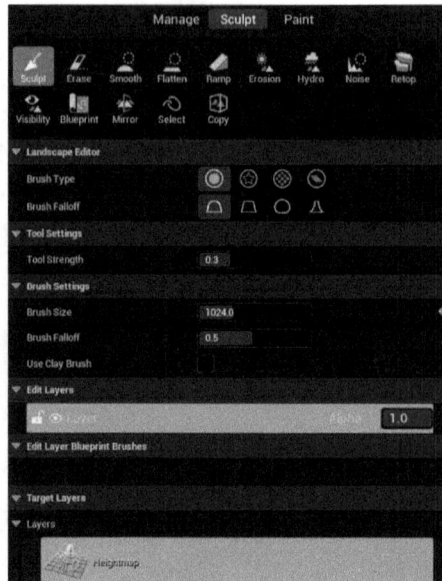

Figure 11.63: *Set the sculpt brush size to 1024*

Click anywhere on the landscape, and you will notice the selected area's terrain rise as seen in *Figure 11.64*:

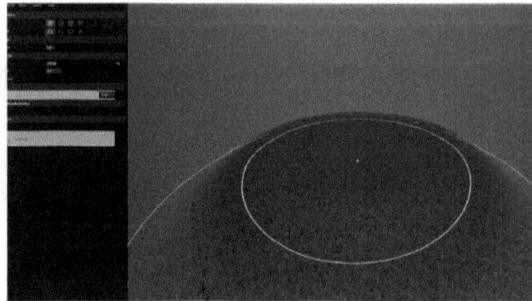

Figure 11.64: *Raising the terrain by clicking anywhere on it*

Hold *Shift+Click* and you will notice it sink as shown in *Figure 11.65*:

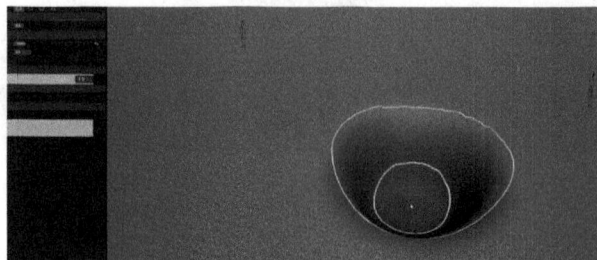

Figure 11.65: *Sinking the terrain by Shift+clicking anywhere on it*

Next, in the **Landscape** tab, under **Sculpt**, select **Flatten**, as shown in *Figure 11.66*. **Flatten** essentially is a brush that allows us to flatten any part of the terrain, especially useful when parts of the terrain need to be leveled, with equal elevation, as we need them to be in castle's courtyard grounds.

Figure 11.66: Select the Flatten tool to level the ground

Figure 11.67 shows two applications of the **Flatten** tool. In one instance, it was applied over the elevated ground; in the other, over the sunken terrain. The end result is what could eventually evolve into a cliff.

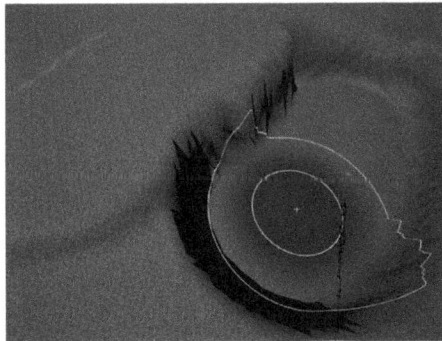

Figure 11.67: The Flatten tool applied on both elevated and sunken terrain surfaces

Note how the elevation difference between the higher and the lower terrain results in a rough transition, with shadows that are most certainly not very smooth. The best way to smoothen this abrupt difference, is by selecting the **Smooth** tool (*Figure 11.68*) and then brushing with it over the two types of terrain (*Figure 11.69*):

Figure 11.68: Selecting the Smooth tool

The following figure shows the smooth tool applied over the rough terrain transitions:

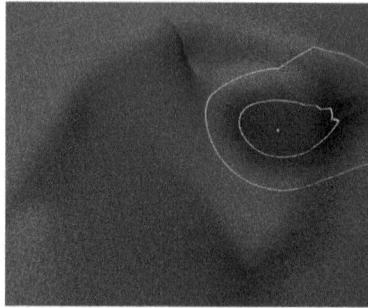

Figure 11.69: *The Smooth tool applied over the rough terrain transitions*

Now, it is a good time to slightly elevate the terrain with sculpting, right where we placed the trees in the earlier steps, while using the Flatten tool to even the terrain within the designated area, as shown in *Figure 11.70*:

Figure 11.70: *Using the Landscape mode's tools to create a nice, even terrain beneath the trees we placed earlier in Foliage mode*

Combining the above techniques

By combining all of the above techniques, paired with patient dedication and attention to detail, eventually, your level design process should resemble the concept reference image from *Chapter 7, Fantasy Castle Project Breakdown and Planning*. In *Chapter 13, Fantasy Castle Interactive Blueprint Actors*, we will be revisiting a lot of these processes, for the purpose of finetuning, optimizing and finalizing, but in this chapter, we can already see the resemblance to our end goal. *Figures 11.71 to 11.76* show some of the author's work progress during this stage of the project. At this point, it was also a good opportunity to bring the Greek God Statue from the book's earlier project into this project's asset collection.

Figure 11.71: *Almost there — visually speaking*

In the following figure, the concept shows certain aspects of the entire environment:

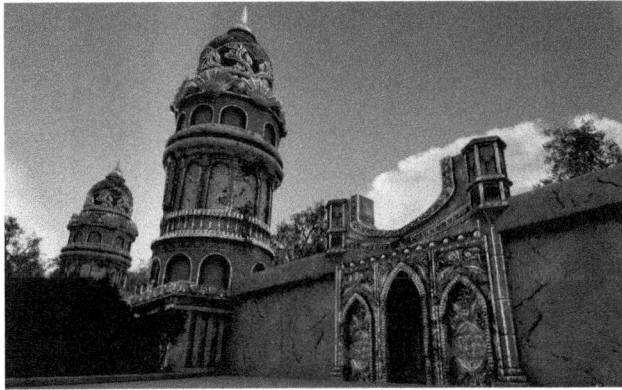

Figure 11.72: *Some parts will require imagination since the concept showed us only certain aspects of the entire environment*

The following figure shows the view from the castle's grounds:

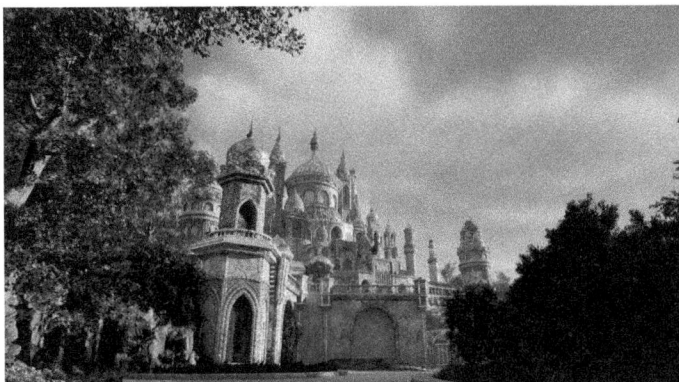

Figure 11.73: *The view from the castle's grounds*

The following figure shows the Greek God Statue:

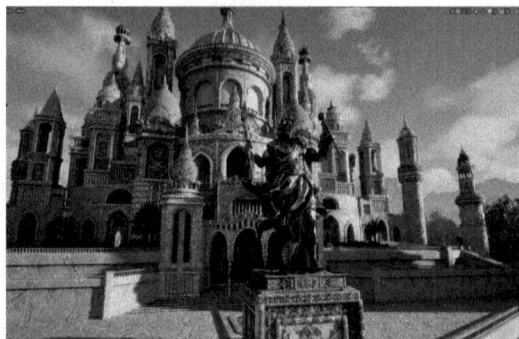

Figure 11.74: The Greek God Statue seems to fit right in

The following figure shows a view from an angle the concept did not show us:

Figure 11.75: The view from an angle the concept did not show us

The following figure shows the view from the castle:

Figure 11.76: The view from the castle

Conclusion

We created the Fantasy Castle Project, then we proceeded with importing the assets created in previous chapters, categorized, and organized them within our project's **Content** folder structure, while being efficient in the way we handled the large number of assets. We created a Master Material, from which we derived close to a hundred Material Instances, while assigning to it custom parameters that allow us to finetune each Material Instance's properties individually..

From there, we assigned all the Materials to their corresponding Static Meshes, which in turn were used modularly, combined with each other, in ways that resemble *Chapter 7's, Fantasy Castle Project Breakdown and Planning* reference image's breakdown. We explored the different options available to us for combining multiple meshes into one, considering the pros and cons of each method.

We did use the Landscape and Foliage modes to slightly enrich our scene, mainly for visualization purposes, while we also took advantage of both Quixel Bridge and some of the freely available Unreal Marketplace assets to enrich our Foliage and terrain asset libraries.

At this point, the level has a very strong visual resemblance to our end goal, yet there is still a lot more work to be done on this project. In *Chapter 12, Fantasy Castle Character and Interaction Blueprints*, we will set up our own character while we will create interactive Blueprints and a mini game. In *Chapter 13, Fantasy Castle Interactive Blueprint Actors*, we will finalize and optimize the entire level, including lighting, interactive actor placement, geometry, and Foliage optimizations, while in *Chapter 14, Fantasy Castle Mini Game Blueprints*, we will package the project into an executable.

Points to remember

- Proper and efficiently organized folder structure is of paramount importance when working with a large number of assets.

- While having a lot of assets, there is a need for only a few (or even one) Master Material, from which multiple Material Instances can be derived, therefore facilitating better performance in runtime.

- There are many methods to combine multiple meshes into one, each with its set of advantages and disadvantages.

- Brief look at Foliage mode.

- Brief look at Landscape mode.

- Be creative; do not rely 100% on the concept; use your imagination and creativity.

Exercise

1. Create your own level with a new landscape, complete with some Foliage. Combine multiple meshes into modular building parts (towers, archways, entire buildings even) and create your own fantasy castle, or maybe even a small town!

Join our book's Discord space

Join the book's Discord Workspace for Latest updates, Offers, Tech happenings around the world, New Release and Sessions with the Authors:

https://discord.bpbonline.com

CHAPTER 12

Fantasy Castle Character and Interaction Blueprints

Introduction

In this chapter, we will be working with Blueprints. We will take the default Third Person template and modify it for this project. We will replace the character model, while we will add some useful features to the character Blueprint, such as switching between first and third-person views, toggling a character light on and off, and switching between walking, running, and sprinting.

Structure

The structure followed in this chapter:

- Modifying the Third Person template's character Blueprint
- Changing the character mesh
- Third Person character Blueprint
- Creating sprint, walk and run functions
- Creating a zoom in/out functionality
- Creating a player light that can be toggled on/off
- Switching between third and first-person views

Objectives

This chapter's objectives are to expose and engage the reader in Blueprints. It is worth noting that this is addressed to entry level users, as Blueprints can get quite complex, to the point that one could write an entire series of books on the subject. However, this chapter should provide anyone with a good entry point to the wonderful world of Blueprints.

Modifying Third Person template's character Blueprint

Before getting started, let us list all the features we will be adding to the character Blueprint:

- Replace the character model
- Add a first/third person view toggle functionality
- Add a mouse wheel scroll zoom in/out functionality
- Add a toggle walk/run functionality
- Add a sprint functionality
- Add a character light toggle functionality

The first thing we will need to update is the end user input. The easiest way to do this is by navigating to the top of your main Unreal Editor window, selecting **Edit,** and then clicking on **Project Settings** as shown in *Figure 12.1*:

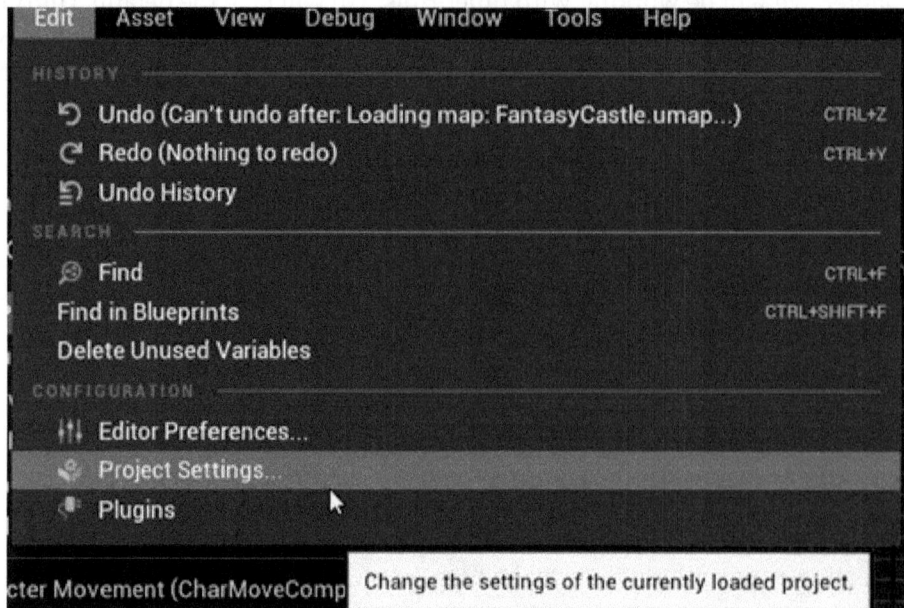

Figure 12.1: Project Settings

Once the **Project Settings** window pops up, scroll down and navigate to **Input** under the **Engine** category, on the left-hand side, as shown in *Figure 12.2*:

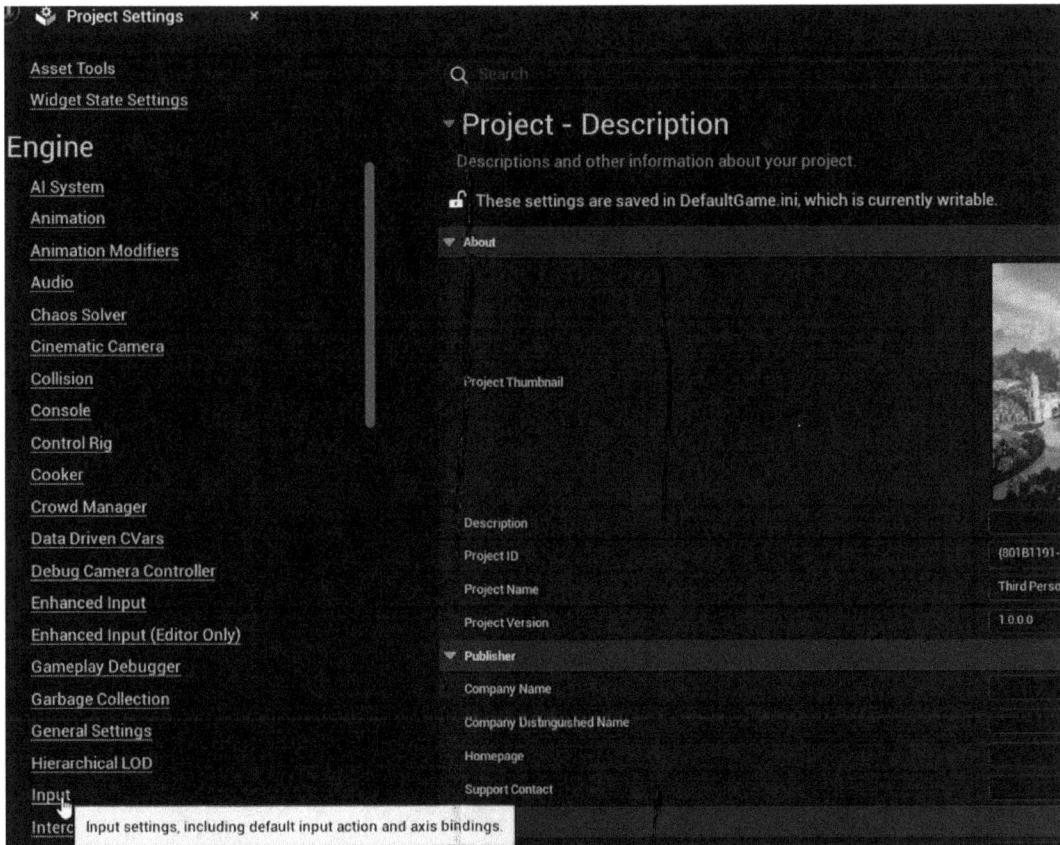

Figure 12.2: *Project Settings*

Now, under Bindings expand **Action Mappings** and click on the add icon (circle with + in it). Then, name the newly added mapping `Sprint`, expand it, and assign `Left Shift` as its input, as shown in *Figure 12.3*:

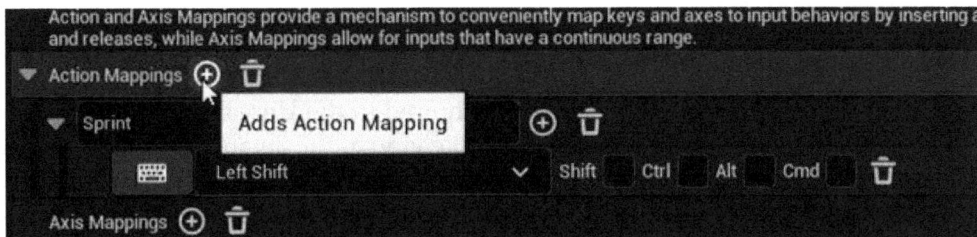

Figure 12.3: *Adding your first custom input*

Repeat these steps until your input **Action Mappings** look identical to the ones in *Figure 12.4*:

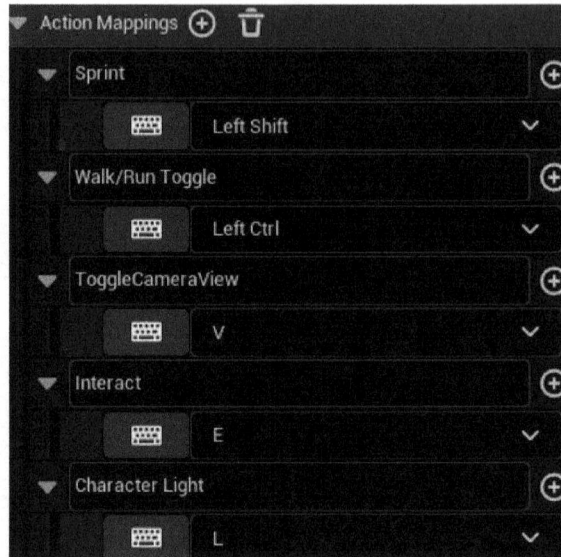

Figure 12.4: Complete list of Action Mappings

Now repeat the same step for **Axis Mappings**, which is right below the **Action Mappings**. Add a new mapping, name it **CameraZoom**, and assign the **Mouse Wheel Axis** as its input, as shown in *Figure 12.5*:

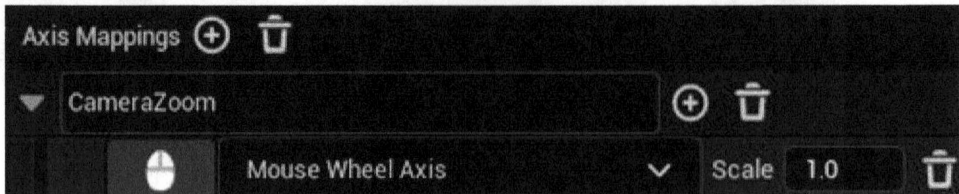

Figure 12.5: Complete list of Action Mappings

Changing the character mesh

If you are relying on using character models acquired in the Unreal Engine Marketplace, most of the time, they are rigged with the same skeleton as the default characters provided with the engine's templates, which means it is rather easy to import them into projects and use them right away. But sometimes your projects might require that you work with characters that need some extra work before being ready to use, characters that might have a different skeleton — even if most of the time with a similar bone structure — than the default ones.

In that case, you would need to follow a process, called **retargeting** in which essentially you identify the similarities between two different skeletons, link these similarities and ultimately allow one to use the other's assets (such as animations and more).

For this project's purposes and theme, the author created *Sumati*, a 3D character model (*Figure 12.6*), by using Reallusion Character Creator 4 and Maxon ZBrush:

Figure 12.6: Meet Sumati!

If you are interested in learning more about retargeting, keep on reading. If you want to simply use the already retargeted model provided with the project, then reading this section of this chapter is not required.

If you are importing a character, then you are looking to import an FBX file. When importing an FBX, we previously encountered the different options you are presented with, but these were specifically for Static Meshes. Now, since we are importing a character model rigged with a complete skeleton, we are importing a Skeletal Mesh and not a Static Mesh. As such, ensure your **FBX Import Options** popup utilizes the settings displayed in *Figure 12.7*:

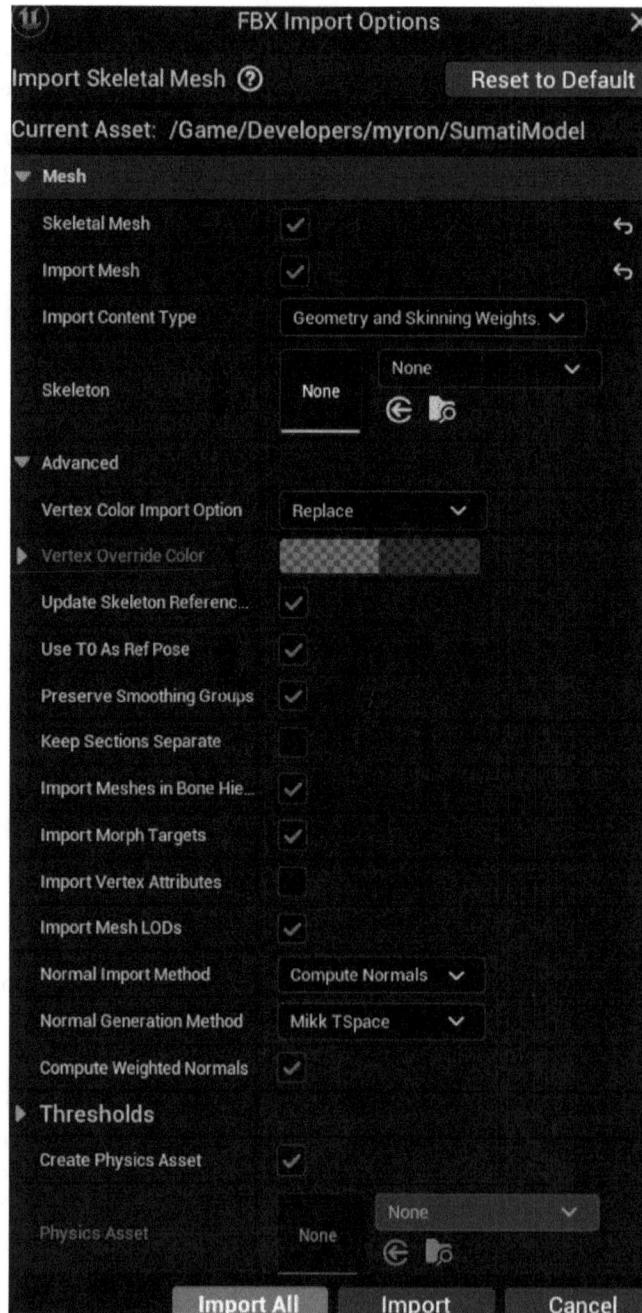

Figure 12.7: FBX Import Options for a Skeletal Mesh

Next, in your Content Browser, navigate to **Content/Characters/Mannequins/Rigs/**, select and right click on **IK_Mannequin**, and then select **Duplicate**, as shown in *Figure 12.8*:

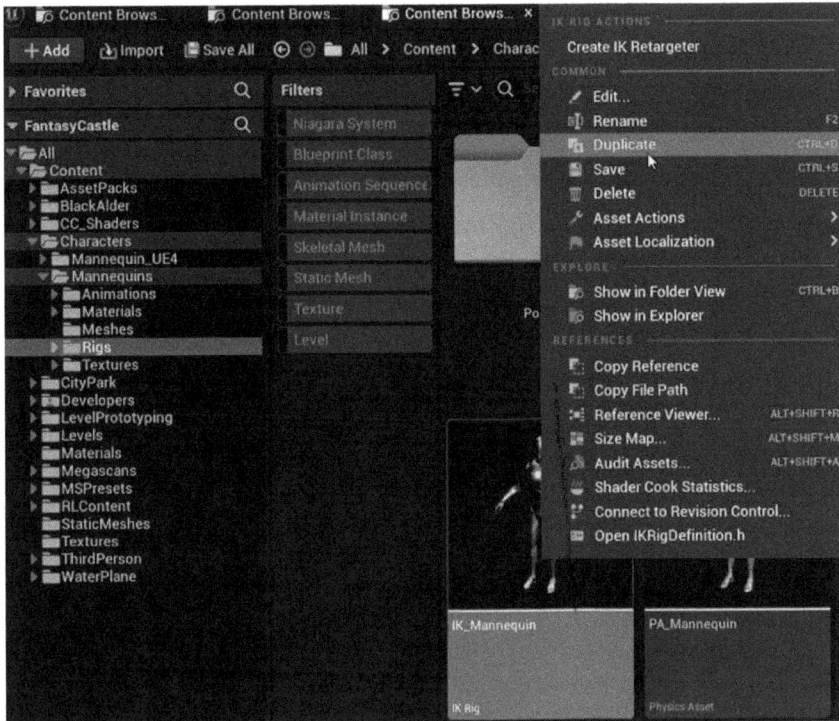

Figure 12.8: *Duplicating the IK_Mannequin rig*

Rename the duplicated **IK_Mannequin** asset to IK_Mannequin_For_OurModel. Now double click it to open it. It should resemble what is shown in *Figure 12.9*:

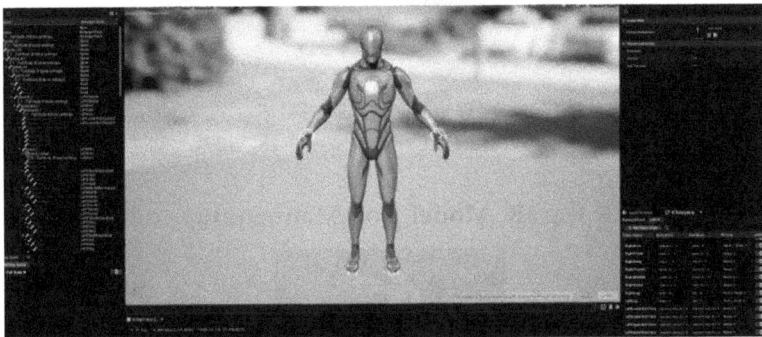

Figure 12.9: *What you see when you open the duplicated IK_Mannequin rig*

On the lower right-hand corner, under the IK Retargeting tab, remove the **LeftLowerArmTwist01** chain by clicking on the trash bin icon, as shown in *Figure 12.10*:

Figure 12.10: *Removing a chain from the IK Rig*

Keep repeating this action until the chain under **LeftLeg** is **LeftClavicle**, as shown in *Figure 12.11*. Do not forget to save after you are done.

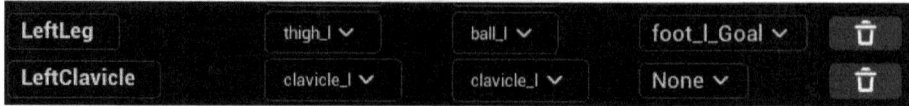

Figure 12.11: After you deleted several chains, the one under LeftLeg should be LeftClavicle

Now right-click on an empty space in your Content Browser, navigate to **Animation**, then to **Retargeting** and from there select **IK Rig** as shown in *Figure 12.12*:

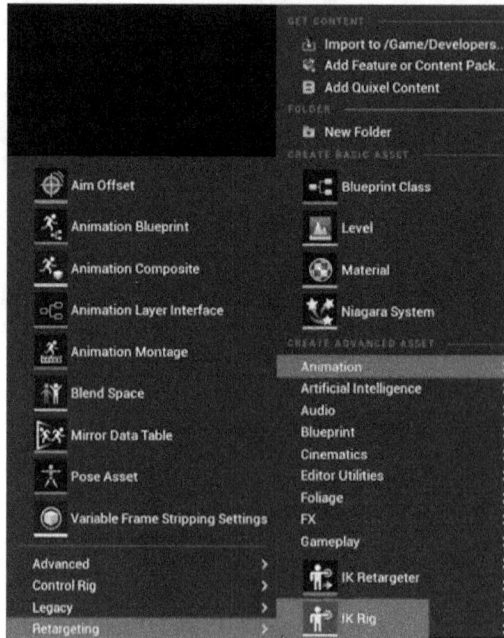

Figure 12.12: Creating a new IK Rig

Name the newly created **IK Rig IK_Model_For_Mannequin**, as shown in *Figure 12.13*:

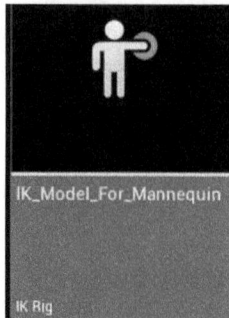

Figure 12.13: Creating a new IK Rig

Double click the newly created **IK Rig**, and in the preview tab on the upper right corner, under **Preview Mesh** set **Preview Skeletal Mesh** to `Sumati`, as shown in *Figure 12.14*, if you are using the provided project files, or to any other Skeletal Mesh you might have acquired and imported:

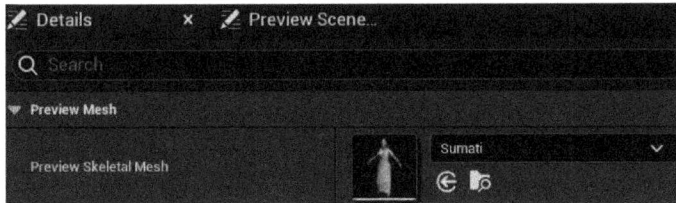

Figure 12.14: Assigning the desired Skeletal Mesh in the newly created IK Rig

On the lower left side of the same window, under the **Solver Stack** tab, click on the +**Add New Solver** button, and then select **Full Body IK**, as shown in *Figure 12.15*:

Figure 12.15: Adding a Full Body IK

Now, right click on the **pelvis** bone, found in the upper left corner of the same window, under the **Hierarchy** tab, and select **Set Root Bone on Selected Solver**, as shown in *Figure 12.16*:

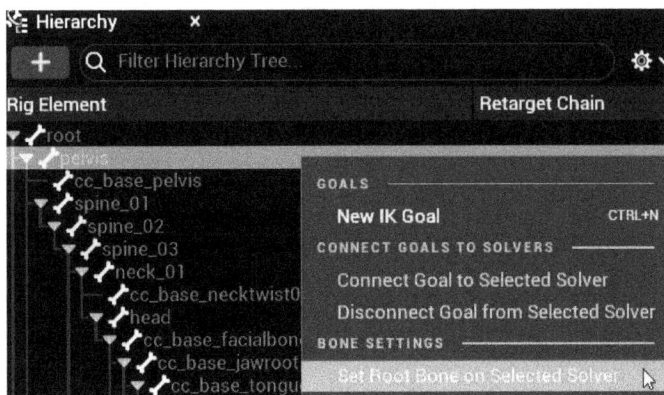

Figure 12.16: Setting the pelvis bone as the root bone

Right click on the **pelvis** bone once more, this time select **Set Retarget Root,** as shown in *Figure 12.17*:

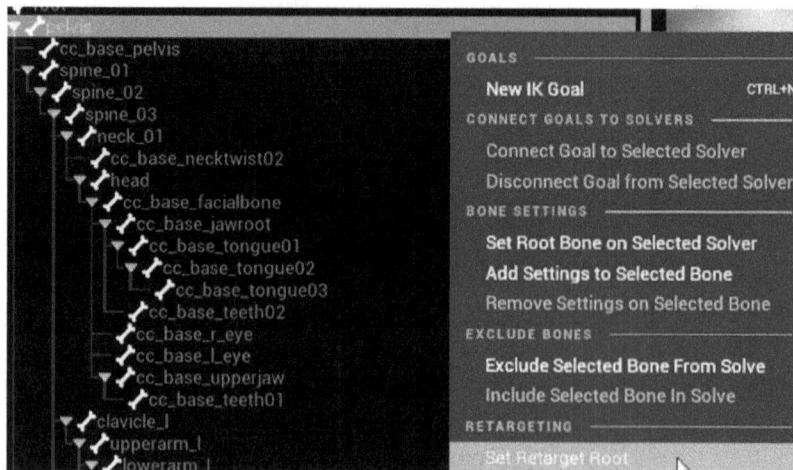

Figure 12.17: Setting the pelvis bone as the Retarget Root

Right click on the **pelvis** bone yet again, this time, select **New Retarget Chain...** as shown in *Figure 12.18*:

Figure 12.18: Selecting New Retarget Chain

In the **Chain Name** field type **Root** and then click on **Add Chain**, as shown in *Figure 12.19*:

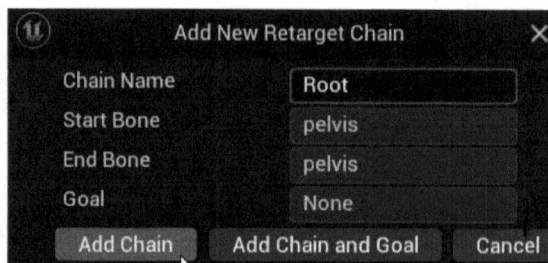

Figure 12.19: Chain Name should be Root, click Add Chain

Now, we will follow that process several times. Right click on the `spine_01` bone and select New Retarget Chain, this time, use **Spine** as the **Chain Name**, and then once more, click **Add Chain**, as indicated in *Figure 12.20*:

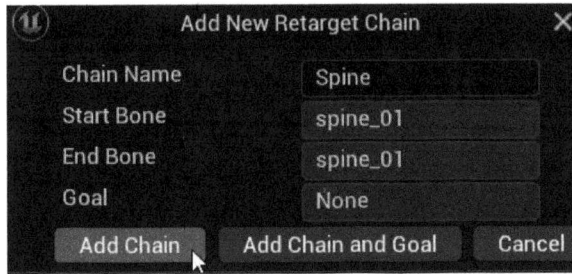

Figure 12.20: *Adding further Retarget Chains*

Quickly jumping on the lower right-hand corner of the window, under the **IK Retargeting** tab, on the **Spine** row, click on the **End Bone** and select `spine_03` from the drop-down menu, as shown in *Figure 12.21*:

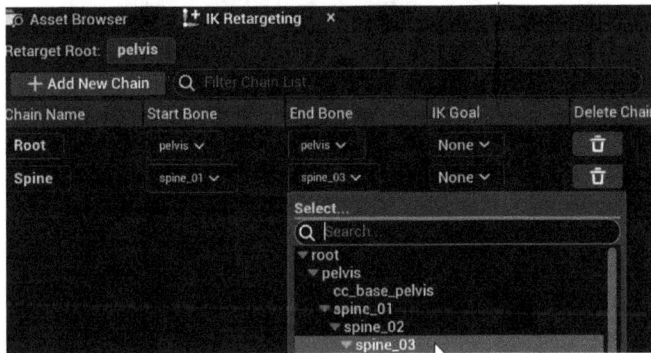

Figure 12.21: *spine_03 is the End Bone of the Spine chain*

We repeat this process in a similar fashion with plenty of other bones till we have essentially defined every chain that includes the set of bones we will reference when retargeting between two skeletons. To expedite the process, you can look at *Figures 12.22* to *12.24*. You will want to be right clicking the same bone as listed in each figure's **Start Bone** field, then select New Retarget Chain and using the **Chain Name** listed in each figure, to finally click **Add Chain**:

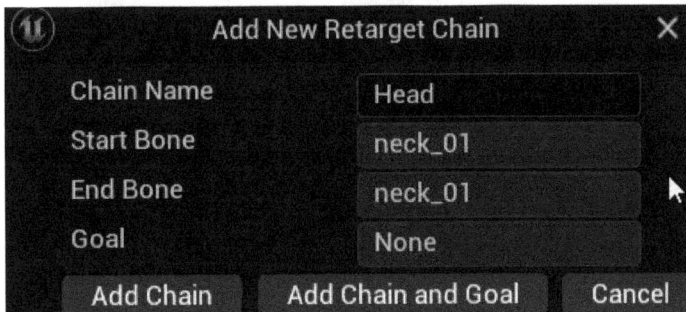

Figure 12.22: *The Head chain*

Figure 12.23 shows the **LeftClavicle** chain:

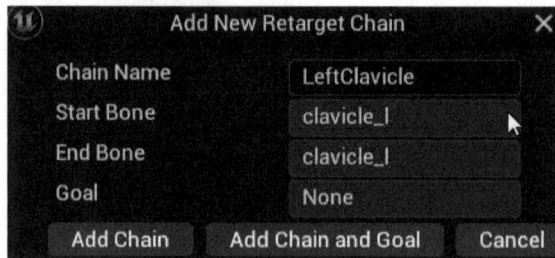

Figure 12.23: *The LeftClavicle chain*

Figure 12.24 shows the **LeftArm** chain.

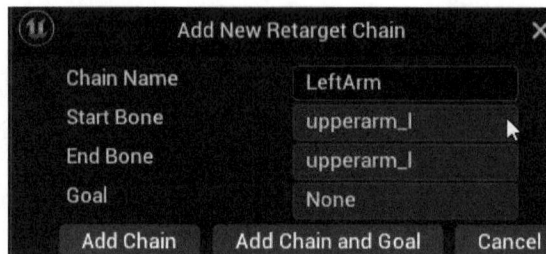

Figure 12.24: *The LeftArm chain*

For the next one, select three bones (by holding *Ctrl* while clicking on bone names), specifically select **pinky_01_l**, **pinky_02_l** and **pinky_03_l**. Right click on them, New Retarget Chain, and use the same as shown in *Figure 12.25*:

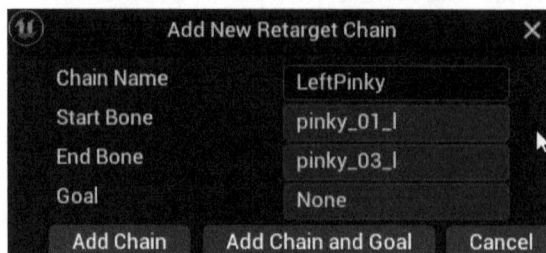

Figure 12.25: *The LeftPinky chain*

We will repeat this approach for all the finger related bones. To expedite the process, *Figures 12.26 to 12.28* indicate the first bone to select in the **Start Bone** field, and the last in the **End Bone** field. Select both the first and the last and all the bones in between the two, and then right click any of them, select New Retarget Chain, and set the names shown in the figures:

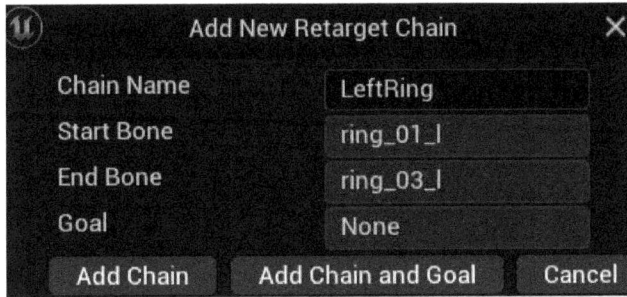

Figure 12.26: The LeftRing chain

The following figure shows the LeftMiddle chain:

Figure 12.27: The LeftMiddle chain

The following figure shows the LeftThumb chain:

Figure 12.28: The LeftThumb chain

Now select and right-click on **hand_l** and select **New IK Goal**, as shown in *Figure 12.29*:

Figure 12.29: New IK Goal for hand_l

Back at the IK Retargeting tab on the lower right, at the **LeftArm** row, set **hand_1** as the End Bone and set **hand_1_Goal** as the IK Goal, as shown in *Figure 12.30*:

LeftArm	upperarm_l ∨	hand_l ∨	hand_l_Goal ∨	🗑

Figure 12.30: Updating the LeftArm chain's End Bone and IK Goal fields

Now, repeat all the steps from *Figure 12.23* to *Figure 12.30* for the right side of our skeleton. It will all be the same with the exception that all the _l suffixes will be _r and all the chain names, instead of using the *Left* prefix, will be using the *Right* prefix. For example, in *Figure 12.30*, the right-hand counterpart would be RightArm, upperarm_r, hand_r, and hand_r_Goal.

Once you have successfully completed the right side, we can move on to the legs of the skeleton. Right click on the **thigh_1** bone, New Retarget Chain, as shown in *Figure 12.31*:

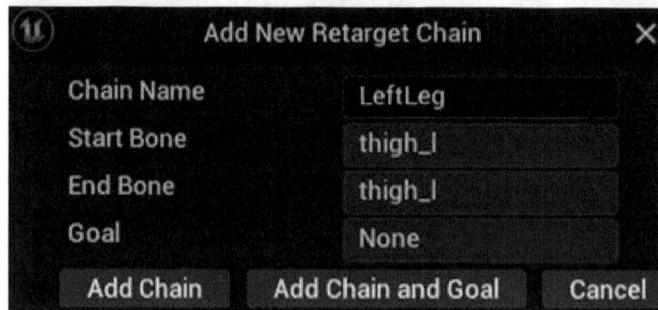

Add New Retarget Chain	✕
Chain Name	LeftLeg
Start Bone	thigh_l
End Bone	thigh_l
Goal	None

Add Chain   **Add Chain and Goal**   **Cancel**

Figure 12.31: The LeftLeg chain

Next, ensure that your **LeftLeg** row is identical to the one in *Figure 12.32*:

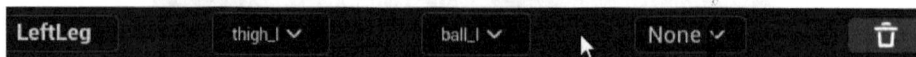

LeftLeg	thigh_l ∨	ball_l ∨	None ∨	🗑

Figure 12.32: The LeftLeg chain's row settings

Repeat the same steps for the right leg, as shown in *Figure 12.33* and *Figure 12.34*:

Add New Retarget Chain	✕
Chain Name	RightLeg
Start Bone	thigh_r
End Bone	thigh_r
Goal	None

Add Chain   **Add Chain and Goal**   **Cancel**

Figure 12.33: The RightLeg chain

The following figure shows RightLeg chain's row settings:

Figure 12.34: The RightLeg chain's row settings

Next, right-click on **ball_l** and select **New IK Goal** as shown in *Figure 12.35*.

Figure 12.35: New IK Goal for ball_l

Then click **Assign Goal** as shown in *Figure 12.36*. Repeat the same for **ball_r**.

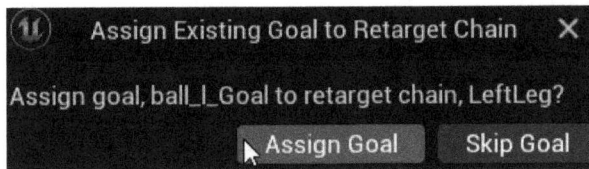

Figure 12.36: Assigning the IK Goal

Back to the **Hierarchy** tab on the left, type in **ik_foot** in the search box, as shown in *Figure 12.37*:

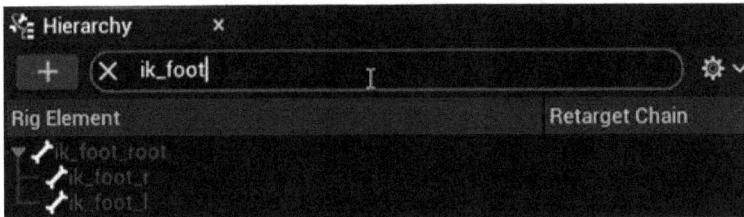

Figure 12.37: Find the ik_foot elements

Right-click on **ik_foot_root** and select New Retarget Chain. Name it **FootRootIK** as shown in *Figure 12.38*:

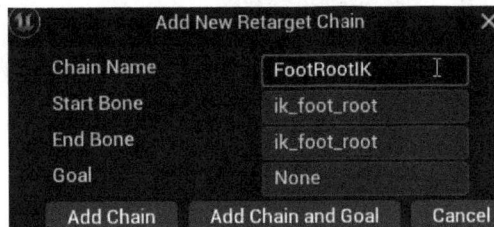

Figure 12.38: FootRootIK retarget chain

Then add a new retarget chain on **ik_foot_l**, name it **LeftFootIK** as shown in *Figure 12.39*:

Figure 12.39: LeftFootIK retarget chain

Repeat the same for **ik_foot_r**, name it RightFootIK.

Returning to the **Hierarchy** search box, type in **ik_hand**, as shown in *Figure 12.40*:

Figure 12.40: ik_hand

Right-click on **ik_hand_root**, create a new retarget chain and name it **HandRootIK**, as shown in *Figure 12.41*:

Figure 12.41: HandRootIK

Next, create a retarget chain for **ik_hand_gun** and name it **HandGunIK**, as seen in *Figure 12.42*:

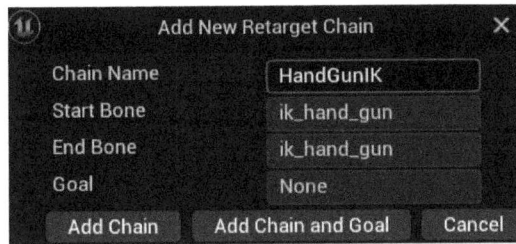

Figure 12.42: *HandGunIK*

Also, create a retarget chain for **ik_hand_l**, name it LeftHandIK, and the same for **ik_hand_r**, which you will name RightHandIK.

If you have done everything correctly, your **IK Retargeting** tab should look identical to the one in *Figure 12.43*:

Figure 12.43: *The finished IK Retargeting tab*

Next, right-click in the Content Browser, navigate to **Animation**, then **Retargeting**, and select **IK Retargeter**, as shown in *Figure 12.44*.

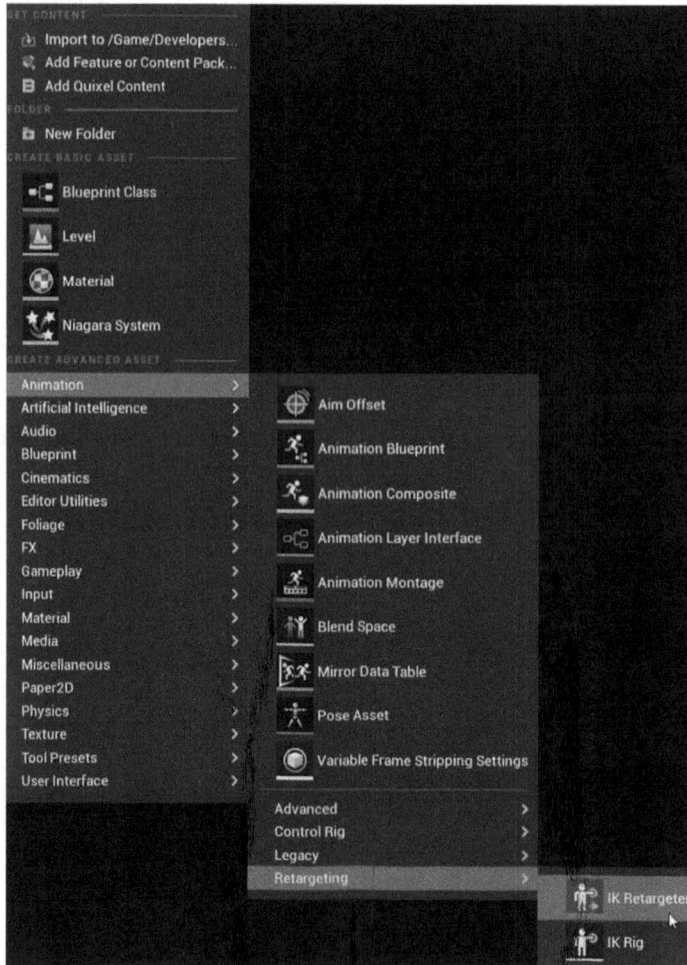

Figure 12.44: *Creating a new IK Retargeter*

Name it **OurModel_To_UE5** as shown in *Figure 12.45*:

Figure 12.45: *Naming the newly created IK Retargeter*

Double click the newly created file, and under the **Details** tab use the same settings as in *Figure 12.46*. Save and close when you are done.

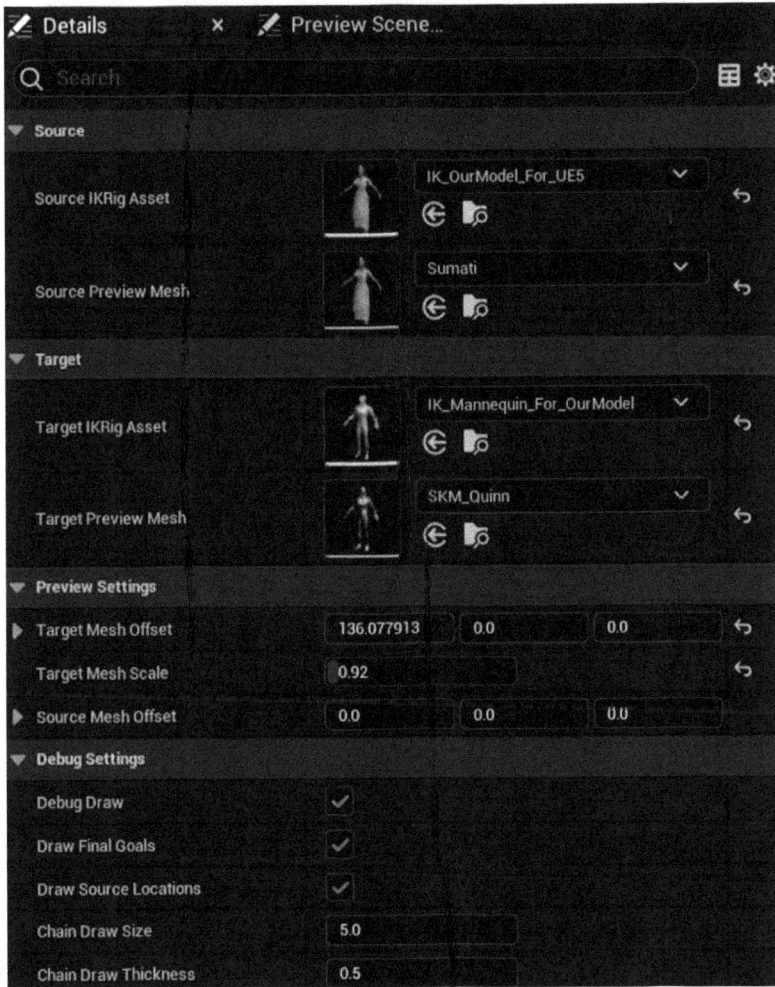

Figure 12.46: The settings you should use for OurModel_To_UE5

Repeat the process shown in *Figure 12.44*, this time name the newly created **IK Retargeter UE5_ToOurModel**, as shown in *Figure 12.47*:

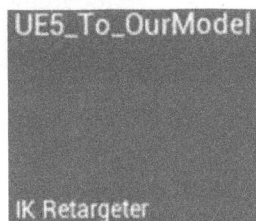

Figure 12.47: Naming the new IK Retargeter UE5_To_OurModel

Figure 12.48 shows the settings you should use for the IK Retargeter we just created:

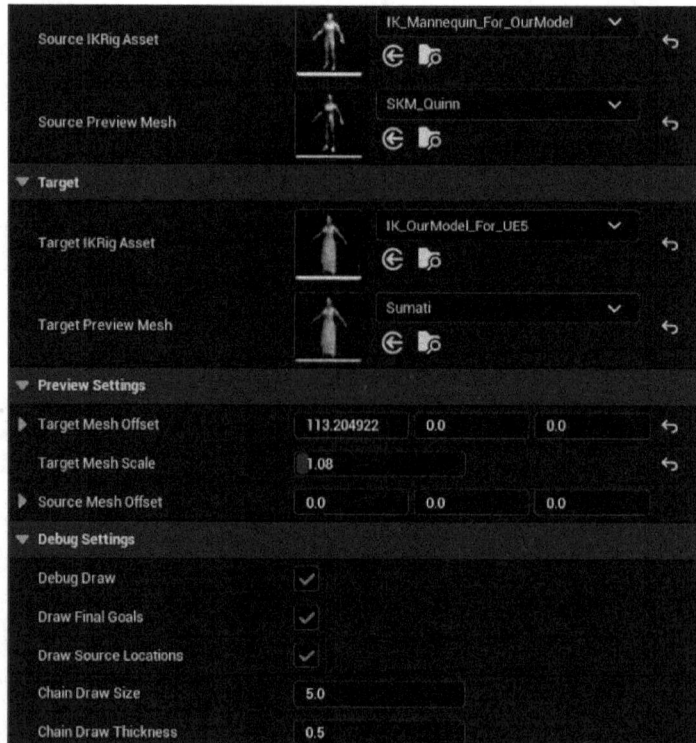

Figure 12.48: In a way, it is the same as Figure 12.46 but with reversed Source and Target

Navigate to **Content/Characters/Mannequins/Animations/** and right click on **ABP_Quinn** and select **Retarget Animation Assets** and then **Duplicate and Retarget Animation Assets/Blueprints** as shown in *Figure 12.49*:

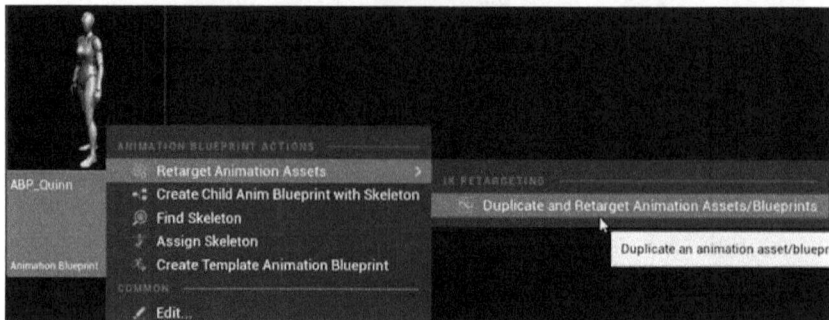

Figure 12.49: Duplicating and retargeting Quinn's animation Blueprint and associated animations

A new prompt will pop up. Under **IK Retargeter**, on the upper right-hand side, select **UE5_To_OurModel**, as shown in *Figure 12.50*. Change the folder to **Content/Characters/Sumati/**:

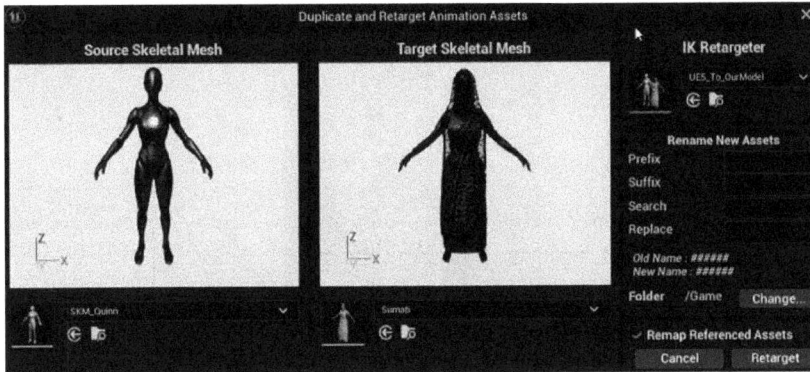

Figure 12.50: *Duplicating and retargeting Quinn's animation assets to Sumati's*

Now save all files, and we are ready to begin modifying the Third Person character Blueprint.

Third Person character Blueprint

In the Content Browser, navigate to **Content/ThirdPerson/Blueprints** and double click BP_ThirdPersonCharacter. On the upper left corner, under the Components tab click on **Mesh (CharacterMesh0)**, as shown in *Figure 12.51*:

Figure 12.51: *The Character Mesh Component within the BP_ThirdPersonCharacter Blueprint*

With the Mesh Component selected, on the upper right-hand side of the screen, under the Details tab, change the **Mesh** to **Sumati**, while using **ABP_Quinn** as the **Anim Class**, as shown in *Figure 12.52*:

Figure 12.52: *Replacing Quinn with Sumati*

Now, if you play in the Viewport, you will be controlling Sumati as your playable character, as shown in *Figures 12.53* and *12.54*:

Figure 12.53: Sumati as a playable character in game

Figure 12.54: Sumati running

Compile the Blueprint and save it. You may recall earlier in this chapter, we modified the project settings and added some new input mappings. Now it is a good point to develop the functionalities these inputs will be controlling.

Let us start with modifying the character's walk/run cycle. By default, the Third Person template provides a walk and a run animation, but it does not provide a sprinting one. Naturally there are plenty of great packages on the Unreal Engine marketplace, providing you with some excellent locomotion-based animations. However, for this project's purpose, we just need a simple sprint animation. The author is not an animator by any means, and that is a testament to the Unreal Engine's versatility, as we will duplicate an existing running animation, slightly modify it to look like a sprinting animation, and use that.

In the Content Browser, navigate to **Content/Characters/Mannequins/Animations/ Quinn/** and select and right click on **MF_Run_Fwd** and select **Duplicate** as shown in *Figure 12.55*:

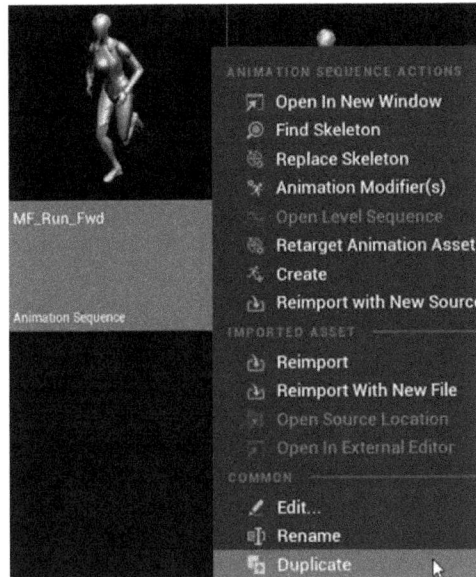

Figure 12.55: Duplicating Quinn's run forward animation

Name the newly created animation **MF_Sprint_Fwd,** as shown in *Figure 12.56*:

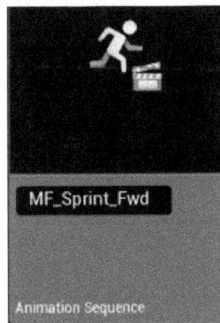

Figure 12.56: Name the duplicated animation MF_Sprint_Fwd

Double click to open the newly created animation. Firstly, pause the animation loop, by pressing the pause button as shown in *Figure 12.57*, then press the backwards arrow all the way to the left, to ensure you are in the animation sequence's first frame.

Figure 12.57: Pause the animation cycle loop

Next, position the camera in the main Viewport in a way that allows you to look at the character from the side, as shown in *Figure 12.58*:

Figure 12.58: *This is what the first frame of the default run animation looks like*

On the upper left corner of the window, under the Skeleton Tree tab, click on spine_03 to select it, as shown in *Figure 12.59*. Back in the center of the screen, in the Viewport, select the rotation gizmo (shortcut *E*) and rotate the spine by 20 degrees to the front of the model, as shown in *Figure 12.60*:

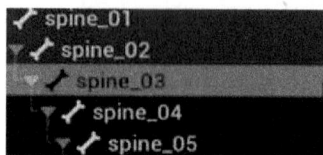

Figure 12.59: *Selecting spine_03*

Back in the center of the screen, in the Viewport, select the rotation gizmo (shortcut E) and rotate the spine by 20 degrees to the front of the model, as shown in *Figure 12.60*:

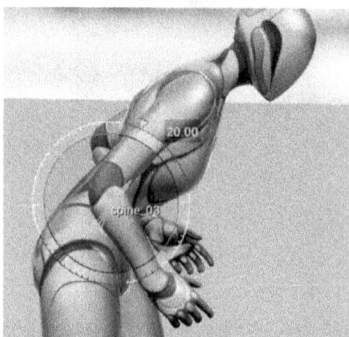

Figure 12.60: *Rotating spine_03 20 degrees to the front*

Next, in a similar way, select and rotate spin_05, rotate it backward by 15 degrees, as shown in *Figure 12.61*:

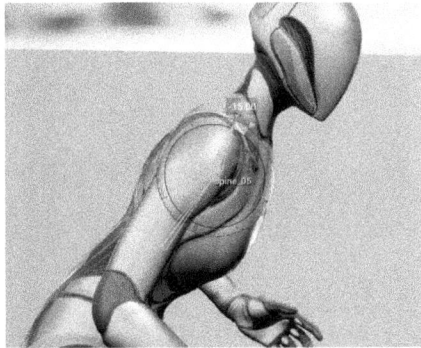

Figure 12.61: Rotating spine_05 backward by 15 degrees

Similarly, select **head** and rotate it backward by 15 degrees as well, as shown in *Figure 12.62*:

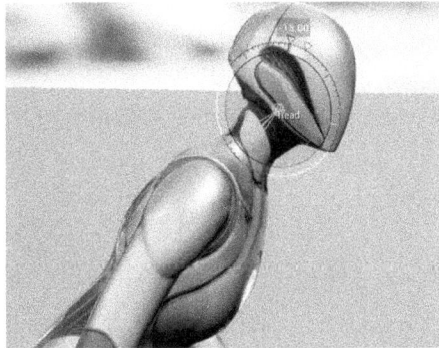

Figure 12.62: Rotating head backwards by 15 degrees

Now, on the top center, click on the **+Key** button, as shown in *Figure 12.63* and then save the animation.

Figure 12.63: Press the +Key button to register all the changes you just performed

The end result should look similar to the one in *Figure 12.64*, which you can compare to *Figure 12.58* to notice the difference between the two.

Figure 12.64: Compare the resulting sprint pose with the running pose in Figure 12.58

Next right click in the Content Browser, and navigate to **Animation**, then select **Legacy** and click on **Blend Space 1D** as displayed in *Figure 12.65*.

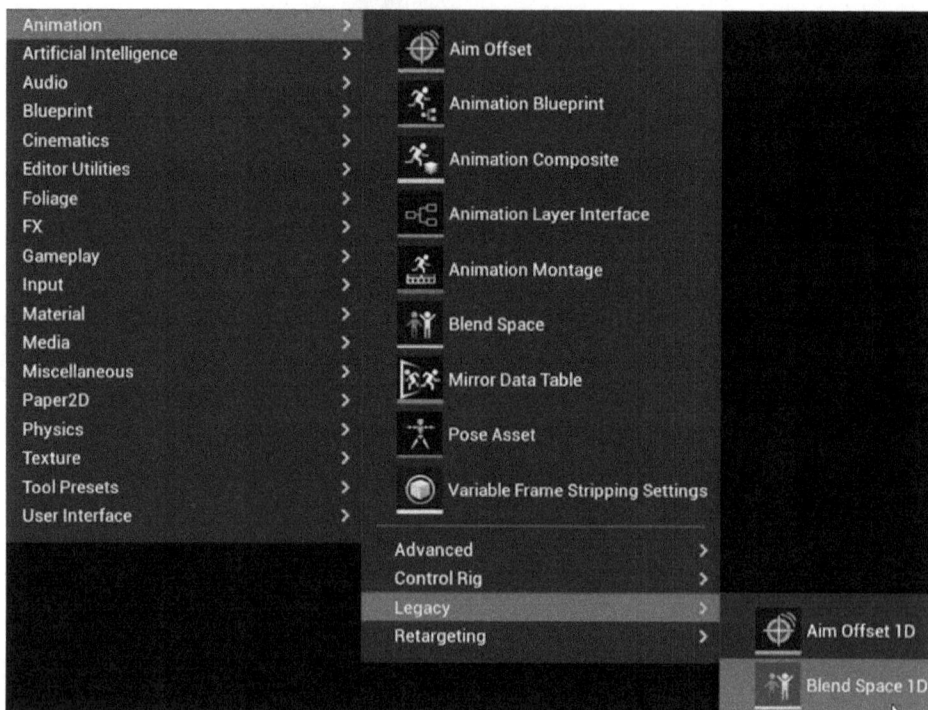

Figure 12.65: Creating a one-dimensional Blend Space

You will be asked to pick a skeleton, pick **SK_Mannequin** as shown in *Figure 12.66*. Name the newly created blend space **BS_Walk_Run_Sprint**.

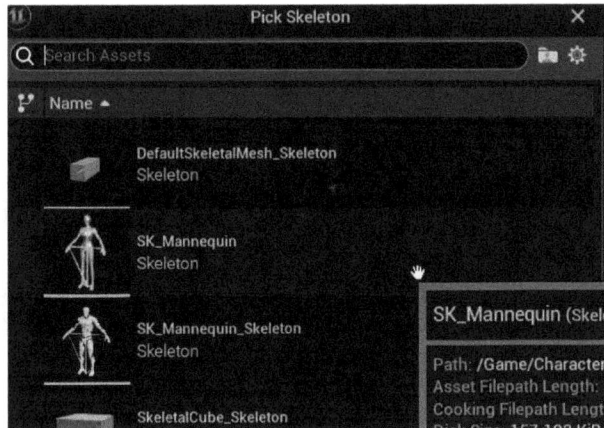

Figure 12.66: Selecting the Mannequin skeleton

Essentially, the Blend Space, as the name indicates, is a way to blend different animations together. The reason we use it is to blend between animations in different locomotive states, specifically walking, running, and sprinting.

Open the newly created blend space and click on the **Asset Details** tab on the upper left corner. Use the same settings as shown in *Figure 12.67*:

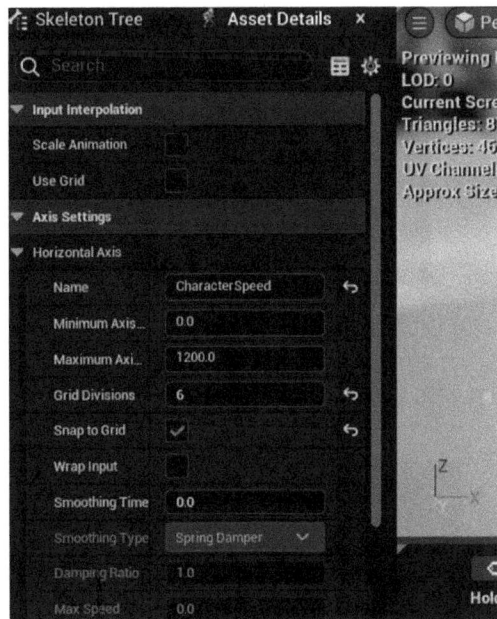

Figure 12.67: Use the settings shown

Essentially, we just created a grid that will be divided into 6 points, with a total length of 1200 units on a straight line. *Figure 12.68* displays that line:

Figure 12.68: Straight line with four points, 0 being the point all the way to the left, 1200 all the way to the right

On the lower right corner of your window, under the **Asset Browser** tab, search for `walk in place` as shown in *Figure 12.69*:

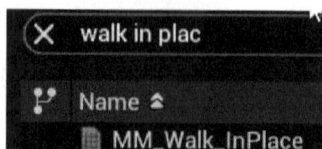

Figure 12.69: Searching for walk in place

Click and drag **MM_Walk_InPlace** to the leftmost point of the graph on the center lower part of the window, as shown in *Figure 12.70*:

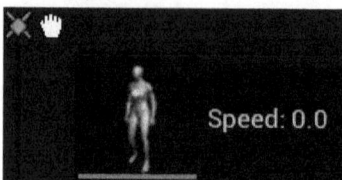

Figure 12.70: Dropping the MM_Walk_In_Place animation in the graph's leftmost point

Back in the **Asset Browser** tab, type in the search field **mf_** and you will get the results shown in *Figure 12.71*:

Figure 12.71: Searching for animations with the mf_ prefix

Click and drag **MF_Walk_Fwd** to the second vertical line from the left in the graph, as shown in *Figure 12.72*:

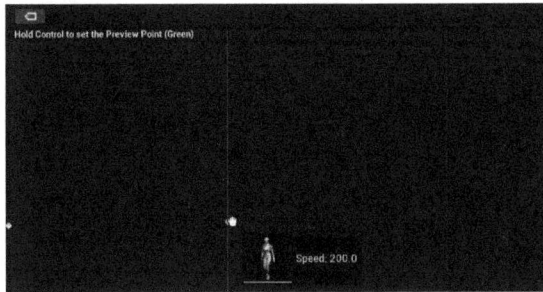

Figure 12.72: *Placing MF_Walk_Fwd to the 200 value point*

Click and drag **MF_Run_Fwd** to the fourth vertical line (the middle) from the left in the graph, as shown in *Figure 12.73*:

Figure 12.73: *Placing MF_Run_Fwd to the 600 value point*

Click and drag **MF_Sprint_Fwd** to the sixth vertical line from the left, all the way to the right in the graph, as shown in *Figure 12.74*:

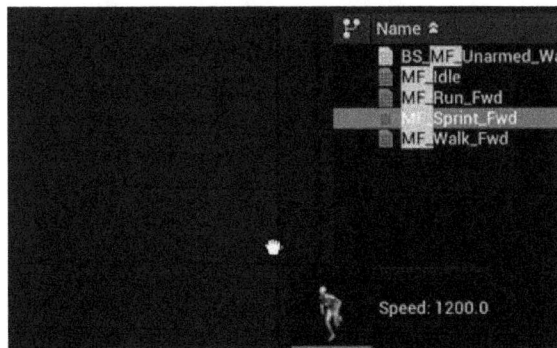

Figure 12.74: *Placing MF_Run_Fwd to the 1200 value point*

Before proceeding, right click on that last point we just placed, and set the **Rate Scale** to 1.6, which means the animation will be playing 1.6 times faster than originally, thus giving a better sense of sprinting. This step is shown in *Figure 12.75*:

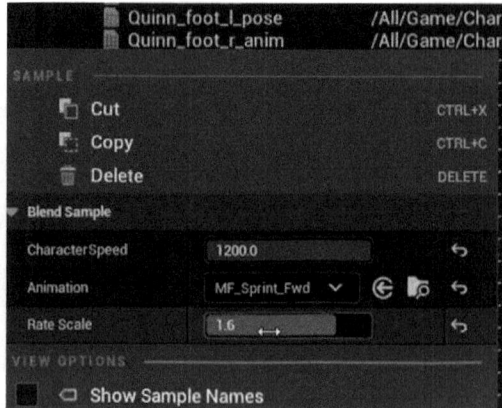

Figure 12.75: *Increasing the sprint animation's playback speed*

Next, save and close the blend space asset. Back in the Content Browser, navigate to **Content/Characters/Mannequins/Animations/** and double click on **ABP_Quinn**, which is Quinn's **Animation Blueprint,** as shown in *Figure 12.76*:

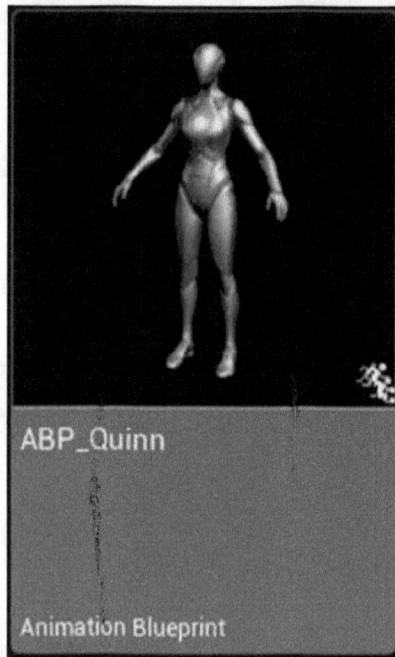

Figure 12.76: *Quinn's Animation Blueprint*

On the upper right corner of the ABP's window, under the **Asset Override…** tab, expand **ABP_Manny** until you can see **Walk/Run**, which you then expand as well, and then you place the **BS_Walk_Run_Sprint** blend space we just created in the corresponding field, as shown in *Figure 12.77*:

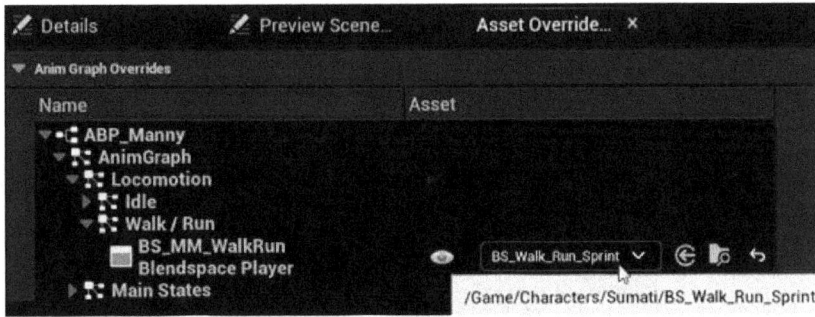

Figure 12.77: *Assigning the blend space we created to Quinn's Animation Blueprint*

Hit compile on the upper left side of the window, save, and close. Now, we are ready to start editing the Blueprints in the BP_ThirdPersonCharacter Blueprint class.

Creating sprint, walk, and run functions

Back in the Content Browser, navigate to **Content/ThirdPerson/Blueprints/** and double click on BP_ThirdPersonCharacter. Right click anywhere on an empty space in the Blueprint's Event Graph, and search for **input sprint**, select the only result you find there, as shown in *Figure 12.78*. This is the Sprint input mapping we assigned at the beginning of this chapter, in *Figure 12.3*.

Figure 12.78: *Searching for Input Sprint*

The resulting node is what is displayed in *Figure 12.79*:

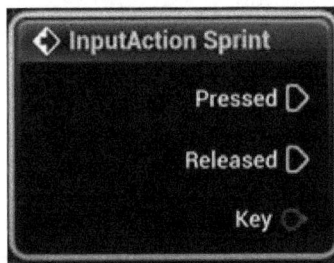

Figure 12.79: *The Input Sprint node*

Next, we will need to create variables and functions, which will help us define what constitutes the beginning of a sprint, as well as the end of one.

On the middle-left side of your Blueprint editor window, press the add function button (white circle with a + icon) and name the newly created function **StartSprint**. Repeat this step and create one more function, naming it **StopSprint**. Refer to *Figure 12.80* for these steps:

Figure 12.80: Adding StartSprint and StopSprint functions

A bit lower, under the **FUNCTIONS** section, there is the **VARIABLES** section. Press the add button there (white circular icon again) and create a new variable, named **IsCharacterSprinting?** as shown in *Figure 12.81*. It has to be a **Boolean** variable, meaning it can be either True or False.

Figure 12.81: Adding a IsCharacterSprinting? Boolean variable

Now, create a **SprintingSpeed** variable, this time, it has to be a **Float** type since we want to be able to use decimal values. To change the variable type, click on **Boolean** to expand the drop down menu and select **Float**, as shown in *Figure 12.82*:

Figure 12.82: Adding a Float variable

Now, double click on the **StartSprint** function so we can start writing it. While having the **StartSprint** function open and visible in the main view of the window, on the upper left corner of the Blueprint editor window, where the **Components** tab is, you can see a Component named **Character Movement (CharMoveComp)**. Click and drag this Component somewhere in the function's graph, as shown in *Figure 12.83*:

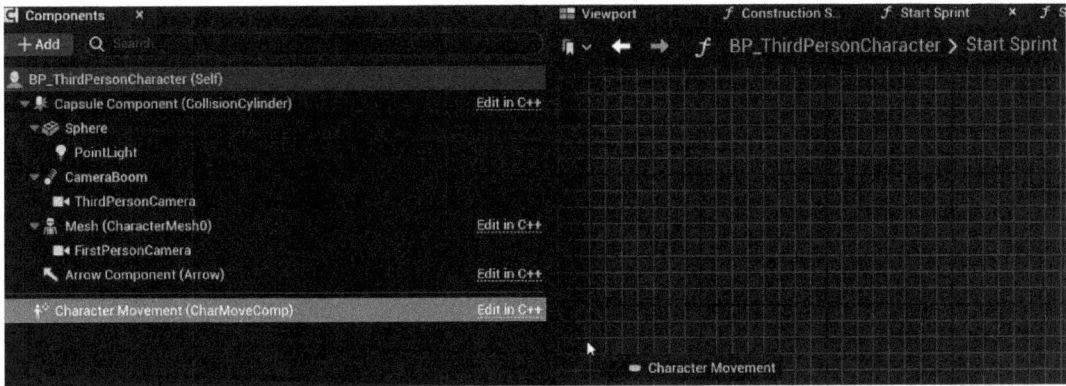

Figure 12.83: Adding a Character Movement reference in our StartSprint function's graph

Next, drive a cable from the Character Movement node's output pin into the empty space, and then type in **set max walk**, and select **Set Max Walk Speed** as shown in *Figure 12.84*:

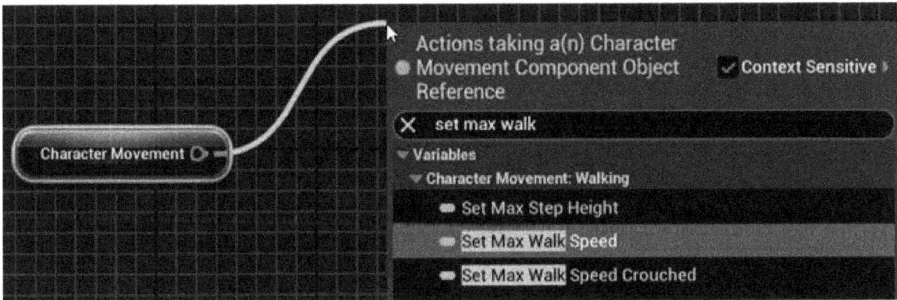

Figure 12.84: Set Max Walk Speed

Then click and drag the **SprintingSpeed** float variable we just created a while ago into the function graph, select Get SprintingSpeed, then click and drag the Boolean variable **IsCharacterSprinting?** into the function graph, select Set IsCharacterSprinting? and then connect all the resulting nodes exactly as shown in *Figure 12.85*:

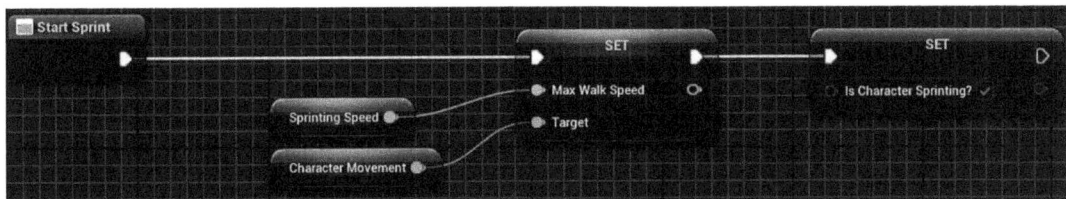

Figure 12.85: Our StartSprint function is now complete

Similarly, create a **CurrentSpeed** float type variable, and much like in the previous steps, complete the **StopSprint** function's Blueprint graph to look identical to the one displayed in *Figure 12.86*:

Figure 12.86: Our StopSprint function is now complete

Note the little check mark missing in **StopSprint** function's **IsCharacterSprinting?** set node.

By replicating the previous steps, we can now create several new functions and variables. More specifically, here is a list of the functions to create next (with the listed names):

- **ToggleWalk**
- **ToggleRun**
- **ToggleFirstPersonView**
- **ToggleThirdPersonView**
- **CharacterLightOff**
- **CharacterLightOn**
- **CalculatePlayerTotalScore**

Here is a list of the variables to create next, with the listed names and variable types:

- **IsCharacterRunning?**, **Boolean**
- **IsCharacterWalking?**, **Boolean**
- **WalkingSpeed**, **Float**
- **RunningSpeed**, **Float**
- **IsThirdPersonViewActive?**, **Boolean**
- **IsCharacterLightOn?**, **Boolean**
- **PlayerNumberOfGoldStatuesCollected**, **Integer**
- **PlayerNumberOfMarbleStatuesCollected**, **Integer**
- **PlayerNumberofGlassStatuesCollected**, **Integer**
- **TimeLeftPointMultiplier**, **Float**
- **TotalScore**, **Float**

Some of these we will be using later, after we have created some other Blueprint functions. Here is what your list of functions and variables for BP_ThirdPersonCharacter should look like (*Figure 12.87*):

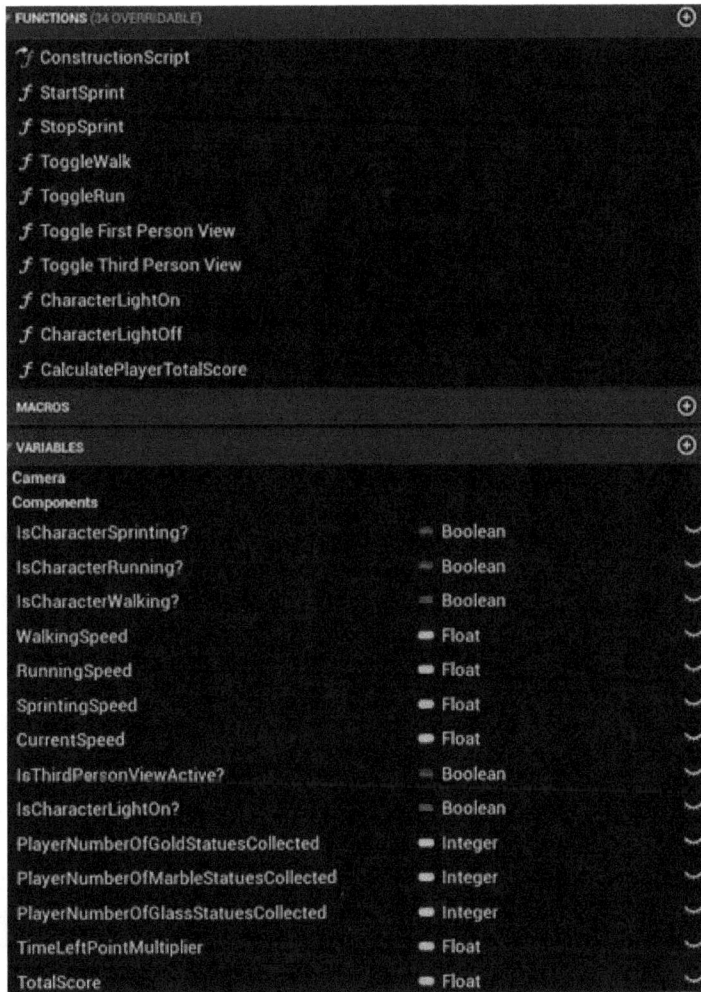

Figure 12.87: Complete list of functions and variables for BP_ThirdPersonCharacter Blueprint

Before proceeding, let us set some default values for some of the variables. Firstly, compile and save the Blueprint. Once it has successfully compiled and saved, let us first define the default value for the **WalkingSpeed** variable.

Click on the variable (on the list of variables on the left side of the window), and then all the way on the right side of the window, under the Details tab, in the **Default Value** category, define it as 400, as shown in *Figure 12.88*:

Figure 12.88: Toggle Walk function's node structure

In a similar way, set the following variables to the following default values:

- **RunningSpeed**: 800
- **SprintingSpeed**: 1200
- **CurrentSpeed**: 400
- **IsThirdPersonViewActive?**: True (check the box)
- **IsCharacterLightOn?**: False (uncheck the box)
- **TimeLeftPointMultiplier**: 10

Next, refer to the following figures, as they represent the node structure for each function's graph, which you can replicate by following the same processes we followed in completing the **StartSprint** function.

Figure 12.89 displays the node structure of the **ToggleWalk** function:

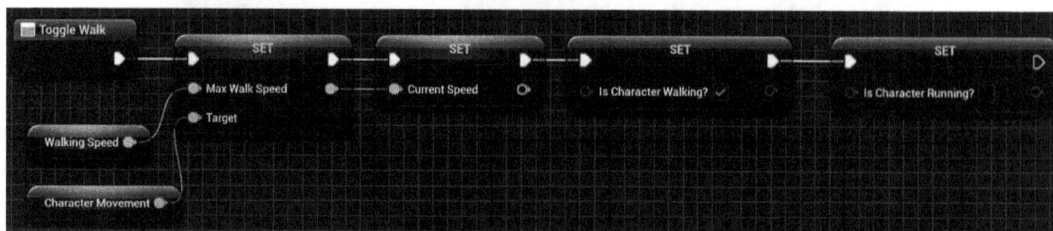

Figure 12.89: *ToggleWalk function's node structure*

Figure 12.90 displays the node structure of the **ToggleRun** function:

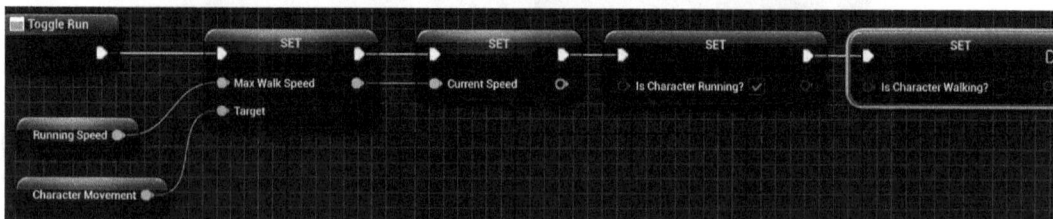

Figure 12.90: *ToggleRun function's node structure*

Before moving on to completing more functions, let us utilize the ones we just finished, starting with **StartSprint** and **StopSprint**. Back to the BP_ThirdPersoCharacter Blueprint's Event Graph, click and drag the **StartSprint** function in the graph. Click and drag the **StopSprint** function as well. Then, connect the **InputAction Sprint** input node's (*Figure 12.78*) **Pressed** output pin to the **StartSprint** function's input pin, and the **Released** output pin to the **StopSprint** input pin. Then select the three nodes (click and drag over them or *Ctrl+click* over each node) and press C to create a comment box around them. Title the comment box as **Sprinting**. All these steps are displayed in *Figure 12.91*:

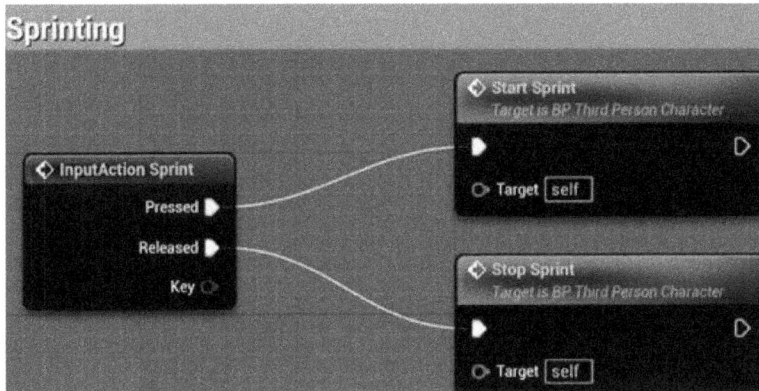

Figure 12.91: Sprinting functionality in the character Blueprint is now complete and functional

You can edit the comment box's colors by selecting it and then modifying its RGB values under the **Details** tab on the right side of the screen, as shown in *Figure 12.92*:

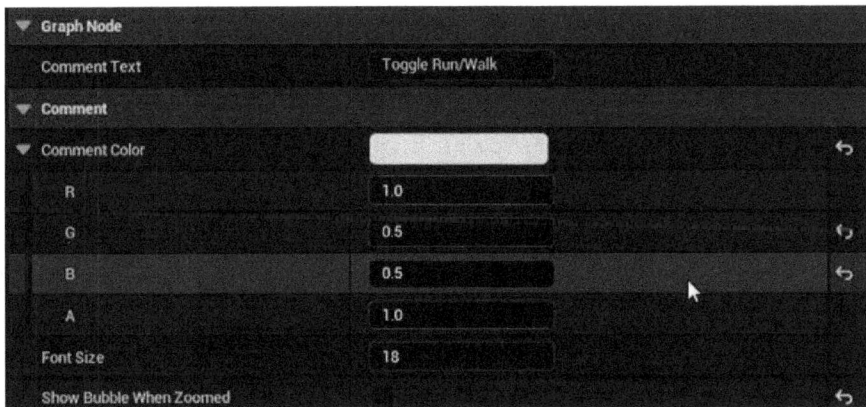

Figure 12.92: Modifying the comment box's color values

Next, right click on an empty space in the event graph and type in **Input Walk/Run Toggle** and create the node. Then, create a **Branch** node to check a Boolean value, by either right clicking on empty space in the graph and typing in **Branch** or pressing *B* and clicking on an empty space in the graph. Click and drag the **ToggleRun** and the **ToggleWalk** functions into the event graph, and connect the **Branch** node's **True** output pin to the **Toggle Run**'s input pin, and the **False** output pin to the **Toggle Walk**'s input pin. Click and drag the **IsCharacterWalking?** variable into the graph, select Get IsCharacterWalking? and connect the resulting node's output pin to the **Branch** node's **Condition** input pin. Connect the **InputAction Walk/Run Toggle** node's **Pressed** output pin to the branch node's execution input pin. Finally, select all these nodes and create a comment box around them (by pressing *C* while the nodes are selected) and name it **Toggle Run/Walk**. All these steps are displayed in *Figure 12.93*:

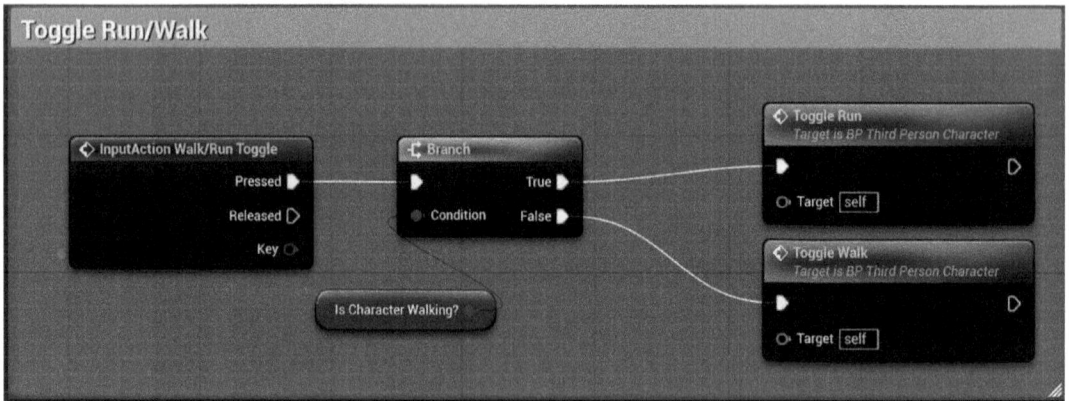

Figure 12.93: Toggle Run/Walk should now be functional

At this point, compile, save, and playtest. Try pressing and releasing the *Shift* key (which is defined as our Sprint Input in the project settings) while moving the character to see how the character sprints and then stops again. Also, try pressing the *Ctrl* key, to switch between walking and running.

Creating a zoom in/out functionality

Under the Components tab on the Blueprint editor's upper left corner, select, click, and drag the **CameraBoom** Component into the event graph, as shown in *Figure 12.94*:

Figure 12.94: Bringing the CameraBoom into the event graph

Next, right click on the event graph, and search for Input CameraZoom, and create that node. Drag a cable from the **InputAxis CameraZoom** node's **Axis Value** output pin and type in multiply or * to get a multiplication node. Then, set the second value of the multiplication node to **-10.0**.

Drive a cable from the **Camera Boom** node's output pin, and type in Get Target Arm Length and create the corresponding node. From that node's output pin, drag a cable and type in + to get an addition node. Connect the multiplication node's output pin to the remaining input pin on the addition node and then drag a cable from the addition node's output pin and type in **Clamp (Float)** to create a clamp node.

Set the clamp node's minimum value to 150 and the maximum to 400. Next, drive another cable from the **Camera Boom** node's output pin and type in Set Target Arm Length to create the corresponding node. Drive the clamp node's output pin into the Set Target Arm Length node's float (green) input pin.

Select all the nodes we just created and used, create a comment box, title it **Allow Mouse Scroll for Zooming in/out**. Compile, save, and playtest to make sure scrolling the mouse wheel results in zooming the camera in and out.

All of the above steps can be easily summarized and followed in *Figure 12.95*:

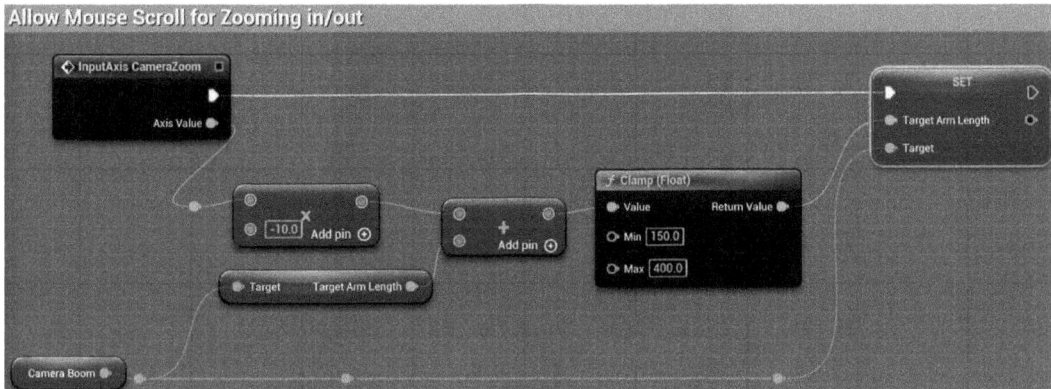

Figure 12.95: Camera zoom in/out functionality

Creating a player light that can be toggled on/off

Players often complain about dark environments in games, especially in dark fantasy games, since artistic direction in such games often requires dark environments to maintain a certain degree of atmospherics required for the game. Developers usually compensate by creating a mechanic that essentially allows players to toggle on and off a light (sometimes in the form of a spell, other times in the form of a torch). We will create a simple light orb (one could say a spell) that the player will be able to toggle on and off.

Before modifying our BP_ThirdPersonCharacter Blueprint's event graph even further, we first need to add some Components to it, as well as create an emissive material for the orb.

First and foremost, under the Components tab, click on the +**Add** button, and add a **Sphere** Component, placed under the **Capsule Component** as shown in *Figures 12.96* and *12.97*:

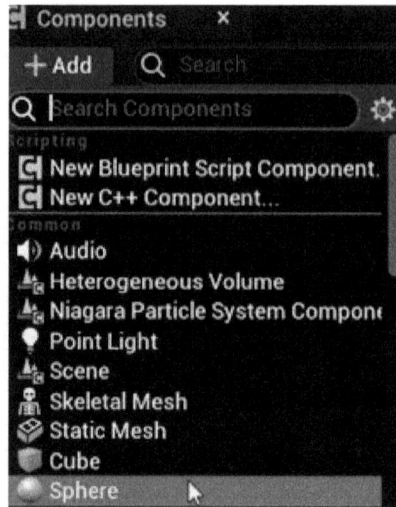

Figure 12.96: Add a Sphere Component

The following figure shows sphere component added under the capsule component:

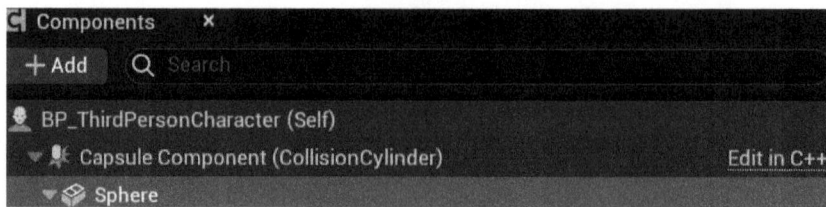

Figure 12.97: The Sphere Component added under the Capsule Component

With the **Sphere** Component selected, this time add a **Point Light** Component, as shown in *Figures 12.98* and *12.99*:

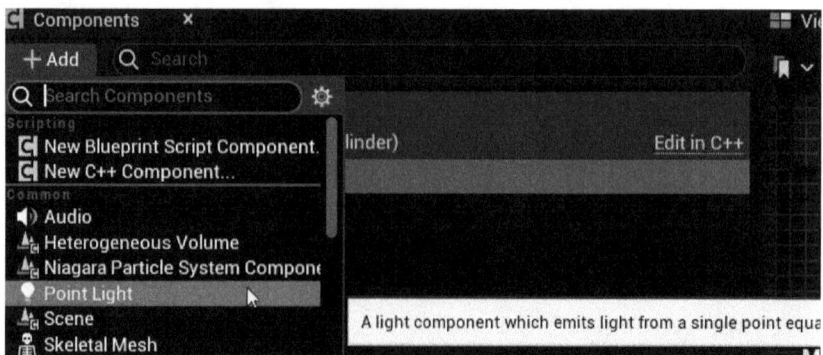

Figure 12.98: Adding the Point Light Component

The following figure shows the PointLight component added under the Sphere Component:

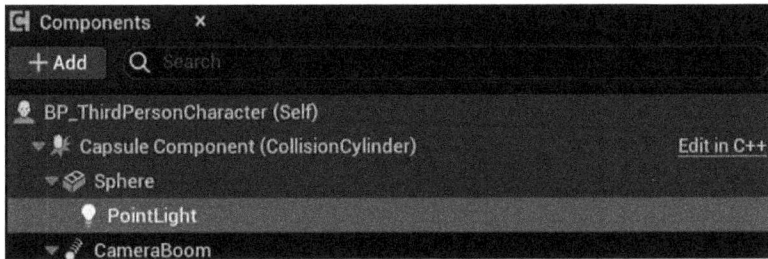

Figure 12.99: The PointLight Component added under the Sphere Component

Since we are in the process of adding Components, let us add one more, even though it is not relevant to the player light. Select the Mesh Component, and while having it selected, add a **Camera** Component, as shown in *Figure 12.100*:

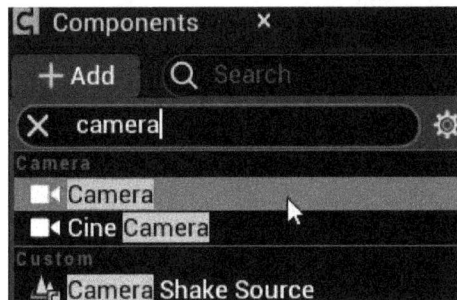

Figure 12.100: Adding the Camera Component

Name it FirstPersonCamera as, shown in *Figure 12.101:*

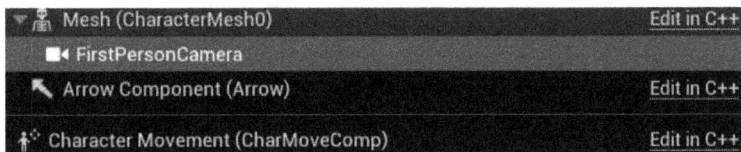

Figure 12.101: The Camera Component, properly named and placed under the Mesh Component as it should

We will resume the Camera Component later, back to the player light function for now.

In the Content Browser, navigate to **Content/ThirdPerson/Blueprints/** and, there, create a new material named **M_CharacterLightEmissive**.

You should be familiar and comfortable with the Materials by now, so refer to *Figure 12.102* for the completion of this material. Once you are done, hit apply and save.

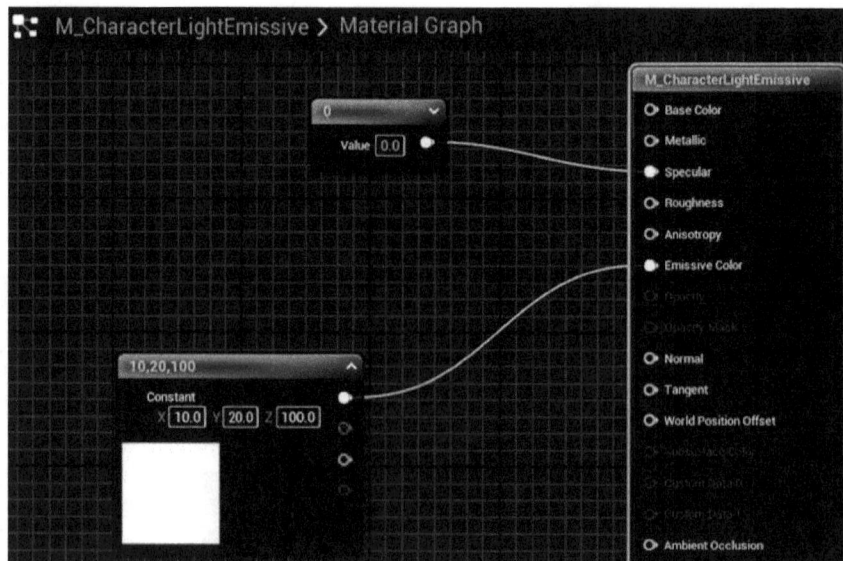

Figure 12.102: The player's light orb material

Next, select this material and apply it on the Sphere Component in the BP_ ThirdPersonCharacter Blueprint, by selecting the Sphere Component, and applying the material to its material field, found under the Details tab on the right side of the Blueprint editor's window. While in the Component's details tab, also set its location coordinates to the same as depicted in *Figure 12.103*:

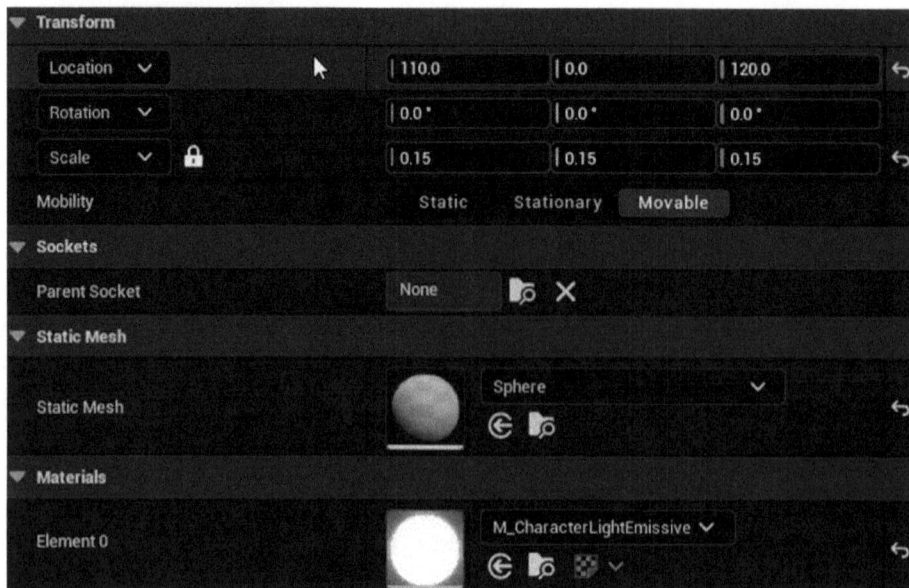

Figure 12.103: The player's light orb coordinates in relation to the character and the light orb material applied to it

Next, scroll down further below in the details and set the **Collision Presets** to `NoCollision`, and even further down, look for **Hidden In Game** and check the box next to it, as shown in *Figure 12.104*:

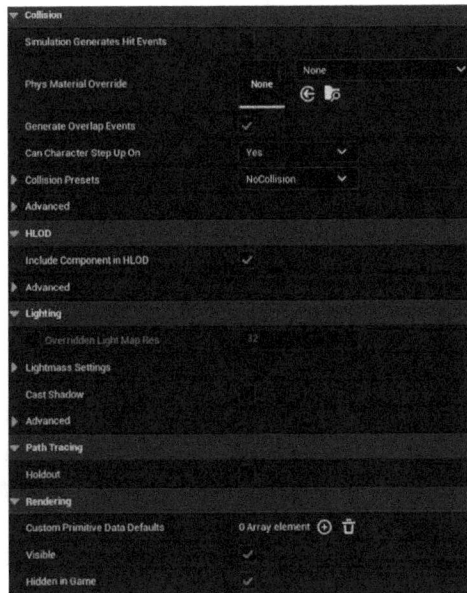

Figure 12.104: The player light orb with NoCollisions, and set as Hidden In Game

Now that the orb is set let us work on the Point Light attached to it. Click on the PointLight Component under the Sphere Component, and under the Details tab, set its **Intensity** to 0, the **Intensity Units** to `Candelas`, and the **Light Color** to a Hex linear value of 8A90FFFF, lastly, setting its **Attenuation Radius** to 768 and disabling its **Cast Shadows** checkbox, all shown in *Figure 12.105*:

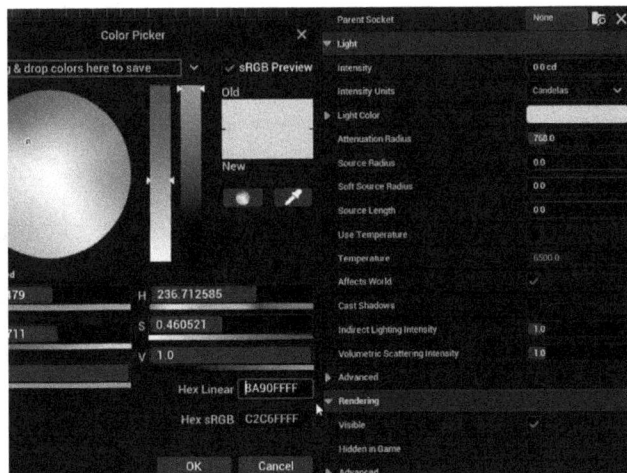

Figure 12.105: The default settings for the Point Light Component

Now, let us double click on the **CharacterLightOn** function, and click and drag the **Sphere** and **Point Light** Components in the graph.

Drive a cable from the **Sphere** node's output pin and type in **Set Hidden in Game** and create the corresponding node, make sure the box next to this node's **New Hidden** is unchecked.

Then, drive a cable from the **Point Light** node's output pin and type in **Set Intensity**, create the corresponding node, and then drive one more cable out of the **Point Light** node's output pin and type in Set Cast Shadows and create the respective node. Set **New Intensity** value to 10, while checking the box next to the **New Value** of the **Set Cast Shadows** node.

Lastly, click and drag the variable **IsCharacterLightOn?** into the graph, then select Set IsCharacterLightOn? and make sure its box is checked. Connect all these nodes as displayed in *Figure 12.106*:

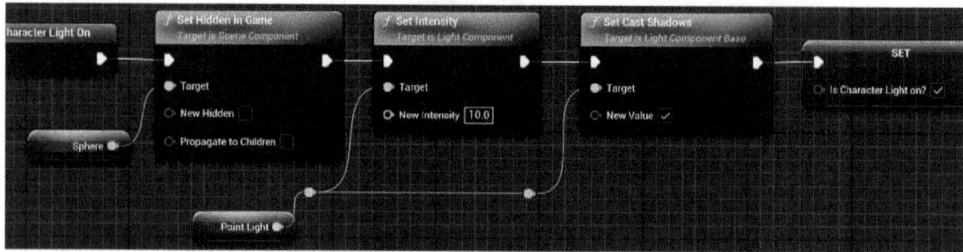

Figure 12.106: *The CharacterLightOn function is now complete*

Now select all the nodes (except the first purple **Character Light On** one) and *Ctrl+C* to copy them.

Double click on the **CharacterLightOff** function, and press *Ctrl+V* to paste all the nodes. Now we will reverse in the node's setting; in other words, Sphere's Hidden in the game will be checked, Point Light's Intensity will be set to 0, casting shadows will be unchecked, and **Is Character Light on?** will be unchecked as well. All are resulting in what is shown in *Figure 12.107*:

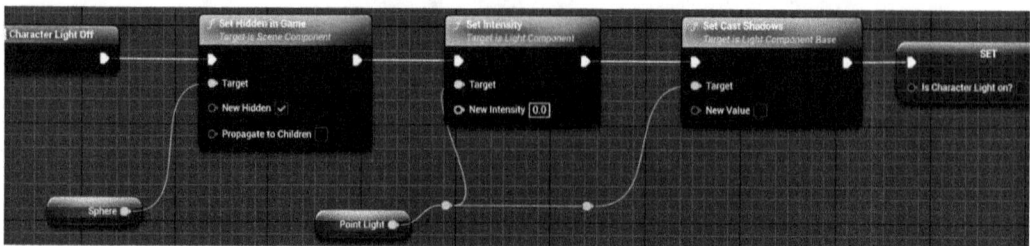

Figure 12.107: *The CharacterLightOff function is now complete*

Back to the Blueprint's event graph, right click on empty space, type in Input Character Light, create the node.

Click and drag the **CharacterLightOn** and **CharacterLightOff** functions next to it, click and drag the **IsCharacterLightOn?** variable in the graph as well, select Get IsCharacterLightOn? and then connect them all with each, as shown in *Figure 12.108*.

Finally, select all these nodes, press C to create a comment box, which you will title as **Character Light Toggle**.

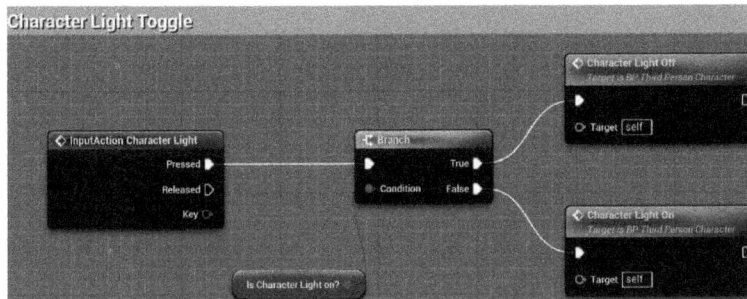

Figure 12.108: Player light functionality should now be ready to test

Compile, save, and playtest, and while playtesting, press *L* since that is the default key to toggle the light on and off. Your result should resemble the one in *Figure 12.109*:

Figure 12.109: Let there be light

Switching between third and first-person views

While we might be using the Third Person template, we should not feel restricted to that, we can easily add a first-person mode as well. An even better option is a first-person mode, where you can still see your character's body when looking down, therefore making for a much more immersive experience.

By default, the Third Person template names the camera attached to the character Blueprint as Follow Camera. Let us rename it to **ThirdPersonCamera** by selecting it under the Components tab, pressing *F2* or right clicking and selecting rename.

Next, let us add a new Camera Component right under the Mesh Component, and name it **FirstPersonCamera**. Now, your **Components** tab should look like *Figure 12.110*:

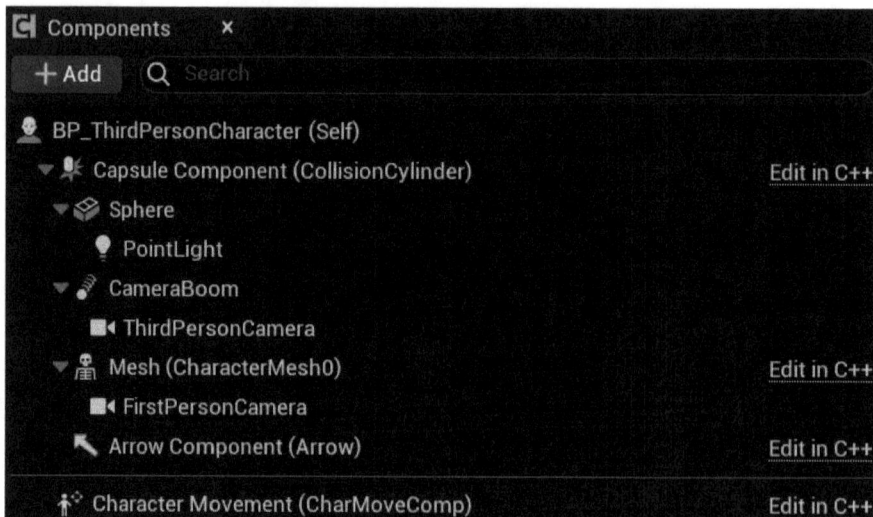

Figure 12.110: Character Blueprint's Components tab

Select **FirstPersonCamera**, and while having it selected, go to its Details tab, look for **Parent Socket**, click, and select **head** as shown in *Figure 12.111*. Also, update its location and rotation values as shown in *Figure 12.111*:

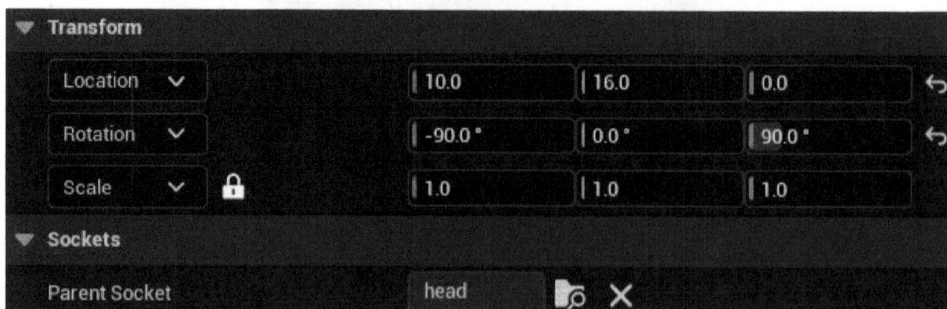

Figure 12.111: First Person Camera Component's details tab

Since the first-person camera Component is attached to the mesh, it will end up being attached specifically to the character mesh's head socket. If you go into the Blueprint editor's Viewport tab, you will notice the camera is literally attached to the character mesh's head, as seen in *Figure 12.112*:

Figure 12.112: Possibly the world's largest body cam!

Next, ensure that the first-person camera Component's **Camera Options** (again under the Details tab) are identical to the ones in *Figure 12.113*:

Figure 12.113: Ensure you have the same settings

Next, double click on the **Toggle First Person View** function, click and drag the **Third Person Camera** and **First Person Camera** Components in the graph, and drive from each one's output pin a cable and type in **Set Active**.

Then right click anywhere on the graph, type in **SET Use Controller Rotation Yaw**, check its box, and lastly, click and drag the IsThirdPersonViewActive? into the graph, and select SetIsThirdPersonViewActive? (Alternatively, you can *Alt+Click&Drag*, and it automatically selects the Set node instead of Get — which you can get by *Ctrl+Click&Dragging* a variable into a graph).

Lastly, connect it all together with the correct checked/unchecked boxes and sequence, as shown in *Figure 12.114*:

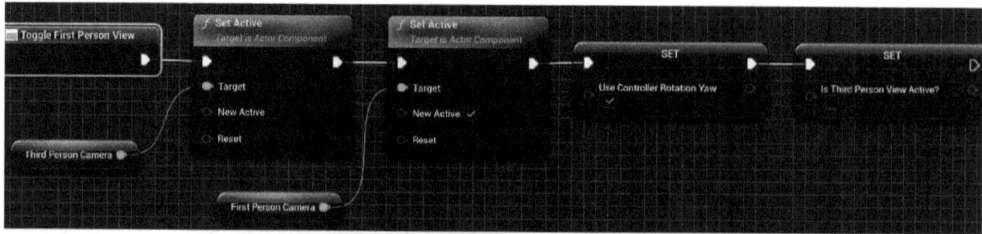

Figure 12.114: Toggling the first-person view should now be functional

Click and drag to select all nodes (except for the first one), copy them, and then open up the **Toggle Third Person View** function and paste into its graph all the nodes we just copied. Then reverse the settings and connect them to the initial node, as shown in *Figure 12.115*:

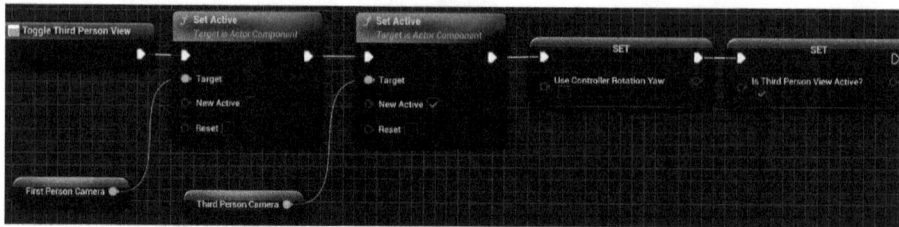

Figure 12.115: Toggling the third person view should now be functional

Back to the event graph, right click anywhere, type in Input Toggle Camera View, create the node, drive a cable from its **Pressed** output pin, and connect it to a **Branch** node.

Ctrl+Click & Drag the **IsThirdPersonViewActive?** variable into the graph and connect it to the branch node's condition input pin.

Next, *Click & Drag* the **Toggle First Person View** function and place it on the branch's **True** output pin.

Now, *Click & Drag* the **Toggle Third Person View** function and place it on the branch's **False** output pin.

Select all nodes, press C to create comment box, title it **Toggle between First and Third Person View Modes**. The result should resemble what is displayed in *Figure 12.116*:

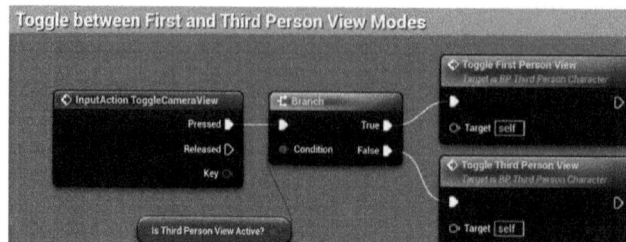

Figure 12.116: Toggling between the third and first-person views should now be functional

Compile, save, and playtest (as per the input mappings we used in the project settings, *V* is the default key to switch between view modes). *Figure 12.117* shows the first-person mode in action:

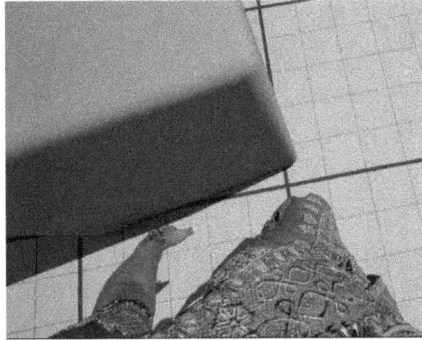

Figure 12.117: First person view in-game!

At this point, we are ready to conclude this rather lengthy chapter. Our **BP_ ThirdPersonCharacter** Blueprint's graph and functionality have been significantly expanded. In *Figure 12.118,* all the brighter comment boxes are the additions we just performed to the default template:

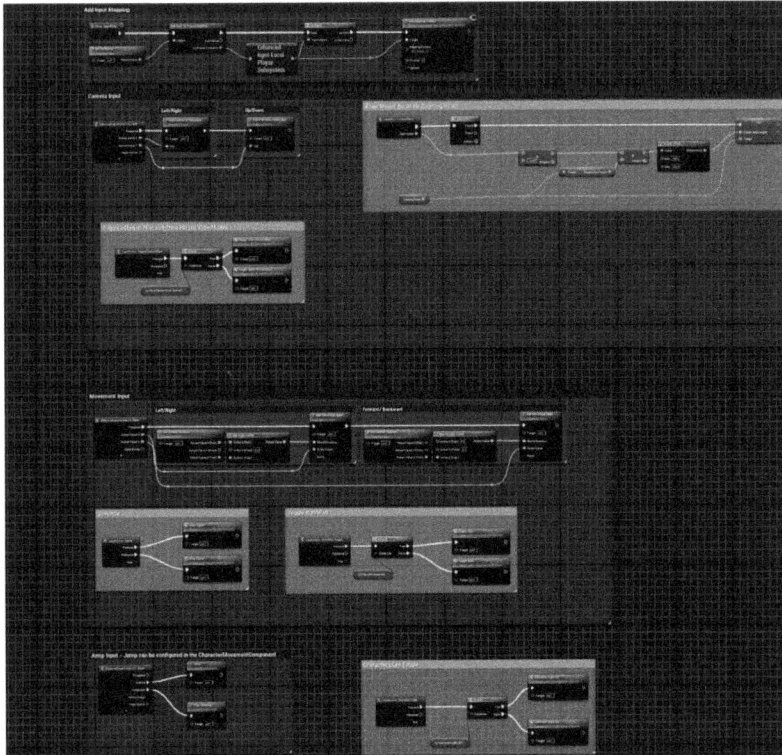

Figure 12.118: Expanding the template significantly

Conclusion

In this chapter, we touched on some very important concepts, ranging from importing custom character meshes and retargeting them, making them fully compatible with the default animation assets, to significantly expanding the capabilities and functionalities of the Third Person template.

We learned how to work with functions, variables and Components in a Blueprint class, while we also learned how to define input mappings through the project settings, and how to use these input mappings within a Blueprint.

At this point, it is worth noting that there are always better and more efficient ways to approach a problem through a Blueprint based solution, but that comes with experience and knowledge. What is presented in this book is meant to target a beginner to early intermediate developer.

In the next chapter, we will be using the same concepts of functions, variables and input actions, to create different Blueprint based actors that will helps collectively create a mini game for the Fantasy Castle level.

Points to remember

- Can import custom character meshes with custom skeletons and retarget them.
- Can define and modify default input mappings through the project settings.
- Utilizing functions, variables, and components within a Blueprint class.

Exercise

1. Try creating your own functionalities, by modifying the existing ones. What if the character could spawn two lights? A red and a blue one? What if you prefer allowing the player to zoom further in or out? Play around with values both in nodes and variables, create new functions and most importantly, be creative!

Join our book's Discord space

Join the book's Discord Workspace for Latest updates, Offers, Tech happenings around the world, New Release and Sessions with the Authors:

https://discord.bpbonline.com

CHAPTER 13

Fantasy Castle Interactive Blueprint Actors

Introduction

In this chapter, we will create several Blueprint actors for the player to interact with as well as actors that when put together, allow the player to play a mini game.

More specifically, we will create a firepit the player can light up and put out and a portal the player can use to instantly teleport between two different locations. We will also conduct some preparational work for the actors we will be developing in *Chapter 14, Fantasy Castle MiniGame Blueprints*.

Structure

This chapter's structure is as follows:

- Creating an interactive firepit
- Widget Blueprints
- Creating a teleportation portal

Objectives

By the end of this chapter, we will learn how to create interactive Blueprint actors, Widget Blueprints, more specifically, create firepits that can be lit on and off, portals that allow the player to quickly traverse between two different points in a level.

Creating an interactive firepit

The first interactive actor we will create is a firepit. When the player is close enough to it, they will be able to light it up or put its fire out, thus allowing them to either brighten the surrounding environment or darken it, depending on their preference.

The first step is to go back to our trusted Content Browser (or Content Drawer, if you prefer) and create a folder under **Content/** named **Blueprints**. Within that folder, create three more, namely **ElephantStatues**, **FirePit** and **Portal**. Your results should resemble *Figure 13.1*:

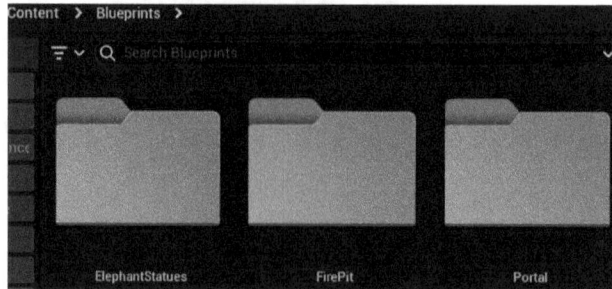

Figure 13.1: The newly created folders

Open up the **FirePit** folder, and right click, and select **Blueprint Class** as seen in *Figure 13.2*:

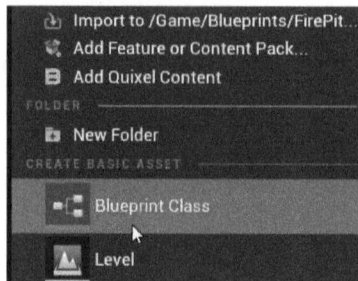

Figure 13.2: Creating a Blueprint Class

You are instantly presented with numerous options, select the very first **Actor** as shown in *Figure 13.3*:

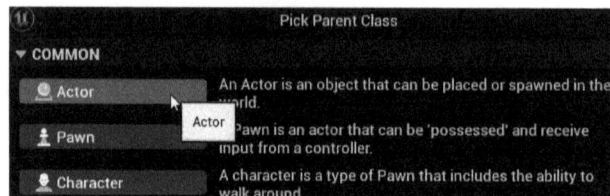

Figure 13.3: Pick Actor

Name the newly created actor BP_FirePit. Double click on it to open it. The first thing we want to do with this actor is assign it a Static Mesh. If you are using the provided project files, then you can look for **SM_FirePit**, located in **Content/AssetPacks/AssetPack15**. It is worth noting that this mesh was created by merging several different Static Meshes from the other asset packs — namely roofs and decorations!

Click and drag the **SM_FirePit** asset over to the Blueprint actor's editor window, and place it right under the **DefaultSceneRoot** in the components tab, as shown in *Figures 13.4* and *13.5*:

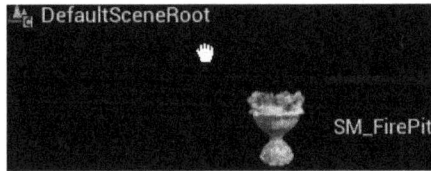

Figure 13.4: Place SM_FirePit right under the DefaultSceneRoot

Having placed the Static Mesh, as shown in *Figure 13.5*:

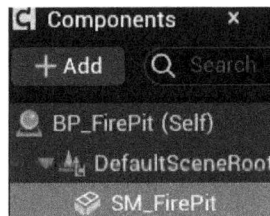

Figure 13.5: The end result after placing the Static Mesh

If you want to add an extra bit of realism, you can also download a Quixel Bridge campfire 3D asset, to use it as the burning wood in the pit, but that is entirely optional. Should you decide to do it, you first get it from Quixel Bridge, then click and drag it right under **SM_FirePit**.

Next, we need to add a flame particle effect. The Unreal Marketplace features an excellent pack with fire particle FX, freely available and found under the permanently free collection. Refer to *Figure 13.6* for more details:

Figure 13.6: M5 VFX Vol.2 is an excellent source of fire themed particle FX, and is freely available

If you are using the provided project files, you do not need to install them. If you are working on a separate project though, proceed with adding M5 VFX to the project.

Next, navigate to **Content/M5VFXVOL2/Niagara/Fire** and look for **NFire_00**, as shown in *Figure 13.7*:

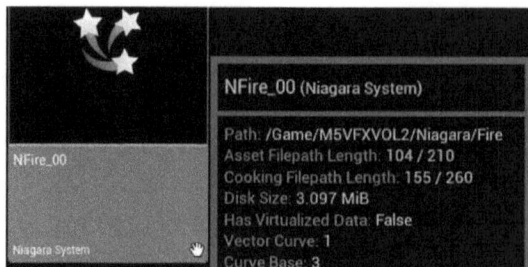

Figure 13.7: *M5 VFX Vol.2's NFire_00 is perfect for our needs*

Select **NFire_00** and drag it under SM_FirePit. Next, add a Point Light component, placed under (not within) **NFire_00**. Finally add a **Sphere Collision** component under the Point Light you just added, as seen in *Figure 13.8*:

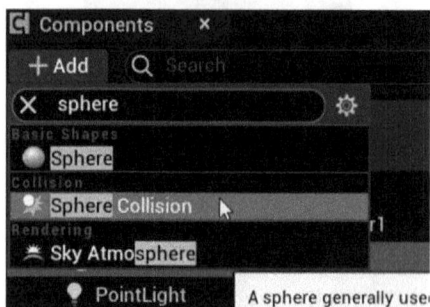

Figure 13.8: *Adding a Sphere Collision component*

Your BP_FirePit's component list should now be complete and looking identical to *Figure 13.9*:

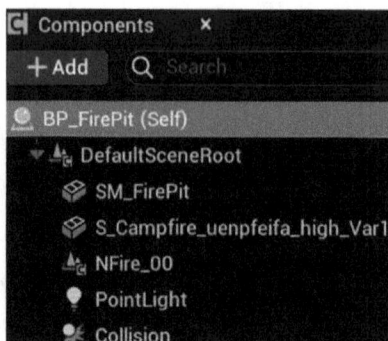

Figure 13.9: *The list of components in BP_FirePit*

Widget Blueprints

At this point, it is appropriate to shortly pause our BP_FirePit creation and focus on Widget Blueprints. Widget Blueprints are what is used to display information on screen, in other words, it is what is mainly used in UI. For this book's and this project's purposes, we will be using very simple widgets, but overall, they can get quite complex, allowing UI designers to achieve some astonishing UI content.

In our Content Browser, under **Content/Blueprints/FirePit/** right click and select **User Interface** and then **Widget Blueprint** as shown in *Figure 13.10*:

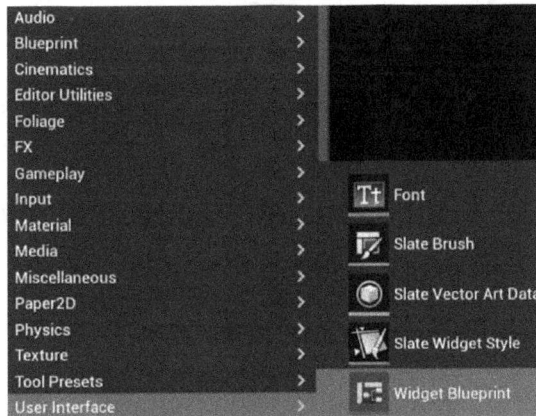

Figure 13.10: Creating a Widget Blueprint

Then select User Widget and name the newly created widget WBP_FirepitUIToLight and double click to open up the asset. On the upper left corner, under the **Palette** tab, search for **border**, as shown in *Figure 13.11*:

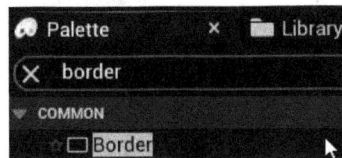

Figure 13.11: Search for border

Click and drag the result into the empty space in the center as shown in *Figure 13.12*:

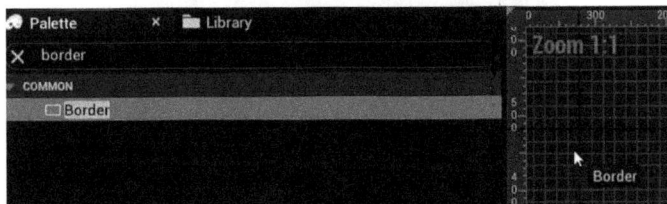

Figure 13.12: Add the border to the empty space

With your newly added border selected under the Hierarchy tab on the lower left corner of the widget editor, navigate to its details tab on the right-hand side of the window, and look for **Horizontal Alignment** and **Vertical Alignment**, as well as for the **Brush Color**. Use the same settings as shown in *Figure 13.13*:

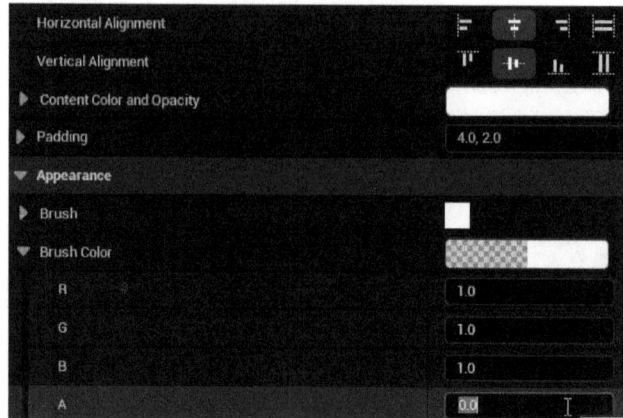

Figure 13.13: *The settings for the border we just created*

Back to the **Palette** tab, search for **text** as indicated in *Figure 13.14*:

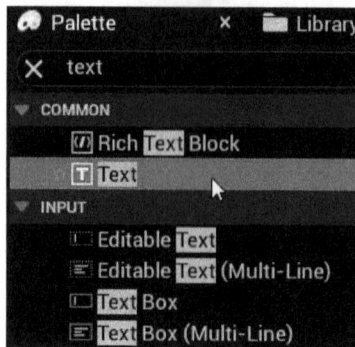

Figure 13.14: *Searching for text*

Click and drag **Text** over the border, in the central window, as shown in *Figure 13.15*:

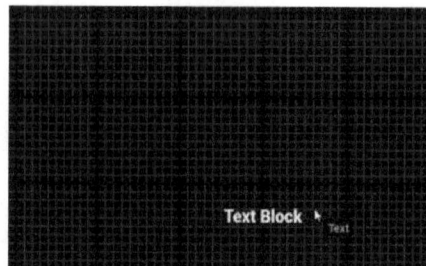

Figure 13.15: *Placing the text over the border*

With the **Text Block** selected, go the details tab on the right, and ensure you have the same settings as those displayed in *Figure 13.16*:

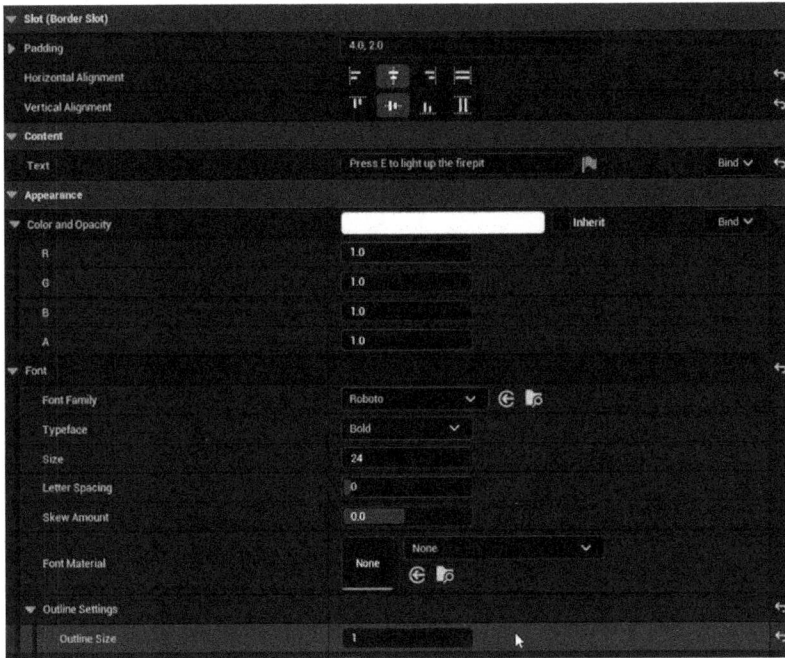

Figure 13.16: Make sure you use the same settings as above for your text block

Your final result should look much like *Figure 13.17*:

Figure 13.17: Simple yet informative

In the Content Browser, right click on WBP_FireputUIToLight and duplicate it. Name the duplicate copy as WBP_FirepitUIToPutOut and double click to open it.

All you need to change is the text content in the text block. Change it to what *Figure 13.18* shows:

Figure 13.18: Change the text to the above

Compile and save if you have not done so already.

Now, we can resume the creation and finalization of our BP_FirePit actor. It is a good time to add the functions and variables we will need for this Blueprint actor. We will do so by following the same methodologies we used in the previous chapter when we added functions and variables for the BP_ThirdPersonCharacter Blueprint.

Create the following functions:

- `LightUpFirePit`
- `PutFireOut`

Then, create the following variables with their respective types:

- `CanFireItUp`, `Boolean`
- `IsFireLit?`, `Boolean`

Figure 13.19 shows the full list. For now, ignore the **DefineWidgets** function, as well as the `FirepitUIToLight` and `FirepitUIToPutOut` variables:

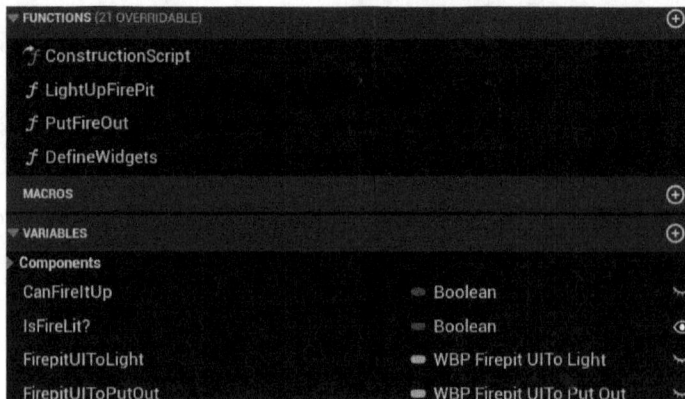

Figure 13.19: *The full list of functions and variables for BP_FirePit*

Anywhere in the event graph, right click and type in **create widget**, select the only available option. While having the WBP_FirepitUIToLight Widget Blueprint selected in the Content Browser (or the Content Drawer) select it to be used in the newly created node, as shown in *Figure 13.20*:

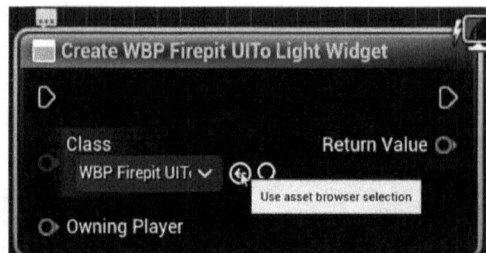

Figure 13.20: *The create widget node in BP_FirePit's event graph*

Draw a cable from the node's **Return Value** and select **Promote to variable**, as shown in *Figure 13.21*:

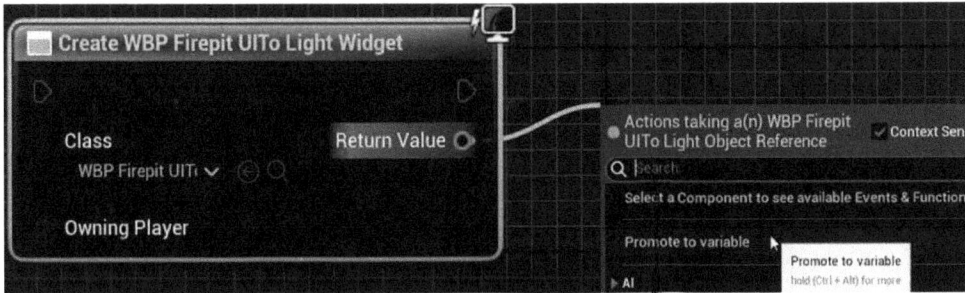

Figure 13.21: *Promoting the return value of the node to a variable*

This results in what is shown in *Figure 13.22*:

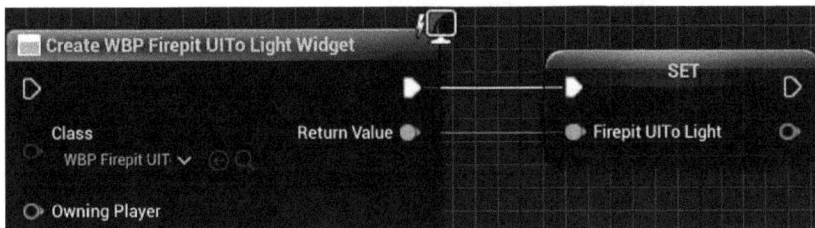

Figure 13.22: *Ready to define this widget within the Blueprint actor*

Repeat the same process, this time for WBP_FirepitUIToPutOut. Then connect all four nodes to each other and to **Event BeginPlay**, by using a **Sequence** node after the **Event BeginPlay**. You can get the Sequence node by either right clicking and typing in **sequence** or by pressing *S* and clicking on the graph. Combining it all together should look as shown in *Figure 13.23*:

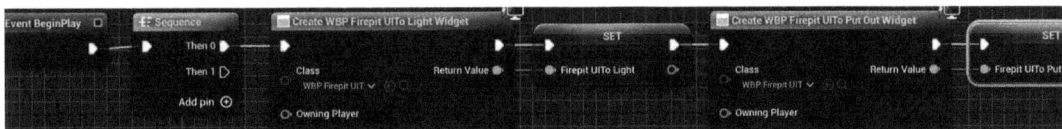

Figure 13.23: *Defining both widgets*

Next, select all the widget related nodes, as shown in *Figure 13.24*:

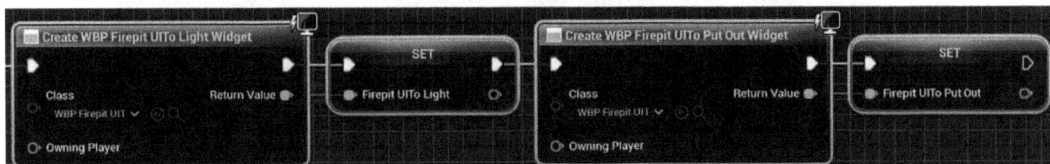

Figure 13.24: *Selecting all the widget related nodes*

Now, right click on any of them and select **Collapse to Function**, as shown in *Figure 13.25*. Name the new function **Define Widgets**.

Figure 13.25: *Collapsing the nodes to Function*

Figure 13.26 displays the result of the previous action. If you double click the **Define Widgets** node, it will take you inside the function, where you will find all the nodes we collapsed to it.

Now you can understand why *Figure 13.19* had a function and two variables we did not bother with then:

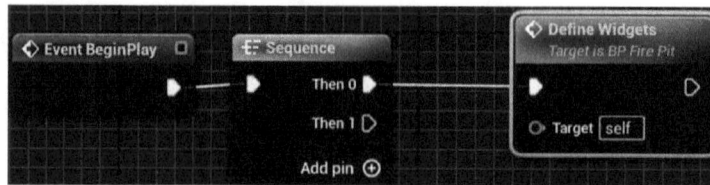

Figure 13.26: *All the previous nodes are nicely compacted within the Define Widgets function*

Now, let us open up the **Light Up Fire Pit** function. Following the same process of clicking and dragging variables and components in *Chapter 12, Fantasy Castle Character and Interaction Blueprints*, we similarly bring in components and variables, while also driving cables into empty space in the graph, or by right clicking and searching any necessary nodes we need to create, try to build the same structure as in *Figure 13.27*:

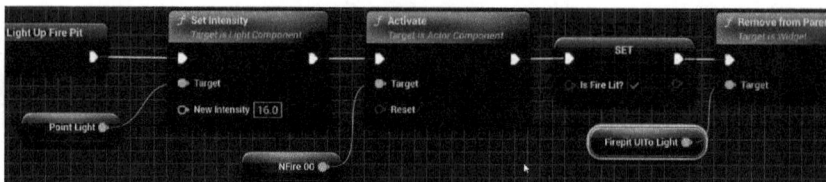

Figure 13.27: *Defining the Light Up Fire Pit function*

Once the **Light Up Fire Pit** function is complete, copy all the nodes and paste them into the **Put Fire Out** function's graph, where we will reverse the settings and make them look identical to the ones displayed in *Figure 13.28*:

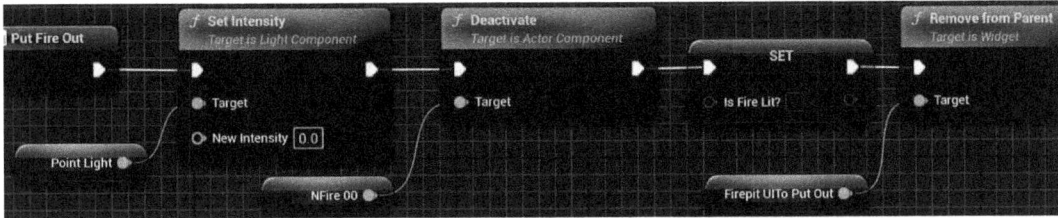

Figure 13.28: Defining the Put Fire Out function

Next, complete the **Event BeginPlay**'s node sequence, as shown in *Figure 13.29*:

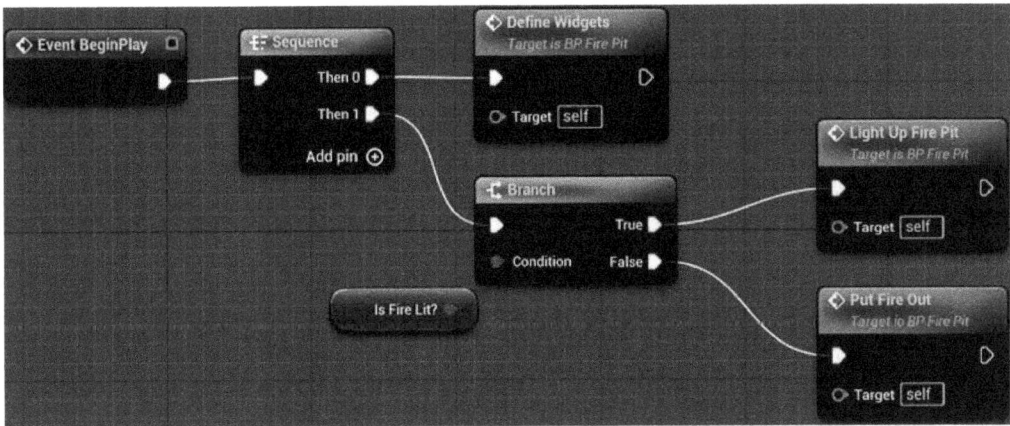

Figure 13.29: Finalizing the Event Begin Play sequence

Next, let us create a system with which when the player is within range, we prompt them to either light up the fire (provided the firepit's fire is not burning) or put it out (provided it is burning).

The way we achieve that is by creating the node sequence you see in *Figure 13.30*. For clarity and legibility purposes, *Figures 13.31* and *13.32* show the same image split into two larger halves.

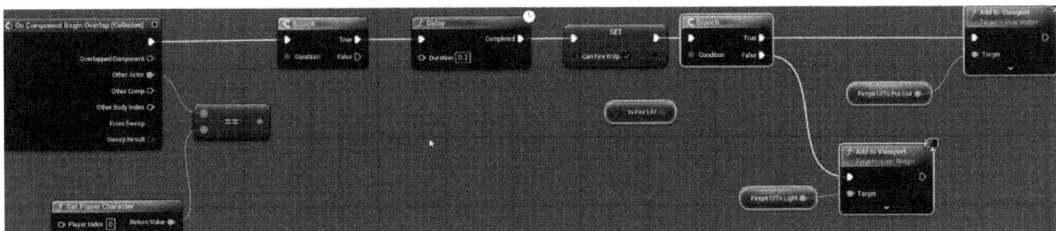

Figure 13.30: Refer to Figures 13.31 and 13.32 for a more legible version of this sequence

Figure 13.31 shows the Blueprint sequence's left half:

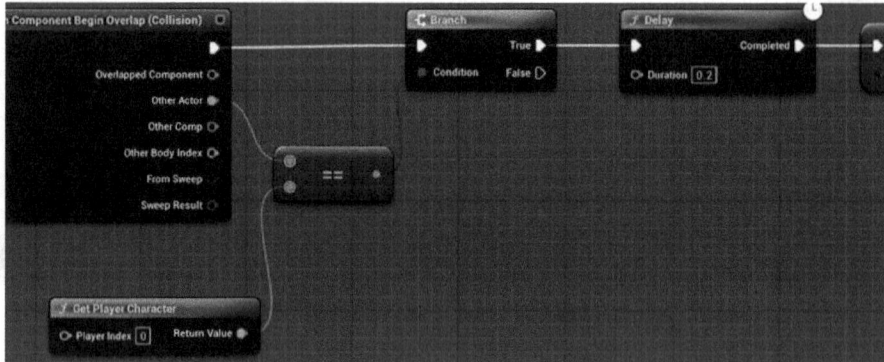

Figure 13.31: *Figure 13.30's left half*

Figure 13.32 shows the Blueprint sequence's right half:

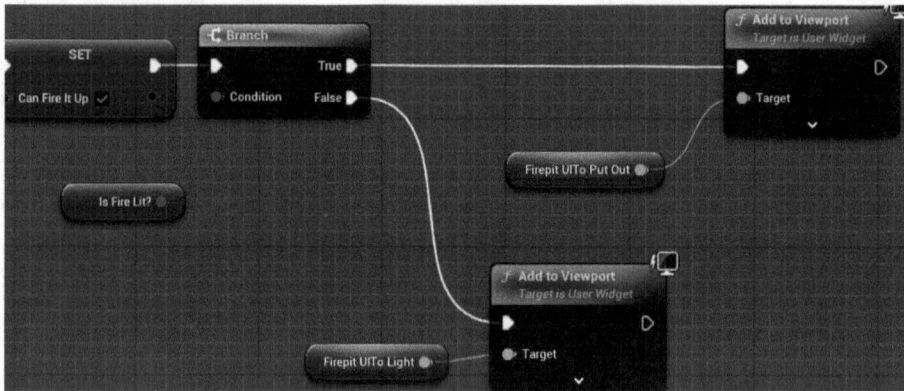

Figure 13.32: *Figure 13.30's right half*

Let us analyze the above figures and see how we can derive each node and each step of the node sequence shown.

We get the **On Component Begin Overlap (Collision)** node by selecting the Collision Sphere we added to the list of components, as shown in *Figure 13.33*:

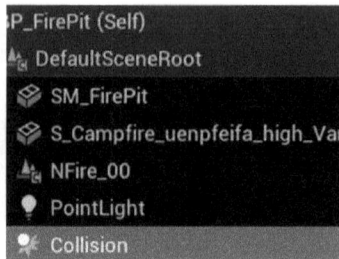

Figure 13.33: *Select the collision component*

Under its Details tab on the right side of the screen, scroll down till we find and click the + button next to On Component Begin Overlap, as shown in *Figure 13.34*:

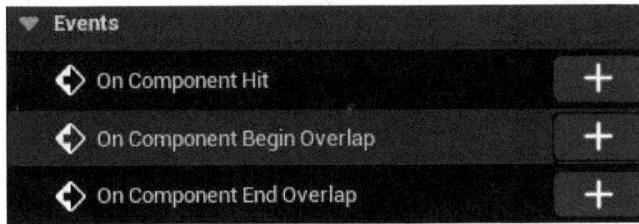

Figure 13.34: Adding the begin overlap node

Next, we right click on the event graph and type in **Get Player Character**, from which we draw a cable and type in **==,** which gives us the equals node, which also connects to the **Other Actor** pin of the begin overlap node. The result of the equals node is then driven to a branch node. In simple words, the logic behind this is that we check what overlaps with the collision sphere around the firepit. If what overlaps with it is the player, and that condition holds true, then we continue to the second half of the node sequence.

Next, we use a delay node just to give the Blueprint a short amount of time (0.2 seconds, the duration of a frame) to check, update and register all these conditions and events. From the delay node we proceed to set the variable **Can Fire It Up** to true. In other words, since it is the player that overlaps with the collision, then the player is within range, so then they can fire the pit up.

From there, we proceed to another branch sequence, which checks the variable **Is Fire Lit?**. If it is true, then we add to the player's Viewport, the widget prompting the user to put the fire out. If it is false, then we essentially present them with the option to fire it up.

In a similar manner, we structure what happens when the player exits the range within which they are allowed to interact with the firepit. In other words, when the Overlap Ends.

Figures 13.35 and *13.36* show the Component End Overlap sequence of events, which we will go over next:

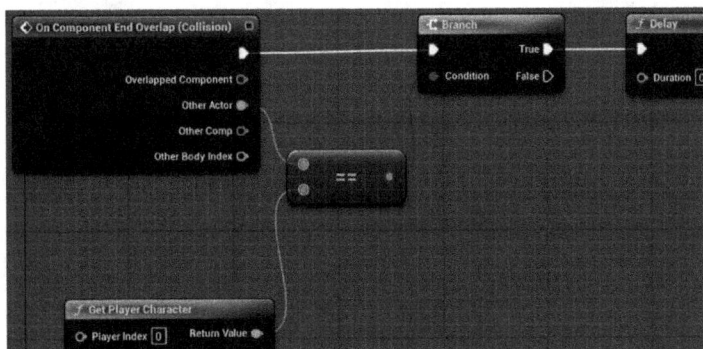

Figure 13.35: The first (left) half of the Component End Overlap node sequence

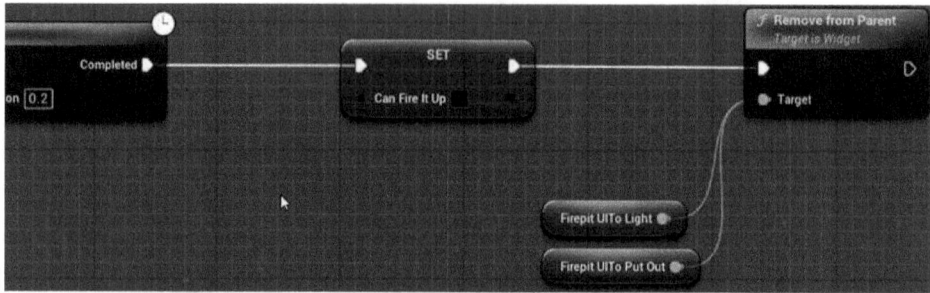

Figure 13.36: The second (right) half of the Component End Overlap node sequence

Let us analyze the Component End Overlap node sequence. Firstly, to get the Component End Overlap node, simply repeat the steps shown in *Figures 13.33* and *13.34* but press the + button for the **On Component End Overlap** instead.

Much like before, we check if the actor that ends the overlap with the collision sphere is the player, hence the equals and branch nodes.

Once again, we use a delay node, just to give enough time to the game to perform its calculations and update accordingly, then proceeding to setting the variable **Can Fire It Up** to false and consequently removing all widgets from the player's view.

In other words, if the player exits what we define as the acceptable range to allow interaction with the firepit, we specify that the player can no longer interact with the firepit, and therefore remove any UI information that prompts them otherwise.

As such, there is only one part of logic left to define and construct; what happens when the player is within range, can interact with the firepit, and decides to press the interact key (which we defined in the project settings' input mappings as key *E* — did so in *Chapter 12, Fantasy Castle Character and Interaction Blueprints*)?

The logic for that is shown in *Figure 13.37*:

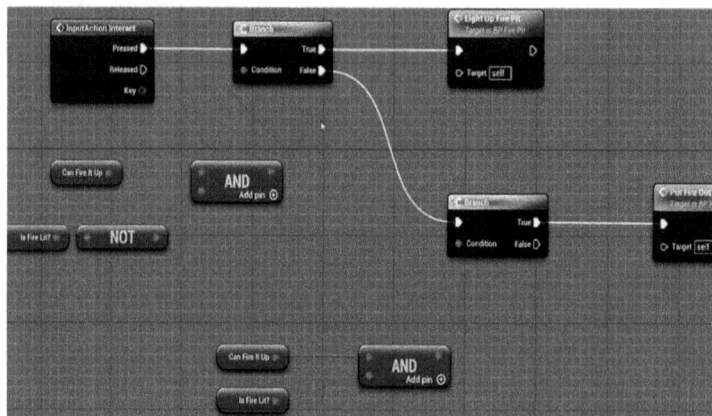

Figure 13.37: The logic defining what happens when the user interacts with the firepit

Figures 13.38 and *13.39* break *Figure 13.37* into two halves, once again for legibility purposes.

Figure 13.38 shows the Blueprint sequence's left half:

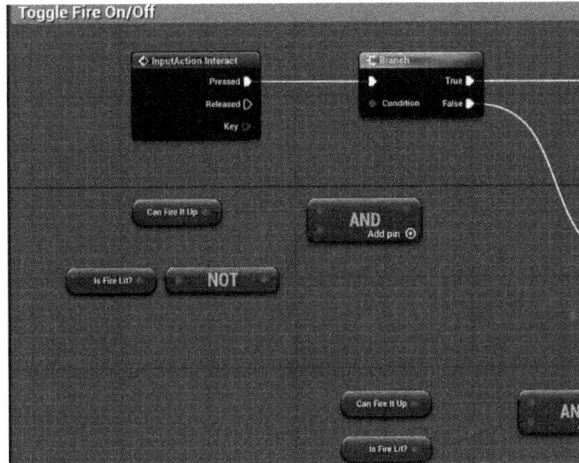

Figure 13.38: *Figure 13.37's first half*

Figure 13.39 shows the Blueprint sequence's right half:

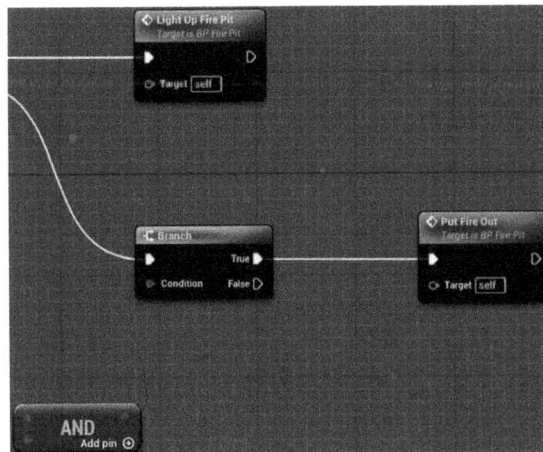

Figure 13.39: *Figure 13.37's second half*

Let us break the interaction node sequence down into smaller, easy to understand parts.

We start with an Input node that corresponds to the Interact input (E), which, once pressed, proceeds to check two conditions: can the player interact with the firepit (**Can Fire It Up**) and (**AND** node) is the fire already put out (**Is Fire Lit?** connected to a Boolean **NOT** node). If both of these conditions are true, then we proceed to execute the function of lighting up the firepit, which, as we previously saw, essentially scales up the Point Light's intensity while also making the fire particle FX active and, therefore visible to the player.

If, however, either of these conditions is false, then the **Branch** node will result in a false result, which consequently sends us to a second **Branch** node, checking again whether the player can interact with the firepit (**Can Fire It Up**) and if the fire is actually lit. If both of these are true, then we execute the `PutFireOut` function, which, as we saw earlier, sets the Point Light's intensity to 0, deactivates the Niagara based fire particle, therefore resulting in a dormant fire pit.

Before declaring the BP_FirePit done, there is one last set of things for us to double check and ensure they are set up properly. Specifically, we need to check the collision sphere's radius, the Point Light's default values and the NFire_00's default status (active or not). Then, we need to check if we need any default values assigned to any of our variables while we also want to expose the `IsFireLit?` variable, allowing a level designer to place the firepit in the level and have it lit by default, thus providing light to the environment.

We check all of the above conditions in *Figures 13.40* to *13.44*:

Figure 13.40: *The collision sphere's radius is set to 128*

The following figure shows Point Light component's assigned settings:

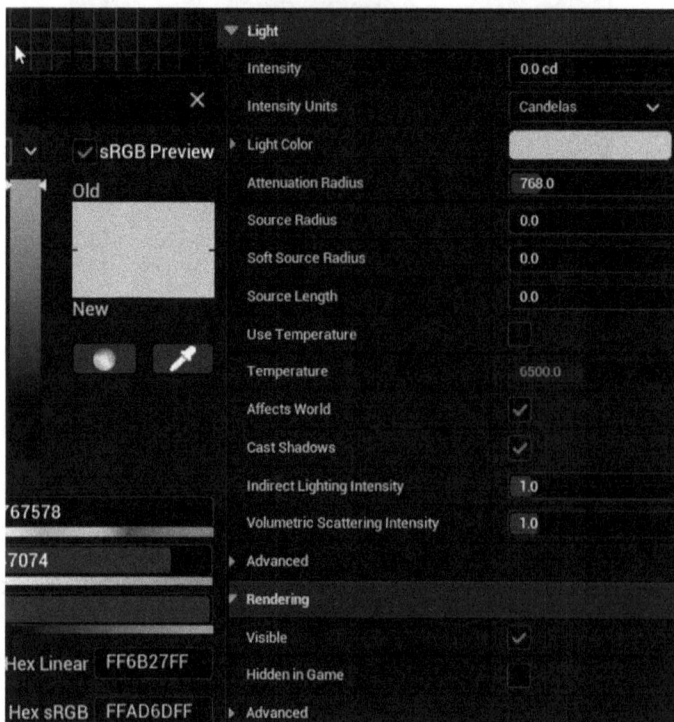

Figure 13.41: *The Point Light component's assigned settings*

In the following figure, fire particle's Auto Activate is disabled/unchecked:

Figure 13.42: The fire particle's Auto Activate is disabled/unchecked

In the following figure, Can Fire It Up is disabled by default:

Figure 13.43: Can Fire It Up by default is disabled, as it should

The following figure shows IsFireLit? variable settings:

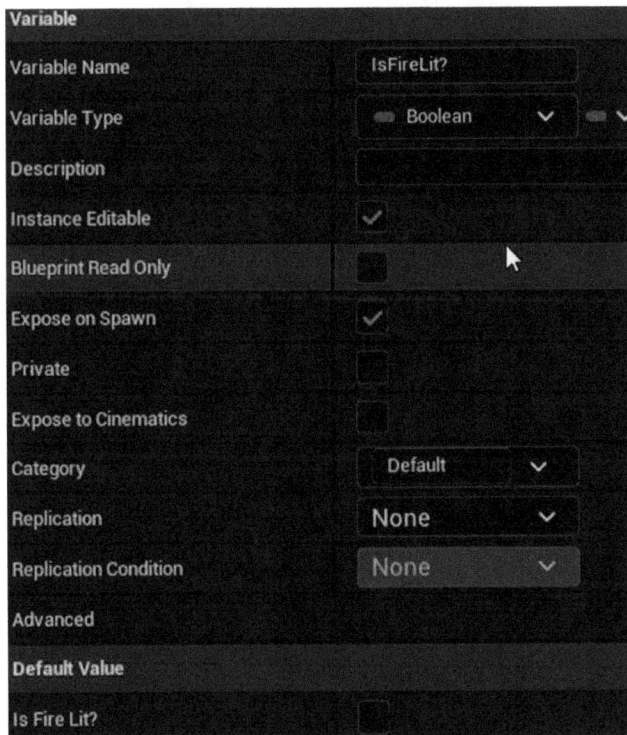

Figure 13.44: IsFireLit? variable settings

Compile and save if you have not already done so. Next, place two fire pits in a level, and set one to be as **Is Fire Lit?** set to true, while the other is set to false (default). Then, playtest the level and try to interact with each.

Figures 13.45 and *13.46* to *13.49* show the fire pit placement in the level and interaction with the player respectively:

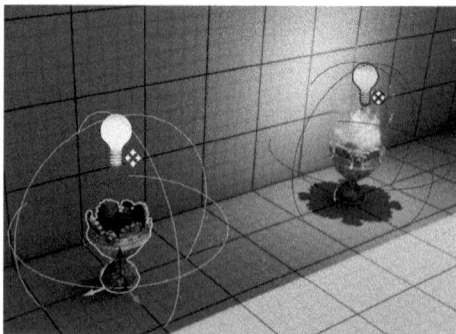

Figure 13.45: *IsFireLit? is unchecked for the left firepit, checked for the right one*

The following figure shows how to light up the unlit firepit:

Figure 13.46: *Success! We are prompted to light up the unlit firepit*

In the following figure, the prompt lit up:

Figure 13.47: *By pressing E, not only it lit up, but the prompt also disappeared as it should*

In the following figure, when approaching the lit up firepit, we are prompted to put out the fire:

Figure 13.48: When approaching the lit up firepit, we are prompted to put out the fire

In the following figure, by pressing E, the firepit's fire is extinguished:

Figure 13.49: By pressing E the firepit's fire is extinguished, while the prompt also disappears

In *Figure 13.50*, we go back to the left firepit and are prompted to extinguish its fire as well, and we do it in first person view (by pressing *V*). In *Figure 13.51*, we press *E* and *V*, thus leaving both firepits unlit and returning back to the third person view. To compensate for the lack of light, we toggle our character's light by pressing *L* (just a great excuse to playtest the previous chapter's mechanics).

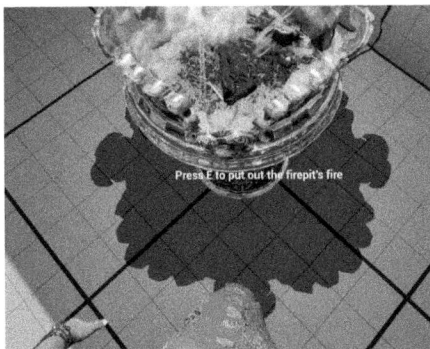

Figure 13.50: Prompted to extinguish the first firepit's fire, while in first person mode

In the following figure, we are back to the third person mode:

Figure 13.51: *Back to third person mode, with both firepits turned off and the character light toggled on*

Creating a teleportation portal

We will create a portal through which the player can teleport to another portal. Essentially for this system to work, a level designer will need to be placing at least two portals in a level, one referencing the other. As the player walks through portal A, it triggers their teleportation to portal B. If they walk through portal B, then they teleport back to A.

First, in the Content Browser, under **Content/Blueprints/**, create a folder named **Portal**. While in the newly created folder, right-click and create a new Blueprint Actor class. Name the newly created class **BP_Portal**. Open this Blueprint class.

Next, while having **DefaultSceneRoot** under the components tab of the Blueprint selected, add a **Scene** component. Now, let us define the portal's visuals, by bringing in several Static Mesh components in the scene. You can select Static Meshes you would like to use from the Content Browser and drag them under the Scene component we just added, while having the scene component selected. This way, all the Static Meshes can be scaled and moved uniformly, by simply controlling the scene component's transform values.

Now add a box collision component. Name this component **Teleportal**. We will be using this to detect when the player overlaps with it, and from there teleport them to the portal's destination.

We also add a simple plane shape, which we size to match the portal. Once we begin placing portals in our Fantasy Castle level, we will be using this plane to assign to it a material that resembles the destination; this way the player has an idea of where the portal might lead them.

Lastly, we add an **Arrow** component, which will help us define the specific coordinates the player teleports to, as well as the direction.

Figure 13.52 shows the list of components the author used, as well as what they all look like together in the Blueprint's Viewport:

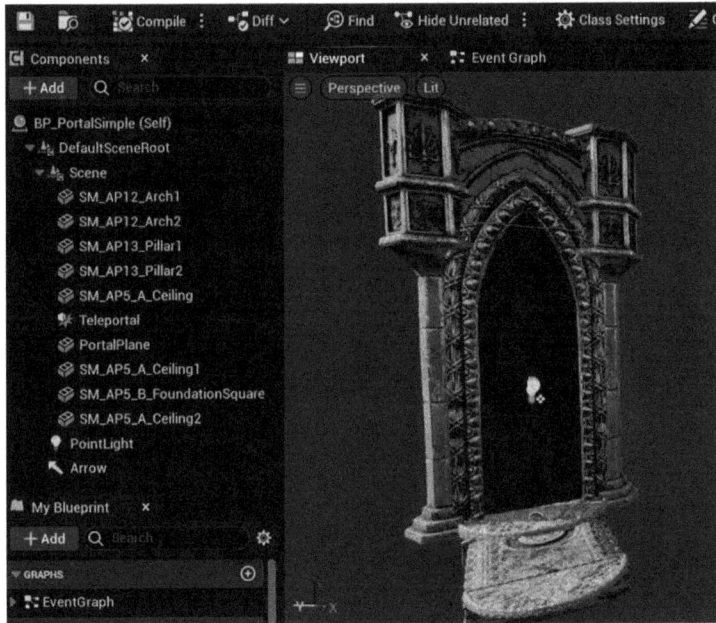

Figure 13.52: The list of components and the visual result of BP_Portal

Now, let us create three variables, such as the ones shown in *Figure 13.53*:

Figure 13.53: The list of variables to create on the left and right, along with whether they are public and instance editable or not

For **PortAltoTeleportTo** and **TeleportToLocation** press the small eye icon. When this icon resembles an open eye, it indicates that the variable is public and instance editable. In simpler terms, you can set this variable's values when placing the Blueprint actor in a level, as you will be finding the variable listed under the actor's details tab, along with the corresponding value field.

For the next step, under My Blueprint tab, in the Functions section, you will see there is a **Construction Script** function. Open it and click and drag the **Arrow** component.

From the arrow node's output pin, drag a cable and type in **Set Relative Transform** to create this node.

Then *Ctrl+Click* and drag the **Teleport to Location** variable, which you connect to the **Set Relative Transform** node's **New Transform** input pin. *Figure 13.54* shows what your final set up in the construction script should look like:

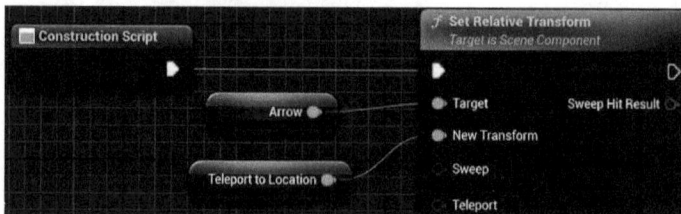

Figure 13.54: *The construction script*

Now select the **Teleportal** component from the Components tab. While having it selected, add a component begin overlap node in the Blueprint's event graph.

Next, create a function named **TeleportTo**. Open the function. *Figure 13.55* shows the first half of the function's node sequence we will create, while *Figure 13.56* shows the second half, once more for legibility purposes:

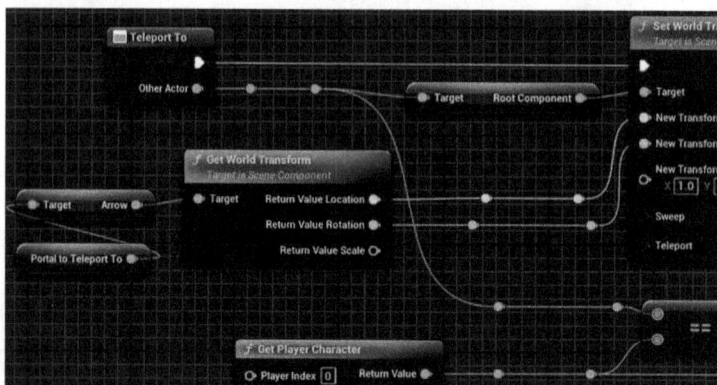

Figure 13.55: *The TeleportTo function's first half of its node sequence*

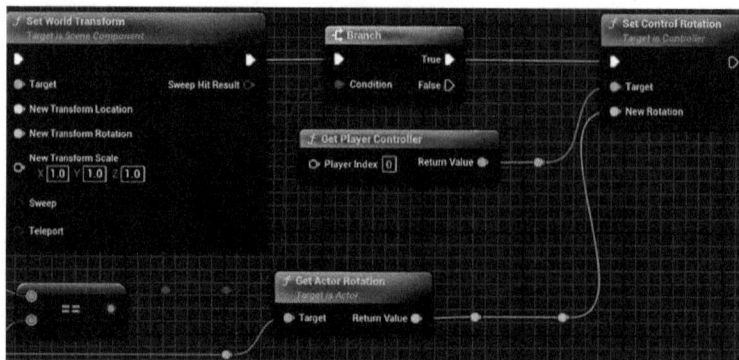

Figure 13.56: *The TeleportTo function's second half of its node sequence*

Firstly, note how the very first node has an **Other Actor** output pin. To get this, you need to click on the **Teleport To** node, and then under its details tab, go to **Inputs** and add an input, which you will name **Other Actor** and the type will be **Actor**, as shown in *Figure 13.57*.

Figure 13.57: *Adding an input to the node*

Figure 13.58, shows exactly how to get the input type:

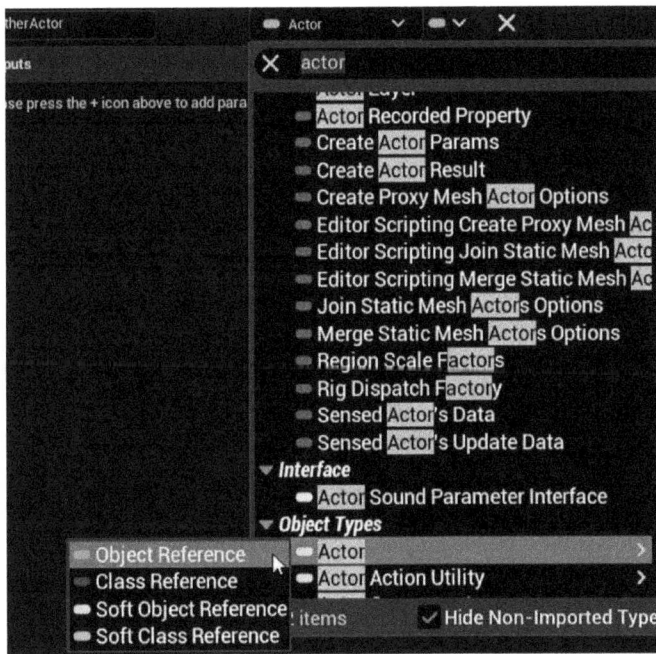

Figure 13.58: *Getting the Actor input type*

The other actor will be needed to connect it to Teleportal's component begin overlap node.

Next, we have brought in the **Portal To Teleport To** variable, from which we get its arrow component, and we drive a cable from its output pin to get its **Get World Transform** node, which will give us this specific arrow's location, rotation and scale in the level/world it is placed.

From the **Other Actor** we drive a cable and type Get Root Component, which then is driven into a Set World Transform node. In the **Set World Transform** node's **New Transform Location** we connect the **Get World Transform** node's **Return Value Location**, and we do the same for the rotation related pins of each node.

Then we drive a cable from **Teleport To** node's **Other Actor** pin that leads into an equals node, which is also connected to a **Get Player Character** node. The equals node's output is then driven into a branch, and the **Branch** node's **True** output is driven into a **Set Control Rotation** node, which uses **Get Player Controller** as its **Target**, and a **Get Actor Rotation**, which is connected to the **Get Player Character** node, as the **Set Control Rotation** node's **New Rotation**.

In other words, we store the world coordinates of our intended portal destination's arrow component and define them as the intended destination for the player. Since this entire function will be connected to the overlap begin node in the main event graph, it means we check if it is the player that overlaps with the teleportal component. If it is the player, then we ensure the player teleports to the new location in the same direction they were walking into the portal, which is forward.

Then, back to the event graph, we connect the function to the begin overlap node, press C to create a comment box, and name it **Begin Overlap**, as shown in *Figure 13.59*:

Figure 13.59: Finalizing the BP_Portal

Compile and save if you have not done so already. Then, place two BP_Portal actors in an empty level, as shown in *Figure 13.60*:

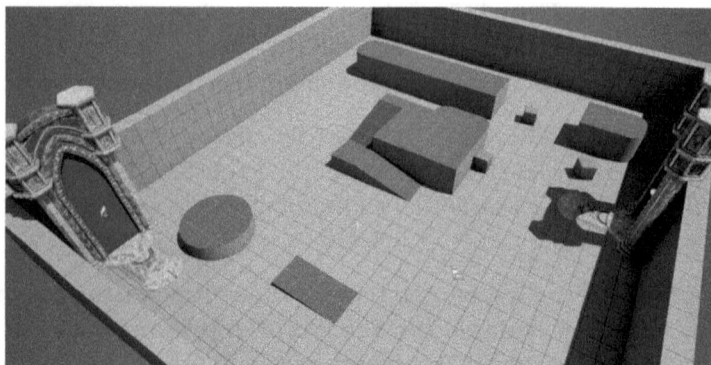

Figure 13.60: Two portals in a map

While having one of them selected, pick the other portal by selecting it in the **Portal to Teleport To** field under the details tab, as shown in *Figure 13.61*:

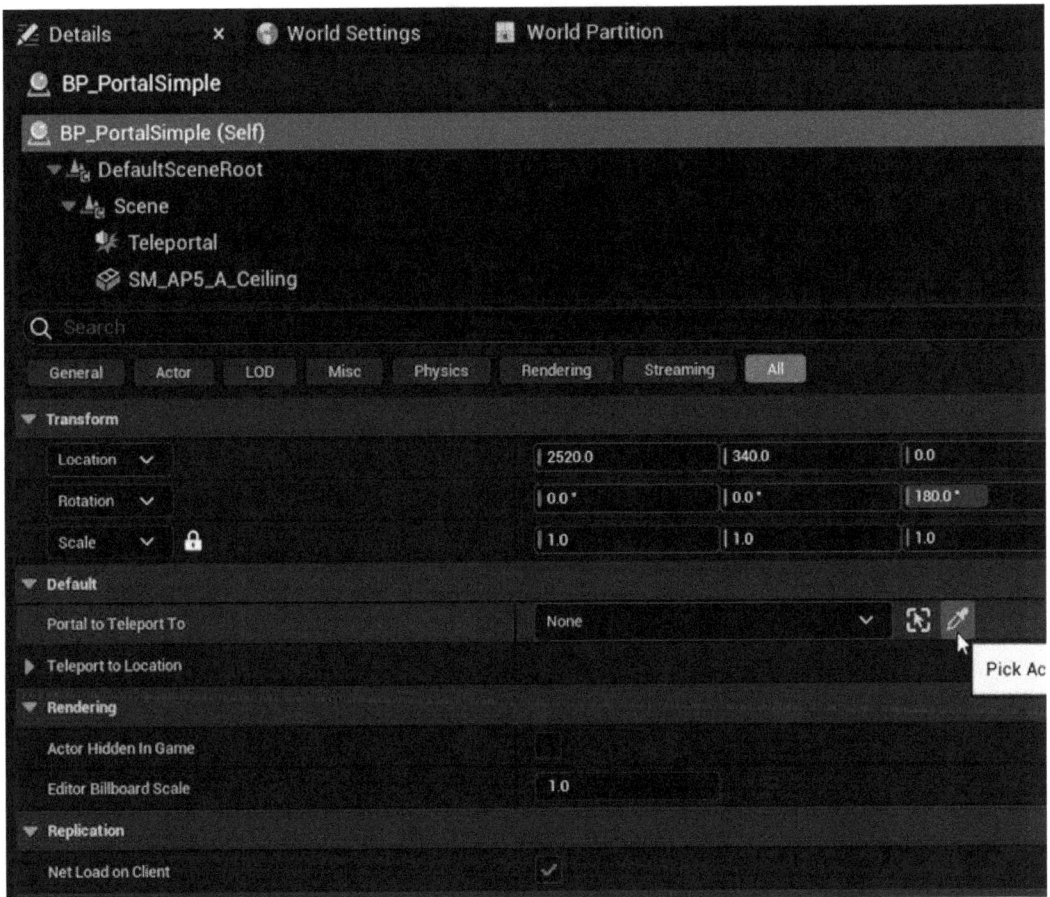

Figure 13.61: Two portals in a map

In *Figure 13.62*, we are zooming in on that field after the second portal has been selected:

Figure 13.62: A closer view to selecting the second portal

Now, we are ready to playtest. *Figures 13.63* and *13.64* show the author's play test results:

Figure 13.63: Going through portal 1…

The following figure shows the play test result:

Figure 13.64: …leads to portal 2

Conclusion

We worked with Widget Blueprints to create some basic UI, while we also created our first interactable actors, such as firepits that can be lit on and off, and portals that can be traversed by the player. We created all that by using functions and variables within our Blueprints.

In the next chapter, we will take what we learned further, and we will create more interactable actors, that will allow us to create a simple mini game, when used with another.

At this point, it is worth mentioning that using this book's resources, such as the project files, will certainly help as you read through the more difficult chapters, such as the one we just covered.

Points to remember

- Sometimes Blueprint actors need to be built in parallel as they might be referencing variables of functions one from another.

- Creating Widget Blueprints for UI.

- Switch nodes and their functionality, properties and application.

- Sequence nodes and their functionality, properties and application.

- User interactions.

Exercise

1. You can duplicate some of these actors we created and start playing around with some of the existing functions or come up with new ones, such as creating your own firepit, that has different colors of flames, such as blue or purple, or instead of fire particles, it has orbs with emissive Materials that match the color of the light they emit.

Join our book's Discord space

Join the book's Discord Workspace for Latest updates, Offers, Tech happenings around the world, New Release and Sessions with the Authors:

https://discord.bpbonline.com

CHAPTER 14

Fantasy Castle Mini Game Blueprints

Introduction

Continuing with interactive Blueprint actors, in this chapter we will proceed to create a mini game in which the player has to collect three types of small elephant statuettes, within a predetermined amount of time. Once the time's up, we will calculate the player's total score, based on the amount and type of statuettes they collected and present them with it, while allowing them to restart and reset the mini game.

A lot of the processes and methods used were already utilized in the last two chapters, so will try to expedite the process as much as possible.

Structure

In this chapter, we will go through the following topics:

- Creating the actors for a mini game
- Starting with the elephant statuettes
- Greek God Statue as an interactable actor
- Creating a countdown timer
- Creating a total score widget
- BP_GameStartActor

- Finalizing the elephant statue actor
- One last addition to BP_ThirdPersonCharacter

Objectives

By the end of this chapter, we will learn how to use some basic array functions while creating all the elements we need for putting together a simple mini game, in which the player collects different types of statues within a specific amount of time, each granting the player different score points.

Essentially, this could be your first game!

Creating the actors for a mini game

Before we get into more Blueprint creation, let us first analyze the mini game we will be having in our Fantasy Castle map. The way it will work is that the player approaches a magnificent version of the Greek God Statue and, when within range, is prompted to activate it to start the mini game, if they activate it (by pressing *E*), then they have a preset amount of time to find and collect three kinds of elephant statuettes; a golden kind, a marble kind, and a glass kind. The goal is to collect all golden statuettes before the clock runs out, while marble and glass statuettes work as bonus points. In addition, if the player collects all of the gold statuettes before the clock runs out, then they get bonus points. At the same time, however, they also get penalized for the time that passes.

The game ends when the time runs out or when the player has collected all golden statuettes. At the end the player is presented with their score and some stats, and if they want, they can reset the game and start all over again.

Now that the reader knows the concept, it can be understood we will need to create the elephant statuette actors, the statue actor that initiates the game, and, of course, the UI to accompany all that.

Since many of these actors are dependent on each other, we will need to develop them in parallel, so in the next couple of sections of this chapter, we will be jumping from developing the elephant statuette to the statue and vice versa.

Starting with the elephant statuettes

Having already completed the fire pit actor earlier in the chapter should help us visualize the needs of the elephant statuette actor. We need to consider that the player has to be within range of the actor, for a message to be displayed, informing them of being able to pick up the actor. If the player interacts (*E* by default) with the actor while within range, then they will pick it up, which essentially means we need to destroy the actor, yet somehow keep a record of it having been picked up.

There is also the matter of updating the player's score as they pick up these statuettes. In addition, we need to consider the fact that there are three versions of the actor, and each one rewards the player with a different number of points.

Another point to consider is versatility. We want to allow for an easy way to change the points the player can score, the points that are subtracted if the time runs out, the amount of time they have, as well as the reward they earn for finishing before the time runs out.

Lastly, we also need to consider that the statuettes need to also communicate with an actor that initiates the mini game, which will also be able to reset the mini game and respawn all statuettes.

Let us begin.

In the Content Browser, under **Content/Blueprints/** create a folder named **ElephantStatues**.

Right click to create a Blueprint actor and name it **BP_ElephantStatue**. Open it and start adding Static Mesh **Components** to define its looks while also adding a sphere collision component, which you will label **Collider**, as seen in *Figure 14.1*:

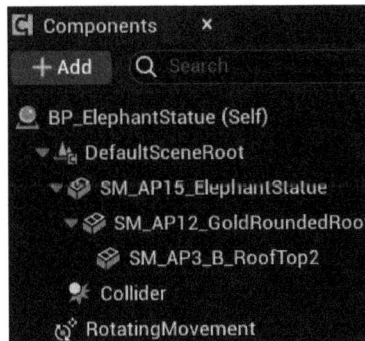

Figure 14.1: The newly created Blueprint actor's component list

You can see the visual result of this component list in the Blueprint actor's Viewport, which looks identical to *Figure 14.2*:

Figure 14.2: The visual representation of BP_ElephantStatue

First, let us create a couple of variables, specifically:

- **TypeOfStatue**, **Integer** type
- **IsAGoldStatue**, **Boolean** type
- **IsAMarbleStatue**, **Boolean** type
- **IsAGlassStatue**, **Boolean** type

Since there are three versions of the same object, we will need to define what these three versions look like in the actor's **Construction Script**. *Figures 14.3 to 14.5* show the complete node sequence:

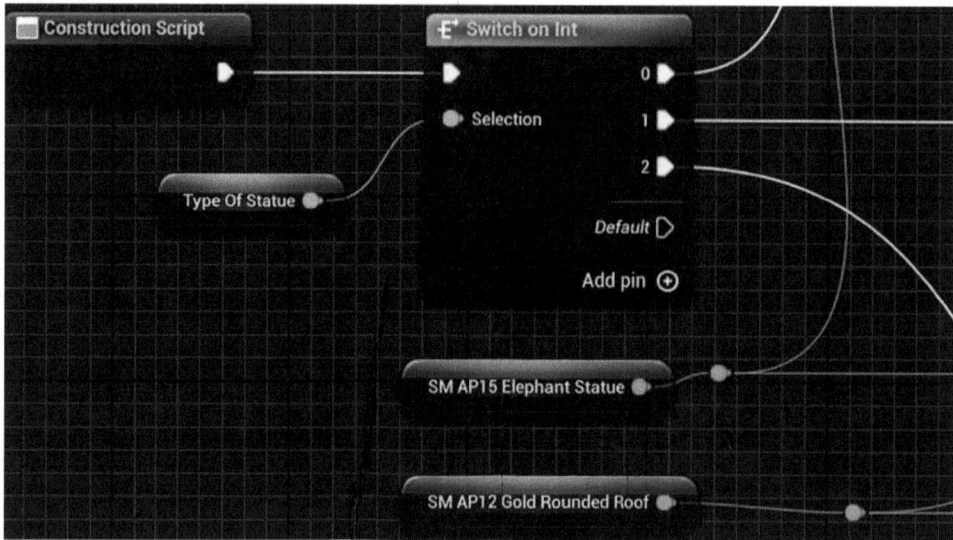

Figure 14.3: BP_ElephantStatuette Construction Script – Part 1

We start by bringing in the **Type of Statue** variable, which is an **Integer** type. The types of statues are gold, marble and glass. Therefore, we can define the **Type of Statue** value of 0 representing the gold statue, 1 representing marble, and 2 representing glass.

We connect the variable node to a switch node that works with integers, and we add pins to have three outgoing execution pins, 0,1 and 2. What the switch node will do, is depending on which value **Type Of Statue** feeds it, it will execute a different path. So, a **Type of Statue** value of 0 will follow the switch node's execution path 0, 1 value will lead to output 1 and so on.

Next, we bring in the Static Mesh components that make up for the actor's visuals. We are using three Static Meshes, one of them will remain gold throughout all the types, but the other two will have their Materials changed depending on the type of statue they are meant to be.

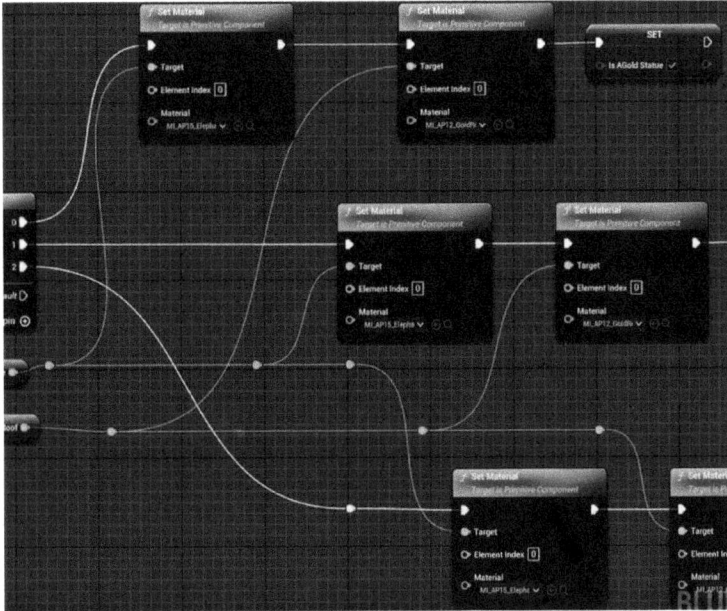

Figure 14.4: *BP_ElephantStatuette Construction Script – Part 2*

So, based on what we just described, the switch node's output pin 0 should lead to assigning gold Materials to the statuette meshes, output pin 1 to Materials assigning marble Materials to the meshes, and output pin 2 to glass Materials.

This is exactly why we use the **Set Material** nodes, and in them, we use Materials that represent each different type:

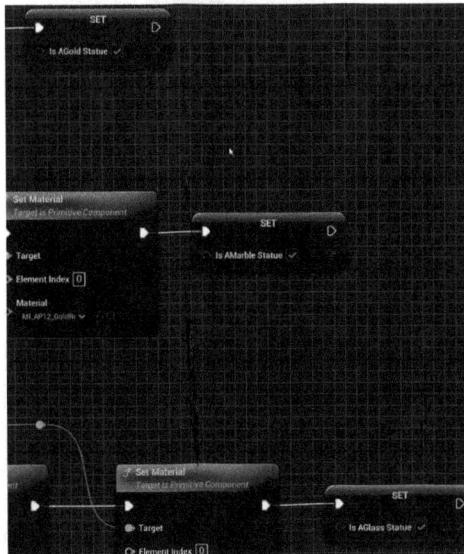

Figure 14.5: *BP_ElephantStatuette Construction Script – Part 3*

Finally, as can be seen in *Figure 14.5*, we end up setting our Boolean variables to the corresponding Materials.

To summarize, if **Type Of Statue** equals 0, then gold themed Materials are assigned to the meshes, and the **Is AGold Statue** Boolean is set to true. If **Type Of Statue** = 1, then marble Materials are assigned to the meshes and **Is AMarble Statue** = true. Lastly, if **Type Of Statue** = 2, glass Materials are assigned, and **Is AGlass Statue** = true.

In addition, we want to expose the `TypeOfStatue` variable, so that we can easily set the integer values when placing the actors in a level. As a reminder, you can expose the variable by pressing the small eye icon next to it, as displayed in *Figure 14.6*:

Figure 14.6: Exposing the variable

Next, we want to create three functions which will be executed as soon as we start playing, as seen in *Figure 14.7*:

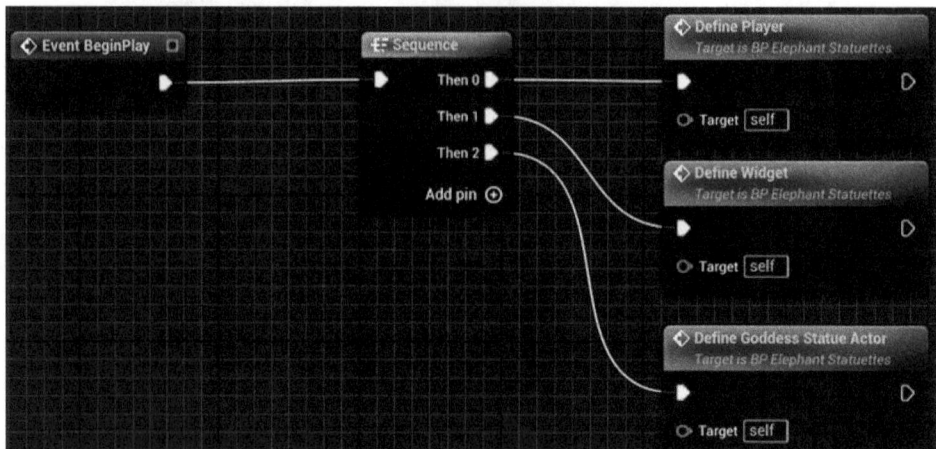

Figure 14.7: Event Begin Play

The first function is **Define Player**, pretty simple and to the point, as seen in *Figure 14.8*:

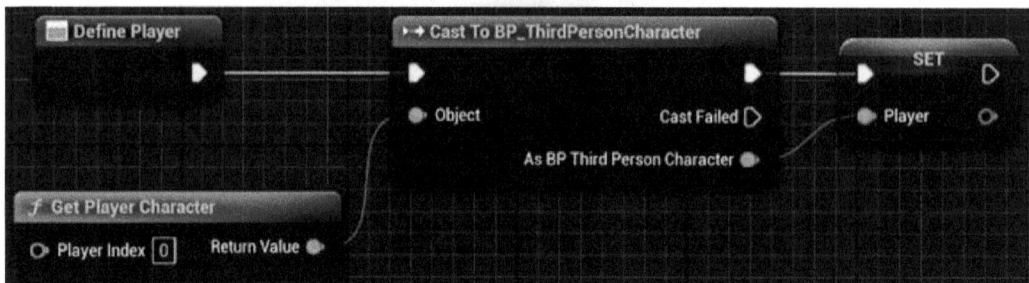

Figure 14.8: The Define Player function

Right click on the graph, type in **Cast to BP_ThirdPersonCharacter**, create the node, drive a cable from its **As BP Third Person Character** output pin, select Promote to Variable name the variable **Player**. Right click on the graph, type in **Get Player Character**, create the node, connect it to the **Cast BP_ThirdPersonCharacter** node's Object pin. Compile, save, done, moving on.

Before proceeding to the next step, it is time we created a Widget Blueprint for the elephant statue actors. All we need to do is select one of the firepit Widget Blueprints we created and drag it into the **ElephantStatues** folder, as shown in *Figure 14.9*:

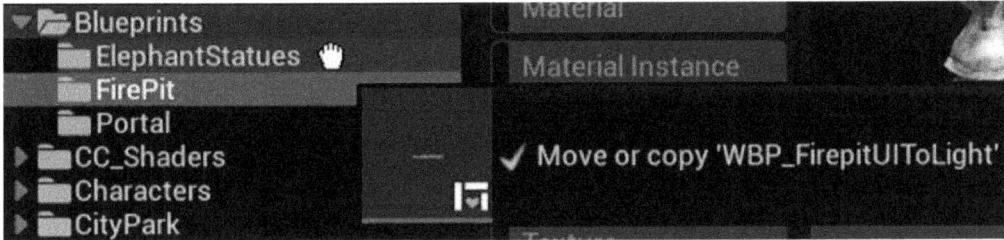

Figure 14.9: *Moving the selected Widget Blueprint from FirePit to ElephantStatues*

Then, when prompted, select **Copy Here**, as displayed in *Figure 14.10*:

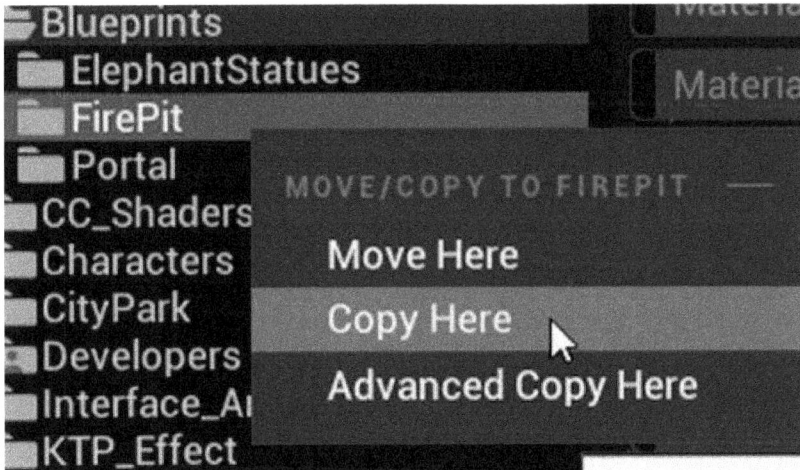

Figure 14.10: *Making a copy of the existing Widget Blueprint*

Then select the Widget Blueprint you just placed in the **ElephantStatues** folder, and either right click and Rename or press *F2*, to rename it to WBP_UIToPickUpStatue.

Now double click the new Widget Blueprint, and all you need to do is change the text displayed to **Press E to pick up the Elephant Statue**.

With the Widget Blueprint done, we are ready to move on to creating the **Define Widget** function, which is shown in *Figure 14.11*:

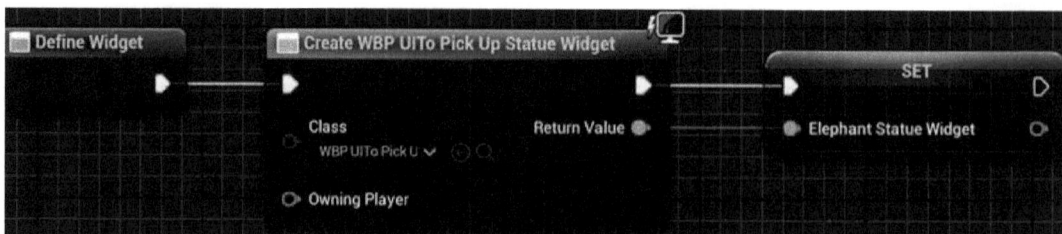

Figure 14.11: *The Define Widget function*

Right click anywhere in the event graph, type in **Create Widget** to create the create widget node, then use the Widget Blueprint we just created in the class field of the create widget node, drive a cable from its return value output pin, and select promote to a variable. Name that new variable as **Elephant Statue Widget**. Lastly, select all the created nodes and collapse to function, naming the newly created function as **Define Widget**.

The next function to create is Define Greek God Statue. In order to create this function, we first need to start the Greek God Statue Blueprint actor.

Before doing that, we can create one more variable in BP_ElephantStatuette, specifically add a variable named **CanPickup** and make it **Boolean**. Compile and save, we will return to this actor later again.

Greek God Statue as an interactable actor

How will this actor work in-game? The player approaches it, while within range, a message pops up, prompting the player to press *E* to start the statue collection mini game. If the player walks away, the message disappears.

If the player presses *E*, the message disappears, a new UI pops up, displaying a time countdown, the number of gold elephants that have been picked up, the number of total gold elephants available in the level, the number of marble and glass elephants — without displaying how many of them are in total, since they are meant to be bonus points.

With the mini game initialized, there is no further interaction to be had with the statue. Once the game is over (whether because the player collected all the golden elephant statues, or because the time ran out), if the player goes back to the statue, they are prompted to press *E* to replay the game. If they press *E*, all the elephant statues are respawned at the same locations they were before, the score and the stats are reset, and the game starts again.

In essence, for the mini game to work, the Greek God Statue actor, the elephant statue actors and the third person character Blueprint class, all will need to communicate with each other and update each other.

Let us get started with the basics first. Inside the **Content/Blueprints/ElephantStatues** folder, right click, create a new Blueprint actor class, name it **BP_GameStartActor**.

Let us bring in all the Static Mesh components that will visually build up the Greek God Statue, assign any special Materials we want, and add a collision sphere component for a start, as shown in *Figure 14.12*:

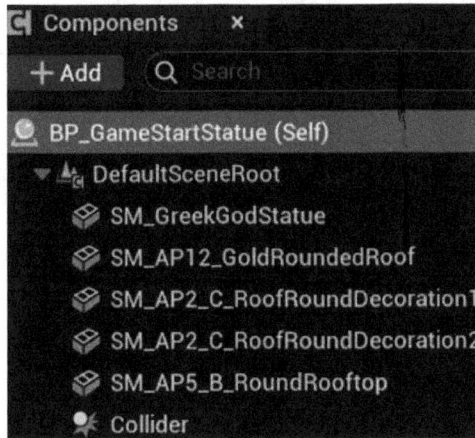

Figure 14.12: The BP_GameStartActor components

Looking at the Blueprint actor's Viewport, we see what *Figure 14.13* displays:

Figure 14.13: The visuals

Before we begin, let us take a look at the functions we will need to execute upon initializing the actor, refer to *Figure 14.14*:

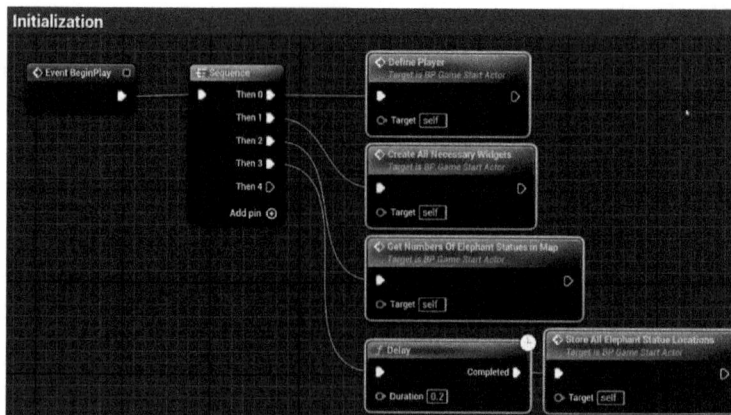

Figure 14.14: Initializing BP_GameStartActor

The **Define Player** function is identical to *Figure 14.8*.

The **Create All Necessary Widgets** function is similar to *Figure 14.11*. However, there are a lot more widgets to define here, and these widgets require a little bit more work. Let us get them done, and then we can resume the work on BP_GameStartActor.

The first Widget Blueprint we will need is similar to the ones we created so far, so follow the same instructions as in *Figures 14.8* and *14.9* however, this time, you will name the duplicated/copied Widget Blueprint as WBP_UIToStartMiniGame, and you will replace the text with what is shown in *Figure 14.15*:

Press E to start statue collection minigame

Figure 14.15: The message that will prompt the player to start the mini game

Next, duplicate the Widget Blueprint we just created and name the duplicate WBP_UIToReplayMiniGame. *Figure 14.16* shows what the message will be in this widget:

Press E to replay statue collection minigame

Figure 14.16: The message that will be prompting the player to replay the mini game

Creating a countdown timer

Now, let us create the countdown timer UI. Create a new user Widget Blueprint (*Chapter 13, Fantasy Castle Interactive Blueprint Actors, Figure 13.10* in case you forgot how to do that) and name it WBP_PlayerTimerStatues. Open it, and in the widget editor's Palette tab, search for Canvas Panel, click, and drag it into the main window.

Then, search for **Text**, click, and drag it over the Canvas Panel in the main window. On the upper right corner of the window, under the **Details** tab, on top, check the box **Is Variable** and name it **CountdownTime**, as shown in *Figure 14.17*:

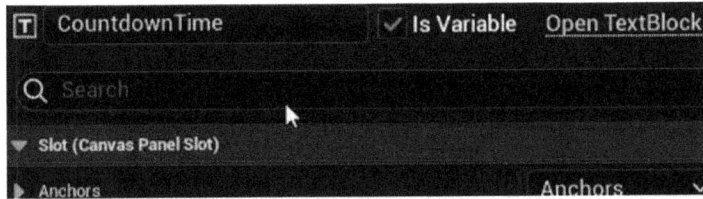

Figure 14.17: CountdownTime text variable

Next, a bit lower, click on **Anchors** and select the one that indicates the text block will be in the upper right corner (as shown in *Figure 14.18*):

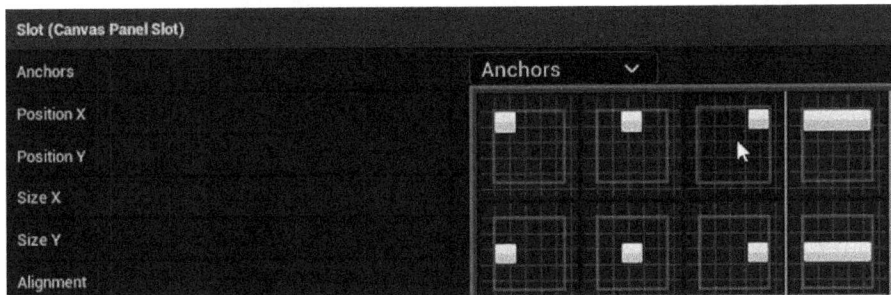

Figure 14.18: Anchors

For the rest, use the same settings, as shown in *Figure 14.19*:

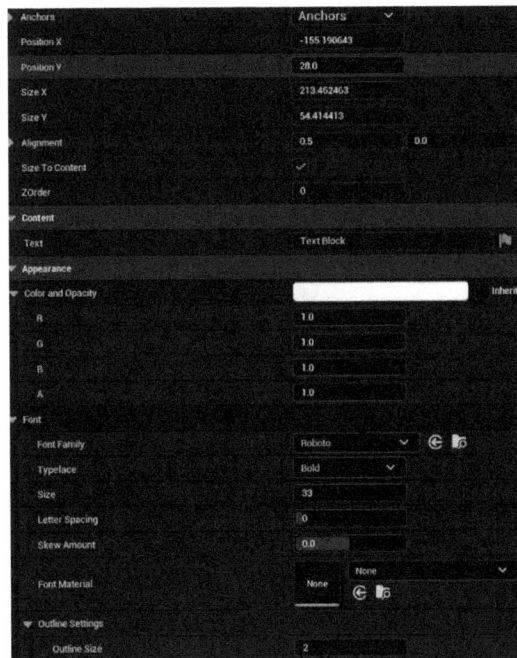

Figure 14.19: Use the same settings as shown here

Next, click on the **Graph** icon in the upper right corner, as shown in *Figure 14.20*:

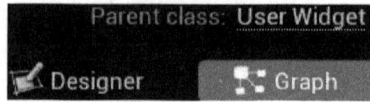

Figure 14.20: *Click on Graph*

As you can see, the window now is very similar to a Blueprint actor's editor. First, create two variables, the ones shown in *Figure 14.21*:

Figure 14.21: *The variables you need to create and their types*

Back to the Widget Blueprint's event graph, right click, type in **Custom Event**, create the node, and then let us replicate what is shown in *Figures 14.22* and *14.23*:

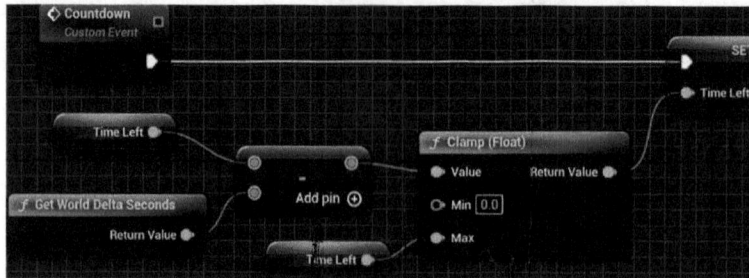

Figure 14.22: *Countdown Event – Part 1*

Ctrl+Click and drag the **TimeLeft** variable into the graph, draw a cable from it, type in **-** or subtract, then right click, type in **Get World Delta Seconds**, create that node, and connect it to the second input pin of the subtract node.

Drive a cable from the subtract node's output pin, type in **Clamp (Float)**, create the node, plug **Time Left** to clamp node's **Max**.

Alt+Click and drag the **Time Left** variable into the graph, plug the clamp node's **Return Value** output pin to the set node's **Time Left** input pin.

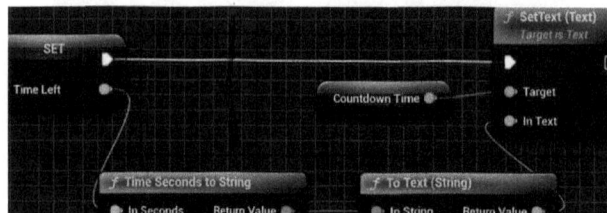

Figure 14.23: *Countdown Event – Part 2*

Next (refer to *Figure 14.23*), drive a cable from the set node's **Time Left** output pin, right click, type in **Time Seconds to String**, create a node, drive cable, type into **To Text (String)**, create node.

Ctrl+Click and drag the **Countdown Time** variable, drive a cable from its output pin, right click, type in **Set Text (Text)**, create a node. Drive To Text node's **Return Value** to Set Text node's **In Text**.

Do not forget to drive a cable from Countdown node's output execution pin to **SET** node's execution input, and from that to Set Text node's execution input. Compile, save.

Back to BP_GameStartActor, create a variable named `MiniGameDuration`, of **Float** type, and expose it (*Figure 14.24*). Compile and save.

Figure 14.24: One more variable to create in BP_GameStartActor

While adding variables here, let us create one more **Float** type variable named `TimeItTookPlayerToFinish` (*Figure 14.25*). Compile, save.

Figure 14.25: Yet another variable to create in BP_GameStartActor

Back to WBP_PlayerTimerStatues 's event graph, right click in the graph, create one more custom event node, name it **ResetTimer**, and follow *Figure 14.26* to complete it:

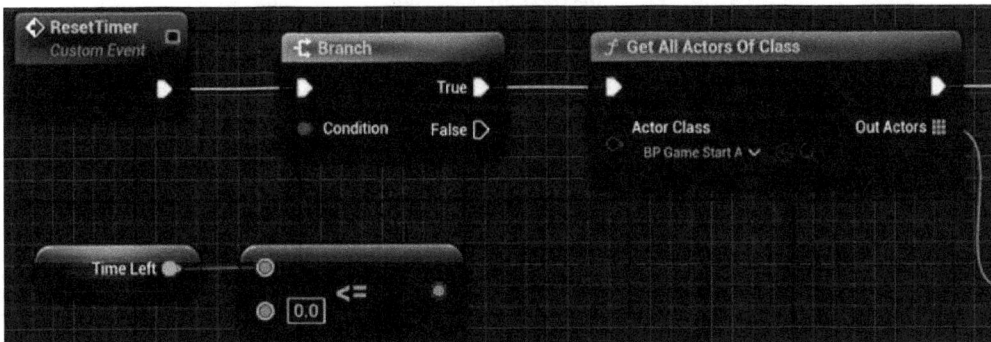

Figure 14.26: Reset Timer custom event – Part 1

Drive a cable to a branch node, *Ctrl+Click* and drag the **Time Left** variable, drive a cable from its output pin, type in <=, create a node, and drive the output pin to the branch's **Condition**.

Drag a cable from the **Branch** node's **True**, type in **Get All Actors of Class**, create a node, and make sure **Actor Class** uses BP_GameStartActor.

Continue by referring to *Figure 14.27*:

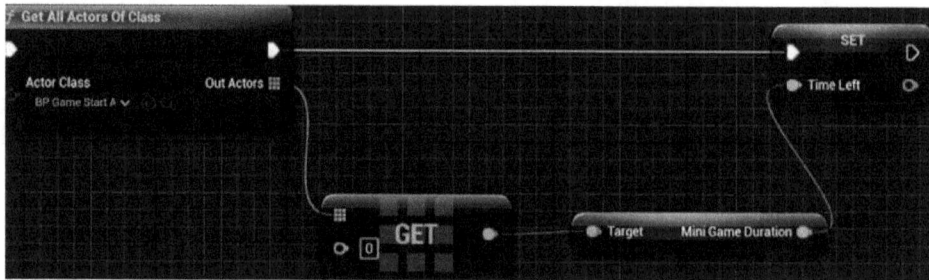

Figure 14.27: Reset Timer custom event – Part 2

From the **Out Actors** array output pin, drive a cable, type in **GET**, create a node, drive cable, type in get Mini Game Duration, and create a node. *Alt+Click* and drag the **Time Left** variable, drive the **Mini Game Duration** node's output to the set **Time Left** node's **Time Left**, and connect the execution line between **Get All Actors of Class** and **SET** as shown in *Figure 14.27*. Compile, save.

Next, find the **Event Tick** node in the event graph, drive a cable and type in **Countdown**, create the node. It should look exactly like *Figure 14.28* shows:

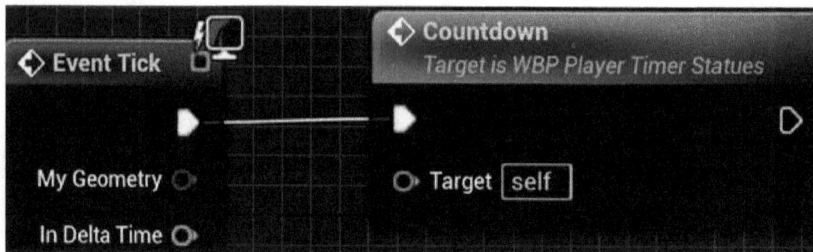

Figure 14.28: Event tick

Next, find the **Event Pre Construct** node in the event graph, as shown in *Figure 14.29*:

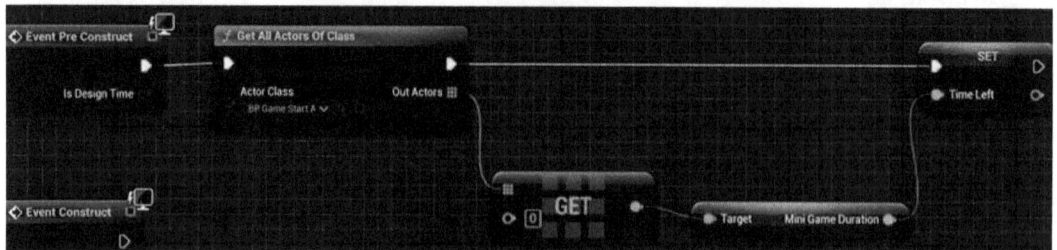

Figure 14.29: Event Pre Construct

Compile and save; you can now close this Widget Blueprint.

Creating a statue collection HUD

In this section, we will learn to create a statue collection **Heads Up Display (HUD)**. Right click in the Content Browser, create a new user Widget Blueprint, and name it **WBP_PlayerScoreStatues**. Double click it to start editing. Now that you are familiar with bringing elements to the widget designer, bring in all of the following elements as shown in the widget's **Hierarchy** tab, in *Figure 14.30*:

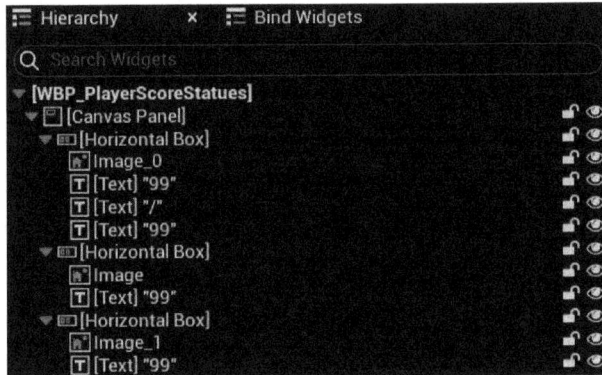

Figure 14.30: WBP_PlayerScoreStatues – Hierarchy

Visually, it should look similar to *Figure 14.31*:

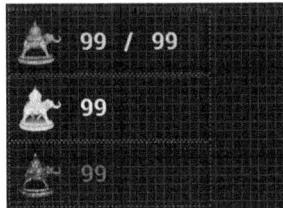

Figure 14.31: WBP_PlayerScoreStatues – what it looks like

Figures 14.32 to *14.34* will show the detailed settings for each of the elements in the Hierarchy, this way you can replicate the result seen in *Figure 14.31*:

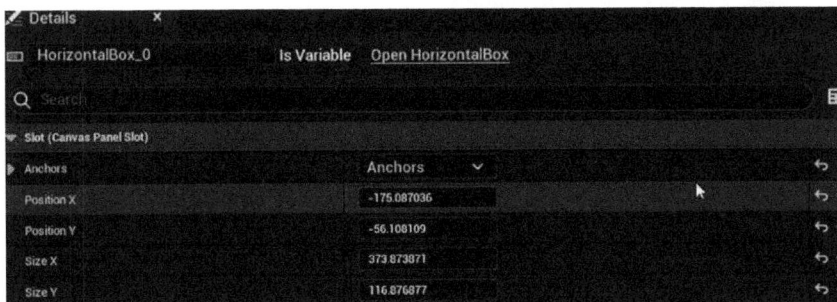

Figure 14.32: Details for HorizontalBox_0

The following figure shows the details:

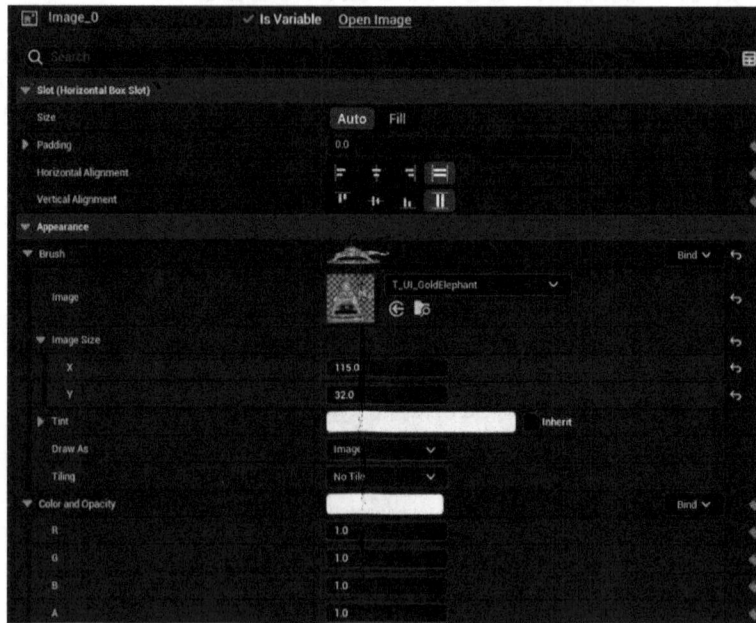

Figure 14.33: Details for HorizontalBox_0

The following are the details for TextBlock_1:

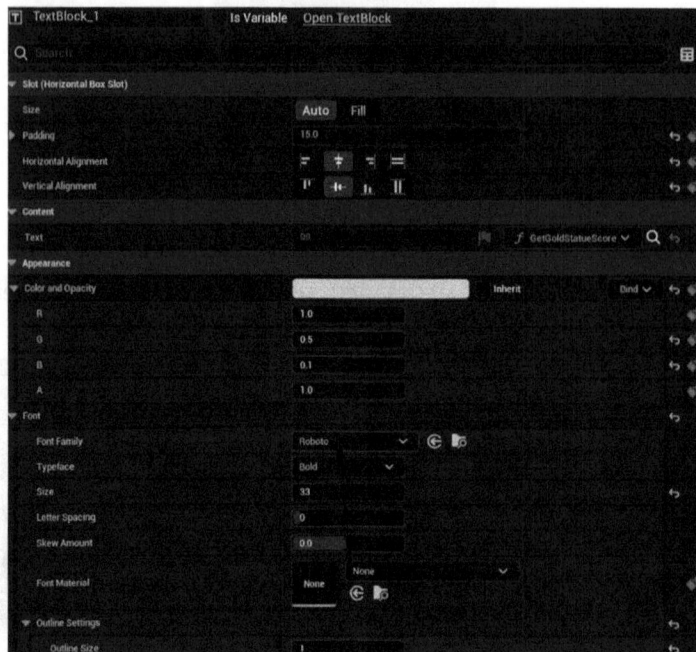

Figure 14.34: Details for TextBlock_1

For **TextBlock_1**, under **Content** in the **Text** row, click on **Bind**, and then select **Create Binding** as shown in *Figure 14.35*. This will result in creating a function. Rename the function into **Get Gold Statue Score**:

Figure 14.35: Event tick

In the **Get Gold Statue Score** function's graph editor, replicate what is displayed in *Figure 14.36*:

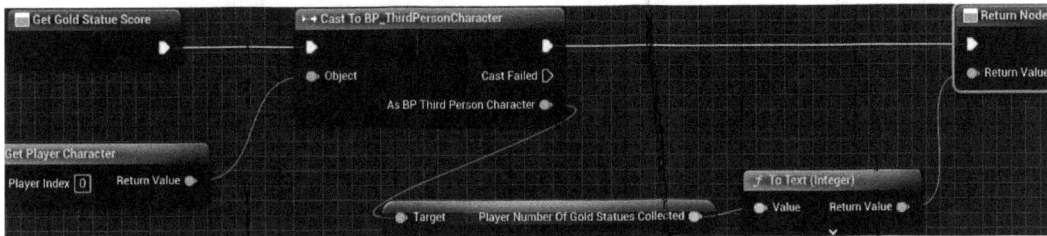

Figure 14.36: Get Gold Statue Score function

Back in the Designer window of the Widget Blueprint, continue with the details for each member of the widget's Hierarchy. Follow *Figures 14.37* to *14.38*:

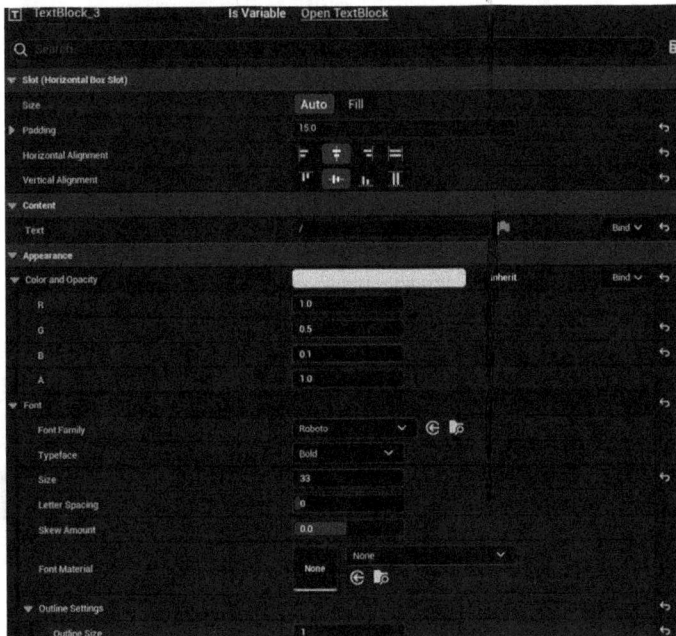

Figure 14.37: TextBlock_3 settings

The following are the details for TextBlock_4 settings:

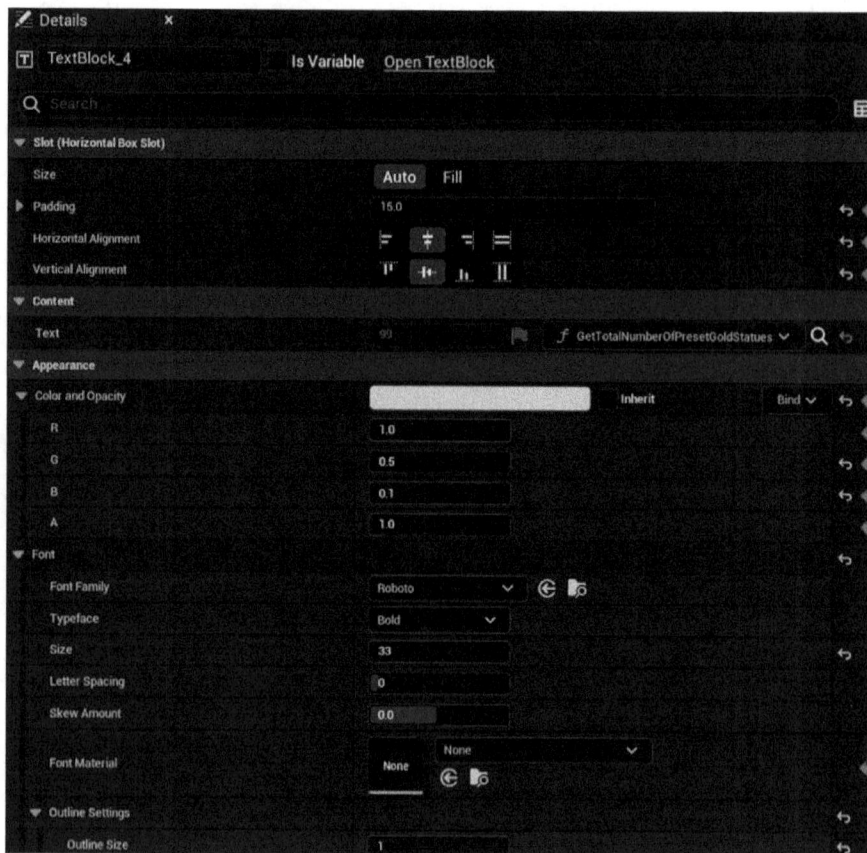

Figure 14.38: TextBlock_4 settings

A bind is needed for **TextBlock_4**'s text, so replicate *Figure 14.35* to create a new function for it. Name the function Get total Number of Preset Gold Statues and replicate the node sequence displayed in *Figure 14.39*:

Figure 14.39: Get Total Number Of Preset Gold Statues function

You can easily replicate the rest, as it follows a similar pattern. For reference purposes, *Figures 14.40 and 14.41* show the sequence node of the remaining functions for this widget, which are once again created by binding the text that represents the respective type of elephant statues collected.

Note: The cables in the following figures are not nicely stretched out, for the purpose of being able to fit the entire node sequence in one image.

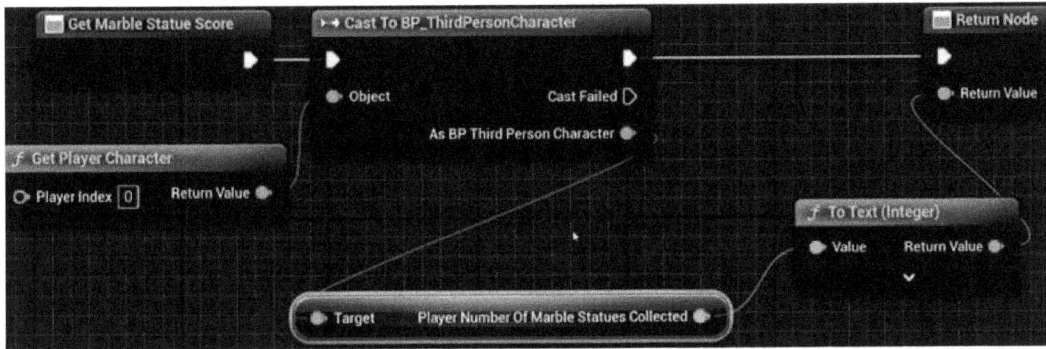

Figure 14.40: Get Marble Statue Score function

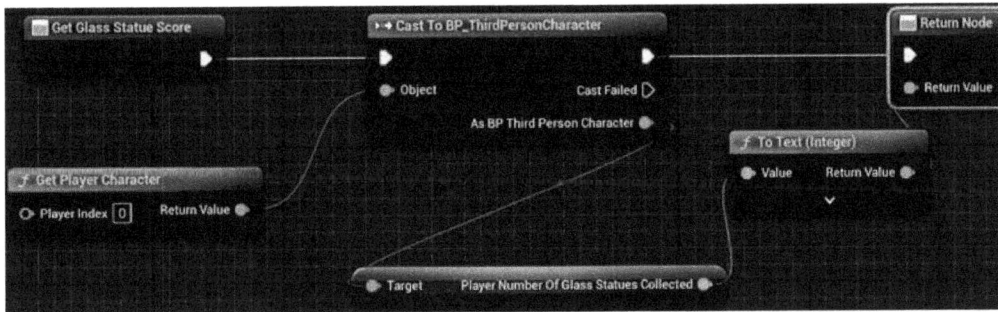

Figure 14.41: Get Glass Statue Score function

Creating a total score widget

One last Widget Blueprint to create. Duplicate the one we just finished, WBP_ PlayerScoreStatues and name the duplicate as WBP_PlayerTotalScoreStatues.

For the most part, it will be the same, with the difference being that with this we will show the total number of marble statues that were in the level, as well as the total number of glass statues that were in the level. In addition, we will show the time it took the player to complete the mini game, and finally we will calculate and display the total score, while also prompting the player to press X to close the window.

For the purpose of expediency and practicality, we would not go over all the steps, as you can follow and replicate the steps we took for the gold statues' stats and apply them to the marble and glass statues. Similarly, you can add the texture and text which you will bind for the time, as well as for the total score.

Instead, let us dive straight into the sequence nodes the functions for calculating the time and total score use, as well as the sequence node in the event graph for closing the window.

Starting with the **GetTimeTookPlayerToFinish** function is displayed in *Figure 14.42*:

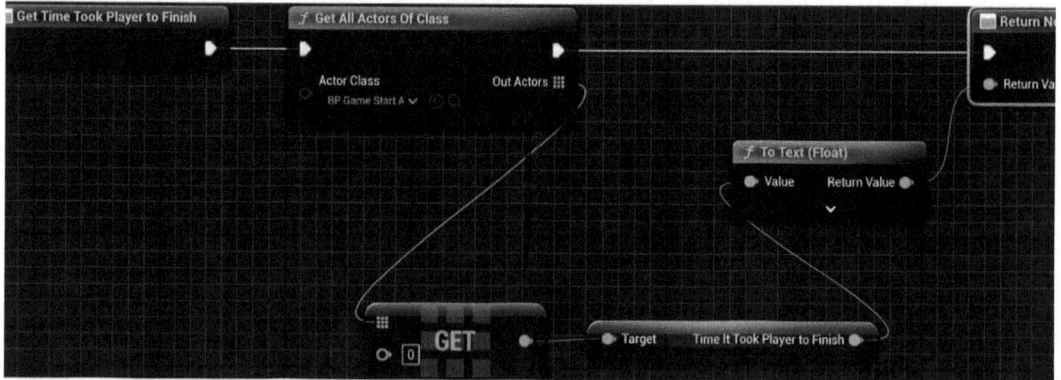

Figure 14.42: *Get Time Took Player to Finish function*

GetTotalScore function displayed in *Figure 14.43*:

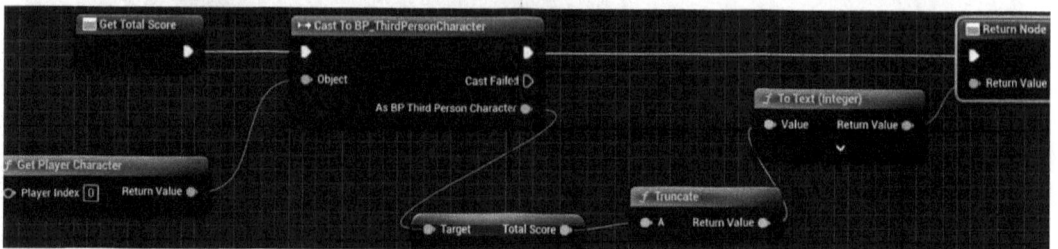

Figure 14.43: *Get Total Score function*

Compile and save.

Returning to the BP_GameStartActor's even graph.

BP_GameStartActor

To make the reader's life a little bit easier, *Figure 14.44* is the same as *Figure 14.14,* allowing us to return where we left off while creating this actor:

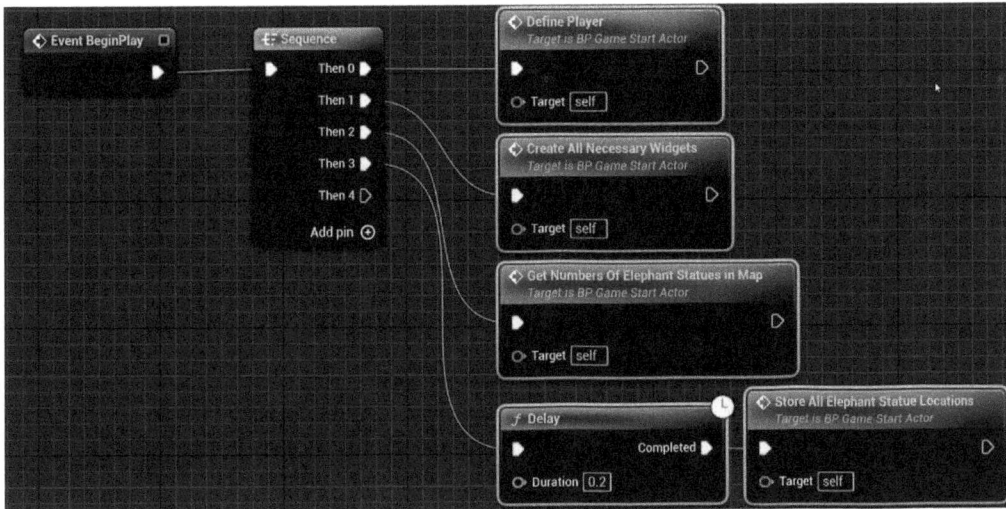

Figure 14.44: *Let us build the rest of these functions!*

In *Figure 14.45*, we complete the **Create All Necessary Widgets** function by utilizing the Create widget node and then promoting to a variable, as done several times before in this chapter. The widgets to use are the ones we just created.

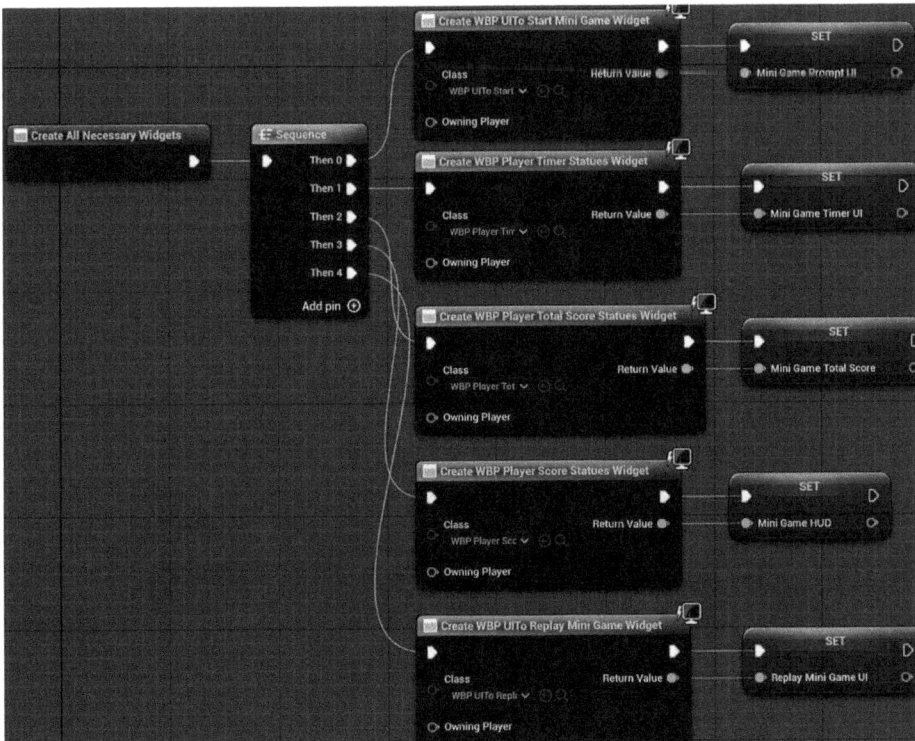

Figure 14.45: *Let us build the rest of these functions!*

Proceeding with writing the **Get Numbers of Elephant Statues in Map**, which is shown in *Figure 14.46*:

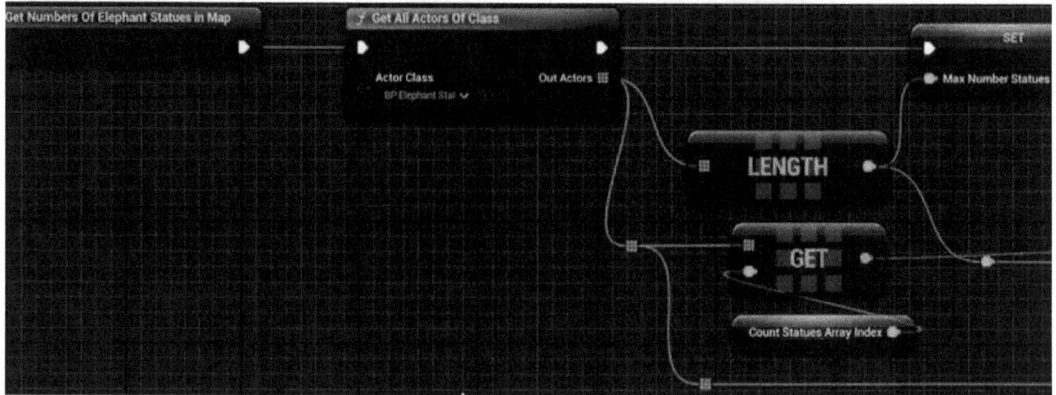

Figure 14.46: *Get Numbers of Elephant Statues in Map function – Part 1*

By now, the reader should be quite familiar with the nodes, as well as with the way in they can be obtained (right click, typing in the name of the node you see in the figures, creating the node etc.), so will be focusing mainly on explaining the logic of the node sequences from here on.

With this function, we get all the elephant statue actors that are placed in a level, and we do so in the form of an array. Then, we use this array to extract its length, in other words, the number of actors it found and gathered (e.g. if we place 5 elephant statues on a map, then the array's length will be 5).

Therefore, we are using the array's length to define the max number of statues. At the same time we use the **Count Statues Array Index**, which is a local variable of integer type (see *Figure 14.47* to learn how to create local variables, as well as which variables you need to create for this function) which we use to update the array's index. If, for example, the array has 5 items, index 0 refers to the first item, index 4 to the fifth.

So, with the help of **Count Statues Array Index** we control which index of the array we will be accessing and extracting.

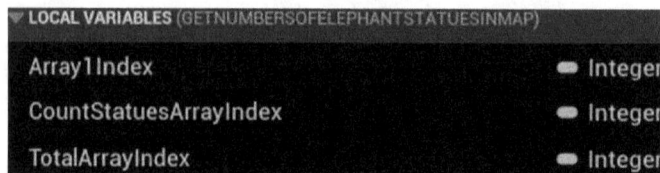

Figure 14.47: *Get Numbers of Elephant Statues in Map function's local variables*

Moving on to the function's second part, as shown in *Figure 14.48*:

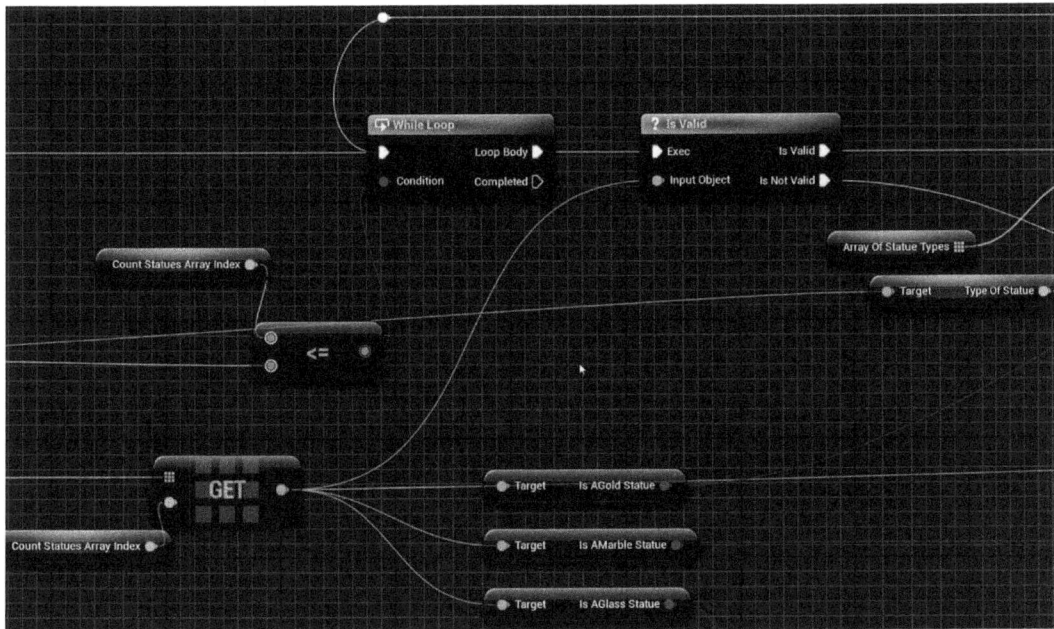

Figure 14.48: *Get Numbers of Elephant Statues in Map function – Part 2*

We check if the array's index is less than or equal to the length of our array. As long as it is less or equal, it means that there are still objects for us to extract from the array. If it becomes equal, it essentially means we have reached the end of the array. Thus, if this condition holds true, then we enter a **While Loop**. In the meantime, every time we extract an object from the array, we call its Boolean variables that define whether it is a gold, marble or glass object (statue).

Moving on to *Part 3* in *Figure 14.49*.

Next, we collect the integer value that indicates the type of statue we have (remember, 0 is gold, 1 is marble, 2 is glass) and place it in an array of integers, named **Array of Statue Types**. From there we move on to a **Branch** node, where we check if the statue object, we extracted from the first array is a gold statue.

If it is, we proceed in incrementing the number of gold statues by one and updated the **Max Number Gold Statues** value.

If it is not, then we proceed in the next branch, which repeats the process, but this time checking whether the statue is a marble one or not. If it is, we increment the number of marble statues by one and update the **Max Number Marble Statues**.

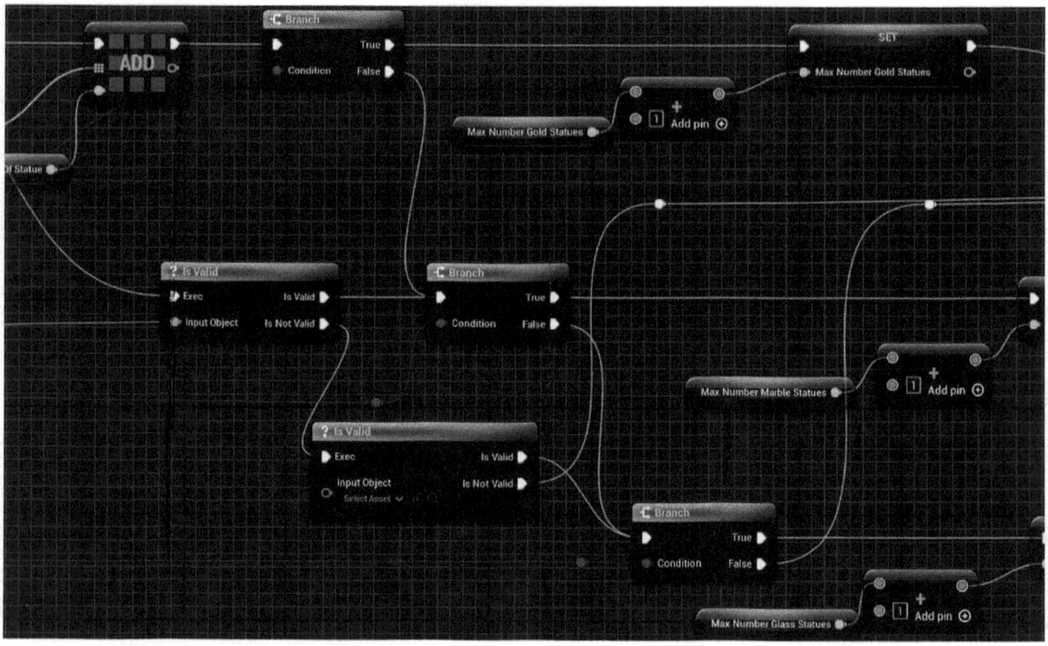

Figure 14.49: *Get Numbers of Elephant Statues in Map function – Part 3*

If it is not marble, then we move on to the next and last branch, which, in a similar fashion, checks if the statue is a glass one, in which case we increment their number by one and update their max number value.

Then, all nodes eventually lead to what is shown in *Figure 14.50*, which is the fourth and final part of this function:

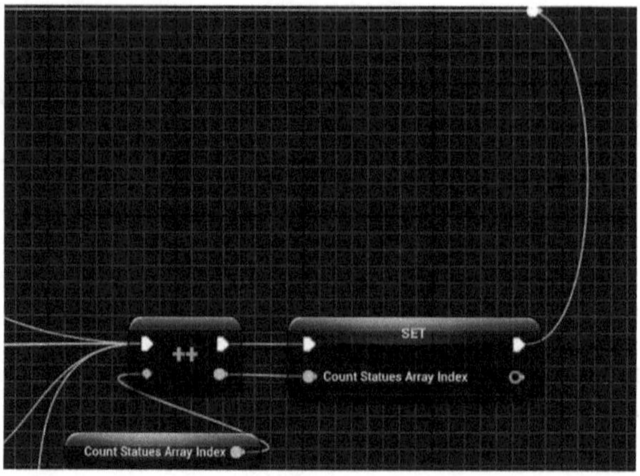

Figure 14.50: *Get Numbers of Elephant Statues in Map function – Part 4*

In this last part of the function, we increment the **Count Statues Array Index** by one, while updating it, and then we go back at the beginning of the loop seen in *Figure 14.48*, where we check if we reached the end of the array or not. If we did, that is where the function stops. If the end of the array has not yet been reached, then it repeats all of the above processes until it reaches the end.

Next, we need to look at how the Store All Elephant Statue Locations function is built.

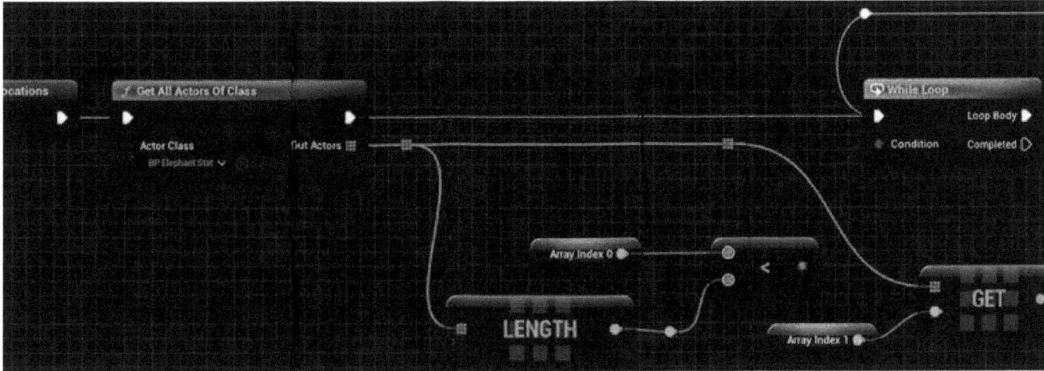

Figure 14.51: *Store All Elephant Statue Locations function – Part 1*

As seen in *Figure 14.51*, once more, we take advantage of the power of arrays. The logic is almost identical to the previous function's; therefore, it should be easier to follow at this point. Moving on to part two of this function, which is displayed in *Figure 14.52*:

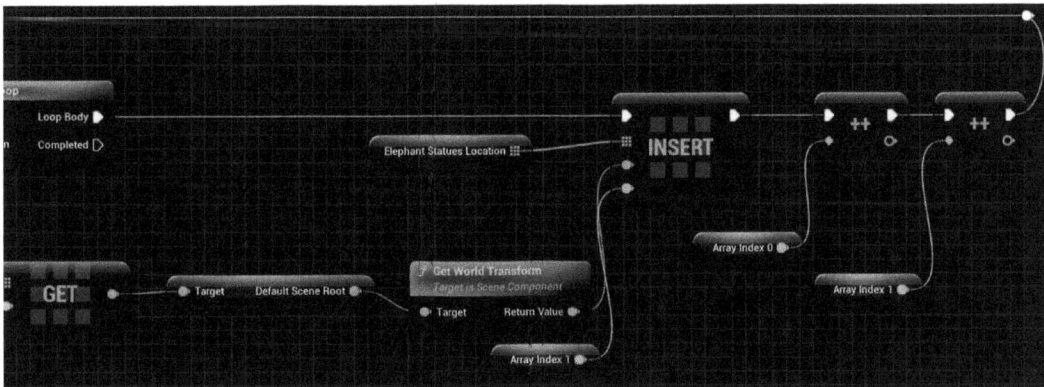

Figure 14.52: *Store All Elephant Statue Locations function – Part 2*

Same as before, but this time, we collect the transform values (location coordinates, rotation and scale values) for each of the elephant statues and store them in **Elephant Statues Location** variable, of a transform type, and specifically an array.

Before proceeding further with the actor's event graph, let us take a look at the finalized variable list and the types used, as shown in *Figure 14.53*:

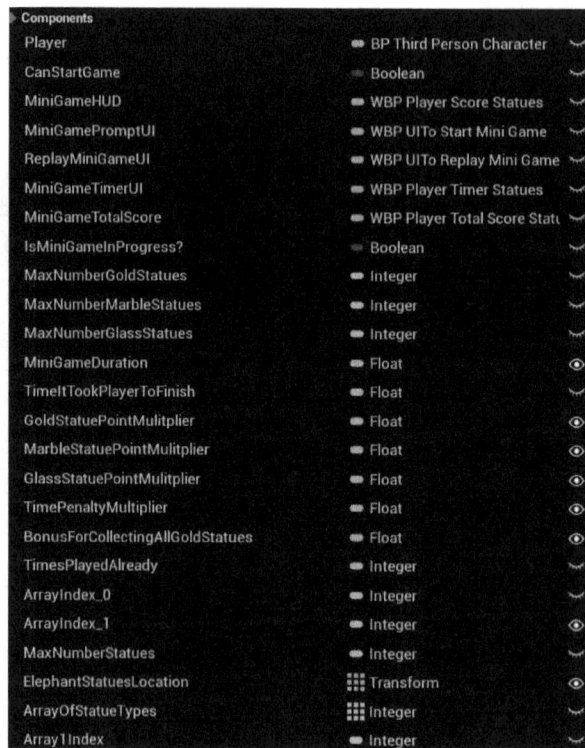

Figure 14.53: *BP_GameStartActor's finalized variable list*

Now, let us look at the final list of functions, as seen in *Figure 14.54*:

Figure 14.54: *BP_GameStartActor's finalized function list*

By now it should be relatively easy to follow any sequence nodes used in this project, so in the next couple of figures, we will be looking into the structure of the functions not yet covered. If there is any node or any other element not discussed before, we will take a closer look at it; otherwise, the figures themselves should be self-explanatory at this point.

Figures 14.55 to *14.64* display the node structures of functions:

Figure 14.55: Start Mini Game function

The following figure shows Check Game Progress function:

Figure 14.56: Check Game Progress function – Part 1

Figure 14.57: Check Game Progress function – Part 2

The following figure shows Stop Mini Game function:

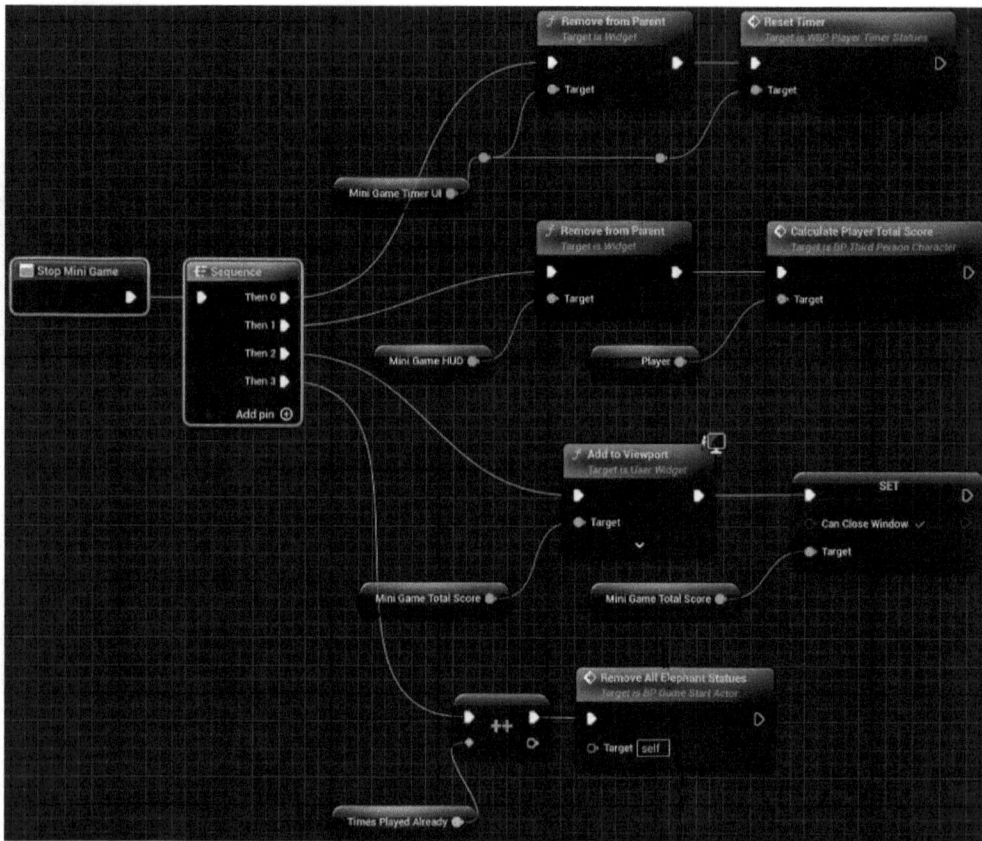

Figure 14.58: Stop Mini Game function

The following figures show the **Reset All Elephant Statue Locations** function:

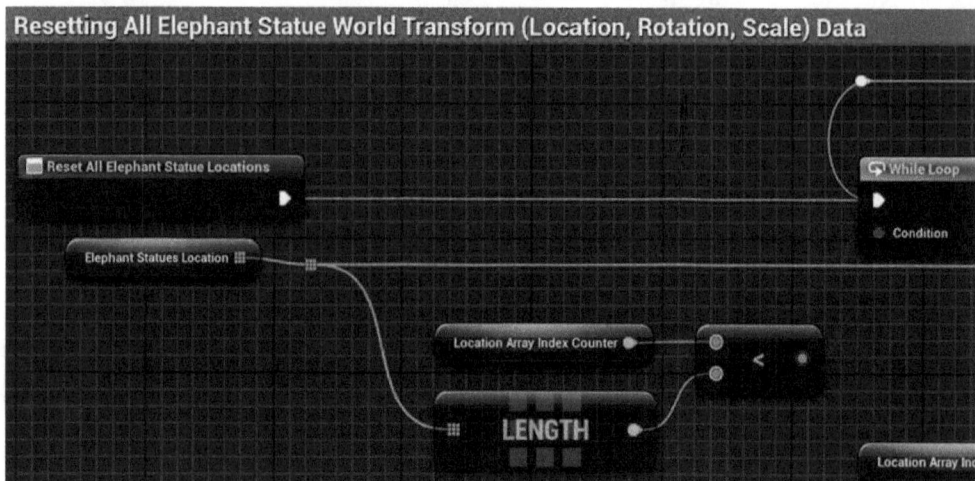

Figure 14.59: Reset All Elephant Statue Locations function – Part 1

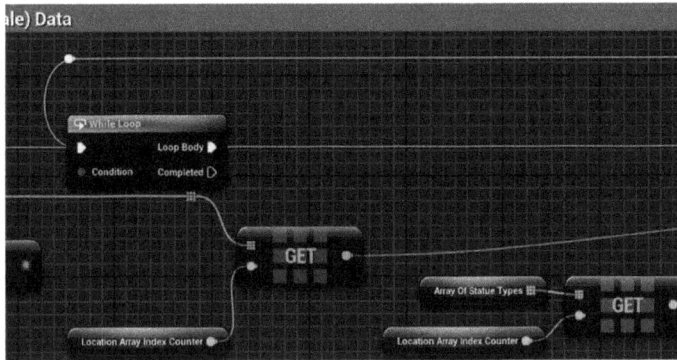

Figure 14.60: *Reset All Elephant Statue Locations function – Part 2*

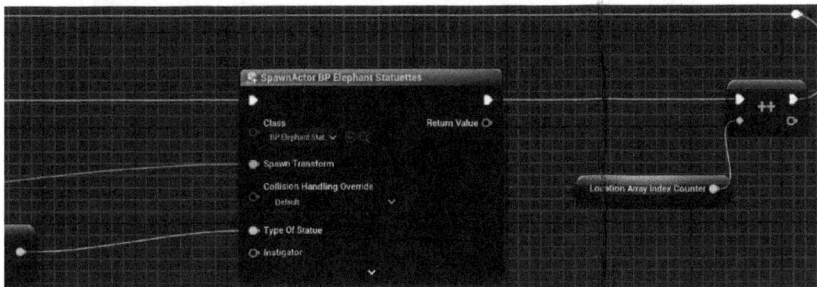

Figure 14.61: *Reset All Elephant Statue Locations function – Part 3*

The following figures show the **Reset Player Scores** function:

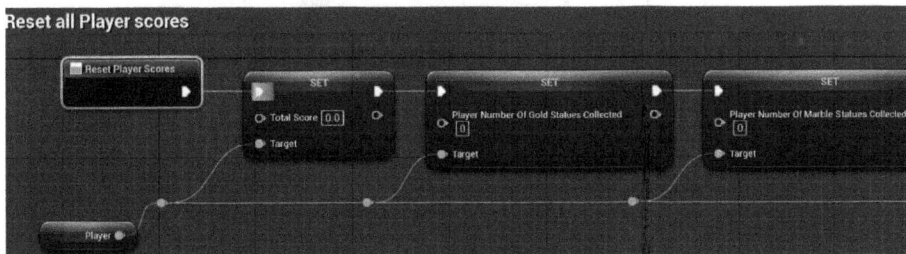

Figure 14.62: *Reset Player Scores function – Part 1*

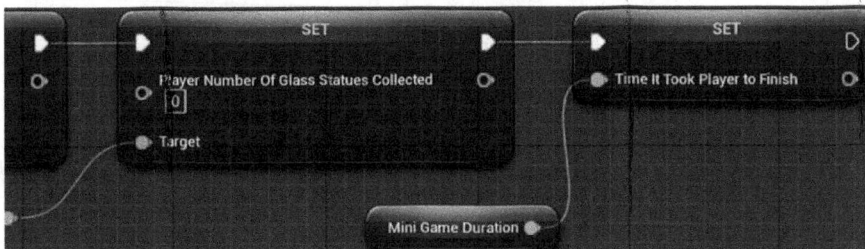

Figure 14.63: *Reset Player Scores function – Part 2*

The following figure shows Remove All Elephant Statues function:

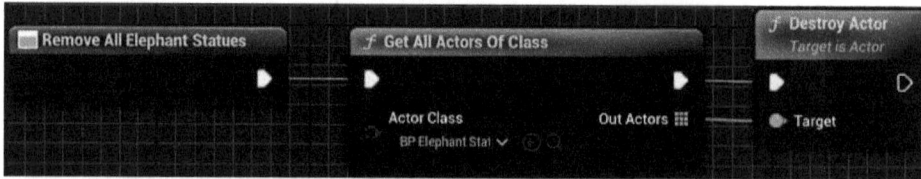

Figure 14.64: *Remove All Elephant Statues function*

Now, let us examine how these functions and variables are used in the event graph. *Figures 14.65 to 14.72 cover that:*

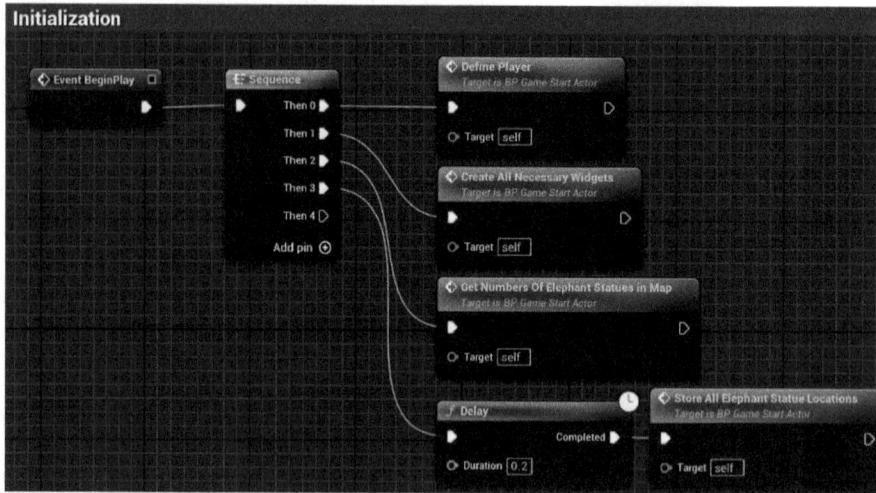

Figure 14.65: *The Event Begin Play sequence once more*

The following figure shows actor's begin overlap sequences:

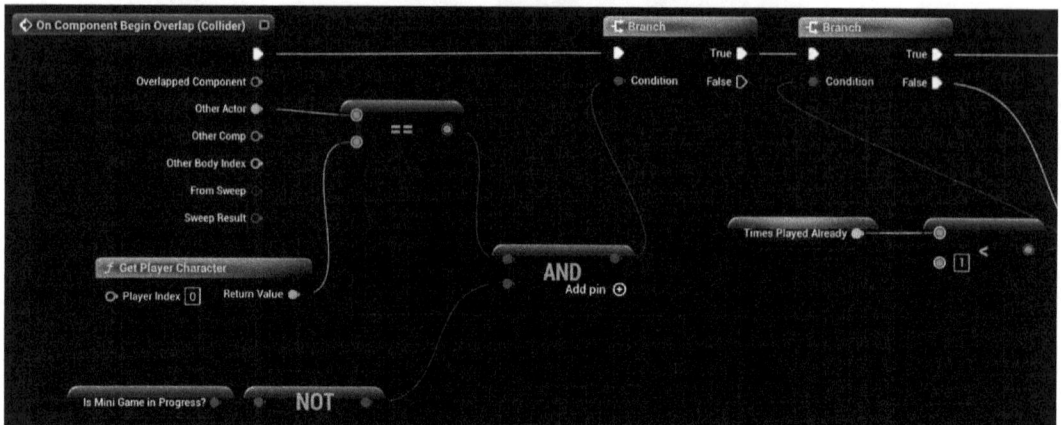

Figure 14.66: *This actor's begin overlap sequences – Part 1*

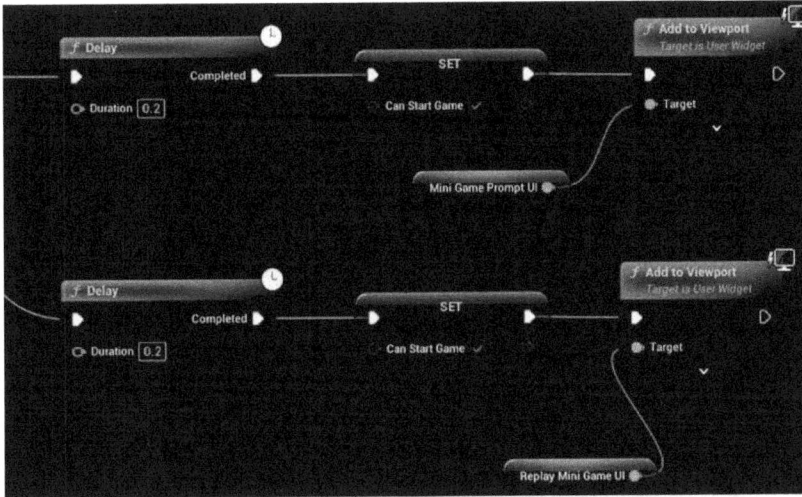

Figure 14.67: This actor's begin overlap sequences – Part 2

The following figure shows the actor's end overlap sequences:

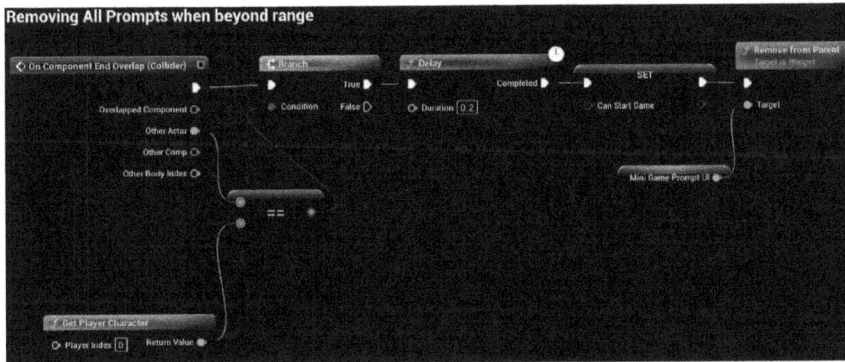

Figure 14.68: This actor's end overlap sequences

The following figures show the Player activating the Blueprint actor:

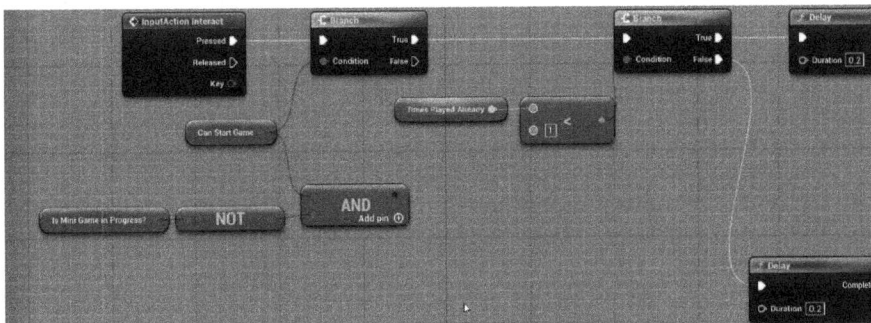

Figure 14.69: Player activating the Blueprint actor – Part 1

Part 2 of Player activating the Blueprint actor:

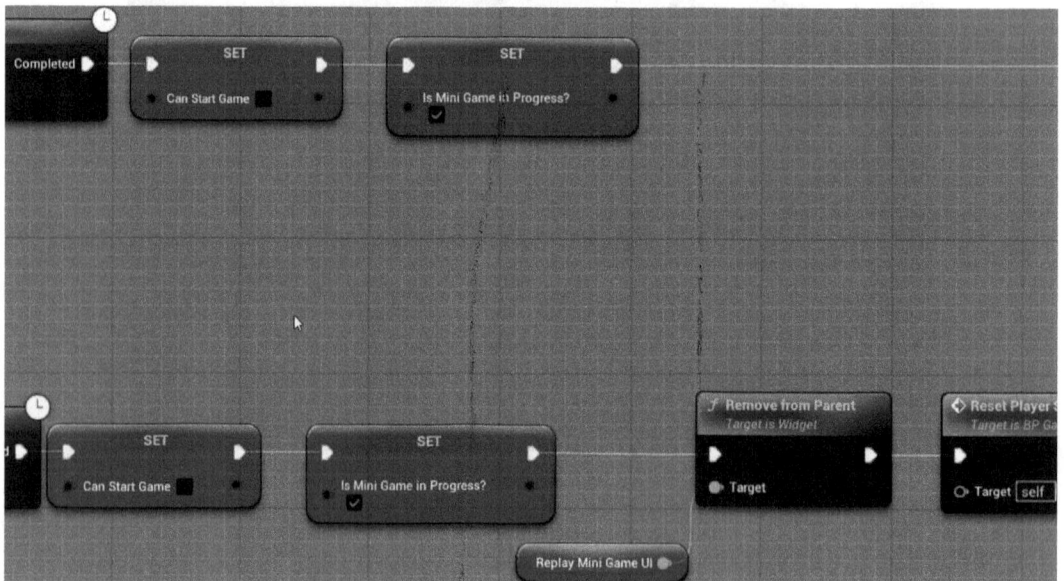

Figure 14.70: *Player activating the Blueprint actor – Part 2*

Part 3 of Player activating the Blueprint actor:

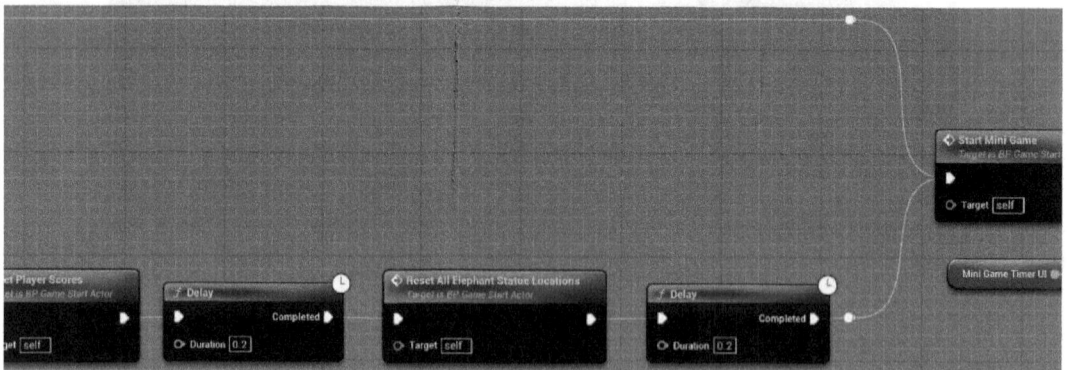

Figure 14.71: *Player activating the Blueprint actor – Part 3*

Part 4 of Player activating the Blueprint actor:

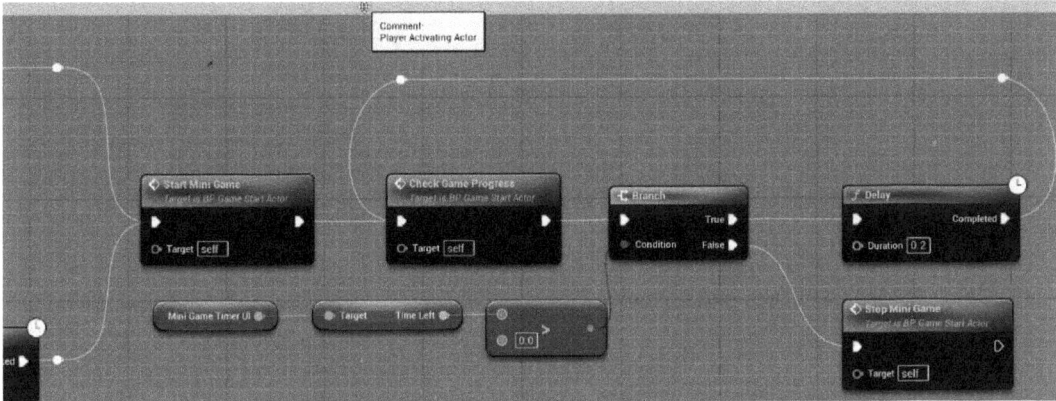

Figure 14.72: *Player activating the Blueprint actor – Part 4*

Finalizing the elephant statue actor

In a similar and expedient fashion, let us look at the final setup of the Elephant Statue Blueprint actor. *Figures 14.73* to *14.79* display the details:

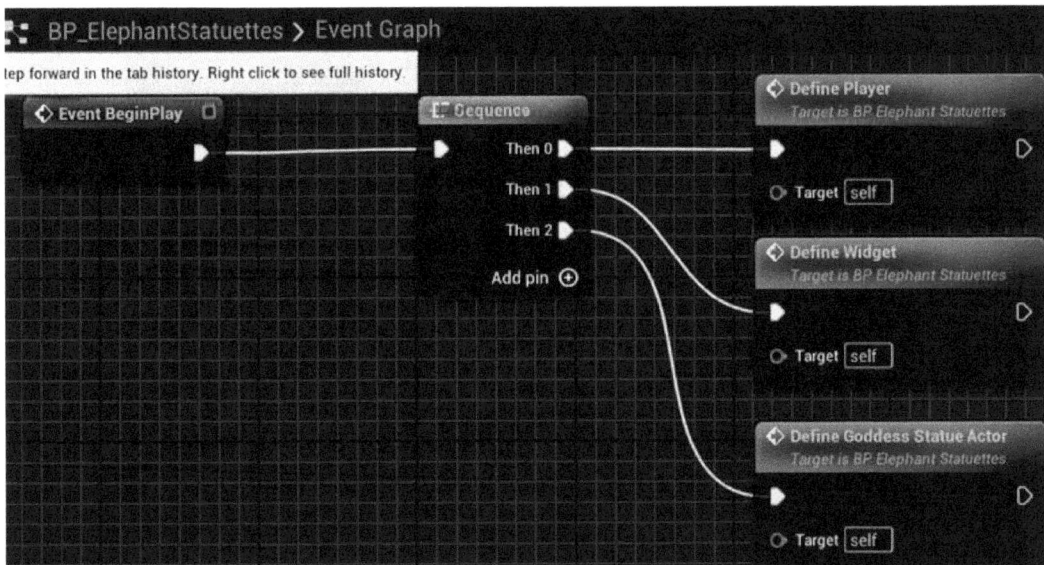

Figure 14.73: *Revisiting the event begin play of the elephant statue Blueprint actor, we already covered the functions shown*

The following figure shows BP_ElephantStatuettes' begin overlap sequences:

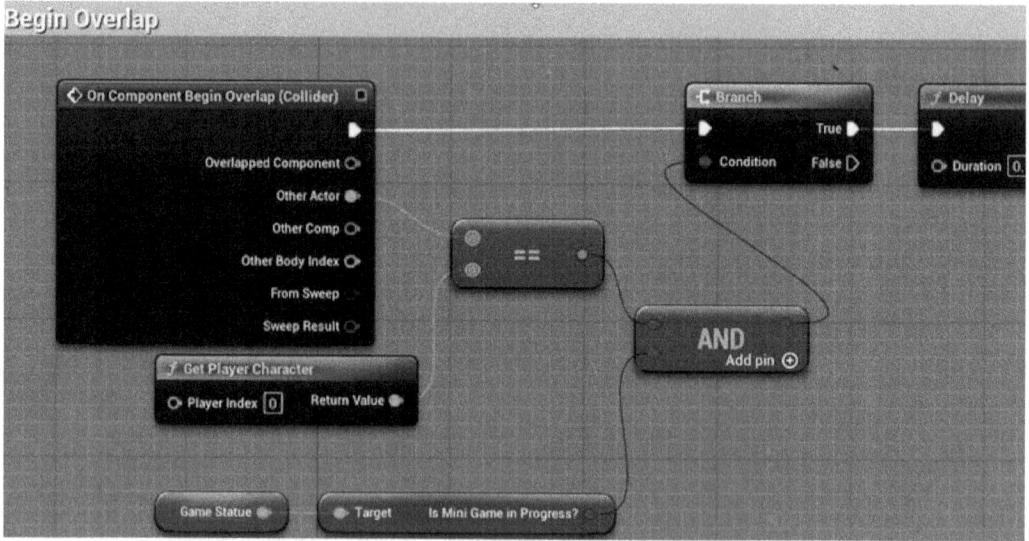

Figure 14.74: *BP_ElephantStatuettes' begin overlap sequences – Part 1*

Part 2 of BP_ElephantStatuettes' begin overlap sequences:

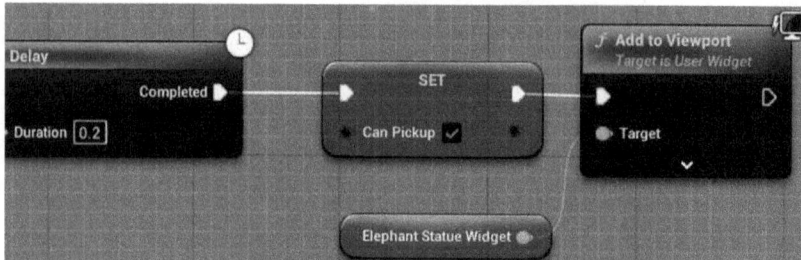

Figure 14.75: *BP_ElephantStatuettes' begin overlap sequences – Part 2*

Part 1 of BP_ElephantStatuettes' end overlap sequences:

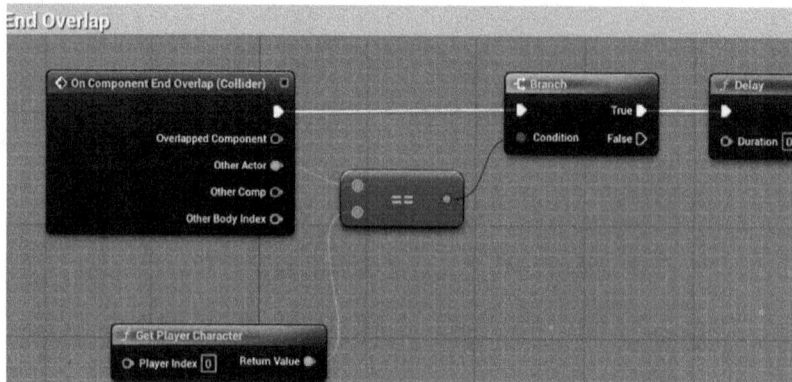

Figure 14.76: *BP_ElephantStatuettes' end overlap sequences – Part 1*

Part 2 of BP_ElephantStatuettes' end overlap sequences:

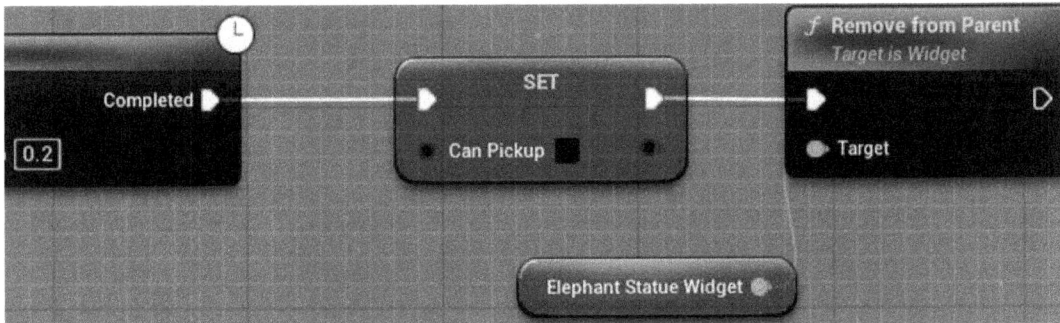

Figure 14.77: *BP_ElephantStatuettes' end overlap sequences – Part 2*

Part 1 of BP_ElephantStatuettes' player interaction sequences:

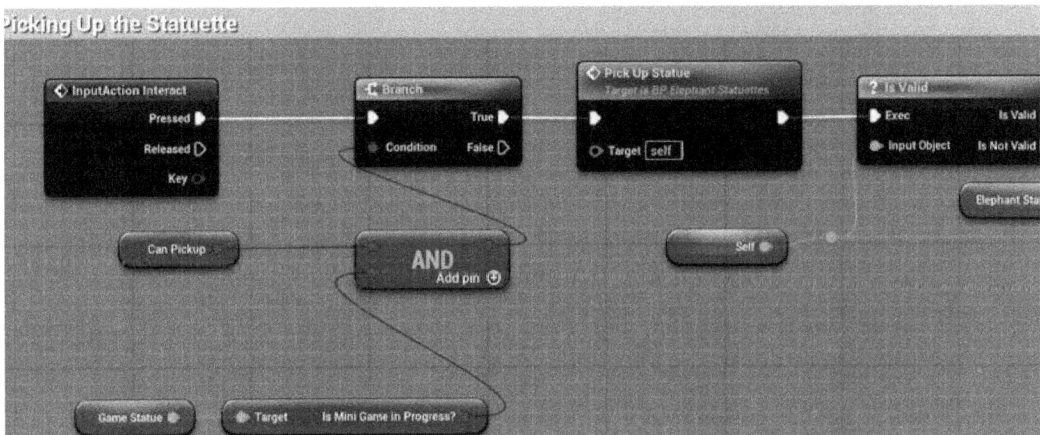

Figure 14.78: *BP_ElephantStatuettes' player interaction sequences – Part 1*

Part 2 of BP_ElephantStatuettes' player interaction sequences:

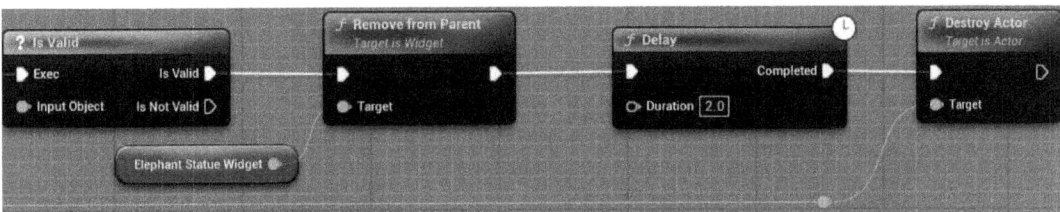

Figure 14.79: *BP_ElephantStatuettes' player interaction sequences – Part 2*

Figures 14.80 and 14.81 display the finalized list of variables and functions for the BP_ ElephantStatuettes actor:

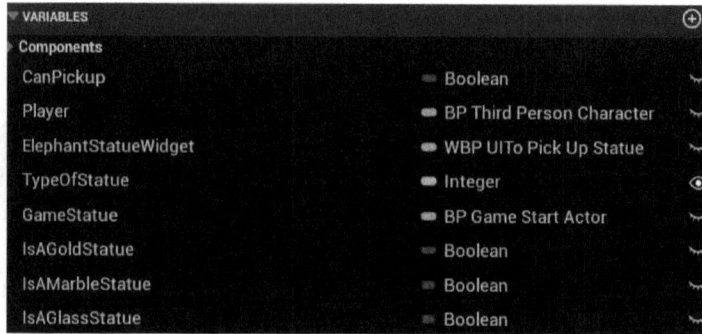

Figure 14.80: *BP_ElephantStatuettes' final list of variables*

The following figure shows BP_ElephantStatuettes' final list of functions:

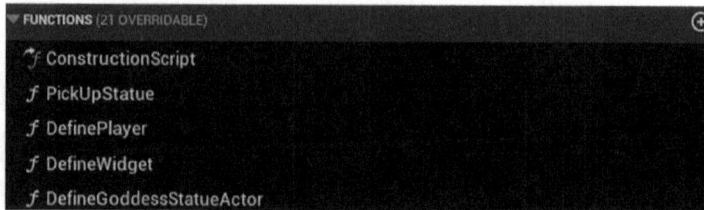

Figure 14.81: *BP_ElephantStatuettes' final list of functions*

One last addition to BPThirdPersonCharacter

We just need to add a function to calculate the player score, and we are pretty much done. *Figures 14.82* to *14.85* show the details:

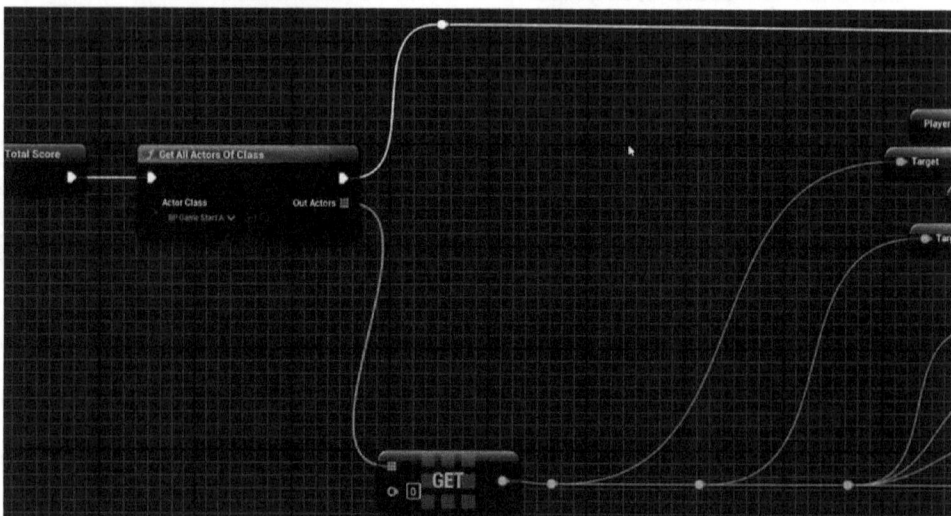

Figure 14.82: *BP_ThirdPersonCharacter's CalculatePlayerTotalScore function – Part 1*

Figure 14.83 shows the second part of the Blueprint:

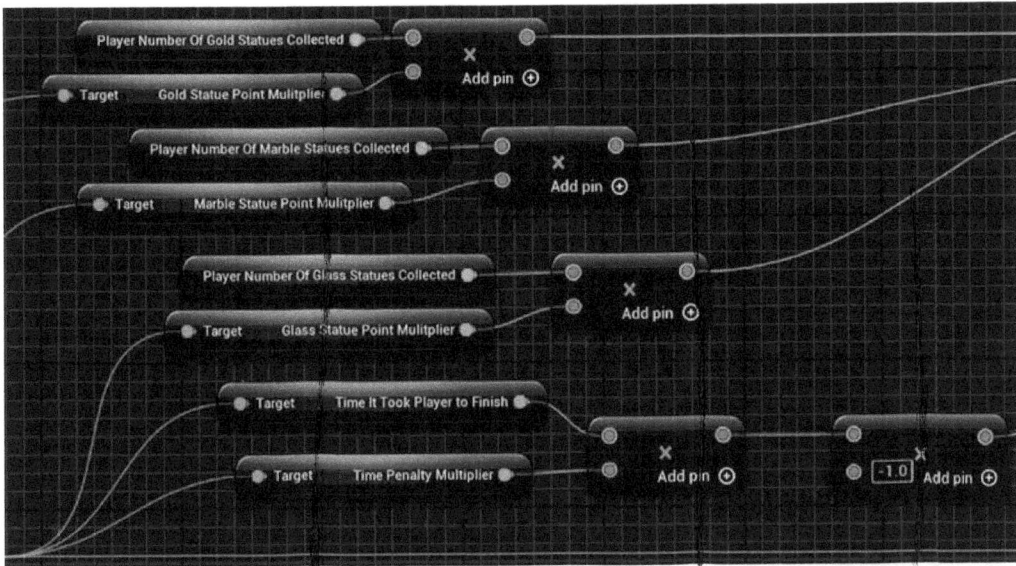

Figure 14.83: *BP_ThirdPersonCharacter's CalculatePlayerTotalScore function – Part 2*

Figure 14.84 shows the third part of the Blueprint:

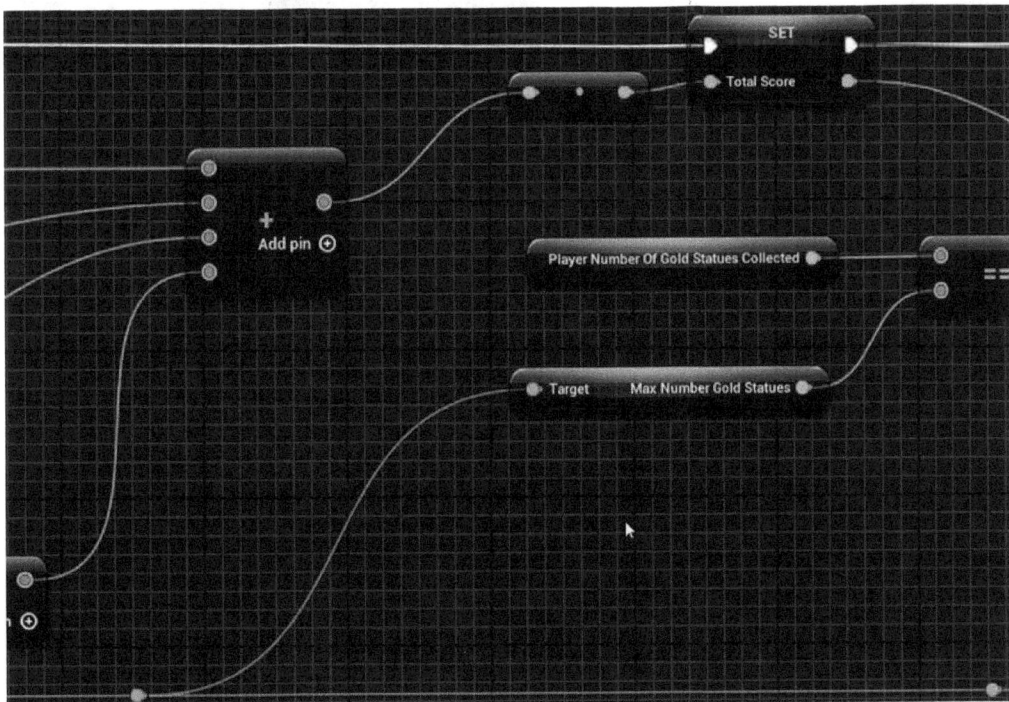

Figure 14.84: *BP_ThirdPersonCharacter's CalculatePlayerTotalScore function – Part 3*

Figure 14.85 shows the fourth part of the Blueprint:

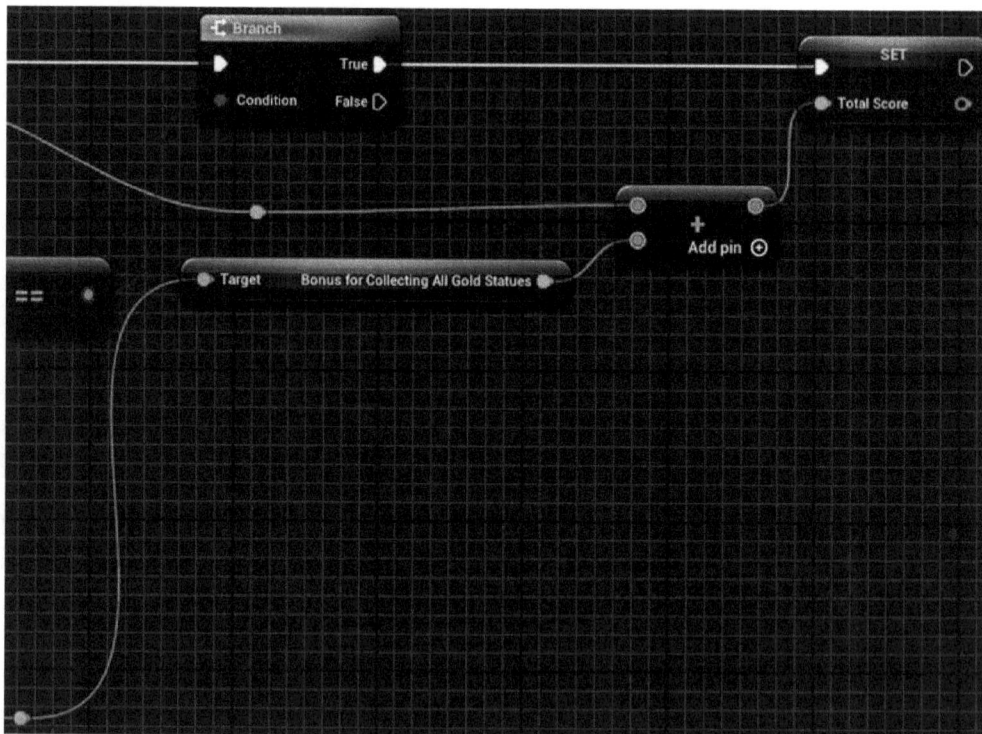

Figure 14.85: *BP_ThirdPersonCharacter's CalculatePlayerTotalScore function – Part 4*

Conclusion

This chapter covered all of the project's Blueprints. There is a lot to remember, including arrays, widgets, functions, and variables, but ultimately it all contributes to creating a mini game.

In the next chapter, we will show how we place all these actors in the Fantasy Castle level, and then we will proceed with optimizing and finalizing the level, and finally packaging an executable version of the project.

Once again, a friendly reminder to use this book's resources such as the project files, as this will help reading through the more difficult chapters such as this one.

Points to remember

- Arrays for storing and extracting object and object data.

- Key points from *Chapter 13, Fantasy Castle Interactive Blueprint Actors*, since it was reused often in this chapter, such as:

o   Parallel development of Blueprint actors.

o   Different node types, their functions, properties, and applications.

o   Blueprint variables.

Exercise

1. Take existing actors and duplicate them, then modify them, such as light being lit when interacting with the Greek God Statue, or creating an additional type of elephant statue and assigning it your own Materials, scoring attributes, and, of course, updating all of the Blueprints to keep track of it.

Join our book's Discord space

Join the book's Discord Workspace for Latest updates, Offers, Tech happenings around the world, New Release and Sessions with the Authors:

https://discord.bpbonline.com

CHAPTER 15

Fantasy Castle Level Finalization and Packaging

Introduction

In this chapter, we will first optimize the level, by eliminating the number of actors in the scene, optimizing the lighting, and any collisions that need improvement. Then we will finalize the Foliage and any landscaping necessary, and finally, we will place the actors we created in *Chapter 14, Fantasy Castle Mini Game Blueprints*, playtest them, and make sure everything works well and that there is a good flow.

Finally, we will finish the chapter and the project by packaging an executable.

Structure

The structure observed in this chapter:

- Reducing the number of actors in the scene
- Batching scene actors
- Landscape and Foliage updates
- Lighting optimization
- Collisions and blocking volumes
- Placement of playable/interactable actors
- Packaging settings

Objectives

By the end of this chapter, the readers will learn how to optimize the level through different techniques, such as batching together multiple objects, optimizing lights and light related actors, placement and testing of actors. Ultimately, this is where we finalize the entire Fantasy Castle Project. Finally, set up and package our Fantasy Castle level in an executable format.

Reducing the number of actors in the scene

Load up the level Fantasy Castle. Depending on whether you use the project files provided in this book or if you decide to build the level from scratch, you will have several actors placed in your scene. The more detailed you like to be, the more actors you will find.

In the author's case, *Figure 15.1* shows the number of actors listed under the outliner, which is a total of 1,549 actors:

Figure 15.1: The number of actors in the Fantasy Castle level

While performance is not bad at all (on the author's PC, at least), we should still optimize as much as we can. Simply put, the more objects there are in a scene, the greater the performance toll there will be to render these objects. Therefore, reducing the number of objects can help significantly with improving performance and framerates.

The most obvious way to reduce the number of objects would be to delete any that might be unnecessary. But we will assume that all of them are necessary; otherwise, we would not have placed them in the level (Although you would be surprised how often a level designer will go over their work and remove quite a large number of objects they first thought necessary, especially when under the pressure of bad framerates).

Another way to deal with rendering fewer objects would be to call them when X amount of distance is between the player and the object. You will notice this technique is being used quite often in large open-world games when you look far away at a specific point, and as you approach that point, objects that were not there start appearing. That can be achieved with draw distance culling, as well as with Unreal's World Partition, which allows you to visualize the world in a virtual grid and, from there, adjust each grid cell's size and settings as far as loading and rendering objects within the cell are concerned.

Another technique often used, which also used to be very time-consuming in the past, is **levels of detail (LOD)**. Essentially, LODs are utilizing lower resolution, but better performing versions of a 3D mesh. Going back to the open-world gaming reference, you often notice that objects that are already visible from a distance seem to be changing shapes as you get closer to them. The Unreal Engine can automatically assign LODs quite easily, relatively fast, and extremely effectively. However, since we are using Nanite for this project, we do not need to worry about LODs, not for the Static Meshes at least (we could use LODs if we had Skeletal Mesh NPCs, though — which we do not).

Let us concentrate our efforts on minimizing the number of actors in our scene while retaining the same visual fidelity.

Batching scene actors

You might recall the ability to merge meshes, we mentioned it in *Chapter 11, Fantasy Castle Bringing it All in Unreal*, specifically in *Figures 11.27* and *11.28*. Let us bring up the **Merge Actors** tab once more (on the top of the window — Tools | Merge Actors). This time, from the **Merge Method** drop down menu, select **Batch**, as displayed in *Figure 15.2*:

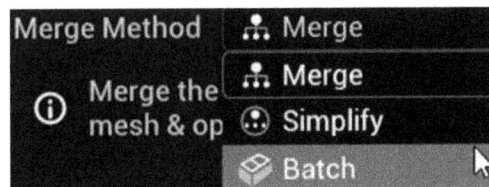

Figure 15.2: Select Batch as the merging method

Next, go to the **Outliner** tab, and sort by **Type**, as shown in *Figure 15.3*:

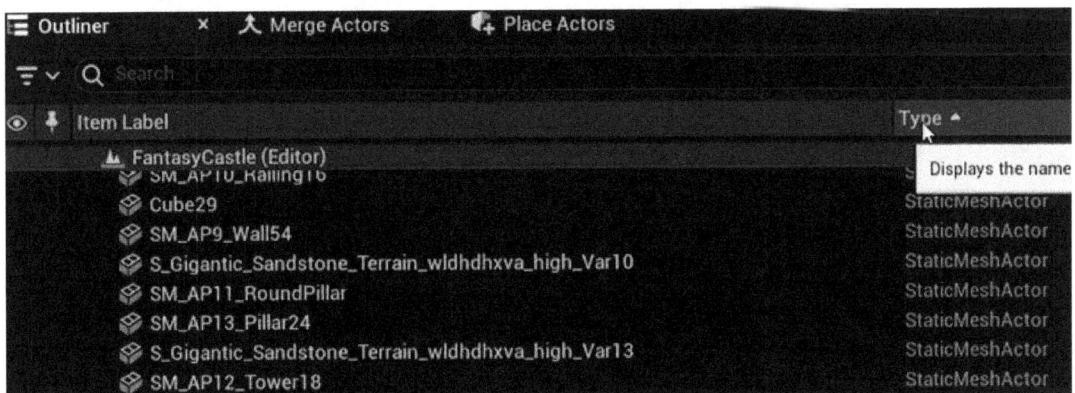

Figure 15.3: Select Batch as the merging method

Next, select all of the Static Mesh actors. Doing so results in having 1,190 actors selected.

Now, back to the **Merge Actors** tab, at the bottom, check the box next to **Replace Source Actors** as shown in *Figure 15.4*. Then click **Merge Actors**.

Figure 15.4: Check the box next to Replace Source Actors

Now, going back to the outliner, we see that the amount of total actors in the scene is 230, as seen in *Figure 15.5*:

Figure 15.5: Compare that number to the one in Figure 15.1

But how does the level compare visually, now that we batched these meshes and reduced the amount of actors? *Figure 15.6* shows the level before batching the actors. *Figure 15.7* shows it right after:

Figure 15.6: The Fantasy Castle level before batching the actors

Figure 15.7 demonstrates the number of total actors in the scene after having batched the actors:

Figure 15.7: The Fantasy Castle level right after batching the actors

Landscape and Foliage updates

Now, it is a good opportunity to revisit the landscape and the Foliage of the level. In this example, since the level is not truly open, instead we restrict the player within the castle grounds, we do not really need a landscape, with the exception of it serving as either a backdrop in the distance or as a surface that blends well with the Foliage placed within the castle's courtyard.

As far as the backdrop is concerned, we achieved some very nice results with the mountain mesh we obtained from Quixel Bridge. Therefore we only need to keep the landscape that is utilized within the castle grounds, as shown in *Figure 15.8*, and maybe a bit of the surrounding, where we can blend it nicely with the other ground-themed Quixel Bridge meshes.

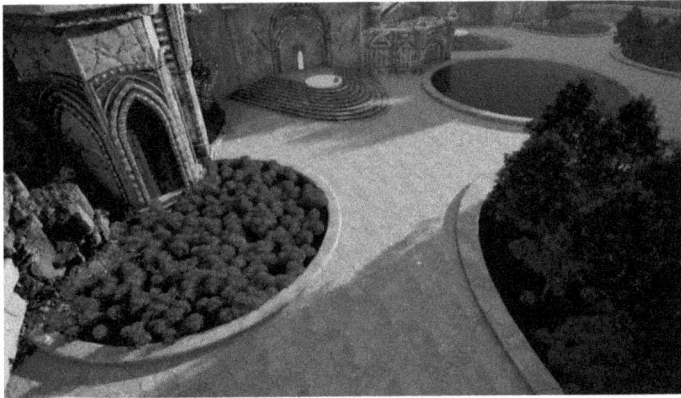

Figure 15.8*: Landscape parts that should be kept*

Press *Shift+2* to enter Landscape Mode, and while in the **Landscape** tab, select **Manage** and then **Delete**. Set the **Brush Size** to 1. Refer to *Figure 15.9*:

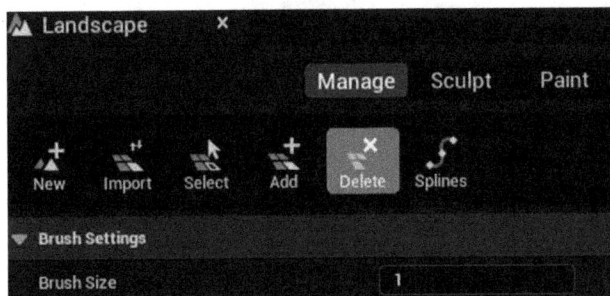

Figure 15.9*: Deleting some landscape segments*

Next, hover over the landscape, and you will notice a bright yellow square highlighting the landscape. If you click on the highlighted area, that is the amount of the landscape that gets deleted. Refer to *Figure 15.10*:

Figure 15.10: If you click on the highlighted area, it will be deleted

Delete all landscape around the broader range of the castle grounds, much like in *Figure 15.11:*

Figure 15.11: What is left of the landscape

Now press *Shift+3* or enter Foliage mode. Using the same processes discussed in *Chapter 11, Fantasy Castle Bringing it all in Unreal,* specifically between *Figures 11.46* to *Figure 11.55,* add or remove Foliage until you are happy with the visual result. However, you do need to finetune the cull distances, be selective about the placement, and be as economical as possible. In *Figures 15.12* to *Figure 15.16,* you will see the author's settings for the Foliage used in the provided project:

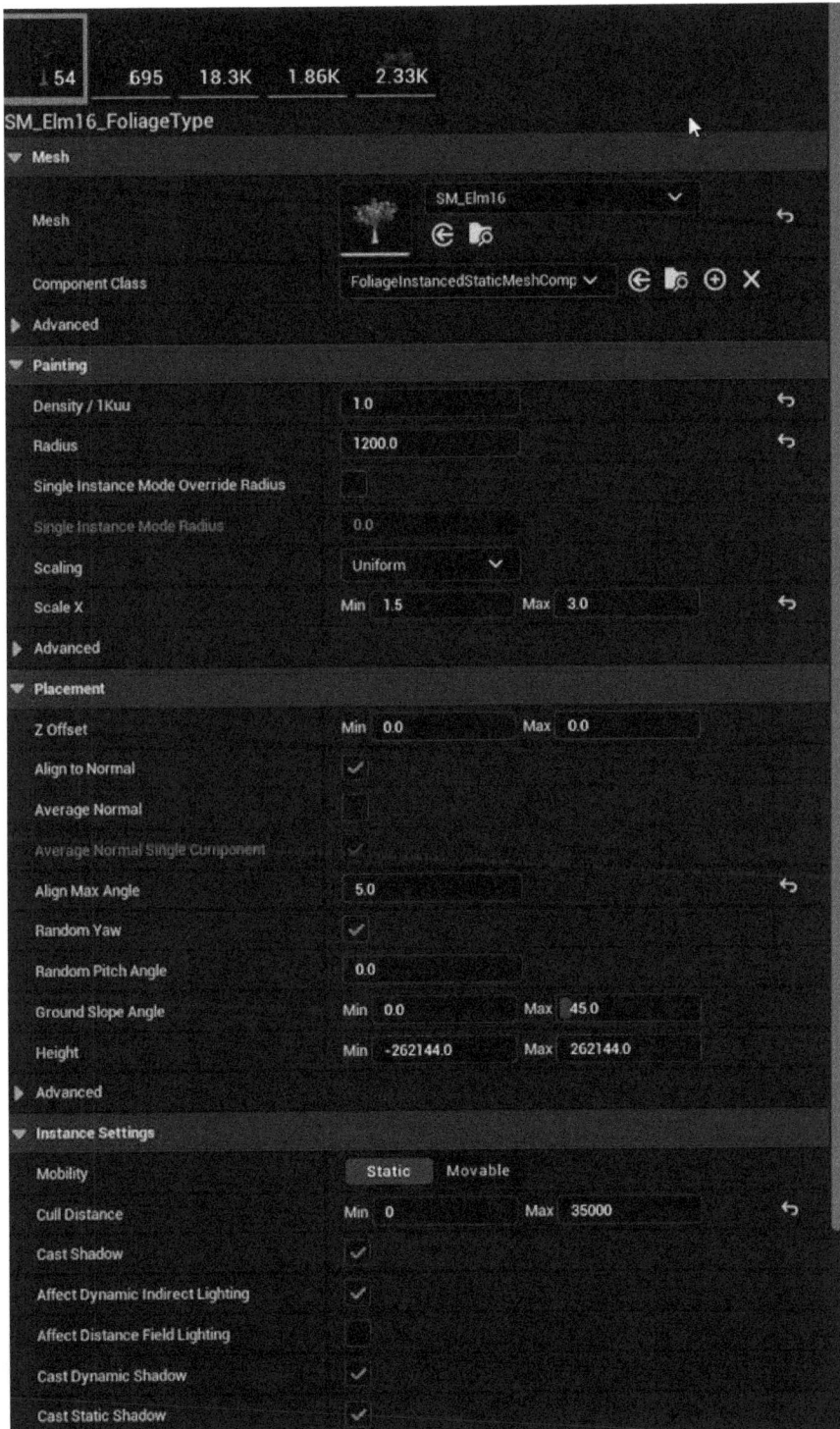

Figure 15.12: Tress to be rendered closer

Figure 15.13 shows more of the Foliage settings:

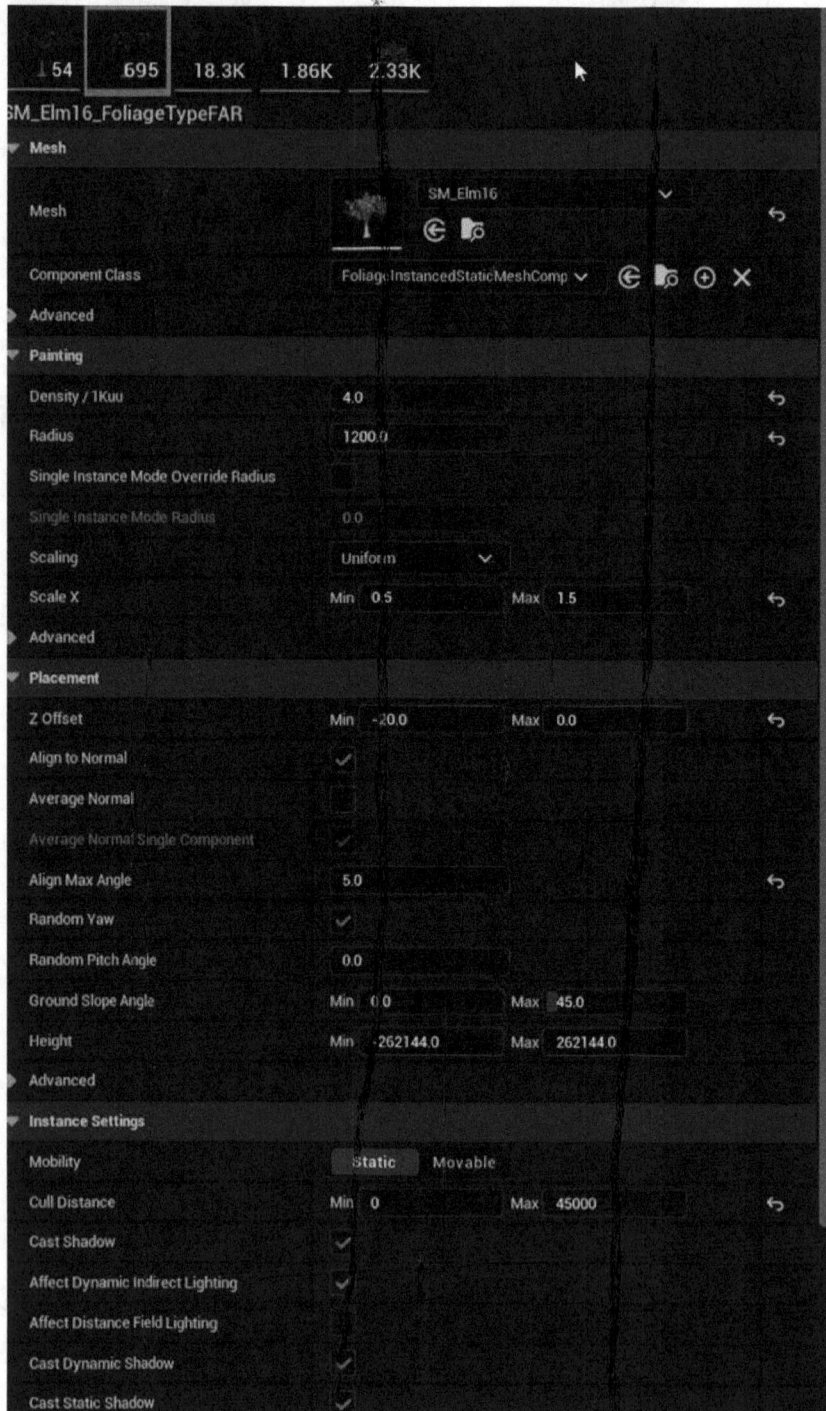

Figure 15.13: *Trees to be rendered in the far distance*

Figure 15.14 shows more of the Foliage settings:

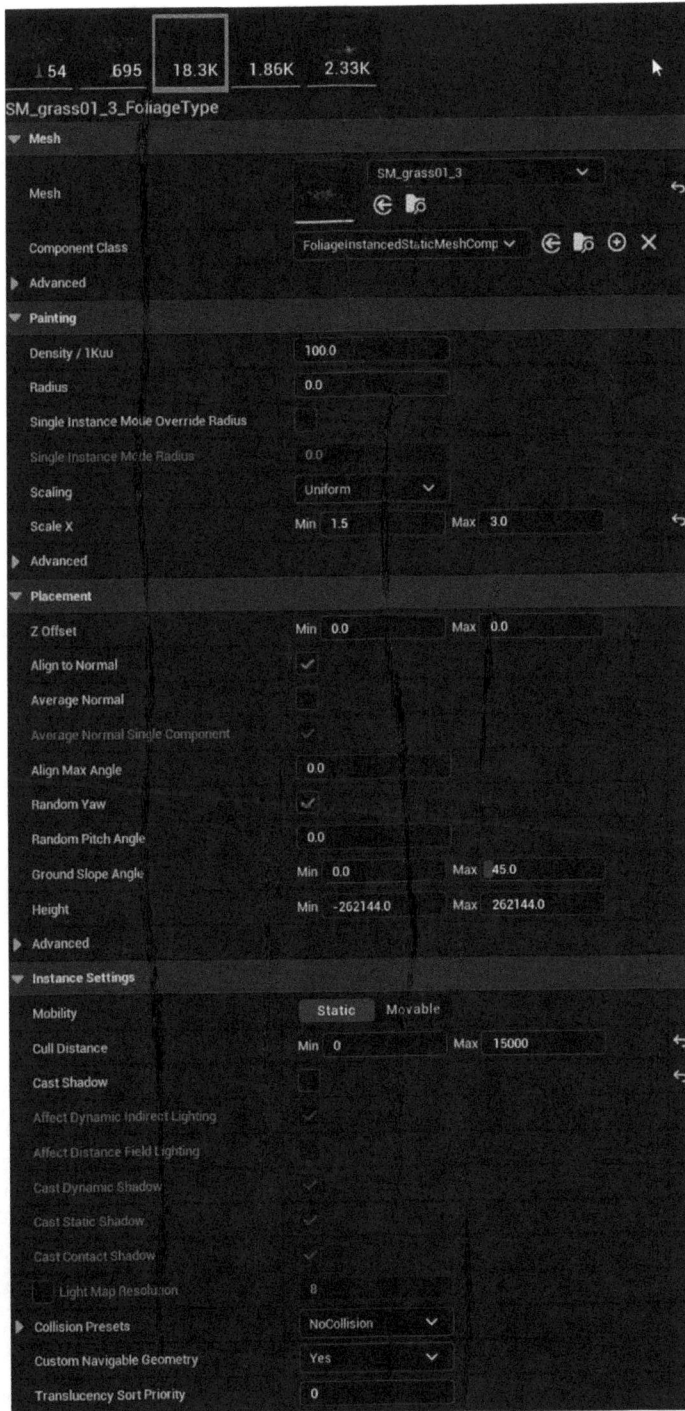

Figure 15.14: Grass Foliage

Figure 15.15 shows yet more of the Foliage settings:

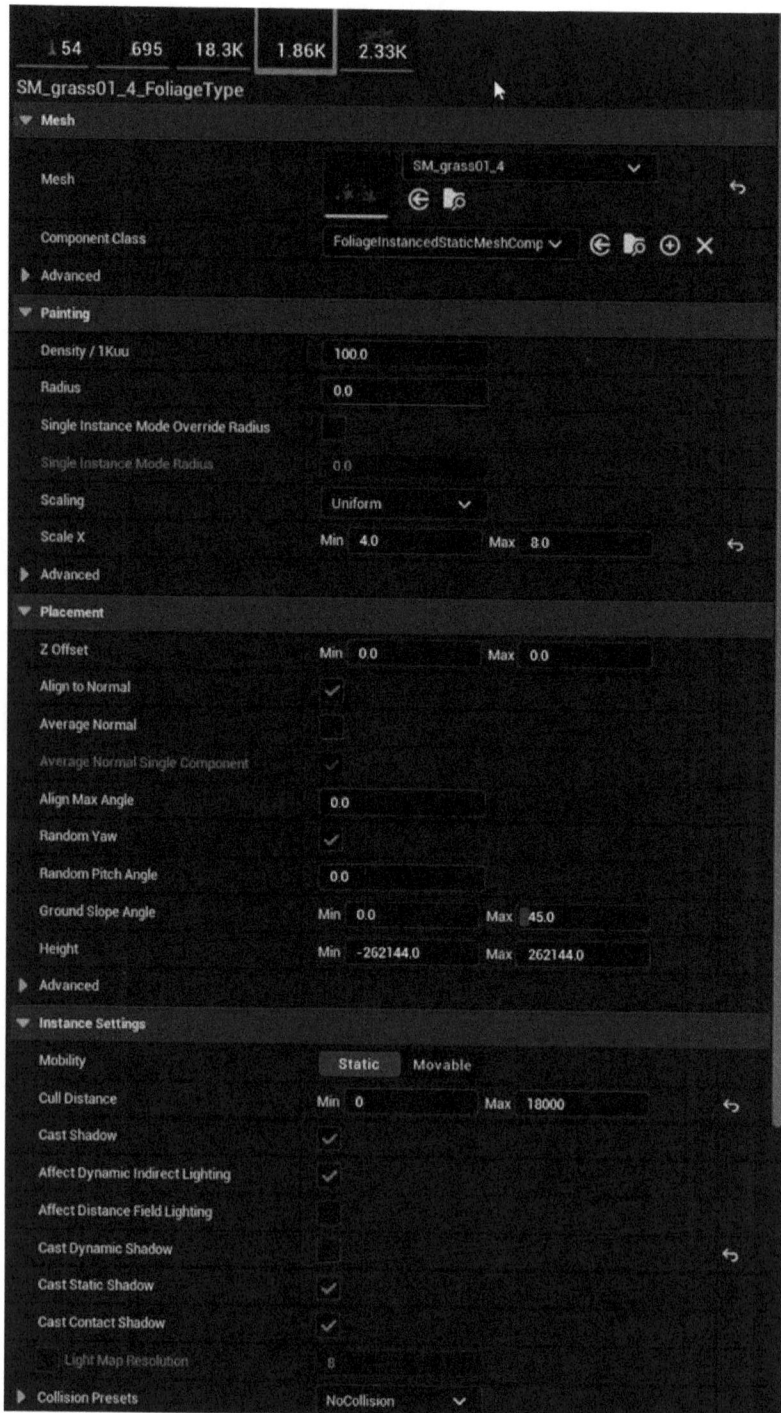

Figure 15.15: *Second type of grass Foliage for variation*

Figure 15.16 further expands on the Foliage settings:

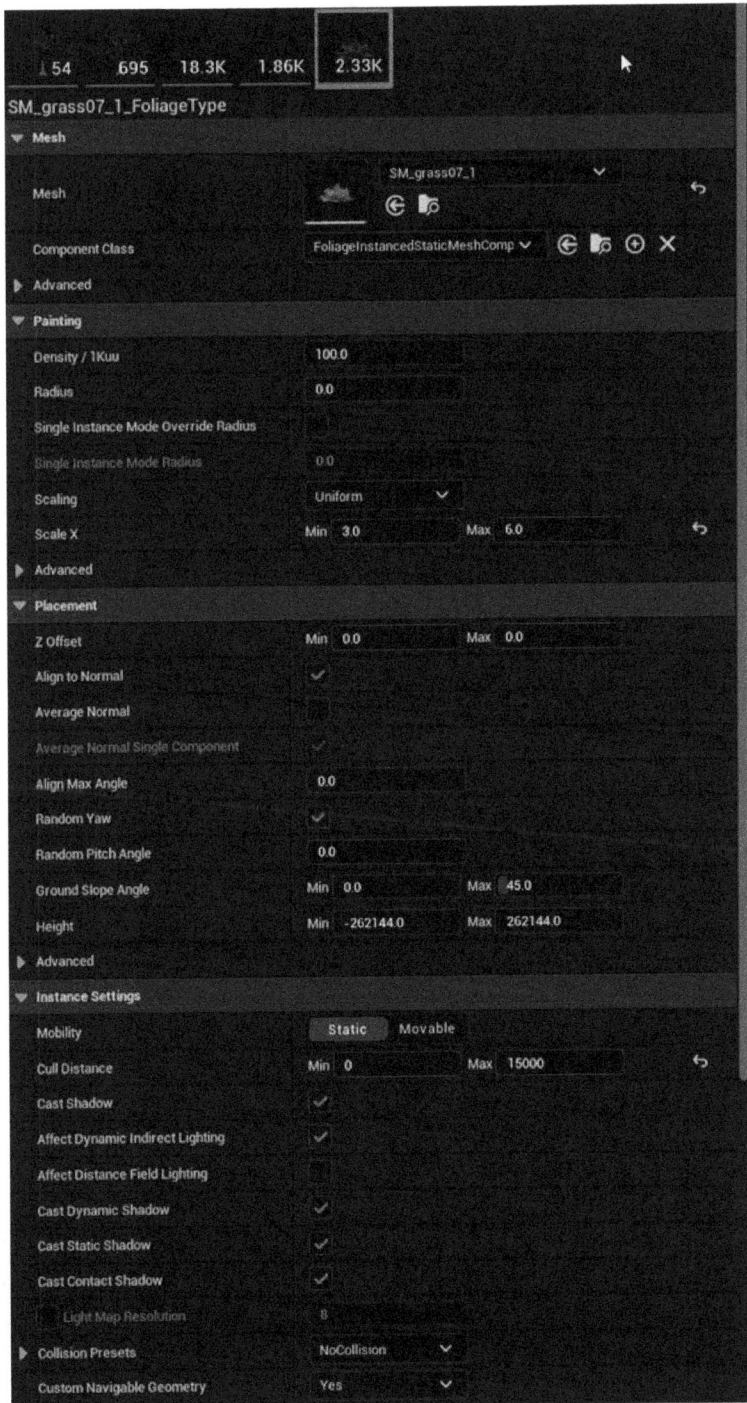

Figure 15.16: *Larger grass Foliage*

Note how *Figure 15.14* features a large number of that Foliage type, yet the shadow cast is disabled, while the cull distance is set to a smaller amount, meaning this Foliage type will not render in longer distances, unlike the tree Foliage used in *Figure 15.13* which is meant to be rendered and seen from far distances.

Figures 15.17 to *Figure 15.19* show the final Foliage result in the author's version of the project:

Figure 15.17: *The Foliage in its final form*

As shown in *Figure 15.18*, one can note the closeup rendering of the grass Foliage:

Figure 15.18: *Closeup of the grass Foliage*

In *Figure 15.19* can be observed how the trees appear in the far distance:

Figure 15.19: Trees in the distance

Lighting optimization

First, let us consider the light sources we have. We have the sun/directional light, which we already edited in an earlier chapter, then we have the Point Lights that are part of the fire pit Blueprint actors we created in the previous chapter, as well as the player light, and lastly, whatever lights we place in any interior areas of the level.

Let us quickly open up the BP_FirePit, then click on the PointLight component, and set the Attenuation Radius to 786 units. Next, type **Distance** in the search field and use the settings shown in *Figure 15.20*:

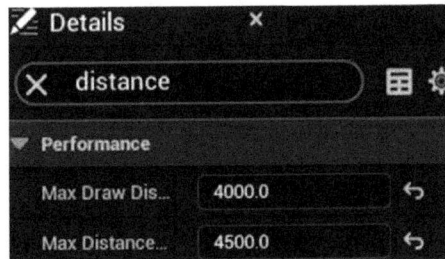

Figure 15.20: Modifying BP_FirePit's light settings

The changes we just performed ensure that once the player is further than 4500 units away from a BP_FirePit actor, the light component of that actor will not be rendering.

If you want to optimize it further, whether due to lower system specs or simply because you want to add a lot more such actors in the level, you can not only decrease these numbers (attenuation radius and max draw distance) but additionally, you can disable Cast Shadows. Just be warned that the further optimized something is, the less appealing it will look.

Similarly, you could disable shadow casting on the player's light we created within BP_ThirdPersonCharacter, but then the visual quality will decrease, and you will have side effects such as light bleeding through geometry, etc. Nonetheless, feel free to play around with such settings, and choose the one that best works for your needs.

The exterior areas of the level do not really need any PointLights or any other lighting, other than what the default basic map already had (directional light, fog, skylight, etc.), but if you created interior areas, even if you lit some of them with BP_FirePit actors, more likely than not, you need to use some sort of ambient lighting. You can use Point Lights, with a rather large attenuation radius, that is not too bright on the intensity and have the Cast Shadows disabled while still using a Max Distance Cull value. *Figures 15.21* and *Figure 15.22* show some examples of such lights the author used in some of the Fantasy Castle level's interior spaces:

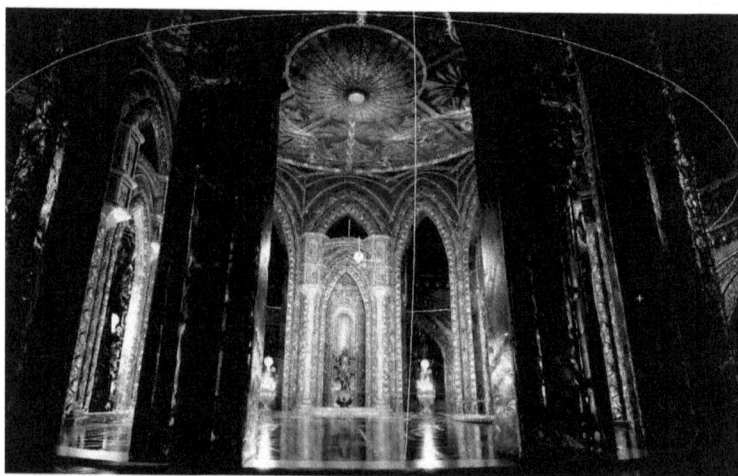

Figure 15.21: Interior Point Light used for ambience in combination with fire pit actors

Figure 15.22 displays some of the interior lighting done for this environment:

Figure 15.22: More interior lighting

The settings used for the light in *Figure 15.23* can be seen in *Figure 15.24*:

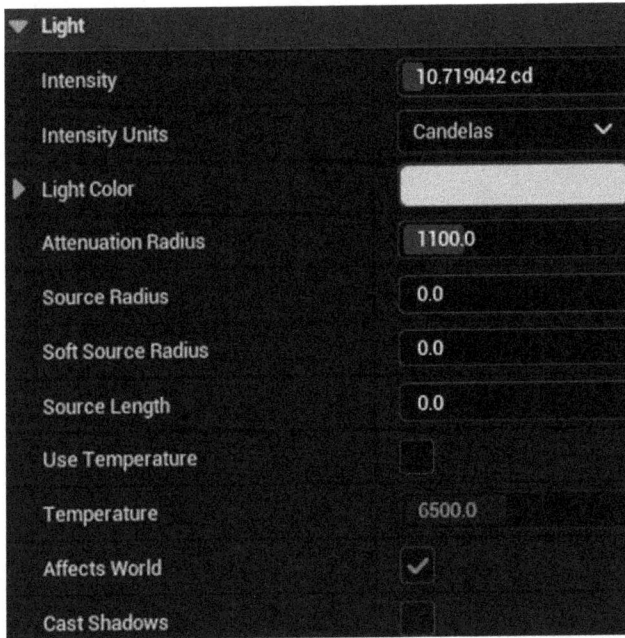

Figure 15.23: *Light settings for ambient Point Light in Figure 15.21*

One other lighting and post processing related optimization you can perform is to add a **Post Process Volume** in the level. Follow *Figure 15.24* for finding them and *Figure 15.25* for the settings used. Also, use the setting shown in *Figure 15.26*:

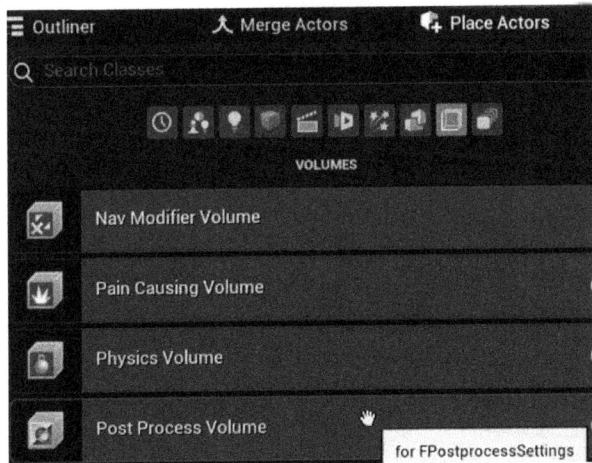

Figure 15.24: *Click and drag the Post Process Volume anywhere in the level*

Figure 15.25 demonstrates the **Post Process Volume** settings that are being used, more specifically, the contrast, gamma, and gain values:

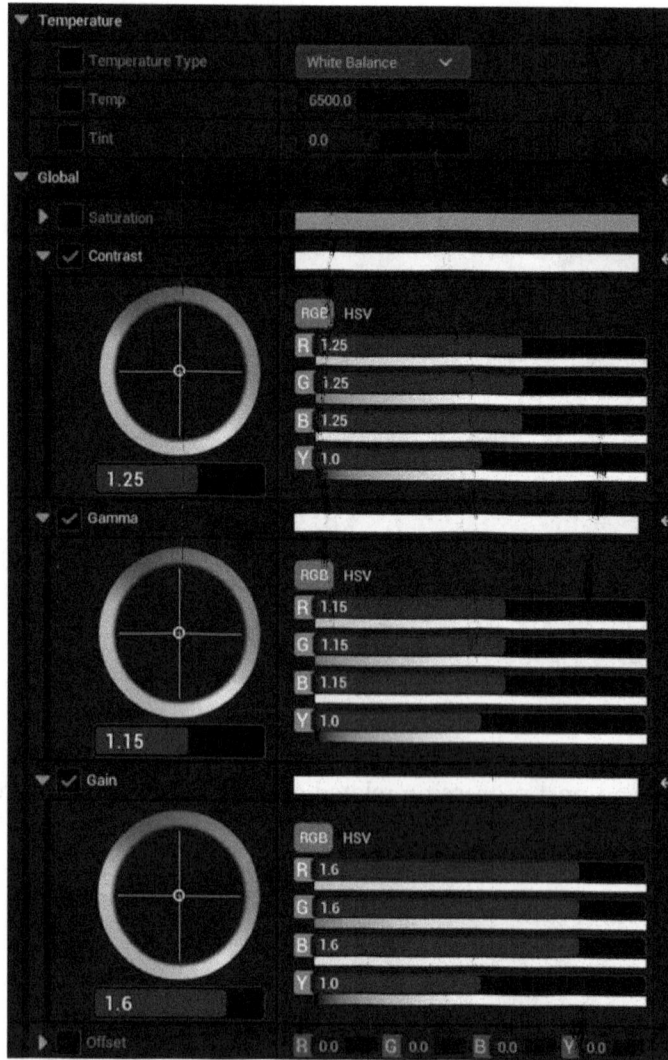

Figure 15.25: The Post Process Volume settings used

Figure 15.26 showcases the post process volume settings that are being used:

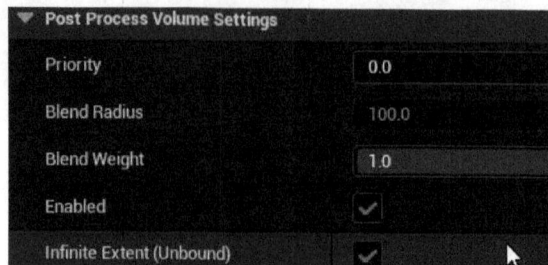

Figure 15.26: Click and drag the Post Process Volume anywhere in the level

Collisions and blocking volumes

When importing the Static Meshes, we enabled automatic collision generation, which, for the most part, works well, but in some cases, such as archways, it does not work as intended since it blocks the player from crossing spaces that should be otherwise accessible. Therefore, it is advised that you pay closer attention to meshes such as archways, arches, doorways, and stairs, and re-generate their collisions. You can do so by double clicking on a Static Mesh in the Content Browser, and then navigating on the top of the window to **Tools,** then **Auto Convex Collision** as shown in *Figure 15.27*:

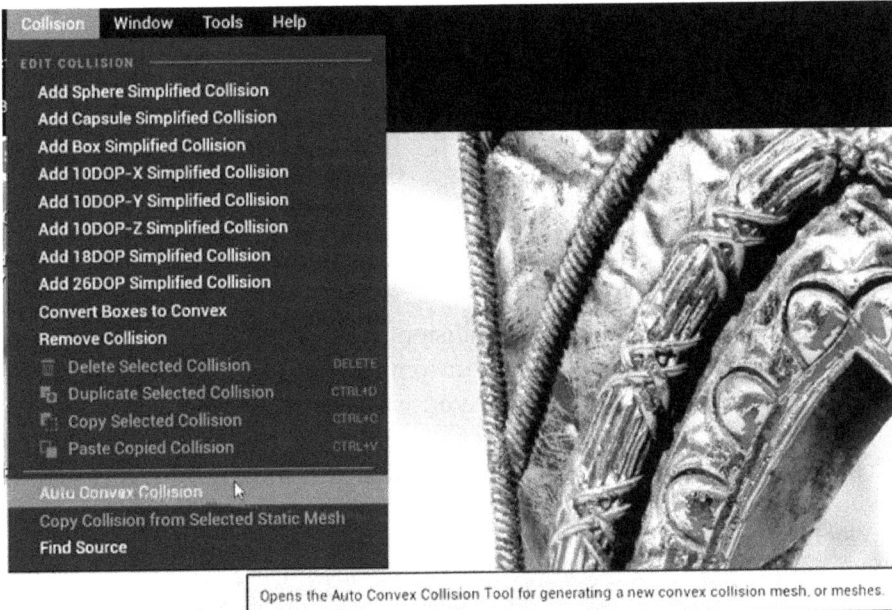

Figure 15.27: Adjusting the collision of a Static Mesh

Then, under the **Convex Decomposition** tab, as shown in *Figure 15.28*, either hit directly apply (sometimes that is more than enough) or increase the **Hull Count, Max Hull Verts** and **Hull Precision** to get a more accurate collision around your Static Mesh, and then again hit **Apply** and of course, do not forget to save once you are happy with your results.

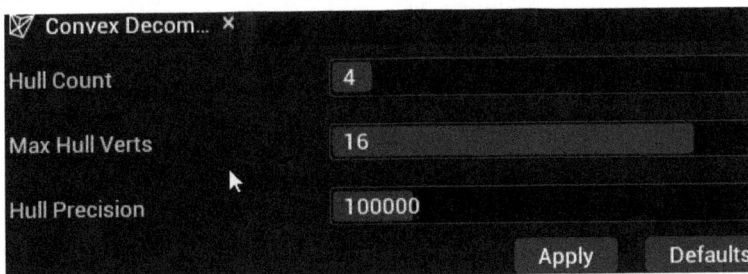

Figure 15.28: Convex Collision settings

After hitting apply, you will notice a green geometry surrounding your mesh, which represents the collision geometry. *Figure 15.29* shows the result of applying convex collision with the default settings (**Hull Count 4**, **Max Verts 16**, **Hull Precision 100000**):

Figure 15.29: Convex Collision application result

Sometimes, you want to place invisible collision in places that visually there is not any obstacle to justify such a collision. It is not uncommon for a game to be blocking the user from accessing certain areas. In this case, you want to use blocking volumes. Blocking volumes are simple geometry, which you can obtain from the same Volumes location we got the Post Processing Volume from, you can click and drag it into the level, and then you can scale it as well as shape (they are rectangular/boxed by default) it, as shown in its settings in *Figure 15.30*:

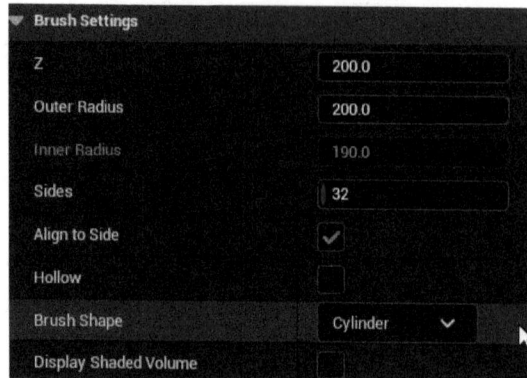

Figure 15.30: A cylindrical shaped blocking volume

The author mainly placed them around the Fantasy Castle, as to avoid having the player exit the castle grounds. Also placed some cylindrical blocking volumes around the Foliage found in the castle's courtyard. *Figures 15.31* and *Figure 15.32* showcase some of the blocking volume placement around the level (the gray lined geometrical shapes):

Figure 15.31: *While challenging to see, the faint gray lined geometry represents the blocking volumes*

Figure 15.32 demonstrates the selected blocking volumes within the map:

Figure 15.32: *All the blocking volumes selected and in Detail Lighting view mode, to make them a bit easier to see*

Placement of playable/interactable actors

This is purely subjective, as there is virtually an infinite amount of interesting combinations you can come up with to ensure that the placement of the statues for the mini game we created in *Chapter 13, Fantasy Castle Interactive Blueprint Actors*, makes for an interesting run.

In the following steps, the author lists his setup, but this is all entirely optional, and it is highly encouraged you to try different setups.

First, we place the BP_GameStart in an atmospheric interior space, giving it a bit of magnificence combined with mystery, such as in *Figure 15.33*:

Figure 15.33: Placing the statue in a nice, centralized, yet not too easy-to-find location

Next, we assign it the following settings affecting the mini game (*Figure 15.34*):

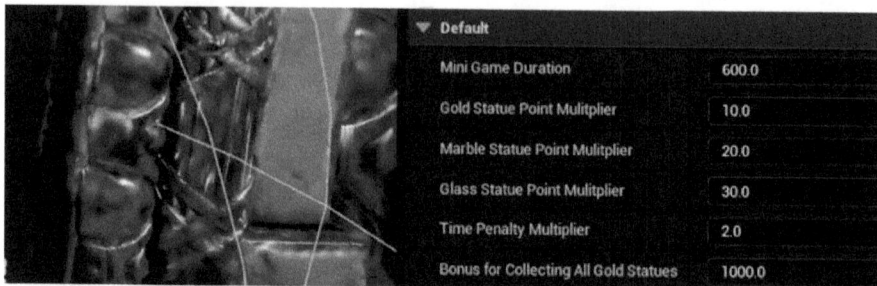

Figure 15.34: BP_GameStartActor's settings in the level

Next, we need to place elephant statuettes all across the map. You can place as many as you want, of any type you want. *Figures 15.35* to *Figure 15.40* show some of the locations the author used:

Figure 15.35: A golden elephant statuette

Figure 15.36 shows an example placement of a marble elephant statuette:

Figure 15.36: *A marble elephant statuette*

Figure 15.37 shows an example placement of a glass elephant statuette:

Figure 15.37: *A glass elephant statuette*

Figure 15.38 shows an example placement of a golden elephant statuette, blending in with the environment:

Figure 15.38: *A gold elephant statuette blending well with the environment*

Figure 15.39 shows an example of the player light function being used in real-time in the game:

Figure 15.39: *The player light function was proven useful in this case*

Figure 15.40 shows yet another example of the player light function being utilized in-game:

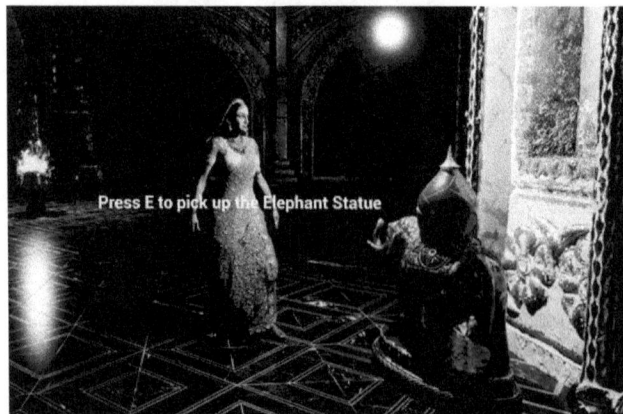

Figure 15.40: *Thanks to the player light function, the end user can locate important actors*

Packaging settings

On the top of the main Unreal Editor window, click on **Platforms** and then on **Packaging Settings...** as shown in *Figure 15.41*:

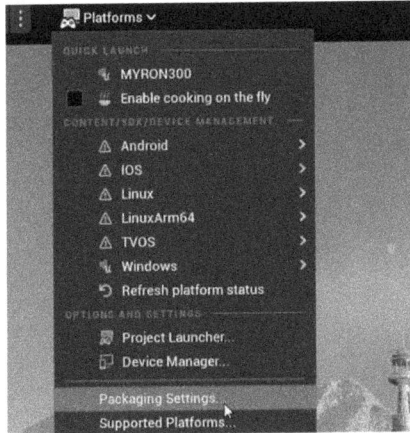

Figure 15.41: Packaging Settings

Next, look for **List of maps to include in a packaged build** and press the add button. Once you have done that, provided you are using the project provided by the author, type **FantasyCastle_Optimized** in the **Index [0]** field, as shown in *Figure 15.42*:

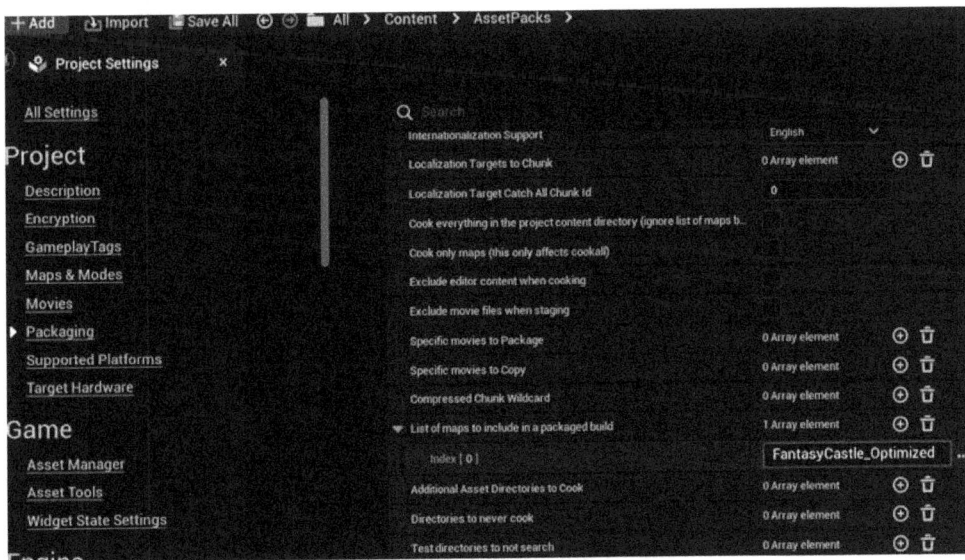

Figure 15.42: Including this map is important

Then, while in the project settings window, click on **Maps & Modes** (close above the packaging section) and use the same settings as shown in *Figure 15.43*:

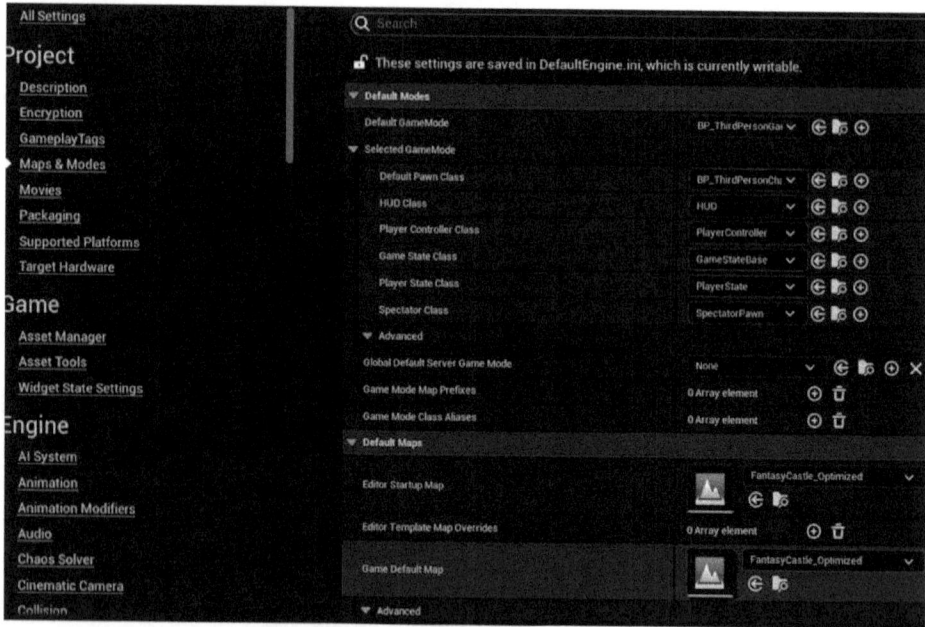

Figure 15.43: Maps and Modes settings to use

Next, close the project settings, and back to the main window, click again **Platforms**, then **Windows** and then **Package Project**, as displayed in *Figure 15.44*:

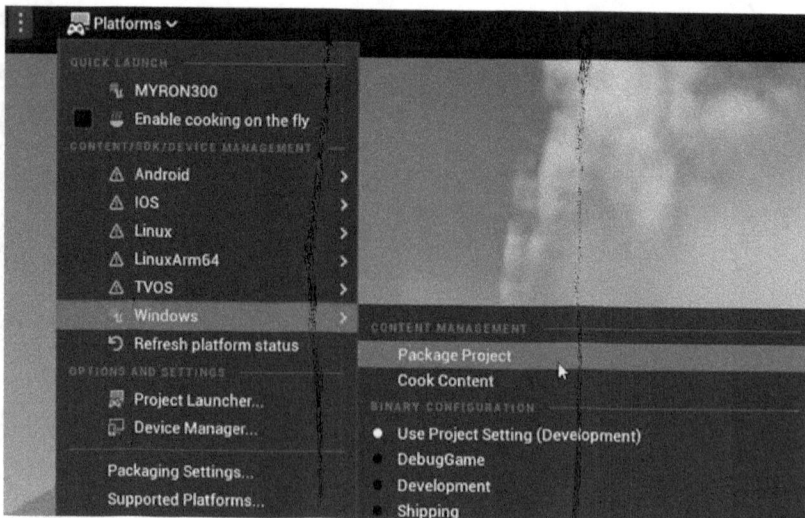

Figure 15.44: Package Project

The packaging now starts, it will take a long while the first time you run it. You will know it is packaging because of the icon on the bottom right corner, the same one as the one shown in *Figure 15.45*:

Figure 15.45: Packaging the Project

In the meantime, you can also keep track of the packaging process, by pressing the **Show Output Log** seen in *Figure 15.45*. This will result in something similar to what is shown in *Figure 15.46*:

Figure 15.46: Packaging's Output Log

Once the packaging is complete, you will be greeted with the icon shown in *Figure 15.47*:

Figure 15.47: Packaging's done! You are ready to run the executable now

Conclusion

We briefly covered some optimization techniques, including LODs, batching actors, and culling distances, while we also went over some lighting optimization techniques, as well as improving collisions. We deleted unnecessary elements, including parts of the landscape, reapplied some Foliage, and optimized each Foliage actor's settings, such as culling distance and whether they cast shadows. Finally, we placed firepits as well as the interactable actors we created in the last chapter.

While all the subjects discussed throughout the book can get a lot more complex, the goal was to expose the reader to a bit of everything and allow them to create something playable. Essentially, at this point, this project, which was also the biggest and most difficult of the entire book, is complete.

In addition, you have an executable that you can show to friends and family, allow them to play your creation and give you any feedback.

Points to remember

- Batching multiple actors in a scene helps minimize the number of actors placed in the world and can be done so without affecting the visuals.

- LODs — even if they are not needed when using Nanite, they can still be useful with Skeletal Meshes.

- Batching actors (instancing objects).

- Light optimizations: max draw distance, attenuation radius, casting shadows or not.

- Post Processing Volumes: they can affect the visuals greatly.

- Blocking Volumes: blocking the player from going to unwanted areas.

- Convex Collisions: achieving more complex collision geometry for meshes such as archways and stairs.

- Before packaging, make sure you include the map you want to package (in this case FantasyCastle_Optimized) in the list of maps to include under the Packaging Settings.

- Ensure you use the correct settings under Maps & Modes in Project Settings.

- Start packaging and be patient, it might take a while the first time!

Exercises

1. Create new levels with a large number of actors and then batch them to see whether your performance has improved or not. Adjust and finetune collisions in Static Meshes. Place several lights in your levels and see how you can optimize them.

   Overall, utilize everything you learned so far and create a level, or even better an entire project of your own! Become active and involved in the Unreal and game development communities (Discord is a great place to start) and start working on projects with other people.

2. If you have created different levels, try packaging with them as the default level.

   The best way to learn is to keep building projects.

Join our book's Discord space

Join the book's Discord Workspace for Latest updates, Offers, Tech happenings around the world, New Release and Sessions with the Authors:

https://discord.bpbonline.com

CHAPTER 16

Statue Scene Introduction to VR

Introduction

This chapter serves as a brief introduction to XR/VR. Development for such platforms can be a complex topic that to be fully covered would need at least an entire book if not a series of books. As such, in this chapter we will only cover the very basics, without focusing on specific devices, Although we will briefly mention some of the most popular ones that the Unreal Engine is compatible with.

Structure

In this chapter, we will discuss the following topics:

- Prepping the Greek God Statue project for VR
- Adding the VR Template to the cloned project
- Testing the VR Template Map
- Different project settings and their impact

Objectives

To introduce the reader to VR development with Unreal Engine 5. We will clone the Greek God Statue project, then add the VR Template to it. After that, we will briefly look at some different rendering settings and the impact they have.

Prepping the Greek God Statue project for VR

Launch the Epic Launcher, and under Library, in the My Projects section, find and right click the Greek God Statue project. Select **Clone**, as displayed in *Figure 16.1*. This will create an identical copy of the project.

Figure 16.1: Cloning the Greek God Statue project

Proceed with selecting a destination folder for the cloned project, similarly to what is depicted in *Figure 16.2*, and when a warning prompt pops up, simply click **Continue**, as indicated in *Figure 16.3*:

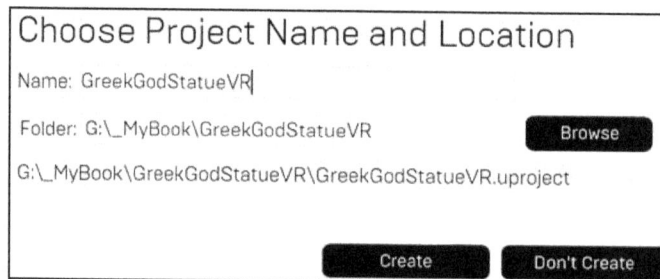

Figure 16.2: Choose a name and destination folder for the cloned project

Figure 16.3 demonstrates a warning when trying to rename a project:

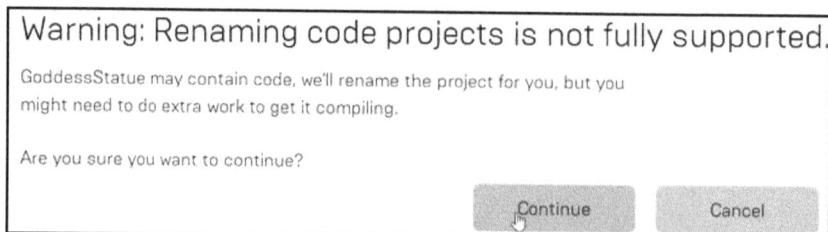

Figure 16.3: When warned about the renaming of the project, simply click Continue

At the time the author created the Greek God Statue, Unreal Engine 5.2 was the latest stable version. At the time the author converted the Greek God Statue to a VR clone, Unreal Engine 5.3 was the latest stable version. Therefore, the author launched 5.3 from the launcher, as shown in *Figure 16.4*:

Figure 16.4: Launching the latest (at the time of authoring this chapter) version of the Unreal Engine

Next, under RECENT PROJECTS select the newly cloned project — ideally, you named it **GreekGodStatueVR** and then click the blue Open button on the lower right part of the window. Next, you will be asked to convert the project, and select **More Options...** as shown in *Figure 16.5*:

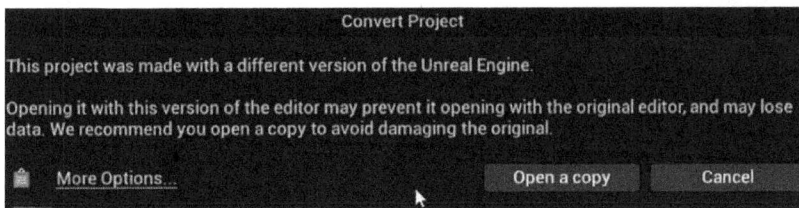

Figure 16.5: More options while converting the project from an older version of the engineer to a newer one

Next, select **Convert in-place,** as shown in *Figure 16.6*:

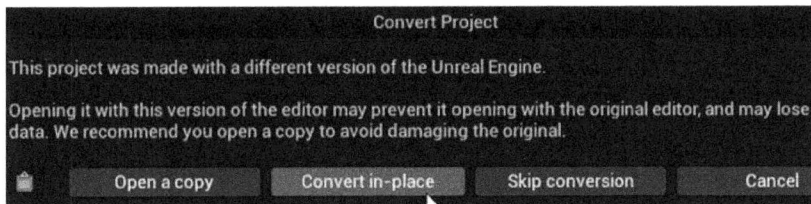

Figure 16.6: Converting the project in-place

Adding the VR Template to the cloned project

Give Unreal a few minutes to prepare the project and compile the shaders. Once the project is loaded, open up either the **Content Browser** or the Content Drawer, and click on the

+Add button on the upper left corner, and then select **Add Feature or Content Pack...** as shown in *Figure 16.7*:

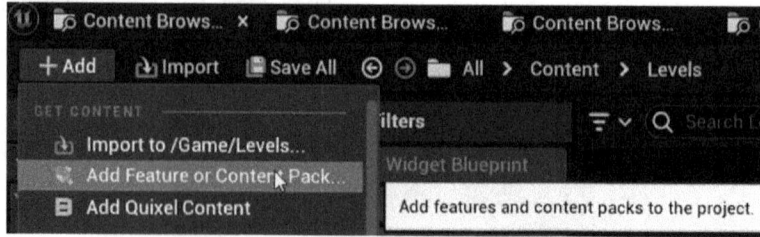

Figure 16.7: *Adding a template to the current project*

A new window pops up, asking you to select the template you would like to add to your current project. Select the **Virtual reality** template and then click **Add to Project** as indicated in *Figure 16.8*:

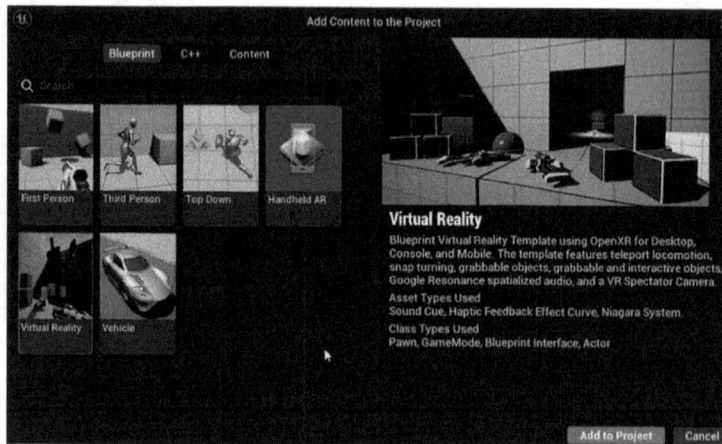

Figure 16.8: *Adding the VR Template to the current project*

Next, Unreal will ask you to enable some missing plugins, which are required in order to be able to run VR. Click **Enable Missing**, as shown in *Figure 16.9*:

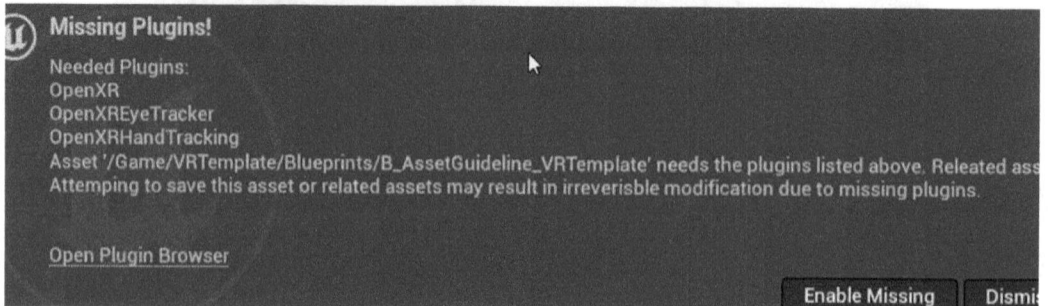

Figure 16.9: *Enabling necessary plugins*

Once you have enabled the missing plugins, you will be asked to restart the editor, as shown in *Figure 16.10*. Select **Restart Now**.

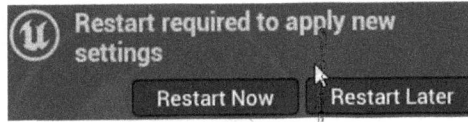

Figure 16.10: *Restart the editor after enabling the missing plugins*

Depending on the VR headset you are working with, you might want to enable some additional plugins, such as the Oculus plugins.

To explore and enable any plugins that might be related to your VR headset, go to **Edit** on the top left, then select **Plugins**, as shown in *Figure 16.11*:

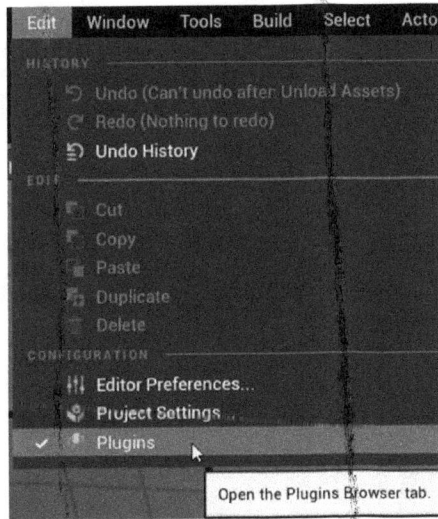

Figure 16.11: *Finding the plugins*

You can either type the name of the plugin you are trying to find, as in the example shown in *Figure 16.12*:

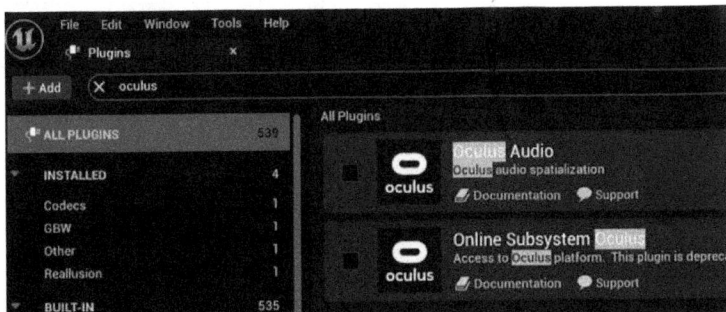

Figure 16.12: *Searching for Oculus related plugins*

You can also navigate to the category you are looking for, such as Virtual reality, as shown in *Figure 16.13*:

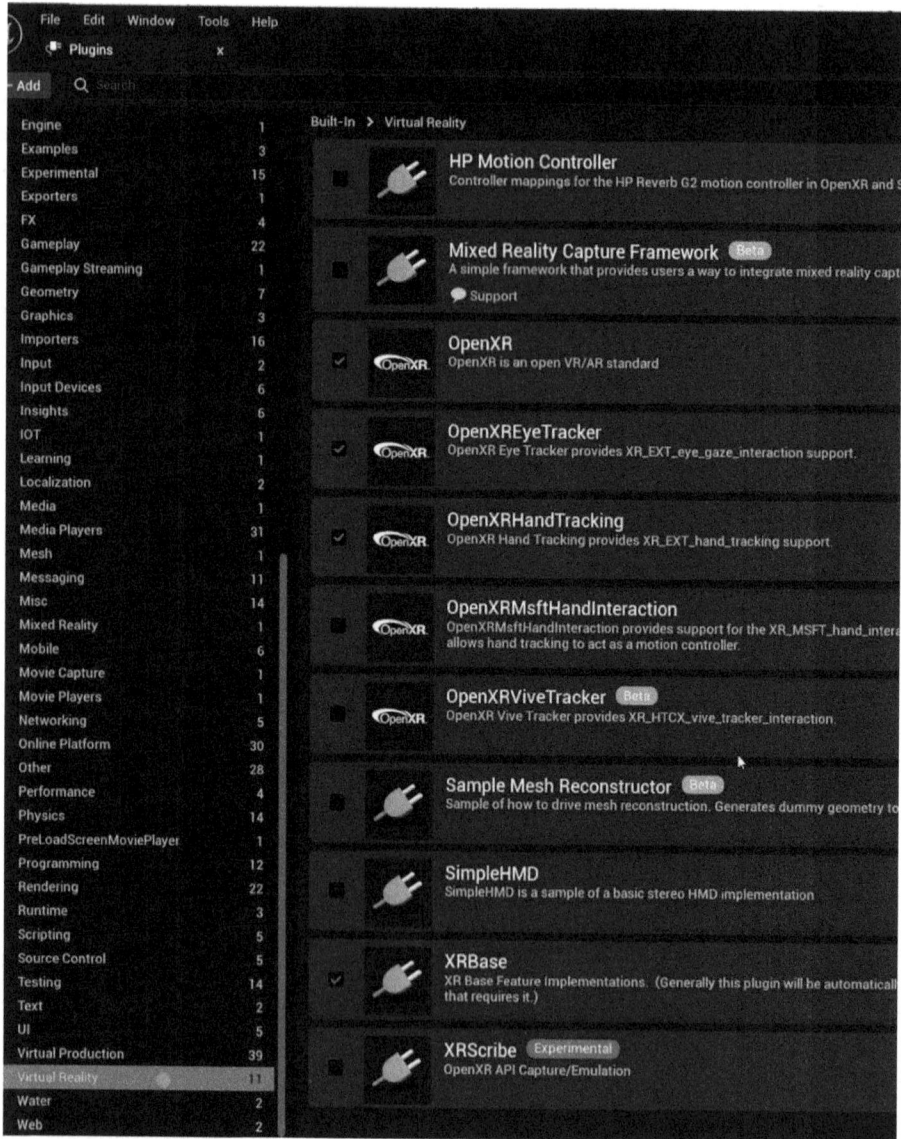

Figure 16.13: A list of several different VR related plugins

Testing the VR Template Map

At this point, it is worth noting that if the reader wishes to try the default VR Template mechanics, you can simply navigate to **Content/VRTemplate/Maps** and open the **VRTemplateMap** level, as shown in *Figure 16.14*:

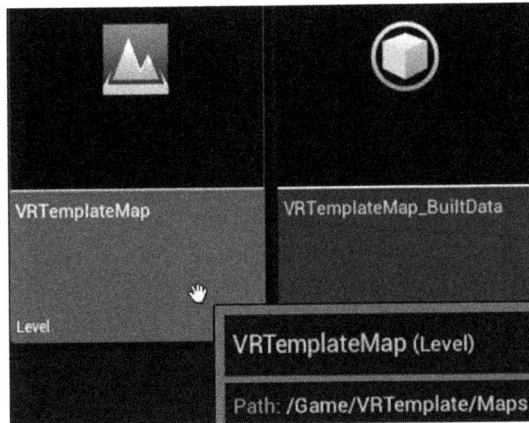

Figure 16.14: Use the VRTemplateMap to try out the default VR mechanics

The template map features physics objects that can be picked up and dropped or thrown, a pair of guns, teleportation mechanics, and more. Analyzing or modifying the VRTemplate's mechanics is beyond this book's scope.

Figure 16.15 shows the sandbox-like map that awaits you for testing out the default mechanics:

Figure 16.15: The VRTemplateMap

To try it out in VR, simply change the play mode by clicking the three dots on the upper left side of the main Viewport, as shown in *Figure 16.16*:

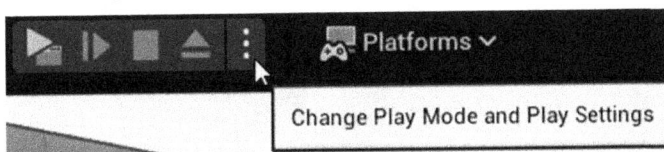

Figure 16.16: Changing the playmode

Then select **VR Preview**, as shown in *Figure 16.17:*

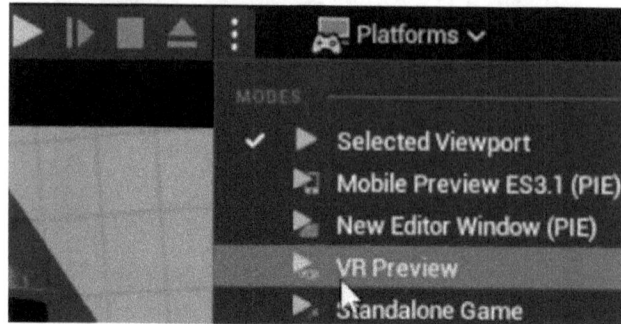

Figure 16.17: Playing in VR

If **VR Preview** is grayed out, as shown in *Figure 16.18*, then either you have not connected your VR headset, or it is switched off. Depending on which VR headset you are using, you will need to ensure it is properly installed and calibrated through its default application (Oculus App for the Oculus Rift or Quest, Steam for Valve Index and HTC VIVE, etc.).

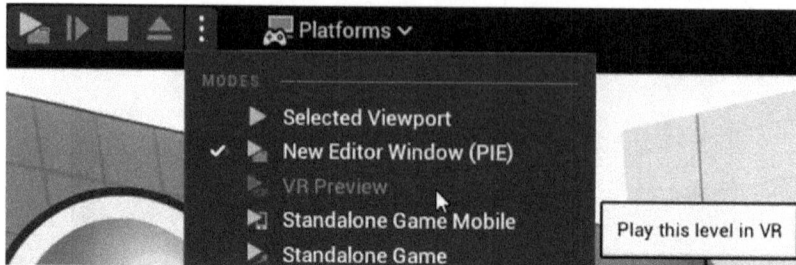

Figure 16.18: Playing in VR is grayed out, possibly because you either didn't connect your VR headset, or it is switched off

Once you successfully run the VRTemplateMap in VR Preview mode, you will be able to see your virtual hands and interact with the objects in the map, similar to the depiction in *Figure 16.19:*

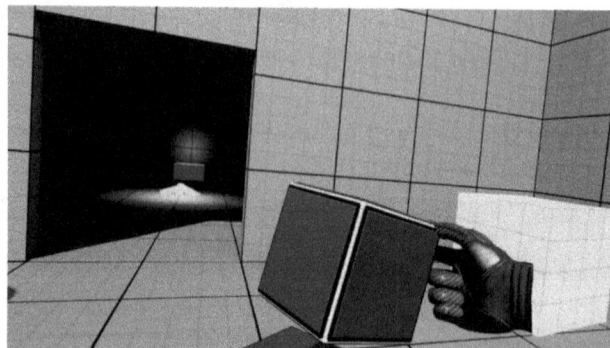

Figure 16.19: Having fun with VR in VR Preview mode

Different project settings and their impact

Since we took and cloned the existing Greek God Statue project, we also kept its original rendering settings, which, quite frankly, are great in terms of visual quality but not the most optimal for virtual reality performance.

As a rule of thumb, when developing virtual reality applications, developers aim for a minimum of 90 frames per second. Optimizing VR applications is quite challenging and most certainly beyond this book's scope, but as a brief introduction to it, it is worth noting that a different type of rendering is prepared, namely Forward Rendering, as opposed to Deferred Rendering.

Deferred Rendering is what our original Greek God Statue project had, whereas Forward Shading is what Unreal Engine's default VR project features. Since we cloned our Greek God Statue project and only added the VR Template's content later, we are still using Deferred Rendering.

To change the rendering to Forward Shading, simply go to **Project Settings**, as shown in *Figure 16.20*:

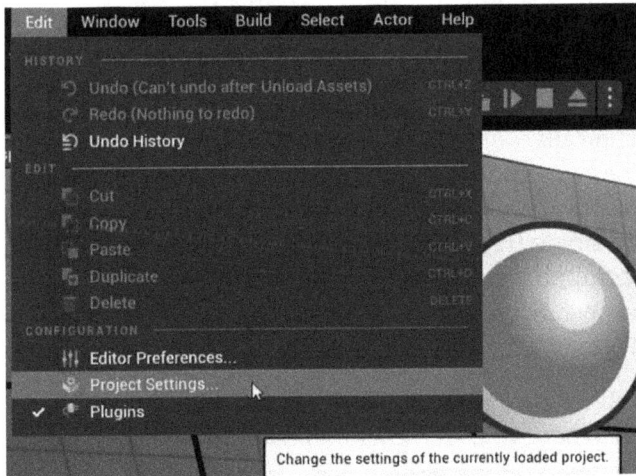

Figure 16.20: *Project Settings*

Next, scroll down on the left-hand side and click on **Rendering**, as depicted in *Figure 16.21*:

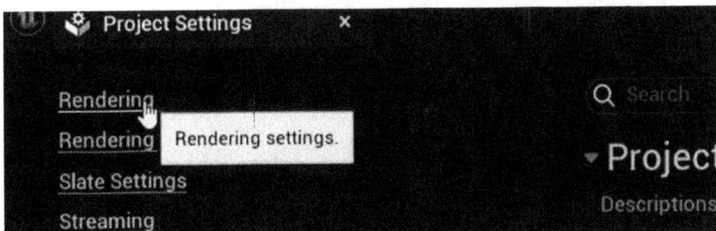

Figure 16.21: *Rendering settings under Project Settings*

Now scroll down until you find **Forward Renderer** and check the **Forward Shading** box, as shown in *Figure 16.22*. For the purposes of this book, let us just say that Forward Rendering is a bit more performance friendly, and with virtual reality, we need to optimize wherever. However, we can, more so than in non-VR development, as bad framerates can have an adverse effect on the end user, such as vertigo, etc.

Figure 16.22: Rendering settings under Project Settings

You will be asked to restart the editor. Do not restart yet. While still under **Project Settings | Rendering**, look for the **VR** section and check the box next to **Instanced Stereo**, as shown in *Figure 16.23*:

Figure 16.23: Enable Instanced Stereo

In virtual reality, technically, a scene gets rendered twice. Once for the left eye and once for the right eye, and the two renders are completed in slightly different angles, which then when combined, give the three-dimensional effect of depth. However, rendering the same scene twice for every single frame can be quite performance demanding. To mitigate this issue, Unreal Engine supports Instanced Stereo rendering, in which the scene is rendered once, along with an instance of itself, therefore rendering it faster, more efficient, and performance friendlier.

Now restart the editor. Load up our Greek God Statue level, found under `Content/Levels/GreekGodStatueLevel`, as shown in *Figure 16.24*:

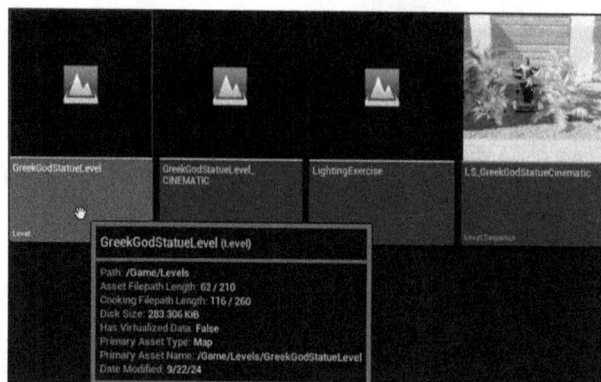

Figure 16.24: Loading GreekGodStatueLevel

The first thing you will possibly notice is that the lighting quality is not as nice as in the original version of the project. The second thing you will notice by getting closer to the statue mesh is that it looks low poly, as shown in *Figure 16.25*:

Figure 16.25: *The God Statue mesh quality has significantly decreased*

While a quick check at the Project Settings will confirm we still have Nanite enabled, the unfortunate truth of the matter is that Nanite, as of version 5.3, is not compatible with Forward Shading. Therefore, any meshes used in a Forward Shading enabled project would have to be created in the older, traditional way, where high poly meshes are used to extract normal maps that are then applied to the lower poly counterparts of these meshes.

In our current project, if your computer system was recently built, chances are you won't have any performance issues by changing the Rendering back to Deferred (simply go back to the Forward Renderer under the Rendering settings and uncheck **Forward Shading,** which we checked as shown in *Figure 16.22*).

However, if this was a fully featured or at least heavier project, such as this book's Fantasy Castle Project, we would most certainly need to retain the Forward Rendering, in order to achieve optimal performance. Naturally, were we to do that, we would need to re-export and re-import all our Static Meshes, as well as their textures, to best match the traditional ways of game asset creation.

For this chapter's purposes, it is entirely up to the reader whether they choose to follow the next and final steps in Forward or Deferred Rendering.

If you revert back to Deferred Rendering, your lighting will have improved, and of course, Nanite's capabilities are once more utilized to the fullest, as shown in *Figure 16.26*:

Figure 16.26: *The God Statue mesh back to its highest quality, with Nanite fully utilized*

Now, while in the `GreekGodStatueLevel`, navigate to **Window** and then select **World Settings** as shown in *Figure 16.27*:

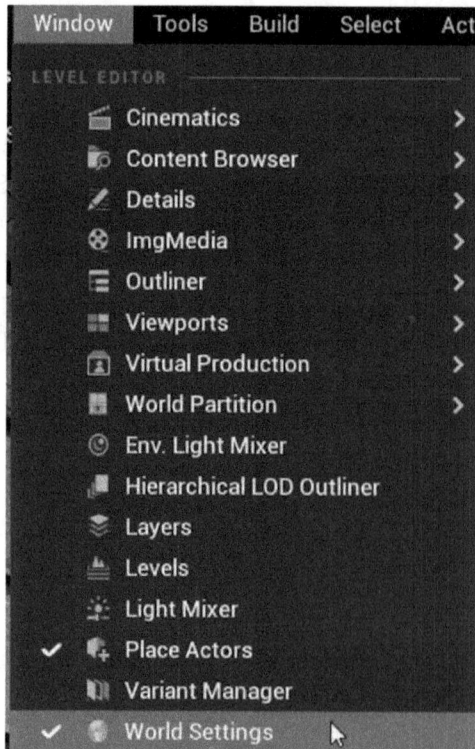

Figure 16.27: *Let us modify the World Settings*

Under the **World Settings** tab, scroll and expand **Game Mode**, and for **GameMode Override** select **VRGameMode**, as shown in *Figure 16.28*:

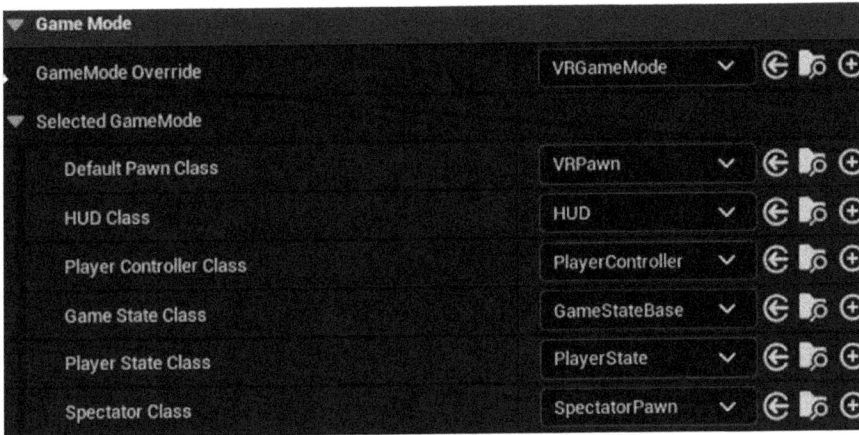

Figure 16.28: Modifying the GameMode and selecting the VRGameMode

Now, simply play in VR more — as depicted in *Figure 16.17*. While there are not any interactions to be had, you will be able to move around the scene in VR, and you will be able to admire the Statue in VR in a life-like manner.

Conclusion

This was a very basic introduction to the wonderful and immersive world of virtual reality. Truth be told, experiencing VR for the first time is an immensely exciting experience, and at first, it is easy to impress end users. However, VR development can be very complex, demanding, and technically challenging to optimize as well as develop mechanics for when compared to non-VR applications. Rest assured, a proper introduction to VR development would require a book dedicated to it.

Points to remember

- You can convert any existing project into a VR project by adding the VR Template.

- You can create a new project with the Unreal Engine's VRTemplate, it will load with the optimal rendering settings by default as compared to converting non VR projects.

- When converting non-VR projects to VR, do not forget to enable the missing plugins Unreal Engine prompts you to activate.

- Ensure you have the proper drivers, applications, and plugins related to the VR headset of your choice.

- Ensure your VR headset is properly connected and installed.

- Ensure your VR headset is properly calibrated and accurately tracking.

- Ensure your VR headset is not switched off or in sleep mode.

- When developing for VR, usually Forward Rendering is preferred, as it is more performance-friendly than Deferred Rendering.

- Forward Rendering does not support Nanite (as of Unreal Engine version 5.3).

- When developing VR content, aim for a 90 frames per second performance (some Oculus headsets support 72 FPS).

Exercise

1. Create new projects based off the default Unreal VR Template project, or convert existing projects to VR. If your computer specs are powerful enough and you are brave enough, try to do the same with the Fantasy Castle Project, however, be warned, it might be a rather heavy/low framerate experience, but you could still create lighter levels, with less assets, just so you can experience them in true, life-like 3D!

Join our book's Discord space

Join the book's Discord Workspace for Latest updates, Offers, Tech happenings around the world, New Release and Sessions with the Authors:

https://discord.bpbonline.com

Index